D1452081

FLASHBACK
Nora Johnson on Nunnally Johnson

ALSO BY NORA JOHNSON

The World of Henry Orient

A Step Beyond Innocence

Love Letter in the Dead Letter Office

Pat Loud: A Woman's Story

Flashback:

Nora Johnson on Nunnally Johnson

Nora Johnson

Doubleday & Company, Inc., Garden City, New York
1979

Quotes from Nunnally Johnson's Roving Reporter columns, 1927. Reprinted from the New York *Post*.

The Lee Side o' L.A. (Personal Glimpses of Famous Folks—Nunnally Johnson). Copyright, 1932, Los Angeles *Times*. Reprinted by permission. By Lee Shippey.

ISBN: 0-385-13406-1
Library of Congress Catalog Card Number 78–18137

COPYRIGHT © 1979 BY NORA JOHNSON
ALL RIGHTS RESERVED
PRINTED IN THE UNITED STATES OF AMERICA
FIRST EDITION

To my children, who will someday have
to understand their parents too.

My heart has followed all my days
Something I cannot name
                    Don Marquis

ACKNOWLEDGMENTS

For sharing memories and stories, many thanks to:

Celia Agar, Gloria Sheekman, Philip Dunne, Felice Paramore, Harry Brand, George Seaton, Sol Siegel, Sara Mankiewicz, Dave Hempstead, George Roy Hill, Monica Kemberg, Gregory Peck, Henry Fonda, Harry Tugend, Joanne Woodward, Olivia de Havilland, Henry King, Natalie Schafer, Peter and Mary Hayes, Marian Thompson, Eleanor Hempstead, Reata Kraft, Lauren Bacall, Marc Connelly, Edith Haggard, Dorothy McKaye, Joel Sayre, Alistair Cooke, Holger Lundburgh, Nora Sayre, Doris Vidor, Finley Peter Dunne, Julian Street, Jean Negulesco, Sylvia Dudley, Harold Bjorkland, Pete Martin, Bob Parrish, Mel and Ann Frank, Merrie Spaeth; and to members of my family, Cecil, Marge and Gene, Dorris, Scott, Roxie, Christie, Alice and Marion. For help in Columbus, I am grateful to Daisy Tucker, Dorothy Smith, Liz Barton, Mamie Rainey, Theodore Smith and Eula Parker.

Also thanks to Charles Silver and the Film Library of the Museum of Modern Art, to Charles Hopkins of the UCLA Film Archives, and to Barbara Humphreys at the Library of Congress for letting me screen Nunnally Johnson movies; to Dr. Gottleib at Boston University's Mugar Memorial Library, where Nunnally's papers are kept; to Bernard Galm of the oral history department of UCLA for access to tapes of interviews with Nunnally, and to Tom Stempel for doing the interviews; to Jim Brown for access to his correspondence about *Henry Sweet Henry;* and to Dick Meryman for transcribed tapes of interviews he did of Nunnally for his own book, *Mank.*

CONTENTS

FLASHBACK
Nora Johnson on Nunnally Johnson

Columbus 1977

In 1977 it is a city of 150,000 in western Georgia on flat land by the Chattahoochee River. The river, which at this point is at the end of a series of falls, has cut so deep a bed that it is invisible from almost everywhere, one isn't conscious of its presence. From the bluffs above you can look down at its muddy waters and sandy shores, and above are overhanging sycamores, live oaks and pecans, some hung with moss. The hot July air smells strongly of baking earth, of dry leaves and grass, and of pulp from the paper mill across the river. There is no pollution of the river or the air, though both look it—but the turgidity of the river is mud and the haze in the sky a heavy humidity that never turns to rain. You could throw a stone, or a Frisbee, over to Alabama. The small city feels like a town, and the town feels closed in—there is none of the sense of motion or travel that moving waters usually impart. People are inclined to stay here. I am told Columbus is the only American city of its size not on a main highway, though there is a daily flight to and from New York—but airports do not form the character of cities as roads once did. Columbus is leisurely and shambly, a single strip with a big sign, "Welcome to Columbus Georgia." Nobody asks to see a baggage check, you could steal a couple of suitcases if you were so inclined.

Columbus is about the same size as Albany or Hartford, or Springfield, Massachusetts, but its feel is quite different. There is

still a "society." My hostess, Daisy, is surprised when she doesn't
see anybody she knows at the airport; usually she does. There is
the intense Southern interest and involvement with kin, family
members keep track of each other, people are pleased to discover
a great-great-uncle in common. It is more important to be "decent" than to be rich, even more important than belonging to the
Methodist Church. People go visiting, ladies have luncheon parties at home or at the country club. Everyone sits and talks to an
extent that can make even the most interested Yankee long to go
out and run around the block. Drinking is still a little naughty in
some circles. Everyone calls the President Jimmy, but for the
most part didn't vote for him (this is conservative territory). No
one says so, but I suspect the Carters aren't quite "quality,"
though "Rosalynn's lovely." There are smiles of relief when I
turn down a polite invitation to drive over to Plains, forty miles
away—Plains is ruined, an embarrassment. One feels it couldn't
happen in Columbus, there is something about the place that
would not tolerate the T-shirt and golden peanut commercialism,
it would simply slide off the surface.

I am told that there has always been a good relationship between the seventy per cent whites and the thirty per cent blacks
—"we were taught to get along with nigras"—in Columbus,
though that good relationship is of course in the Southern context. Not knowing what a waffling liberal they are talking to,
people tread carefully around my presumed Yankee judgments.
Whites and blacks still go to their own churches, they prefer it
that way (and I am startled less by the creeping rate of integration than by the insistence on religion), and the behavior of the
black minister in Plains (who tried to join Carter's church)
didn't help, it was too fast an attempt at change. Blacks object to
certain radical whites going to *their* church and call them "white
Watusis." But in the integrated schools rape of white girls by
blacks is "prevalent"; older couples whose children have left
home dread leaving their neighborhoods (for smaller apartments) because the NAACP will insist the empty house be sold
to a black family, and "they don't keep up the property"; and
even if a white family can slip by the owners will hold out for a
family with college-age children because "the school is too dangerous." On the other hand Julian Harris and the Columbus

Ledger-Enquirer were responsible for breaking the Ku Klux Klan in Georgia, and as for a good relationship—in the wake of the '77 blackout looting—can I really say we do much better? Anyway, Daisy says, it really gets down to quality—there are quality blacks and quality whites. ("Your family," she tells me firmly, "were quality.") She is not a "professional Southerner" who takes issue with anything Northern on principle. But when I ask her the whereabouts of certain old family documents, she flashes, "Burned up during the War" (and in the South there is still only one war), "that's what your Union soldiers did, destroyed your family history." For a moment I am dreadfully embarrassed.

The streets of the town are laid out in a neat numbered grid. Churches predominate, as do the *Ledger-Enquirer* building and the Royal Crown Cola factory. The streets are nearly empty, there are few blacks around and no whites at all, but the temperature is around 100 and as a New Yorker I am still surprised at the ghostly quiet of midday streets in smaller places. The humid air hangs on us like a weight, the grass in the parks is burned away by drought in large areas to reveal streaky earth of a startling brick red. I am here to discover my past. I squint to see what it might have looked like around March of 1897 when James Nunnally Johnson and Johnnie Pearl Patrick, my grandparents, were married. But I hardly need squint: before my eyes a restoration project is taking place that transforms one section of the town to the late Victorian era. ("Why not to ante bellum?" I ask Daisy, and she tells me, quite kindly, that after Sherman's march there was nothing left of Columbus at all.) The restoration is a source of great civic pride and is as costly here as anywhere else. Crumbling Victorian dollhouses go for a hundred thousand dollars and cost another hundred thousand to fix up. Along one section of Broadway, a divided brick street, many are charmingly finished under the stringent regulations of the Historical Society. Porches are hung with flowering baskets, and gaslights, some real, flank doorways. House numbers are written out in script, flags fly from the roofs. Some are gutted and in the process of being rebuilt by their owners, who seem to do a good deal of the work themselves, and the energy going into this project contrasts sharply with the exhausted aspect of downtown at midday. Some of the more splendid houses are restored to museum perfection and one can make a tour of them and their outdoor privies, slave quarters and subterranean kitchens for use when the Yankees come. The houses are of "dogtrot" style, furnished with horsehair sofas and claw-leg tables, and they are hot and musty. Behind one of them, the home of a Dr. Pemberton, is a little restored pharmacy which, it is said, duplicates the one where the formula for Coca-Cola was invented in 1880, a secret which now lies locked in a vault in Atlanta. It is hard to imagine the doctor in this little place with the fig trees outside, cooking up something that is reputed to dissolve dentures in three days. At any rate Coke put Columbus on the map, along with Royal Crown and the first ice machine, which was invented here.

Along the promontory by the hidden river are many gazebos and splashing fountains, though the grass is brown from drought. The riverside suggests, as it is intended to, horses and buggies, decorous picnics, bandstands, ladies with fans and leg-o'-mutton sleeves. At the end of Broadway, overlooking the river's bend, is the Goetchius house—the very house, I am told, where my grandparents were married. Now it is a restaurant, and we eat lunch in that same front parlor, a bright and sunny room with many windows. Eighty years ago it was a few blocks away, in the center of town, and undoubtedly darker and much more furnished; and I imagine their wedding reception after the ceremony at St. Luke's Methodist Church, where she sang in the choir and he first noticed her. At nineteen Johnnie Pearl (known as Onnie) was a delicately gentle beauty, with a touching femininity; Jim, ten years older, a tall and craggy railroad man from Atlanta. It must have been a happy occasion, and packed with kin, since she was one of five children and he one of seven. Where I sit drinking a Bloody Mary they drank—what? Fruit punch? Bourbon? Coca-Cola? Columbus' periods of dryness and wetness have vacillated so rapidly that no one can keep them straight. I know they talked a lot, in their soft drawling voices, and laughed good-naturedly. And that night, before they went to bed, Onnie and Jim must have said their prayers, Jim to please Onnie rather than out of conviction. Then they moved into the first of a series of twelve residences in Columbus.

Everyone traces family trees. I sit at my cousin Dorothy's dining-room table over genealogy charts. Do Southerners do this a lot? "Oh no, it only started with 'Roots,'" she replies oddly. I decide she is joking, which is proven by the painstaking work done by another cousin, copying entries from family Bibles scattered about Georgia and talking to elderly kin with patchy memories. We confirm that both Onnie's and Jim's families have been here since before the Revolution—in fact my great-great-great-greatgreat-grandfather on Onnie's side, La Fayette Elder, came from England to Jamestown in 1620, and others date back to the early eighteenth century. It is even claimed that La Fayette's antecedents can be traced back to the Crusades. Having grown up with the idea that my potato-famine forebears came over in the holds of Irish scows, I am stunned at my grand American bloodlines. With a strange kind of reverse snobbism, neither of my parents ever told me that I am probably qualified to join the DAR, the Daughters of the Confederacy, and the Colonial Dames—"Well, except for one little gap," says Dorothy, "as soon as somebody gets to that other Bible over at Chattanooga and goes out to those other graves at Midway cemetery"—inconveniently located in the middle of a Fort Benning firing range. Instead we try to sort out Onnie's Patricks and Hunters, Elders and Williamses. It seems impossible, they all married so young and had so many babies. If there was a death, the remaining spouse remarried and had another batch. Most of them stayed remarkably close to home; half the population of Columbus must be kin to me. I try to scorn all this as my parents did but I feel the ancestral pull. All those people, all those matings and birthings have made me, there is some connection between what I am now and this great flock of people making careful entries in the family Bibles in Virginia, in North and South Carolina, centuries ago. I recognize it as blind ego—none of them knew I existed—but I don't care, it's too compelling, and Daisy tells me that "the South claims you— it doesn't matter where your mother's people came from, as far as we're concerned you're a Southerner."

I hear that Onnie's father, James Wyatt Patrick, was with Lee when he surrendered at Appomattox Court House, and that James Hunter, a great-great-uncle, managed to father nine children and to survive being hanged by his toes by the Yankees.

From another cousin I hear that Jim's father, Andrew Jackson
Johnson, made ammunition for the Confederate Army. (I am of
course beyond partisanship by now and concerned only with the
nature of quality.) Methodism runs in my veins, surges in fact,
the ones who came from Ireland in the early nineteenth century
were Methodists even before they left the old sod. The occasional Baptist stands out startlingly.

We pick our way through the Lynwood cemetery in Columbus
where Patricks and Hunters lie buried together in family groups.
Sometimes there is a tiny grave next to a large one, a mother and
child lost in childbirth. Rather than headstones there are slabs,
and we tread carefully around them in the dry grass. I am
overwhelmed by their numbers, by the sheer ability of these people to stay together, to stay in the same place, on the same land,
and go to the same church and be buried in the same graveyard.
Of all these dozens only two or three ever went anywhere else,
California for gold or back to England when it didn't work out
here. In this place (which is on the wild side, unlike the tidy
cemeteries I have seen in the Northeast) I truly stand on my
past, if I were buried here myself I would complete a circle.
There is power in such atavism, and a certain sadness (that I
can't quite pass over as ridiculous) that the chains have been
broken by my divorces, by my father's divorces, by my mother's
Yankee blood, by the Polish and Sicilian blood I have passed on
to my children through their fathers, by all of us scattering so
far. (Or have I injected new life and new blood, broken away
from something old and stale?)

Though the past is hard to decipher it seems certain that some
Hunters, Elders, and Patricks were in Columbus when the town
was founded in 1828, on swampland by the Chattahoochee—"a
rough and lawless place" even after the Indians were driven
across the river into Alabama. Duels were frequent, steamboats
on the river formed the only connection with other places. (Two
prominent citizens at the time were a Mr. Lively and a Reverend
Mr. Boring.) In or around 1846 a Mr. George Hunter, Onnie's
grandfather, arrived from South Carolina to visit his brother
James (destined to be hanged by his toes) and his vast family.
George must have been well into middle age, for he had several
grown children. But he was still spry enough to win and marry a

fourteen-year-old girl, Margaret Elder, over the protests of her parents. He then generously gave away his considerable family property in South Carolina, with its three hundred slaves, to his two old-maid sisters, claiming that he was young (which seems questionable) and could support his child wife and the baby on the way. But George died of measles four months later, early in Margaret's pregnancy; at which time Margaret and her child, Georgia (Onnie's mother), seem to have been taken into brother James's family in the Southern manner and raised by them. (Margaret subsequently married a second cousin, Richard Waters, and had four more children.) At nineteen Georgia married James Wyatt Patrick, who fought in the Confederate Army and, after being with Lee when he surrendered, was shot— though not killed—just outside Appomattox by Union soldiers who didn't know peace had been declared. They had five children—Charles, Minnie, Georgia, Maggie May, and Johnnie Pearl.

I ask Dorothy, Maggie May's daughter, about her grandparents. We seem to be an impoverished branch, again the family money has slipped away to siblings; on the eve of buying the very fine Wolforth house, in midtown Columbus, James used the down payment to bail an irresponsible brother out of a "tight." Other Patrick land in Georgia disappeared, possibly after the war. James then died at thirty-nine of "brain congestion," leaving Georgia, like her mother, a young widow, with five small children and no money—though, having fought in the War and being a member of the Columbus Guards Military Company, James was given a splendid military funeral at Lynwood cemetery, attended by his company in full dress suits with white plumes on their hats, who fired salutes at the graveside; which might or might not have helped to console Georgia.

All women could do at that time was use the needle, and Georgia sewed wedding clothes for people in Columbus, a crying need and one that at least helped pay the bills. And, says Dorothy, "she bought bolts of batiste every January, and handkerchief linen, and she did hand-hemstitch every ruffle and whipped the little lace and made the little French knots and embroidery" for all the children's underclothes. Times were so hard that one daughter, Maggie May, had to go and live with friends in the country for two years, and Onnie, the youngest, went to work at sixteen. But this was a family of intrepid women, unafraid of hard work. Besides, they were close and affectionate and bound to St. Luke's Methodist Church by habit and conviction and location—for in the late nineteenth century Columbus was one fifth its present size and truly a town, people lived in what is now the downtown commercial area, went to school and church and each other's houses to "visit" on foot or at most by horse and buggy.

Jim's family sounds very similar, even to the South Carolina root; his grandfather Jonathan Johnson (who was drafted for the War of 1812) came to South Carolina from Virginia, his birthplace, in 1890. Jim was born shortly after the Civil War and went to work at the age of nine, on the roof of the state Capitol in Atlanta. Eventually he went into the family business, railroads. His father and brothers were cabinetmakers (railroad cars used to have a lot of wood interiors) and Jim became a coppersmith and tinsmith for the Central of Georgia Railroad in Columbus. When he married Onnie he was making twenty-five dollars a week and never made much more. Nunnally was born December 5, 1897, and his brother Cecil in 1902.

"They were typical Georgians," Cecil said of his parents, "grinding out a living." Onnie was "very tiny, sweet and gentle. She didn't finish high school. In those days, if a boy misbehaved in school the other students in the class had to whip him. Mama refused and got kicked out." But this is a little misleading—she was in fact a "steel gardenia." "She was truly the commanding general of the four, a fact which they all accepted," says a family friend. "She was never a person to be taken lightly. Her children had the utmost respect for her and her opinions all their days." She made Jim change out of his overalls before coming home. She was a careful manager of their tiny income, and though there was no money to throw away, they moved every two years to a slightly better house, trading up every time. (Daisy takes me to every one or its location. Most are gone now, but I am told that each neighborhood is an improvement over the last one.) There was always a darky, mainly Eula, who came in 1916 and stayed for thirty-nine years. Onnie taught Sunday school and was an earnest public servant, intensely concerned with public education. She was for many years the only, and possibly the first, woman member of the Board of Education; in 1905 she founded Columbus' first PTA, and she was associated with the nurses' association and the Goodwill Community Center. Her main concerns "were to see that the teachers were well treated and properly paid and that the Negroes were actually given education equal to the whites despite the state law on segregation." She eventually owned black housing which she maintained on as high a level as—well, if their skin had been a different color. Or almost.

Jim had "an unusual and delicate sense of humor." He loved Dickens and exasperated Onnie by buying books on the installment plan. When Nunnally and Cecil were old enough, he took them to the public library every Sunday for the week's supply of books. "Read—read—read!" Onnie would explode at the three of them lined up on the porch. "All they do is read!" Jim was the gentler of the pair—he couldn't lay a finger on his little boys, and whipping fell to Onnie during a time when whippings were doled out like grits or Epsom salts. Because of his job Jim was able to get them all passes on day coaches. "They believed in educating us on trips," Cecil said, "so Nunnally and I visited every important building or site, museum and art gallery in Washington and New York. They would never venture into New England . . . because of the carpetbaggers during the Reconstruction days—they just didn't like or trust New Englanders."

Onnie was never far from her three sisters, all of whom were married and had children around the ages of her own, and "visitin'" was constant—"everybody had to see everybody else every week." If someone got in a tight they helped each other out, taking in other members of the family for periods of time if necessary. Hospitality was endemic and "you always cooked enough for guests." Nunnally and Cecil grew up with ten or eleven cousins, most of whom went to the same school and Sunday school. They all lived "downtown" though all over downtown. ("Everybody moved every October," Daisy says. "It was something to do.") Columbus at that time was safe, homogeneous, WASP, and said to be delightful. Social stratification was casual —"If you went uptown you had to put on shoes." Only the Bottoms, a rough black section, was to be avoided. A cousin, Mamie Rainey, writes of this distant paradise:

"One summer our mothers took us on a picnic out back of St. Elmo. Our mothers rode in Aunt May Pekor's horse-drawn surrey. All of us children rode in a mule-drawn wagon. Nunnally and Curtis drove us . . . later they rode us bare back on the mule up and down the road. There were band concerts every Sunday on the court house lawn.

"Aunt Onnie loved a circus. She took the children to meet the circus train when it came in. She then went to the park to see them pitch their tents and cook breakfast. Later they went to the parade. . . . Uncle Joe Benton had an abbatoir and meat market. The boys used to go out there and watch them butcher. They got the cow tails and would put them on us girls. . . . one summer somebody put on picnic excursions on a large boat and we went on one down the river.

"Mama [Georgia Patrick Rainey] and Aunt Onnie used to sing and Aunt May played the piano. . . . Uncle Pekor had the first car in the family. It was a Reo and sat high off the ground. Aunt May had her duster and veiled hat that she wore. Uncle Pekor had a farm across the river in Alabama. Some time on Sunday he would take us over there to pick scuppernongs. . . . The Farmers market was across from the Court House Every morning Aunt Onnie went to market. One of the boys went with her and took their little wagon to take the groceries home. She always bought a watermelon. She didn't fail to go bye to see Aunt May.

"Aunt May had a cow and we girls loved to help churn.

"There has always been a lot of love in our family. . . ."

I try to imagine my father as a child—did anybody recognize him as anything special? "He was the smartest little fellow, sang like a bird too," says his second-grade teacher. (I know him to be tone deaf, bored and even irritated by music.) "Butt-headed," says Cousin Dorothy, which sounds right. An obsessive reader, lying on a bench on the porch or the living-room floor, buried in a book. In his early pictures, dressed as a little angel in a white ruffled dress, later in knickers and jacket, he is immediately recognizable. His small, sharp, deep-set eyes stare from under creaseless lids, even then bagging down over the lashes. At three he is already tipping his head back and staring down his nose.

In family pictures he looks very much like his father, while Cecil looks like Onnie. He looks smart, and difficult somehow, not easy like round-faced Cecil. He is the one with the flinty stare, the look beyond his years. After leaving behind his angel dress he never smiles, whether because of the photographic style of the day or from gravity of nature is hard to say.

Nunnally, Cecil and their cousins all went to the public schools in Columbus through high school. To earn spending money, Nunnally and Cecil delivered newspapers— ". . . we always had enough money for going to the movies or to see a stage show from the second balcony of the Springer Opera House for fifty cents," said Cecil. The Springer is not only still there, it has been most elegantly renovated in Victorian style, with flocked wallpaper, rows of golden lights and a presidential box, another testimony to optimism and civic pride. A brass plaque outside lists some of the greats who have performed there since its establishment in 1871—Edwin Booth, Otis Skinner, Lillie Langtry, Oscar Wilde, Ethel Barrymore, Maude Adams, Irving Berlin, Ruth Gordon—though the period from 1910 to 1915, when Nunnally and Cecil must have gone, seems a little sparse. There were the Dressler sisters, Victor Herbert and assorted wandering minstrels and band concerts. Nunnally remembers the Jewel Kelly Stock Company which put on *Sunset Mine, At the Point of the Sword, Her Majesty's Jewels* and, most notably, *Jesse James,* which he later turned into a picture. The Springer was an operating theater, which in fact Columbus had always had— traveling players and theater companies had come there since 1828—and in the eighties and nineties people had come from all around to see the plays and stay at the Racine Hotel (whose discouraging aspect doesn't in the least daunt the Historic Columbus Foundation, which eyes it as a future project).

However, Cecil continues, "I was the stage-struck one, not Nunnally. When I was a little kid, my friends and I put on a show in our back yard every Saturday. We of course ad-libbed our lines. In 1911 Caruso came to Atlanta in Puccini's *Girl of the Golden West* based on Belasco's play. I fell in love with the story and we did it every week. Nunnally, who was four or five years older than I, saw us and decided to write a better script. That was his first playwriting." Nunnally's only previous works were a few little stories about baseball (to which he was addicted) for the newspaper in 1908 or so.

His life was fairly full. If Columbus was dull, as he later claimed, it was still busy, full of life's tiny rituals, structured to avert solitude. He does not seem to have been a lonely child, writing (as I did) to make connections. He was—if anything—overconnected, cluttered with people and talk and activity and eventually stifled by it.

Cecil says, "In high school he played basketball, baseball, football and tennis. He was excellent in his studies. He took Latin, Spanish and French at the same time for two or three years. In English and grammar he was equally good. He started a literary publication and contributed short stories and poems. When I arrived at high school I was saddled with his brilliance. My English and Spanish teachers kept pointing out what a stupid student I was compared to Nunnally. On the other hand, I was excellent in math and science, in which he wasn't very good. So I decided to be an engineer."

Cecil's wisdom in refusing to compete with his brother is testimony to his ultimate sanity. In high school Nunnally was apparently a success. He was junior class poet and the waggish editor of the Columbus High literary magazine, in which lies evidence of early (though inbred) wit. Classes broke up at his jokes, girls found him hilarious. He was on the basketball team, but he aspired to be either a big-league ball player (first base) or a foreign correspondent in the style of the dashing Richard Harding Davis. He would have liked to go to Yale because of Frank Merriwell. But the genetic instructions which had divided the math from the verbal in the two brothers had been almost abnormally complete in Nunnally's case. He was unable to comprehend math or science in any way. At the end of his junior year, having spent most of the past months chasing a girl who looked exactly like Anita Stewart, he was faced with failing certain exams, particularly science—until he came upon his girl and the (married) science teacher kissing in a classroom. He was hurt, but on the other hand the situation presented an obvious advantage—this was not something the man would want noised about. "Each time I met him in the hall," Nunnally said, "I kind of popped my eyeballs at him." Nothing was said, but Nunnally was exempted from the exam because of "excellent work during the term" and went on into senior year. There was some question as to whether he graduated. As class valedictorian he had written a speech which "they" edited, doubtless removing all the best parts as editors will, and Nunnally protested by not appearing on the stage with the others to receive his diploma. It is agreed that he did graduate, but his schooling ended there. (After his death in March 1977, the Columbus *Ledger-Enquirer*'s obit was headlined, "Columbus High Dropout Nunnally Johnson Dies"—a strange tribute from the home-town paper.)

Following this graduation manqué in 1915 and after a near-fatal bout of malaria and typhoid fever that summer, Nunnally got his first newspaper job. His best friend, Cliff Tucker (late husband of Daisy), was already working on the *Enquirer-Sun,* where his father was editor, and shortly Nunnally was hired as a cub reporter for ten dollars a week. On his first day on the job he "abandoned all thought of becoming a professional baseball player and embraced journalism with a hug that took its breath away." But the first story he did on his own was a disaster. As he described it years later for the paper, "Either a farmer was suing a railroad for running over his wagon or a railroad was suing a farmer for the same calamity. . . . It was a brief story, not more than two paragraphs, but I doubt that in the history of journalism more errors had ever been compressed into such a space of print. . . . I had the wrong railroad suing, if indeed it was the plaintiff. I had the wrong decision. I had the wrong list of damages. I had the name of the other litigant wrong . . . the story was so manhandled that it was impossible to decide which party suffered the greater. Trying to disentangle its ramifications of mistakes, the attorneys finally gave up first in despair and then in disgust. In the end, apparently, it seemed less trouble to forget it than to try to unravel it . . . why I was not thrown off the paper instantly with a warning never to return on penalty of being shot I still don't know. The city editor, I guess, was just about too numb to do anything at all." [Columbus *Ledger-Enquirer,* October 18, 1953.] He stayed about six months until the paper, which was in a bad way financially, let him go because it couldn't afford him.

After that he spent six months in Cleveland, Ohio, where his uncle Charlie Patrick lived, but, he said, "I couldn't get a job. They would have been out of their minds to hire me. I finally got a job in a steel mill there, as a kind of checker. I was so ignorant of how to live away from home. I got a furnished room somewhere in Cleveland. I have no idea where it was, except that I had to get up about five o'clock in the morning to get a streetcar to go out to this steel mill, which must have been fifteen miles out. So I didn't get any breakfast, and there was no place I could find anything to eat at lunch. All those other fellows brought lunches, and I got nothing to eat till seven or eight in the evening, when I took a streetcar back into town. It looked like I was going to starve to death there." He had never thought much about the origins of food or considered that it might not grow fully prepared upon the dinner table. That Onnie scrimped and planned and bought it, that Eula cooked it, were matters he was protected from, as was information about how clean clothes appeared regularly in drawers and closets, how rooms were kept in order, how lawns got mowed and nasturtiums bloomed, what nature of machinery caused an ordinary household to grind forward from day to day. It made him, for the rest of his life, helplessly dependent on women, for it never occurred to him that these things might be done by men. He regarded it all as wonderful and mysterious, magic performed by trolls (or wives).

He had sent out applications to other Georgia newspapers, and the Savannah *Press* offered him a job as a reporter. "That was very good. I liked it there. I lived at the YMCA, which was to me like batching it, man about town." While he was there he joined the Savannah Hussars, a cavalry reserve group, hoping to be sent to Europe. Since he was only seventeen his parents had to sign the papers. He had expected to wear a "real Austrian" uniform, with helmet and jack boots, but instead looked "like kind of a clown soldier, nothing fit me. They had those spiral leggings, which were constantly trailing after me. It was awful."

He was sent to Camp Harris in Macon, where his aunt Georgia and three cousins lived. Cousin Mamie writes: "It was a short distance from our home so Nunnally came over quite often for supper. A lot of times Mama made home made rolls. She buttered them and put them in a ten lb. lard bucket and Cliff rode his bicycle to camp with them for Nunnally.

"Once when Aunt Onnie and Lois Pekor were visiting us, he was to come for lunch. He didn't come so Aunt Onnie, Lois and I rode the Street Car to camp. When we got there he was in the Guard House. They had him picking up watermelon rinds and trash. It broke our hearts and we all three cried.

"Once he slipped out of camp and came to our house. He hid his gun in the woods and Mama gave him some red material to use for an arm band so he would not look like an orderly. I don't know if he was caught or not."

Could the army make a man out of him, with such relatives? He said it did. Besides, Onnie, protective though she was about life's drab details, was not one to sabotage flying the nest. While Nunnally was at Camp Harris, his cousin Dorothy was fighting homesickness at Wesleyan College in Macon. At length she packed up and left. Onnie, in Macon for the day, found her sitting on a suitcase at the station. After hearing Dorothy out, she said, "Dorothy, if you give in to your feeling today, you'll always have to give in to things. If you conquer it, you'll be able to conquer any feeling for the rest of your life." After a short silence Onnie asked her what she was going to do. "I'm going back to school," Dorothy said.

Nunnally's outfit was then sent to Fort Bliss in El Paso to patrol the border against Pancho Villa. It hardly appears to have been exciting, though they charged with swords and Nunnally managed to lose a mule. While he was there he wrote a history of the Hussars (a lost work). It was all rather unrewarding. "I didn't understand horses and horses didn't understand me. Furthermore, though I was keenly anxious to be a leader of men, it was practically impossible to find anyone who would follow me." He got leave to study for an exam to enter Annapolis (there was no money for college, and Cecil worked his way through Georgia Tech) but failed the math section.

Back in Macon, at Camp Wheeler this time, he wrote camp news for the Macon *Telegraph* and was correspondent for the Savannah *Press*. The United States was now in World War I and though Nunnally and his outfit were being trained to go over-

seas, it never happened. Eventually he was sent to an officers'
training camp in Louisville, Kentucky, Camp Taylor, for a
"dreadful hard course" which earned him his commission. Then
at Camp Jackson, in South Carolina, where he was a lieutenant
in an artillery battery, he got to know a man named Steese, who
was the battery clerk. Steese was the assistant night city editor of
the New York *Tribune* and "you never saw a lieutenant suck up
to a corporal the way I sucked up to this corporal because I
wanted a job." Steese sent a note to the *Tribune* (this was before
it merged with the *Herald*) and when Nunnally arrived in New
York he was given a job on the paper.

Before I leave, Daisy drives me out of town to see a peanut
patch and a cotton patch, which we find after some searching
around. While Daisy watches for police, I try to steal a peanut
plant. Its roots are tough, locked into the ground, and all I manage to do is tear off a great hunk of top leaves, which I put on
the floor of Daisy's car. The cotton patch appears to be owned
by a very large black clan who sit nearby on the front porch of
their house. They freeze in place as we drive up. Daisy gets out
and talks to them, then comes back to the car. "Go ahead, I told
them you were from New York." I get out and walk into the cotton patch and in between the rows. There are no puffs of cotton
yet, only pale pink blossoms. I reach down and touch them as
twelve pairs of black eyes follow me. I have probably never felt
so ridiculous in my life. How long is right for a cotton experience? After five minutes or so I walk over and thank them as
they watch me unblinkingly. A couple of them speak a soft word
or two. Back in the car Daisy says, "They probably never saw
anybody from New York in their whole lives. I told them you
never saw a cotton patch before." They probably think I am insane. They neither move nor take their eyes off us as we drive
away.

New York to 1929

In December 1918, a few weeks after the Armistice, Nunnally made the mythic journey to New York. The social chemistry that drew the best literary minds in the country in the same direction has been well documented. We have heard everything about the twenties; if we are of my generation we have longed to live in the twenties and felt deprived that we did not. We sense an irretrievable freshness about that period, a newness that ages even in the description. All those sensitive young men, damp and fuzzy as newborns leaving their hometowns for the city, were infinitely lucky explorers. Nobody would ever again make the first footprint on the beach or the first sounds in a silent landscape. As writers, we even like to think, in certain moods, that the enormous amount of talent here in the twenties was secondary—given such impeccable raw material, any of us could have done it too. The literary ingredients were so good. They had won the First World War and proved that they were on the side of the angels; by doing this they had won the right to throw over that stifling Victorianism they had worn like a corset, which in turn plunged them into the most interesting guilt, conflict and disillusion. And on top of this the night was full of that postwar music nature plays when it is necessary to repopulate, to sew up the social fabric again after the young men have come home. Love and marriage, the smell of success, and a feeling of hope were all in the air. For a writer it was all there, and almost everybody wrote

something—short stories, novels, plays, newspaper stories, essays
grave and humorous, columns, diaries, magazine articles, poetry,
criticism. In the early twenties there were fourteen daily newspapers in New York (now there are three) and twice as many
magazines as there are now. The exodus to Hollywood didn't
start till late in the decade, when the talkies came in; and so
New York in the twenties was the magnetic pole of the writing
business, and Babylon besides—for in that period the city was
really magic.

With his letter of introduction to Hood McFarland, the city
editor, Nunnally went straight to the *Tribune,* where he was
hired as a cub reporter. He was frightened, awkward and extremely innocent, and started out by setting a wastepaper basket
on fire with a burning cigarette. As he later told in the Los Angeles *Times:* "I was so green that I worked for eight weeks without getting a day off. There was a large staff and in the confusion no-one told me to take a day off every week and I was so
scared that I was on hand seven days a week rather than take
chances. Besides that, I had the staff confused. I had only my
uniform and one civilian suit, not yet having accumulated
enough to buy another suit. One day I'd wear my uniform and
the next day my civvies and they thought I was two fellows.
When they discovered I was only one they fired me." [Novem-
ber 27, 1932.]

In February or March of 1919 he was hired for the Brooklyn
Daily Eagle by H. V. Kaltenborn, who was assistant managing
editor. He was to stay there for seven years. Shortly after his ar-
rival he met Alice Mason, editor of the *Junior Eagle,* a ten-page
supplement. Daughter of a Brooklyn church organist, Alice felt,
as Nunnally probably did, that she was there under false pre-
tenses—her mother had gotten her the job by convincing Harris
Crist, the managing editor, that her daughter not only could
write but knew all about type and make-up (an utter fiction)
and that any employer would be lucky to have her. But she
learned fast and held the job. She was a year younger than Nunnally, but to him she was the older, experienced city girl, who
knew her way around town. "He wooed me with a shower of
lemon drops," Alice says, as though I have any idea what she's
talking about. But then that's the sort of thing they went in for

then, lemon drops and crossword puzzles, charades and bubble-blowing.

Alice, a trim and energetic octogenerian with a hair bow who has just gotten her driver's license, lives in a house in the middle of a potato field on Long Island. Our relationship is odd, yet Alice and I must be something to each other, as the younger children must be to my mother. But our family falls outside ordinary definition. Alice last saw me when I was six; she tells me I painted her fingernails for her. I have always thought my older half sister Marge looked exactly like Pop, now I think she looks like her mother. They share other qualities, toughness and a certain recklessness which—at least in Marge's case—temper each other.

I try to look back through Alice's eyes to Brooklyn in 1919—the time warp is deceptive, because Alice looks much younger than her age, and I must keep reminding myself how long ago it all was. What was Nunnally like then? "A great big long-legged kid in a Palm Beach suit and a Panama hat, bouncing along with the stride of youth. He took me with him down to Sheepshead Bay (on an assignment) to the aerodrome . . . it was an innovation. A couple in one plane were married by the minister in another plane. We got caught in the rain and when we got back his trousers—which had been down to there—were up to here." He was the rube, she was the cool career girl. But even though he was shy and awkward, "he was always so funny." Years later, she infuriated him by telling him he looked exactly like Disney's Dopey. She couldn't have picked a more sensitive nerve. One of his early sources of pain was not being handsome, though this never stood in his way with women. He looked in the mirror and saw a plain person, and in those early days a cracker boy, a bumpkin.

Alice presumably was going to show him the ropes, and they were married that year, though before that she "offered to sleep with him and he was too noble—can you imagine anything like that? Not until we were married." This might have been part of being decent. Unlike the mythical male my generation was always hearing about, Nunnally couldn't wait to be married, loved the married state, and never lasted long as a bachelor. It must have been to him a sanctified state, irreligious though he was.

You saved yourself for it. He and Alice were married in Trinity
Church in Brooklyn Heights. "It really was an emotional thing,"
Alice says. "Aunt D. was there with a hat with red currants on,
and Mother had a new hat—just Mother and Aunt D., Nunnally
and me, and the Reverend Dr. Nellish . . . it was just this beautiful church with the rays of sunlight—so much better than a
wedding ceremony with all the fuss. I have very pleasant memories. . . ." One can't help imagining what a wedding in Columbus would have been like, if he'd stayed there and married
the girl who wanted him. Then "on our first night in our little
apartment I fed him creamed frankfurters. He ate them . . . he
wouldn't nowadays. He got very fussy." Fussy or merely sane?
Alice says she wrecked the marriage by being a bad cook and
housekeeper. "I filed things in the middle of the living-room
floor." How did Nunnally go for that? He was very nice about it,
or he seemed to be, then he'd say something innocent-sounding
that cut her down the middle. But then they weren't home much
anyway. "We went out in a bunch—we all took the subway to
the Village. We went to Joe's restaurant, a famous hangout . . .
we danced. . . . Nunnally danced pretty well, though he didn't
like it much. We all got tight, everybody was making liquor. . . .
George Lyndon made something with blackberries and prunes,
the stuff blew up." Nunnally and Alice got theirs from a bootleg-
ger, though Alice and her family, in an early burst of piety, had
signed the pledge not to drink. How did they manage to get up
and go to work (a middle-aged question)? "We had young stom-
achs and good heads."

How long the marriage lasted remains Alice's secret—"we
were married long enough to produce Marjorie. We fulfilled our
destiny in her." Marge was born in 1920, and things went
downhill rapidly after that. The two mothers-in-law were a
chronic problem and "did as much to promote our divorce as
anything." Onnie had been against the marriage from the beginning (since she was against the two later marriages too, one suspects that nobody would have been good enough). "She had a
great deal of influence on him—she didn't want him to marry
just anybody." For some reason she didn't want them to take a
honeymoon, so they went right back to work (and the creamed
frankfurters) the day after their wedding. Alice paid no atten-

tion when Onnie wrote Nunnally that a good Georgia man would never want his wife to work, but gave in on a trip to Columbus when the baby was three months old. "I had the most miserable trip. . . . I was very unpopular, I was tired, the baby'd been cross, they wanted to show me the town. . . . I wouldn't go, I was wrong from the start with Nunnally's relatives. They would expect me to nurse the baby right out in a big circle of relatives." Too many things weren't working out and finally they separated because "Nunnally wanted to be free to write." He took an apartment at 64 West Ninth Street in Manhattan and "we kind of went back and forth till he met Marion [my mother, his second wife]." Onnie came to New York when she got the news of the separation and "had her usual heart attacks. She had them whenever things weren't going her way. We had to rub her hands . . . it was mostly psychosomatic. That kind of sealed it. Mother stuck by us, her children could do no wrong. Though Nunnally said she was the most irritating woman on earth." There was a tiny war between the mothers over who should take care of Marge while Alice went back to work, which Mrs. Mason won; Onnie retreated to Georgia, and Alice got a job on a paper in New Jersey.

In spite of the failure of that brief young marriage, his landscape was, he said, "just glorious, but then, what the hell, I was just out of the canebrakes of Georgia—everything that happened was beautiful to me. And it was the last decade, I suppose, that didn't have a cloud over it—last decade in my lifetime. In the course of time came World War II, the Bomb, and ever since then there's never been a carefree breath drawn. And when I've thought of it I've thought, of course, from the point of view of a newspaperman, a man on the street—there was a time when you could enjoy a good writer, you know. They just seemed to come along periodically at that time and they weren't dismissed and thrown aside, a Broadway butterfly, a house of cards, a big name." During that era of great news reporting (the Dot King murder, the Caruso robbery, the Gerald Chapman trial, the Lockwood investigation, the Black Eagle of Harlem, Gertrude Ederle, the King of the Belgians, Queen Marie of Rumania, the Elwell and Hall Mills Murder cases) Nunnally covered (for the

Eagle) the Wall Street explosion in 1920—being an eager cub, he was the only one in the editorial room that morning and so got his first assignment. As he wrote to Gene Fowler in the fifties: ". . . I came up the stairs at Wall Street to find seven bloody bodies on the pavement right in front of the kiosk. It was the Wall Street explosion but never did a story answer better to Bide Dudley's old line, 'much excitement but could learn nothing.' Nobody knew what had happened except that there were a lot of bodies around and the remains of a horse. If I remember correctly, it was days before it was finally decided that the Communists had planted a bomb in a horse-drawn wagon in front of J. P. Morgan's office."

He covered the Scopes trial in 1924: ". . . in Dayton, Tennessee, with William Jennings Bryan for the prosecution and Clarence Darrow, Dudley Field Malone and Arthur Garfield Hayes defending the young man who was charged, as Bill McGeehan (a sports writer) put it, with 'thinking below the deadline.' Nothing could have been finer than to be in Dayton with Mr. Mencken, Edmund Duffy, Tony Muto and all of our fine friends for the titanic struggle between Evolution and Fundamentalism. I suppose the big moment of my newspaper life was witnessing Clarence Darrow's examination of Bryan as an authority on the Bible. It was hardly a contest."

He also covered the original Fanny Brice-Nicky Arnstein story, which ran on and off for a year or so. As he described it years later in an interview, "Nicky was caught on something called the Leonard Street robbery—some guys stuck up a mail truck and got, I believe, a million dollars' worth of negotiable securities. Presently they came along and arrested Nicky Arnstein and Fanny said he had about as much to do with that robbery as her nephew. But if there was ever a real Runyon character it was Nicky because Nicky was so pleased because he was described as the brains of the Leonard Street robbery. And nobody had ever described him as the brains of anything up to that point. Fanny said he couldn't think his way out of a paper bag. So he didn't deny it, he went into hiding. Fanny was singing, in the Ziegfeld Follies, a song called 'My Man.' Well, that was the stuff to feed the troops, you know. Singing her heart out, 'My

Man.' And Nicky was actually hiding in her home in Scarborough outside the city.

"I covered his surrender. The papers just made fun of the cops because they knew the cops knew where he was and for all kinds of crooked reasons they weren't arresting him. And the *World* would have a box on the front page every day saying, 'Police yesterday searched every wastepaper basket in City Hall without finding Nicky Arnstein.' They would have jokes about this every day. But he decided, for what reason I don't know, to give himself up, and he was going to surrender himself to police headquarters. He was going to come down the West Side and he was going to stop at the Hotel Marie Antoinette, I believe it was, way up on the West Side there and pick up a newspaperman who had been a friend of his, and he was going to give him a story.

"Well, he did—but the thing was that he decided to give himself up on St. Patrick's Day, and he came down the West Side and there was something like twelve thousand cops marching up Fifth Avenue, and they cut off all the cross-town traffic and there was Nicky in this car trying to get over to the East Side to get down to Centre Street. And they said, 'Get back, get back,' and so he'd go down ten more blocks . . . he finally [got there] and gave himself up at Tombs Magistrate's Court, I guess it was. Anyway, I came and I was the only newspaperman there. I guess they were all looking for him uptown and he was waiting there with a lawyer and a couple of other guys. The court was empty. And then a guy came in, and this was the first time I'd ever heard such kind of talk. A little fat fellow, called Dutch, a plainclothesman, he came in and he was boiling. He walked over to Nicky and he said, 'You son of a bitch, ten minutes later and I'da had ya, ten minutes and I'da gotcha.' Now there was a ten-thousand-dollar reward for anybody capturing Nicky Arnstein. And Nicky said, 'Dutch, I'm sorry, I couldn't wait.' This conversation between the crook and the cop was a revelation to me . . . it was like that fellow yesterday who blew the two-foot putt, he would have won the tournament and thirty thousand dollars."

In 1922 he was given a daily column, "One Word after Another." That he was a humorist had become clear to those in charge and now as a roving reporter he could comment on whatever struck him as outrageous—urban tribal customs, the literary life as in this revealing bit: "The writer without the capacity for indignation faces a difficult and discouraging future. He sees all about him special writers, editorial writers, cartoonists, all of those who write or address a public more or less personally absorbed in some spirit of striking out at this or that. Those who strike out at the most popular bugaboos are the most successful. The unindignant man envies them . . . their ability to become exercised over matters which in all probability will never touch them, or only very slightly . . . the unindignant ones, myself for example, struggle along without seeing, more than very infrequently, a cause for emotion."

Like all columnists of the period, he often included a poem, and he was particularly taken by the work of an eleven-year-old marvel named Nathalia Crane, a sort of prodigy poetess who became the center of a literary furor. The best known of this prolific child's work, the title poem of one of her three books, was *The Janitor's Boy*.

> Oh, I'm in love with the janitor's boy
> And the janitor's boy loves me
> He's going to hunt for a desert isle
> In our geography.

> A desert isle with spicy trees
> Somewhere near Sheepshead Bay:
> A right nice place, just fit for two,
> Where we can live alway.

She was almost alarmingly gifted.

> A flower flamed, a parrot screamed
> Night spread her peacock tail
> And beauty tripped the platform of
> That lilac-tinted vale.

Or, yet more baroque:

> Drawn from the silt of the ages
> Blastoderm girthed to destroy
> Turning the least of the laddies
> Into a hangman's boy.

Nunnally gave Nathalia a lot of space, printing not only her poems but interviews with her and columns of curly appreciation such as the following affectionate spoof of her astounding vocabulary ("the word hasn't been written that she can't rope, throw, tie and brand in record time") as used in her book, *Lava Lane:*

> About the best I can do is list a definition of these words as I know them now, and see later how accurate I have been. So:
>
> *Cicatrix:* A lady that has something to do with a wall.
> *Lecturne:* where you, or anybody else, lectures.
> *Campaniles:* plains.
> *Pylons:* (1) big snakes; (2) big girders.
> *Porphery:* one of those fish that follow a ship.
> *Verdi:* a composer of grand opera.
> *Teasel:* where one teases.
> *Regnant:* a condition.
> *Nullah:* to cancel something.
> *Plim:* slang for Plam.
> *Sarcenet:* (absolutely unknown)
> *Sindon:* a little cinder.
> *Tamarind:* a little orange.
> *Cincture:* a bellyband for a horse.
> *Blastoderm:* a prehistoric animal.
> *Fane:* (unknown)
> *Barracoon:* what you hide behind when they begin shooting.
> *Sistrum:* what you catch rain water in.
> *Cygnet:* a ring with your initial on it, or if bought from a pawnshop, with somebody else's initial on it.
> *Trireme:* a sharp lecture for doing something wrong.

The only other person who got so much space was another little girl, Marjorie.

But the *Eagle's* editor denounced Nathalia as a hoax. He said that her father, himself a failed poet and former newspaper editor, had cooked the whole thing up with a group of bored but talented friends—William Rose Benét, Elinor Wylie, Faith Baldwin, Louis Untermeyer. "Since poets of the first rank rarely make enough to eat on, it was hard to understand why they should turn their stuff over to somebody else, even a child," Nunnally

said. But the managing editor had decided that was what happened, and the result was a running debate in the paper, with reporters attacking Nathalia on the front page while Nunnally
tried to defend her in his column. Headlines in the *Eagle* read,

> Edwin Markham Brands Nathalia Crane's Claim to Author-
> ship a Hoax: Honorary President of Poetry Society writes
> the Eagle He Is fully Convinced "Wonder Child" Did Not
> Write Poems—Believes 6 Young, Distinguished Poets Are
> Authors.

> John V. A. Weaver Joins Markham in Doubting Nathalia
> Wrote Verses: Prominent Young American Poet Says He
> Has Talked with Girl, Who Gave No Evidence of Spiritu-
> ality or Unusual Intellect.

> Nathalia Crane's Poems Strikingly Resemble William Rose
> Benét's: Critics Find Remarkable Similarity Between Writ-
> ings of Famous Poet-Journalist and "Wonder Child" Exists
> in Both Words Used and Choice of Subjects.

In this last story the writer compares Nathalia's work verse by
verse to Benét's and finds a "haunting similarity." Other journalists and editors (including Nunnally), it was further charged,
had acted as agents and promoters for Nathalia, writing prefaces
to her books and printing her poems in their columns. In the
midst of all this Nunnally got tired of the whole situation and
quit, saying, "I didn't want to work for anybody I didn't like,"
though, as Marion explains it:

"An elderly spinster on the *Eagle* took exception to his writing
about Nathalia as if there was a dirty relationship between the
two. She really ranted on to some extent. I don't think there was
any such thing. Nunnally was always fond of children, and took
this one up. I do remember his telling me that Nathalia's mother
had made him a proposition, saying her husband no longer
approached her with sex. I don't remember that Nunnally quit
because of Margery's rancid implications. I thought he was ambitious, and the *Herald Tribune* (where he went next) was a step
up as to money and prestige."

The whole controversy fizzled away inconclusively, leaving
hints and unanswered questions hanging. But Nunnally's friend-

ship with the child was real. She wrote him quaintly worded notes inviting him to dinner at her parents' house in Brooklyn, telling him he could choose what he wanted to eat (lamb or roast chicken) and that she would have his brand of cigarettes on hand.

A year or so before this, encouraged by Catharine Brody, a girl friend who had written some fiction for *Smart Set* (the old Mencken and Nathan magazine), Nunnally had started to write short stories. He submitted one to *Smart Set* ("Scarehead") and they bought it for twenty dollars. He wrote four or five more before *Smart Set* folded up and Mencken and Nathan started the *American Mercury*. On the side he wrote for confession magazines, a popular genre at that time—"I confessed for both sexes, becoming quite a hand, in fact, at revealing my past as a betrayed factory girl." Again encouraged by Catharine and her roommate, Marian Spitzer (both *Globe* reporters), and the agent Otto Liveright, he tried the *Saturday Evening Post*, resubmitting one they had previously turned down. They took it. The *SEP* became his market though "it was like selling out to the Establishment," besides which, rather like *The New Yorker* later on, you couldn't offer rejected *SEP* stories to any other weekly, such as *Collier's* or *Liberty* (though the monthlies *Redbook* and *Cosmopolitan* might accept them), because the *SEP* format was so specialized. You either joined their stable or you didn't. Nunnally's stories suited the *SEP* in their timeliness, the very quality that has caused them to lose their glitter over the years. They were witty and current and "very popular among the customers," says Joel Sayre, long-time magazine writer and old friend. "He had a big following until the depression hit."

The short-story market has shrunk so it is hard to imagine what it must have been then. Writers could not only make their names but pay the rent and the speakeasy bills by writing short fiction. People bought magazines anxious to read their favorite writers, and they wanted to read fiction, not fact (today it is quite the opposite). Not only were there more magazines (besides *The New Yorker, McCall's, Redbook*, the *Ladies' Home Journal, Good Housekeeping*, the *Atlantic* and *Harper's*, which are still around, there was the *SEP, Collier's*, the *American*, the *Woman's Home Companion, Liberty, Vanity Fair, Smart Set*, the

American Mercury and the pulps *Bluebook, Everybody's* and *Adventure*) but each magazine printed more fiction. *McCall's*, which now prints one or two stories per issue at most then printed five or six. The pay could be terrific. By the early thirties Nunnally was making $2,500 for a short story and $750 for a non-fiction article; he was offered a contract by *Cosmopolitan* for six stories in a year, $3,000 each. (I note this in some pain since I was paid $2,500 by *McCall's* for a short story in 1976, and presently have a *Cosmopolitan* contract for four articles in a year, $3,000 each. On the other hand book contracts are much higher now than they were then, though fiction lags behind non-fiction.)

There is something hypnotic about the moment a writer first tries fiction. It is a risky thing to do, really, and one might wonder why a competent reporter and successful light columnist would bother to do such a thing. Probably in those days, when they were less burdened than we are by self-scrutiny, it just seemed like another trick to play with words, another balancing act, a new way to play. They were so young, and everybody was doing it—most writers do try a variety of things until they find one or two that feel right to them. But unlike reporting, which is fueled by a hunger for information, or essays and criticism, which come from an observing and reflective turn of mind, fiction—like humor—comes out of pain. Nothing relieves that odd build-up of pressure like fiction, nothing accomplishes so well the act of turning some tangled wound into a separate and orderly experience. In no other form has a writer so much power—he can make up an entire world and the people in it. Without facts, he is free to build his own reality which, if he is successful, will be more real than the real one. It is risky because he must do the whole job—it all depends on his vision. There are no facts of intrinsic interest to counterweigh a bad presentation, no book or play or movie to discuss and criticize and prop oneself against, no stage or screen or actor or director to bear more than half the weight. It is a real solo flight, a nervy walk in space.

Landing from this trip means getting through to somebody else, the smarter the better, which is why immediate acceptance by a good editor can do such wonders. Nunnally sold his first story to Mencken and Nathan (Mencken was his personal god)

and continued to sell almost unfailingly for ten years. The times
and his talent fitted together. He wrote stories quickly if not easily, bright and droll chapters out of his experience. They are
neatly constructed and close to farce in tone. He arrived at a
working comic formula early and stuck with it. They do not attempt a great deal but handle competently what they do attempt.
The pain, being thrown into shadow by the humor, hardly shows
—at least in the early ones, though at the end of the twenties
and early thirties, when he wrote the last ones, undealt-with
anger against women comes out. But by then he was married to
my mother.

In the fall of 1923 Marion Byrnes came to the *Eagle* (long
after Alice had left). Marion was the youngest of four children
of a Catholic educator and his non-Catholic wife, with whom
she was still living in Bayside, Queens. After two years at
Wellesley and two at Barnard, she went off, like everyone else, to
work on a newspaper. She was pretty and gutsy, and lucky
enough to have a family who had not only encouraged but
insisted on her education, but let her live at home after college
without charge or interference (except for her mother's tendency
to be appallingly rude to any young man who came into the
house). For the first year on the *Eagle* (when Marion earned
fifty cents a "stick," which amounted to four to seven dollars a
week) she and Nunnally were only acquaintances. Then she
got the assistant editorship of the Sunday magazine (strong on
success stories, the big thing then) for thirty-five dollars a week;
she moved from the city room across the hall to "where the critics
and the society editor and Nunnally were. My social position
changed." In this new and wonderful place everybody sat around
and did crossword puzzles. In spite of her being one of the few
around who had been to college, everybody did puzzles faster
than Marion in what sounds like kind of a daily contest. One day,
in exasperation, she simply filled all the letters in haphazardly
and announced that she had won. Nunnally was impressed and
further fascinated when she told him what she had done and,
possibly to discover the source of such inscrutable behavior, took
her out to dinner and then asked her to marry him afterward,
over rum at his apartment.

But Marion was already engaged to Les, a real estate man. He wasn't around much, he spent weeks at a time at his housing development in New Jersey, though their understanding had never stopped Marion from going out with other men. But she had agreed to marry him and live in California. When she told Nunnally that he said, "I'm just a clown, all I'm good for is making people laugh." She consoled him, and for six months there was a standoff while she tried to decide which one to marry. At the end of this time Les, who does not appear to have been terribly acute, left for California on business and told Marion he would wait there for her to come along and marry him. This settled the whole thing—after a few letters back and forth Marion wrote him a Dear John and said she was going to marry Nunnally.

It doesn't sound as though either of them suffered much over any of this, up to this point. They went out constantly, with each other and friends, to night clubs and theaters and speakeasies. They drank quarts of booze. Everything was—and this is one of the things we envy about the period—enormous fun and a little crazy. Although Nunnally was undoubtedly hurt by being turned down by Marion on the first try, he wasn't really as pathetic as he sounds, though of course he would have liked her to think so. I am told that women hurled themselves at him. He had had at least one serious affair since the separation from Alice besides Marion and a lady named Cynthia, and probably more I'll never know of. His personal magnetism made them forgive not only his drinking (for, though he didn't drink much, he was very badly affected by what he did drink), which sometimes necessitated either toting him home or putting him on a sofa for the night, but an appalling tactlessness on his part when he told them about one another and even took two of them out to dinner at the same time—a girl with whom he was heavily involved was horrified to find herself at dinner along with the beautiful Marion, who was clearly in the lead at that point. The girl went home in misery, having been told without words that the affair was over. Why he was so bad at a balancing act at which some men are expert (or so I've been told) or why he was—if he was—so insensitive to the feelings of the women in his life is hard to say. For a man who loved women so—which he did, he adored them—he was astonished when he hurt their feelings, pained that he could be so heavy-handed. Pete Martin, in a *Saturday Evening Post* article about him twenty years later, tells this story:

"He was having lunch, during an interim between marriages, with a young woman who had decided that the time was at hand to reproach him for certain shortcomings which she felt were seriously affecting her life. But unaware of this solemn purpose, Johnson had ordered a carefree meal, being particularly pleased to find shad roe in season.

"This he realized, once the emotional scene was launched, was a mistake, for a hearty appetite is obviously incompatible with drama. But the roe was so fresh and well-cooked that he found it impossible, between sighs, to resist a slow but steady attack on it. The young woman stood this brutish behavior as long as she could.

"'Look at you!' she said bitterly. 'Our very lives at the cross-roads, and you there smacking your lips like a pig!'

"'I'm terribly sorry, honey,' he assured her in genuine distress. 'If I'd known it was going to be like this, I'd have ordered something I didn't like.'"

Marion left the *Eagle* shortly after Nunnally did. She wanted the editorship of the Sunday magazine and, when she didn't get it, left in a smart of injustice. It happened that her sister Margaret, recently divorced, had just gotten into a show called *Mayflowers* and swept her younger sister in with her. (Marion's only previous stage experience had been in a review called *Hitchy-Koo* while she was at Barnard, for which she had been asked by one of the Shuberts—but refused—to appear in the nude.) In the chorus, they danced something called the Grecian Bend (around forty-five years later, I watched them demonstrate it, with bursts of giggles and provocative little kicks, on a summer evening in a house in Vermont). Nunnally, now on the *Herald Tribune,* was very amused by the whole thing and came to the stage door every other night, often with a crony, Julian Street or Stanley Walker.

Toward the end of the run Marion's father died and the family circumstances changed considerably. Her mother had been left with very little money and her sister, divorced with two little boys, none at all after the show closed; they all packed up and went to stay with a brother in San Francisco, and Marion went to live with an aunt and uncle in Forest Hills. By now she had a job as assistant editor on *Success* magazine, but it must have been a forlorn period for her, particularly when she suddenly got a telegram from Nunnally saying he couldn't marry her because he was in love with Cynthia and had been all along. She spent a dark weekend, but on Monday morning he phoned her with an explanation that was eventually to become dreadfully familiar— "I was drunk, didn't you know that?" Being drunk was better than being gone—they both knew that, and things wobbled on for another six months. Half a dozen times he said to her at the end of the evening, "It's no good, I love somebody else." During this period he moved into an apartment at 11 West Fiftieth (now Rockefeller Center), two large rooms on the fourth floor which Cynthia helped him furnish. "He was planning to be married to somebody," Marion says, "though he wasn't sure who."

One day he suddenly proposed to her at lunch. His divorce from Alice was—something; started, almost over, practically final, and like a character from one of his own stories, he wanted to marry Marion that night. After work they went to the newly furnished apartment, had a few drinks, and then took a taxi to Portchester. Their newspaper friend Barr Gray went along, presumably to steer them in the right direction, for they were fairly stoned and very merry. After being married by a justice of the peace in Portchester, they took another taxi back to the apartment. This was all "probably in 1926" and Marion had just made it under the line, because "girls had to get married by twenty-five and I just made it."

The next morning, while they were still in the nuptial bed, Cynthia phoned. Nunnally told her that he and Marion had been married the night before, and Cynthia, who apparently had not expected this, burst into tears. He covered the receiver with his hand and said to his bride:

"She's crying. You'd better leave."

Most women would have raised hell at such a direction, but Marion, being almost abnormally obliging, got dressed and went out. When she came back several hours later she found Nunnally depressed to the point of grimness—he had made a terrible mistake, he should have married Cynthia. For several months he was furious with her and at himself, "angry and grouchy most of the time." He drank more than ever and went out with other girls, while Marion threatened to leave and the loyal Barr held the marriage—if such it was—together. Finally she quit *Success*, took two hundred dollars she had saved and went to San Francisco to join her family.

During this period, February and March of 1927, Nunnally phoned her every night, promising total reform. It was her he wanted after all. Whether his decision was brought about by absence or some change in the relationship with Cynthia remains a mystery. Letters he wrote Marion during this period are truly love letters, begging her return. "I wish, wish so much, you'd give me some assurance of your love and intention of coming back. It seems that you don't mention it nearly enough . . . it is not one of those Forest Hills-to-50th-Street separations, or Shelton-to-50th-Street. It is definite—oh, so God damn definite. It has shaken me clean through. . . . I have a bellyful of liberty, and I want somebody to come home to."

At the same time, along with news of friends and work he wrote: "I had lunch with Lois Long and Peter Arno the other day. . . . My God, Morris Markey has written a book! Oh my God! . . . the New Yorker finally bought that burlesque ad thing, 'A Wallflower at a party of Morons' and sent me a check for $60, which was unexpected and welcome."

He had no hesitation about telling her of his busy social life: ". . . a sizable crowd went out for a little drinking. At midnight while in Helen Morgan's night club I realized that this girl and myself had been transferred bodily to somebody else's party. . . . I had lunch with Janet today at the Crillon. . . . Janet won't appear at the Algonquin with me because she's afraid she'd have to answer a lot of people who say, 'is Nunnally Johnson soft on you?' . . . Jane and I had dinner at Jack Kennedy's and then to her show 'Barker' and later Julian and Narcissa came and sat a while and the three of us went over to Roseland where I did a story about taxi dancers."

But Marion, staying in San Francisco with her family, "somehow never looked for a job in California." They were closer than they had been in months, in spite of the three thousand miles between, and she was still very much in love with him. After four weeks she agreed to come back and he wired: ". . . TOO HAPPY

NOW FOR WORDS AND PRAY YOU WILL LEAVE TUESDAY CEREMONY
TAKES PLACE THE DAY YOU ARRIVE AND THERE WILL NEVER BE ANY
QUESTION ABOUT THIS ONE LOVE TO MARGARET AND BEG MRS.
BYRNES TO FORGIVE ME." [She did.]

The idea was that, since the first marriage hadn't worked out
very well, they would try another one. There had been some
question about the finality of the divorce from Alice and the va-
lidity of the first marriage. But I prefer the way my mother explains it—if Portchester doesn't work out you try someplace
else. A plan to marry in Philadelphia, on a day he had an ap-
pointment at the *SEP*, aborted, even though Marion had bought
the ring herself. But shortly after they settled on Hackensack,
where Barr had a friend who was a judge. "We went out on the
bus, cold sober," Marion says. "I wore a fur-trimmed maroon vel-
veteen suit I'd bought for forty-five dollars. It was very becoming." Afterward the three of them again returned to the apartment. This second marriage, in 1927, "was much more normal.
People came over to the apartment. . . . Nunnally was writing a
column a day [for the New York *Evening Post*]. We went out
every night to night clubs or the Dizzy Club," a speakeasy where
journalists hung out.

Marion didn't go back to work. "I decided to be just a housewife . . . he put no pressure on me." But she probably has forgotten (or is defensive with her feminist daughter), for he had
written her when she was still in California: "I went over to the
Eagle yesterday and talked to Rodgers. I told him the situation
and how I felt I was either going broke wiring you or going
crazy worrying about you. We agreed that when you come back
you should not take a job, that if you wanted to write, or wanted
to free lance work around, just for your own satisfaction and at
your own pleasure, or even show business again, that would be
all right. . . . Cleveland commented that you were essentially
domestic and I was surprised, because it has been my belief that
nobody but myself ever thinks of you that way. We scarcely
meant kitchen-bound. But that you are happy in a home. Well,
I'll make one for you."

Growth is patchy and uneven, both in children and the minds
of women. Marion, who had lived with complete freedom and
independence for several years, saw nothing odd in her husband

and her past employer deciding whether or not she should work. (She still doesn't.) "I couldn't have held a job anyway, we were out at night clubs until four in the morning." The way things turned out, it wasn't really an issue with them, or not a visible one, anyway. Life was good in the Hackensack marriage. There were a lot of friends around, Holger Lundburgh, Marian Spitzer Thompson (who claims to be Nunnally's "oldest continuous friend") and her husband Harlan, Joel and Gertrude Sayre, Edith Haggard, Finley Peter Dunne and his wife, Lindsay Parrott, Thyra Winslow, Julian Street, Heywood Broun. The walk-up at 11 West Fiftieth was small but comfortable, with a tiny kitchenette. They went to Europe every year. It is a revelation, fifty years later when we all seem to feel poor, to find how much they could afford on their small salaries in the twenties. (Peter Dunne—then a columnist on the *World*—says the word at Costello's was that fifty dollars a week was not serious dough but sixty was.) An all-around reporter made thirty-five dollars a week, and on that he could afford a pleasant two-room apartment in the Village, for instance, as well as restaurants, theaters and speakeasies. By 1927 Nunnally was selling stories to the *SEP* fairly regularly so he and Marion were well fixed—besides, newspaper people got all sorts of freebies, theater tickets and rounds of drinks at Texas Guinan's or Barney Gallant's or Bleeck's, the newsmen's hangout. Not only did they do better than we do, they didn't seem to be as heavy with worry as we are. Holger Lundburgh, long-time correspondent for the Swedish news bureau and old friend of Nunnally's and Marion's, says, "People met more often and more easily, the food was not expensive, there was always somebody to help out in the kitchen, taxes were low. . . . New York was such a miraculously happy place. People laughed in a different way, and they could live graciously on very little. It was a homely town, a kindly town. Nunnally fitted so well into that time, that city—he liked it, he understood it." He reached out to it, loved and was amused by its eccentricities.

By now he had shed his old awkwardness. "When I met him in 1924 at Faith Baldwin's, he was shy and self-conscious," says Edith Haggard, long-time literary agent and another old friend. "But he grew to have such poise. It was the one way—the only way—he really changed." By the late twenties everything had come together for him, though Marion hung back somewhat. "It was a queer marriage," says Holger. "They had vast differences." She was shyer and more reticent by nature, but besides that, he was the one who got all the attention, he had all the wit and success. A subtle change of emphasis had taken place, now it was clear that Nunnally was going to make it. She was beginning to see that hers would be reflected glory. But that was all right really, she always let him have his way, even when he disappeared for a night or two. "I usually or always let Nunnally have his head about things. I realized he was a creative artist and had to have experiences in order to expand." As for the drinking—well, what drinking? It's all in your point of view. Marion drank along with him and held it a lot better. But "every night we went out was a peril—once I grabbed him just before he was hit by a taxi in Times Square." But there began to be talk of "fleshpots"— Nunnally wasn't writing as much as he should, and Marion would occasionally write one of his columns when he had a hangover. Nunnally had talked of moving to the suburbs in 1927 or earlier, of buying a house in a quiet neighborhood that would be good for his work and for Marge when she was with them. A curious episode decided it. Cecil had come for a visit and the three of them went to a party after a week of night life that would have felled the strongest. At some awful hour Marion left by herself, which she did occasionally when she was unable to dislodge Nunnally. At dawn Nunnally and Cecil came in, and Cecil was crying. In the morning Nunnally said, "We'd better move to the suburbs." (Cecil says that Marion made the suggestion.) But some cloud had passed over. They bought a house in Great Neck, on Long Island, and moved there in 1929.

New York 1926-1932

After the *Eagle*, Nunnally spent a year on the *Tribune*, now moved uptown and merged into the *Herald Tribune*, doing—like Frank Sullivan on the *World*—mostly human-interest stories. "Most papers at that time had a fellow who specialized in lost dogs, sea serpents, and men who predicted the end of the world," Nunnally said. Stanley Walker was the city editor at that time.

Of all the papers in town, "The *Times* was number one," Nunnally said in an interview. "Most newspapermen thought the *World* was the number one newspaper, except that it was folding up. Benchley said the reason it was folding up was that there were too many stories that began, 'Up the dark stairs trudged a lonely figure.' But the *Herald Tribune*, which I landed on in '26, '27, something like that, that was the elegant paper. Typographically it was the best-looking paper in town. The *Times* was always gray, smudgy. And the New York *World* was never very good-looking. But the *Herald Tribune* used the upper and lower case type, beautiful make-up. It was kind of an elegant newspaper."

One Sunday evening he was assigned to cover the evening service at St. Mark's in the Bouwerie. As he described it in a letter to Gene Fowler years later:

"This looked like nothing whatever to me. In fact, I thought somebody was simply humiliating me in some way. So when nobody would listen to my protests, I said to hell with it, and went off to a very lively party in Brooklyn. Around ten o'clock that night I called the desk from the party, reported that there was no story in it, and got goodnight. When I woke up around noon the next day and picked up the paper, there on the front page with a two-column head below the break was a story with a headline something like: Girls Dance Barelegged Around Altar. When I got hold of the *Times* I saw what had happened. The son-of-a-bitch on the *Times* had actually gone down to the church. The Reverend Dr. Guthrie had staged some kind of druid ceremony in his church and a half-dozen fat-legged female members of the parish had shuffled around the altar in cheesecloth. The *Herald Tribune* had picked up the *Times* story from an earlier edition."

Unable to think of an alibi, he went in to see Endicott Rich, the city editor.

"When he asked me what had happened and I told him that I didn't know, we both looked at each other in bewilderment. First I said that I had a pew around a corner and couldn't see very well . . . but when he pointed out to me that St. Mark's was a perfectly square church, like a big block, I fell back on the suggestion that perhaps I had left a little early . . . he was such a kind-hearted man that he simply could not bring himself to believe that I was telling him such a flat lie as I was telling him. I went down to Bleeck's and had another drink and figured that if I kept out of sight the whole thing would blow over. But the combination of religion and sex blew the story not over but up, and somebody got Bishop Manning to denounce the Reverend Dr. Guthrie and his didos, and the story ballooned again that day . . . then followed one of those noisy controversies over church organization and the power of the Bishop and the responsibility of the vicar and God only knows what else.

"Each of these stories began with the mention of the Reverend Dr. Guthrie 'around whose altar barelegged girls danced in cheesecloth,' and day after day Mr. Rich would look over at me with the appealing look of a faithful dog, begging for some sort of explanation, and each time I could only shake my head sadly, like a colored man caught in a watermelon patch with seeds all over his face . . . it seemed to me that this story would never die. In one form or another it went on for weeks."

In fact it went on for years as the Reverend Dr. Guthrie "galvanized by all this attention, staged other antics in his church, and each and every story identified him again as the ecclesiastical impresario who had introduced cheesecloth on the altar. And every time . . . I was harrowed not by a bad conscience but out of shame for the stupidity that kept me from thinking up a decent alibi. Five years ago when the Reverend Guthrie finally passed away, again identified as the rector who had the barelegged dames etc., I breathed a sigh of relief at his passing."

In 1927 he left (though not for that reason) and went on to become "The Roving Reporter" on the New York *Evening Post*. These columns are stronger and funnier than "One Word After Another" In them he intermittently becomes Luther Hook, an imaginary alter ego invented in the *Eagle* column. Luther Hook is, depending on the circumstances, a Middle-aged Veterinarian; a *distrait* French Journalist; a Member of the Old Firm of Hook, Line & Sinker; a varnish salesman; the Onetime Indoor Racquets Champion of the World; an Old-time Diamond Star, an Old Political War-horse Prominently Identified with Both Parties, the Eclipse Editor of the *Eagle*. With or without these disguises he comments on a variety of local oddities, reporting that, among other things, chestnut vendors are really unemployed character actors, top-floor apartments are best for parties because there is nobody upstairs to shush you, the middle of Manhattan Bridge is the best place for "wooing" followed by the little park at the foot of Montague Street, it is theoretically possible to have eight wives in this country without breaking the law, New York is the only city that names two-dollar sandwiches after girls and makes taxi drivers soul-conscious, and, in '27, the Algonquin round table had gone down without a bubble to no one's regret. He further reports that by 1928 many night clubs have become Chinese restaurants, that the old duffer playing croquet in south Central Park is Alex Woollcott, that brunettes have higher blood pressure than blondes, that exercise has maleficient effects, that parlor games (anagrams, Guggenheim, charades, duck-on-a-rock and bubble-blowing) are bigger than ever and that lion-milking fad is hard on cows. He tells enchantingly of the uncontrolled Eighth Avenue subway:

"The last vestige of the city's control over the new Eighth Avenue subway, now in course of construction, apparently disappeared yesterday with the opening at Fiftieth Street and Sixth Avenue of a hole from underground.

"Two laborers emerged into the daylight, blinked once or twice, and then hailed a policeman.

" 'Whatsa da street?' asked one.

" 'Fiftieth,' replied the officer.

" 'Fiftieth!' exclaimed the man. 'Whatsa da avenue?'

" 'Sixth.'

" 'Sixth!' Utterly astonished, he conferred furiously in Italian with his co-worker and raised his hat respectfully to the policeman. 'Excusa da interrupt,' he said. 'We gotta da wrong street an' avenue. Please fill uppa da hole.'

"They disappeared back into the tunnel and Patrolman Andrew Riordan shoved the macadam pavement back into place.

" 'There's no question about it,' he stated, 'they've lost control of the subway. It's all over town. They've got those boys digging down there in the dark and frequently they lose their compasses. The next thing they know they are emerging around the Battery.'

"A survey of the situation showed that Patrolman Riordan was not exaggerating. Excavations in 217 different parts of New York, several in Staten Island and Queens, were described by residents in the vicinity as 'the new Eighth Avenue Subway' and a map of the line drawn up on the basis of these reports disclosed that when completed it will be seventy-five miles long and will traverse every important avenue and cross street in Manhattan, most of the Bronx and parts of Queens and Staten Island. It will make three stops at Fifty-first Street and Park Avenue.

"The gravest aspect of the situation, however, is that one end of the tube has been completely lost. A contractor and seventy men set out last December with orders to dig south as far as Rector Street, where the contractor wanted to get off. It was calculated that they should arrive around May 1. They have not arrived yet."

He tells of an unbroken chain of speakeasies from the Battery to Sixty-first Street, recommending the ones with the "old-fashioned vicious saloon quality." After the move to Great Neck he writes of nerve-racking country noises—twittering birds, crying babies, radios, owls; New Yorkers, he says, are hooked on their grime and racket, even after driving miles to the country for a picnic they eat lunch sitting on the running board (if you don't know what that is, ask someone over forty-five). He gives us some foolproof plots for confession stories. It is all very light. In his Swan Song column, he regrets that he hasn't accomplished more in the three years he wrote the column, such as ending a war (but it was already won) or settling the coal strike (but it was already settled). But "Johnson never felt very strongly on a subject more than one day at a time. . . . Johnson gets no fun out of effort unless something comes out of it. If Johnson could write for a week and at the end of that time some annoying institution crumpled up and collapsed, that would be very jolly. But they don't collapse; they thrive and wax fat on the feeble poisons that writers dip their arrows in; and Johnson can find no fun in tossing pebbles, his pebbles at least, against stone walls . . . so Johnson made an effort at clowning around, just kidding back and forth. . . There is no way of diverting attention from one's more solemn inabilities like clowning around."

There are several columns written from Paris, where he and Marion went several times by cabin boat, staying six weeks or so. As far as Nunnally was concerned, Paris was a lot like New York —"he didn't like strange places where he didn't know people," says Marion. "He had no ear for languages or music and no interest in art or shopping, so he sat all day at the Deux Magots or the Brasserie Lipp with his American cronies." But she didn't complain—"I tried to do everything to please Nunnally." They always stayed at the Hôtel d'Angleterre et Jacob on the Left Bank, where they had a big room for five dollars a night, with WC down the hall. While Marion shopped or went to museums, Nunnally walked or sat around with Austin Parker, Julian Street, Cam Rogers, or Edmund Duffy, his old friend, the cartoonist for the Baltimore *Sun*, soaking up the expatriate culture peculiar to the period—and everyone found his way to those cafés and into his columns, James Joyce, Hemingway, Djuna Barnes, Josephine Baker. In *SEP* articles, he contrasted French literary life with American:

"'You know,' he said, 'I ain't used to the way they go at literature over here. In New York, or even Fort Gaines, or at State

University, if I said, "Well, I don't like Sinclair Lewis, or
Theodore Dreiser, or Ford Madox Ford," they'd say, "Don't you?"
and I'd say "No," and then they'd say, "Well I do." If I said "Well
I like Sinclair Lewis, or Dreiser, or Ford," they'd say, "I don't
care for him," and that would be all there was to it. . . . But here
if I say "Well, I don't care a great deal for Marcel Proust" five of
them leap up and double up their fists. . . . I always thought literature was peaceful.' "

After three years of steady employment on the *Post,* after a
brand of agony familiar to most writers, Nunnally decided to
give up his weekly pay check of a hundred and forty dollars and
try to make it as a free lance. If fiction writing is risky, trying to
live on the proceeds is rather like sky diving. But writers are constantly trying to figure out how to finance the writing they really
want to do, and sometimes the jump is worth taking. He had
been selling stories steadily and now he figured he and Marion
could make it if he could sell one story a month. For some time
he had written in a rented hotel room and now, after the move to
Great Neck, he continued to do the same thing, working every
day from nine to six.

The *SEP* stories (around forty-five of them) have lost over the
past fifty years what I'm sure was at the time an authentic
burnish. Nunnally himself found them, in '69, "unreadable—
windy and overwritten." Well—certainly in need of cutting and
certainly of a style and nature far from that of the seventies.
They are for amusement only, comic melodramas, silent movies
in words. They hold interest not for the writing—which he was
to far surpass in Hollywood—but for what they say about him,
being the only writing he ever did solely from ideas which
sprang into his own head, tailored to nothing but a broad magazine market.

They take place in New York, in newspaper offices, speakeasies, prisons, delis, Grand Central Station, backstage at the
Follies, or apartments off Sixth Avenue, or else on the porches or
in the ice cream shop of a town called Riverside (Columbus).
The conflicts are city versus small town, hick versus sophisticate
usually in contest over a girl. Girls are irrational, superstitious,
adorable, stubborn, cold as ice, indispensable and irresistible;
they can't drive, they make dreadful puns, they become soddenly

adoring when in love. One of the worst is Rough House Rosie, who is given to sinister practical jokes.

" 'I wonder if Ira understands me; if he sees, as I know you do, the real me; the me that is just a little fey, a pixie, with the heart of a child and the spirit of an elf. Not a girl like other girls, Carter, but one of the little folk, perhaps. S'help me Hannah, there isn't a bad, malicious idea in me, Carter—only, only I'm lonely, Carter—awfully lonely. There ain't many like me, Carter. I'm not quite human. I'm by myself—a sprite, you might say; and all I want, all I ask, Carter, is for somebody who will see that—as you see it, I know—'cause I'm lonesome.'

" 'Now, now, little girl!' he objected, much moved.

" 'All I want, Carter, is a playmate—a playmate that understands me a little, that can see that when I'm mischievous it is only the pixie strain in me.' "

The young men—our heroes—bumble in assorted ways. They are often like Mr. Gibbons—"nineteen, as callow as a calf and given somewhat to the pimples of adolescence. His eyes are wide, round and humorless, but his hair is slick with the grease of a bear; and if that is not a wing collar and a jazz-bow tie he is wearing, then we are all mightily mistaken. One suspects, moreover, that in his major garments he has counterfeited that rakish roominess of collegiate apparel by equipping himself with a suit about three sizes too large. A harmless-looking young man, with, indeed, a most disarming and ingenuous smile, he has elected to wear here, however, the aloof air of superior elegance."

In some of the early stories the hero's gaucheness comes from his misuse or overuse of words. In "The Laughing Death" a young man (who of course is trying to get the girl) hooked on crossword puzzles uses words like "ai" and "hoy" and says things like "your prattle roils me." In another the young man infuriates his girl's father by splitting infinitives, and in still another a young doctor's tongue is constantly tangled around medical terminology: " 'Well, Nott says,' he began again, 'for thyroid inefficiency potassium permanganate by cachet is permissible. Some authorities say not.'

" 'Nott?' she asked encouragingly.

" 'No, not Nott—not, n-o-t, not; not Nott, N-o-t-t, Nott. But—

well, some authorities say don't.' He laughed embarrassedly. 'It sounded like a pun, didn't it?'"

Incomprehensible though he is, the girl is patient and he gets her in the end. Words are tricky and powerful, you have to get control of them; probably in some circles (like Columbus), if you know too many of them, they think you're a freak—like Nathalia Crane, who won his admiration by her ability to "rope, throw and tie" the English language. In some stories the hero is a writer or reporter, he's gotten control of the recalcitrant English language and is using it to further his own ends—one young man gets the girl by writing about her. But in two other stories the hero-writer is crazy, absolutely deranged in one and a violent hypochondriac in the other. "Then, while she stood paralyzed with fright, his twisting body turned over and he stared up at her, and through all of the anguish that held his eyes, through all the pain and misery that gripped him, there shone a light of unmistakable triumph.

"'I've got it,' he gasped. 'I've got it—and you said it was imaginary!' His voice, strained and hoarse, rose in the victory of vindication. 'You—all of you—you all said I was crazy—and now I've got it! I've got appendicitis!'

"She waited for no more. Her nerves shaken, her lips holding back a little hysterical sob, she ran, leaving him curled in a ball on the roof against the penthouse. Stumbling down the stairs, she threw open the door to the apartment, and half a dozen lingering guests looked up.

"'He's dying!' she panted. . . ."

This is Nunnally at his worst. There are twists—in "Straight from New York" a silly local Shriner and a smooth hip New York journalist compete for a girl and the Shriner gets her (bumbler beats out wordsmith). Things get worse—in later stories an accident-prone young man does everything wrong, he sits on his girl's dog and kills it and then leaves her in remorse; in "The Wizard" a young man who has been helping his girl's father with household repairs manages to blow up the entire house and—not surprisingly—loses the girl. (When the hero does get the girl, he always wants to get married *tonight*—and somewhere like Hackensack.)

In '30 and '31 women really get the business. In "A Woman at

the Wheel" he tells of their basic inability to drive, and "The
Woman's Touch" is fascinating about male and female roles. The
husbands in this story (some of the later ones are about marriage) set out to debunk the old myth that women are basically
clean and neat and men are dirty, sloppy and incapable of taking
care of themselves. The fantasy is very funny. "I could just see
the way she thought we were living. All our food we got out of
tin cans, which we opened by leaping on them with our teeth
and rending them apart with growls. If by any chance we ever
got any fresh stuff, we just gobbled it raw, and our eggs we ate
with the shells on, because we didn't know any better. We never
took off anything but our hats when we went to bed, when we
took a shower we hung everything on the stove, except our
shoes, which we put in the ice-box. Afterwards we dried on the
sheets. We slept cater-cornered, and on the springs, or maybe
even the slats. When finally we set out for work, we had our
vests on backwards, we wore each other's hats, and our pants
were inside out. In fewer words, we lacked that woman's touch."

At a cabin shared by three couples, one husband sets out to
prove that he can wash all the dishes, three times a day, much
more quickly and efficiently than the women. The challenge is
taken up amid hoots of laughter, but he is miraculously successful. The wives, rather than being pleased at getting out of the
drudgery, grow more and more depressed as their function is
taken over by a man. They mess up as many dishes as they can
find but Ed washes them all (with a hose, it is discovered) and
turns out to be a whiz at dusting, bedmaking and sweeping besides. After the vacation Ruth, Ed's wife, loses her self-
confidence more and more as Ed rubs it in about how efficient he
is. She drops plates and cries as Ed occasionally flies through a
household job to remind her of his expertise. His friend
straightens him out—Ed must get off Ruth's turf if he wants to
keep his marriage. Besides, it just isn't natural to a man—"No
matter how good a man can do certain parts of housework, for
instance, the fact remains that it is work that a woman can do
best. When a man's trying it, he's trying something that he just
isn't naturally fitted for. It's like putting a cheap car to seventy
miles an hour. You can do it, but you can't hold it. It's simply unnatural to him, and he just can't last it the way a woman can."

Anyway "Nature's just designed woman for that kind of thing, and in the long run she'll always be the one who does it best." They end up happily with Ruth botching up the housework as she always did. But in "Nightmare" the husband, exasperated by his wife's insecurity, says, "Can't women ever make a statement . . . without getting it corroborated? Don't they ever believe anybody's going to believe them?" In "Will You Please Stop That," one of a handful of light essays in the *SEP* (one of which, "Sugar in Corn Bread," became rather well known), the tone becomes chilling. It lists what is wrong with wives: they are idiots about money, they don't fill out check stubs, they mangle the Sunday paper, they borrow razors and quote old love letters at the dinner table. They are secretive, inept and basically criminal —they steal other people's seats in restaurants and ashtrays in Europe. There are some husband-faults too, but they are less emphasized. In this excerpt I can hear my mother's voice. He is telling of letting his wife read some of his previous complaints, and her reaction.

". . . I likewise put the blast on her habit of keeping her bedroom at all times as though three or four slovenly burglars had passed hurriedly through, a matter which depresses a husband greatly, since men are by nature much neater and more orderly than women. But reading them over my wife shook her head calmly, totally untouched by the devastating irony of those paragraphs.

" 'I wouldn't bother with those incidents,' she said.

" 'Why not?' I asked.

" 'Because,' she explained, 'they've been mentioned before.'

"Then I leaned forward eagerly, feeling that I was on the verge of some vital discovery in the realm of feminine reason or logic. 'You mean,' I said, 'that if an unpleasantness, as we may describe it, has once been brought into the open, has been discussed publicly in any way, everything immediately becomes jake—is that it?'

" 'Well,' she said, 'it's already been talked about.'

"So there you are. I throw that nugget of reason or logic into this account gratis. Once a problem has been exposed to notice it ceases to be a problem. The instant someone made a formal complaint regarding the property rights of his safety razor, everything was cleared up. Wives thenceforth were free to borrow their husbands' razors openly and with a clear conscience."

Three of the stories were O. Henry Memorial Award stories—"I Owe It All to My Wife," 1923; "The Actor," 1928; and "Madame Irene the Great," 1930. The last two are in the collection *There Ought to Be a Law* which was published in 1931 to fairly good reviews. "His yarns are funny and crackle with wisecracks" (New York *Times*, April 12, 1931). "Mr. Johnson's characters have a touch of the comic universal citizen who distinguishes the work of Peter Arno and Gluyas Williams" (Brooklyn *Eagle*, March 15, 1931). But the Baltimore *Sun* said about "New York—My Mammy": "He has a capital theme in the trials of a typical New Yorker who is sent to Georgia to represent his firm and is overcome by homesickness. But here he exaggerates his situations and characters until the whole impresses the reader with a sense of unreality. It is too serious for burlesque, yet too distorted to be faithful portraiture. Obviously, Mr. Johnson runs the risk of falling between two schools. Pure burlesque has a legitimate appeal, but where burlesque mingles with reality the reader may have a just complaint that too great a strain is placed on his credulity."

This story could have been lovely, and it almost is, if he had let it get as serious as it was meant to be. But he veers from the deeper feeling. "The Actor" is one of the best; here he is writing about the theater people who amuse him enormously. Reginald Peacock, well-known actor, spots his boyhood sweetheart in a restaurant (he lost her to the licensed pharmacist her father hired for his drug business). They come together as though ten years had never happened and agree to marry, until his suburban love makes the mistake of asking him what line he's in— Peacock, whose name has been flung on every billboard in Jersey, his picture in every paper! "Dull, blind, stupid little moron," mutters Peacock, restored to his natural vanity. It is very deft, very Somerset Maugham, and he is far enough from the subject to see it with an accurate eye.

For Nunnally, the mastery and control of words meant success, manhood, freedom, all the things he wanted so badly. Writers have different concepts of words. I knew one who in his boyhood wrote them on bits of paper and locked them in a box, as though someone might steal them (later he had trouble cutting). My words for writing seem to bubble up rather slowly from some swamp of the mind, a sort of La Brea tar pit, a process over which I have little control. But Nunnally's, I imagine, swirled around in a blizzard of gibberish and nonsense (for he loved puns and odd names) challenging him to capture them and put them in order. (When I think of blizzards of words I think of Onnie, who hardly ever stopped talking, and a lot of other people in Columbus, as a matter of fact. Nunnally grew up among incessantly chattering women. His father said very little, but what he said was knifelike.) I suspect this is why he craved form and was so happy writing movie scripts, for scripts are (or were when he was writing them) the tightest form of all—so tight they almost go beyond words, because at best the words give way to the visual, and so every word in them must be exactly right; and so to him this was the ultimate taming, the highest form of control. He never tried a novel, for he knew the form was too sprawling for him to be comfortable with.

He was a controlling conversationalist, too—you listened to him, you played straight man. If the talk veered away from his chosen subject, the areas where he felt at home, he would discharge clouds of what appeared to be boredom and irritation but was probably fear of being ignored because of not being good-looking enough, or "callow as a calf" or whatever. The perfect use of words was his masculinity, but there was a kicker here too. Years later, as a Hollywood scriptwriter, he called what he did "cabinetmaking"—the profession, as it happens, of all the men in his father's family; Nunnally was the first one who didn't work with his hands. He made a joke of his own lack of dexterity, saying he couldn't even change a light bulb; and I wonder about members of the first generation who make such a dramatic switch, and if they are guilty about dealing with intangibles, like blizzards of words, that can't be picked up and held. That the blizzards could be converted into a great deal of very tangible money was important to him, and also has to do with his choosing Hollywood.

In Great Neck, things were only fair. It had been chosen because friends who lived there recommended it—Marian and

Harlan Thompson, Ben Hecht, Sam Hellman (another *SEP* writer), Groucho, and Stanley Walker. "It was after the Fitzgerald and Lardner days," says Marion, "but Great Neck was tradition." The house, which they bought for fifteen thousand dollars, was English half-timbered, on a quiet street in a quiet neighborhood. Marion had her home and a live-in maid besides, but Nunnally, who commuted into town to write, sometimes didn't come home and didn't telephone to explain. Why? "I got drunk." It happened about once a month, and Marion, who had lost one baby a year or so before and was trying to start another, was alternately mad and depressed. "I knew I was married to a very odd man. I tried to tell myself he made up for it by being so amusing." There was more talk about fleshpots and Nunnally suggested they go to Miami Beach. Marion objected but was talked into it. They lived in a hotel at first, then rented a house. Just before the depression, they built a house of their own.

In Florida celebrityhood was starting, in a small way, with the publication of *There Ought to Be a Law*. Mr. and Mrs. Nunnally Johnson are seen (in the paper) on the beach, at the opening of the Jockey Club at Hialeah, displaying a rare cluster of staghorn moss. Marion wears "becoming" little skullcaps, wide white pants and sandals. She looks vulnerable, somehow, a person to whom something is going to happen, but I may be tinting the picture with my own ink. Nunnally looks serious in his sunning togs and rather sexy. Photographed together, there is too much space between them. The interviews are of course only with him. He is referred to as America's foremost "rising young humorist . . . the wit and nonsense which characterize his magazine stories and articles seem part and parcel of his personality." An interview in the Atlanta *Journal* says: "In Mr. Johnson's opinion Lady Luck has perched on his shoulder consistently. He has had few of his stories rejected . . . and has a play about half-written, but he has never written a novel.

"'Couldn't do it, and it wouldn't even be good business,' he said. 'I make as much on one story as I would on an entire book. So I can't see any good reason for writing one. Even if I could do it, I think a humorous serial would be great, but it's hard enough to keep your humor sustained in a 5,000 word story. P. G.

Wodehouse is the only man who can write humor in book length, and he does it superbly.

"'I hate to read my stuff after it's in print. It's depressing. I always think how dumb it sounds, and how much better Ring Lardner could have done with the same subject. If you like your own work, you have a Narcissus complex, and that's fatal.

"'I write directly into the typewriter, after having thought out the entire plot from beginning to end. I can't dictate; I must perform some actual labor. It must be the peasant strain in me.'"

A local magazine says, "Mr. Johnson is typically an American. And his stories are typically 'in American.' He finds among his own people sufficient story ideas to keep him busy the rest of his life.

"'That's why I could never live in Europe,' he says."

They loved Florida—the climate, the swimming, the tennis, the deep-sea fishing. They had a "delightful and friendly sort of home, one story built around a patio." Over the mantel was a Gauguin painting of two dark and flower-decked women sitting on the grass, and the colors in the room were taken from this painting. In this pleasant place Marion finally got successfully pregnant—in this place I have never seen, I was started.

But by this time, 1932, the depression had caught up with the magazine business. In that year the *SEP*, which had bought as many as twelve stories a year in the past, only bought three. The magazines had thinned to half their size, each now printing four instead of twelve, which made the competition—Lardner, Tarkington, Fitzgerald, J. P. Marquand, Kenneth Roberts, Sam Hellman, Sinclair Lewis, Joseph Hergesheimer—far more formidable. Besides, the *SEP* didn't protect its writers during the depression as *The New Yorker* did with advances and drawing accounts, which was why *The New Yorker* kept its best writers (O'Hara, E B. White, Perelman, Thurber) during this difficult period and the *SEP* lost theirs to Hollywood, where the money was. In '69 Nunnally said that he would have preferred to stay in New York, he liked the freedom of his life in Great Neck and Miami, but "that classy field" had simply closed down; it was "the end of short stories as an important field of American writing."

He had, by this time, tried his hand at both movie- and

playwriting. In 1926 he had worked on *For the Love of Mike*, a
silent with Claudette Colbert and Ben Lyon, made in New York.
Leland Hayward produced it and Frank Capra directed. Nunnally said, "I wrote scenes. Capra would tell me, he had a kind
of casual way of doing things, he'd say, 'They find this baby, and
leave it on the doorstep.' He would give me a kind of rough outline of what he wanted, and I would write it . . . it just wasn't
anything much. It was a kind of *Abie's Irish Rose* affair . . . it
completely passed out of my consciousness. A year or so later, I
was driving from Paris down to the South of France, and I
stayed overnight at Lyons. My wife and I were taking a stroll
after dinner. In front of a movie theater [there was] this poster
Ces Gosses, a French expression for his goslings, his kids, and I
recognized Claudette's picture on this thing, and I looked at it
and thought, 'My God, this must be the picture I worked on.' I
don't know whether my name was on it or not. That was my first
introduction to the movies, and it was just nothing because it
never had any bearing [on my career] or it didn't teach me anything at all. It was just something that happened and that was
the end of it."

It wasn't really—few New York newspapermen-humorists
brushed with the movie business in those days without it turning
out to be a portent for the future. In 1927 *The Jazz Singer* came
out, signaling the beginning of the talkies; that same year Herman Mankiewicz, *Times* drama critic and "the Voltaire of Central Park West," was hired by Paramount to recruit anybody he
knew to go to the Coast and make upward of three hundred dollars a week. Mank had been out there since the year before, writing captions for silents, but missed the talent and companionship
of the newspaper guys in New York. Besides the depression, it
was Mank's function that changed the face of humorous writing
in this country—"The new spirit of the talkies was the twenties
moved west in the thirties" (Pauline Kael, *Raising Kane*). Nunnally had great admiration for Mank, whom he later called the
most brilliant man he had ever known. "Mank had a very impressive presence when I first saw him," he said in an interview,
"when I was about twenty-three or twenty-four and so was he,
but he was four times as sophisticated as I was. Christ, I was a
cracker, two or three years out of the army. But Mank had a

background of scholarly family, of really superior intelligence around him . . . we were both newspapermen. Our point of view or attitude was that of the newspapermen of the twenties in New York, which prevented, in my case, my ever taking sides, of never being very strong for a cause, even when I believed in it. . . . Mank and I viewed things more or less from the same point of view. We didn't pass moral judgments on people or we wouldn't admit it, anyway."

Nunnally couldn't resist Mank's summons, particularly since other newspapermen—Ben Hecht, Oliver Garrett, Dudley Nichols, Jim McGuinness—were making it out there on what was known as the Paramount Fresh Air Fund for New York Newspapermen. Having no long-term ambitions about the movie business, he arranged to do his *Evening Post* column from California, and he and Marion went out on a six weeks' contract with Paramount.

It wasn't much of a six weeks. "We took a furnished apartment in Hollywood," Marion recalls, "one room with a kitchenette and a Murphy bed. It was all Chinese. The only companions I remember were Herman Mankiewicz and Reine Davies, Marion's sister, who worked for Hearst as a sort of business manager. Wilson Mizner was another, he was one of the great humorists of Hollywood at the time." Nunnally's work was pretty much of a fizzle. Walter Wanger called him into his office and said, "Look, here are our stars: Adolphe Menjou—we'll begin by calling his picture *Starving in Spats*—Richard Arlen—Richard Dix, the All-American boy. Pick out one of the stars and do a story for him." None of this came to anything, and when the six weeks were over they went back to New York.

But Hollywood as a phenomenon was irresistible to Eastern newspapermen—Eastern anything, as a matter of fact. (Joel Sayre says, "Hollywood was *the* American newspaper news source beginning in 1921 with the Fatty Arbuckle scandal and the James Desmond Taylor murder.") I can't find out if Nunnally had gone to California before the six-week trip (I suspect not) though he wrote about Los Angeles long before with acerbity in his *Eagle* column (as seen through the eyes of Luther Hook, "the same who made the first dawn-to-dusk flight by trolley from Jamaica to Freeport").

"Los Angeles, Cal., Aug. 15.

"The following scene took place in the dining room of my hotel this morning.

"A kindly-looking old man with his kindly-looking old wife had ordered two plates of raw meat for breakfast.

"'We are among the oldest inhabitants of Los Angeles,' I heard the old gentleman say to the waiter, 'and when we say we want raw steak, raw steak is what we want.'

"The waiter returned with what looked to be two perfectly proper dishes of raw steak. The next second two pistol shots rang out. I heard a thud as the waiter dropped to the floor—dead.

"'Now,' I heard the kindly old man say, 'now I reckon you'll bring me raw steak when I ask for it.'

"'Come, come, father,' I heard his wife say.

"'What!' cried the old man. 'You question my judgment?' and another shot rang out. The kindly old lady fell into the steak."

"Los Angeles, Cal., Aug.

"I was the guest of a fine old Los Angeles family at dinner last night, and after the meal the father called his children around him and said,

"'Would you like Daddy to read you a bedtime story?'

"'Goody!' exclaimed little Moron, the youngest. 'I was just saying to sister that if you didn't I was going to shoot you.'

"The mother laughed indulgently. 'He says the cutest things, sometimes,' she said to me.

"Father got out his bedtime story book from the arsenal room.

"'Once,' he began, 'there was a little bunny named Tommy Bunny and he had a sister named Flaming Youth, and Flaming Youth was a heavy drinker. One night she took some opium instead of liquor and shot little Tommy Bunny right through the old ko-ko.'

"'Goody, goody,' cried Methyl, the little girl. 'I'd have shot him too, if I'd been there.'

"'No,' cried little Moron. 'I'd have to shoot him.'

"They got out their 32's and potted away at each other until both were dead."

But the *Evening Post* columns during that six weeks in 1927 were first hand, and he reported that Los Angeles speakeasies are about as exciting as the Public Library's genealogy room, that only three are open till midnight and there is no hashish; that "there is nothing so odd as the movie business"; that one feels Hollywood buildings will crash to the ground if leaned on; that California divorces have hilarious cruelty charges, such as the wife who claims that her husband wakes her up at 4 A.M. splashing in the pool; that Hollywood has more feminine beauty per square inch than any other community between the two oceans; that California has a "partiality for seers and dingy mountebanks"; that Californians are mad for folding beds. Besides, "there isn't a chili con carne counter in the city that isn't under the impression that it is the spit 'n image of the Alhambra, Taj Mahal, Morro Castle, St. Paul's, or the Doges Palace in Venice. . . . Which [New York movie palace] is an Egyptian temple, with a tall, somber sheik pacing slowly, continually and thoughtfully on the roof, visible to all below against the sky and an electric crescent moon a bit clearly upheld by a stick? Which of them is a Chinese palace, with Mandarins selling tickets and proudly and quite unself-consciously presenting in its heathenish interior a picture of the life of Christ? . . . The ice cream stores are lofty, awesome vaults, greatly like Robert Edmond Jones' settings for *Macbeth* with fronts ornamented with gadgets tastily smeared with a pastry bag. The hardware stores are out of old Madrid. The restaurants are Runic. The haberdasheries are Punic. The peanut stands are after the Siamese."

And in this land of Oz "Office boys get paid off in century notes . . . when the star wants a stick of gum he crams a ten-dollar bill into the slot machine . . . the chauffeur idles away the time by tossing double eagles at a crack in the sidewalk. [Even doormen prattle in six figures.] 'We're prepared to sink two hundred thousand in Bow's next picture. Rex Fairface gets twenty thousand a week and his horse gets five. Tom Mix averages 17,000 a week. Mary Gulch, the scenario writer, put six $5000 checks in the bank in one month. It costs a thousand a week for the upkeep of Pickfair, Doug's home. A good title writer gets $5000 a week. . . . Doug gets a half million a picture. The Chinese theatre cost a million dollars. Mary Philbin gets five thousand a minute. The Million dollar theatre cost a billion. Mary

Pickford gets a trillion a week. Tommy Meighan gets a quadrillion.

"'Easy!' said the doorman. 'Maybe more.'"

Nunnally, who had been stage-struck since his early days in New York, had a go at dialogue writing for Broadway in *Shoot the Works* (1931), a Heywood Broun depression "co-operative" whose purpose was to provide work for unemployed stage players and mechanics. He couldn't resist a chance to work with the greatly admired Broun who, he said, "was a big city figure and a kind of character. Broun could get into any taxi and he'd hear, 'How are you, Mr. Broun?' Heywood was an enormous awfully badly dressed man, with a mop of hair, and chuckle and good humor, and he wrote an interesting column and for some reason everybody seemed to know him. Like G. K. Chesterton, who was also enormous and rumpled and celebrated. Somebody said to him, 'It must be wonderful that no matter where you go everybody knows you.' And Chesterton said, 'Yes, and if they don't know, they ask.' That's the way it was with Heywood. He was one of the gods of our world. Like George Kaufman.'"

Broun financed his review almost entirely by himself, and the likes of the Marx brothers, Helen Morgan, Eddie Cantor, Al Jolson, Sophie Tucker, Bea Lillie, George Jessel, George Murphy and Imogene Coca appeared in it intermittently for nothing. High-minded as this purpose was, Nunnally says slyly in an *SEP* article that he suspects Broun really put it on so he could get on stage, an ambition Nunnally shared. Their sketch was "one of those my-God-my husband affairs. . . . I had but to walk on and say, 'Yes, dear, I have had a hard day at the office,' whereupon the telephone rang and the wife screamed, 'My God, my husband!' The line then was, 'What shall I do?' after which this caller crawled under an extraordinarily large bed with the four previous clandestine callers, including Mr. Broun, and sang 'Sweet Adeline.'"

But Nunnally didn't get the part. Though he had long masked his Southern accent with a "superb cosmopolitan polish," it was likely to reappear under stress, a "murky mumbling reminding hearers of an elderly and probably slovenly Negro calling something unintelligible from the bottom of a well," which was probably what would have happened on stage anyway. Nunnally's dialogue goes unrecorded, but the whole venture was fun if a little dizzy. He was called on to teach baby talk to twenty-four chorus girls and help think of wah-de-dah-dahs for a hotsy singer. On opening night "the principal actor in the cast managed to avoid every line I had written." But though he calls that opening "the beginning of my exit from the American theater" he ended up as stage-struck as ever and was to keep returning to Broadway intermittently for the rest of his life.

By 1932 everything pointed to a move to Hollywood. The stories kept coming back from the *SEP*—"I felt like a pitcher who was cutting the corner of the plate, and they were calling them balls." Merritt Hulburd, story editor of Paramount and past editor of the *SEP*, offered this explanation in a letter:

"When I made a party call on the boys at the *Post* [*SEP*] last Monday, I heard that one or two of your yarns had been put on the skids. If you won't take it amiss, I'll tell you what their frank reaction was. They are very much afraid that you are going serious on them, pulling a 'Lardner' or something. For God's sake, let's have back that old rascal Johnson, with his merry twinkle and his roguish smile! I know it's a case of 'don't laugh, boys, the poor guy is being smothered with mortgages'—but that's what you get for being a humorist. You've got to laugh though your bank is breaking."

A few months later Hulburd made Nunnally an offer of three hundred dollars a week to go and work for Paramount in California. "Let's take it," Marion said. "It's three hundred dollars a week more than we have now. I know you'll make it." The decision was made and this time it was for good. When they left New York in 1932, it was truly the end of an era.

Hollywood   1932-1938

The trip out was, Nunnally said, "a little humbling . . . when Oliver Garrett went out, when Dudley [Nichols] went out, you heard these stories: they were put on the Twentieth Century Limited with a drawing room, fruit and liquor, they were transferred in Chicago in a limousine to the Chief, and then they were met in San Bernardino by a limousine. But all they said was if I showed up at Paramount on a certain Monday morning, I could go to work. They wouldn't even pay my way out." He said he borrowed money from his two agents for the trip, though Marion doubts it—"after all we owned two houses, we weren't all that broke. He was always what seemed unnaturally scared about money." Whichever it was, they went out on the Chief, in a compartment, and rented a tiny two-room house off Vine Street in Hollywood. Marion asked him if he was nervous, and he said he wasn't in the least. He had been looking at pictures and wasn't impressed by the dialogue—he knew he could do better. While she gestated and set about housekeeping in this strange, hot place, he went back to work at Paramount.

Though "in two weeks you knew the dramatic form" (of scriptwriting) there was a lot of other lore to master. Nunnally— along with many of the best literary minds of his generation— was part of a wave that was to change the picture industry from a baffled giant trying to cope with the phenomenon of sound to that most spectacular teamwork it represented later in the decade. But in those early days nobody knew quite what to do with writers. Nunnally was among the first to arrive and found that the producers, faced with the fairly new problem of dialogue, felt more secure assigning several of them to one picture ("they always thought three lousy writers would equal one good writer"), sometimes, deplorably, without one another's knowledge—"a murderous and brutal practice." Sometimes they assigned writers to work—on speculation—on properties they didn't own, and it was abuses such as these which led to the formation of the Screenwriters' Guild. In one strange instance a producer named Harold Hurley assigned each of the characters in a certain story to a different writer, in this case Henry Hathaway, Joe Mankiewicz (Herman's brother—by then "the Mankiewiczes were outnumbering the management"), Nunnally and two others. Nunnally actually got a character and a half, a sailor and his parrot. Each one was supposed to think of funny things for his character to say, then they were to meet and put them together—a project which, not surprisingly, withered and died.

The town was full of teams, and the newly arrived writers from the East were invariably assigned collaborators. On Nunnally's first picture, *Bedtime Story* with Maurice Chevalier, he worked with Waldemar Young, a veteran titlewriter of the silents, "a very nice and able man" who was content to let him do the writing, casting out a suggestion from time to time; and the second, *Mama Loves Papa*, was with Arthur Kober, the "continuity man" to Nunnally's "diologue man." The function of Kober, who had been there longer, was to supply a periodic Cut, Fade In, or Wipe, for which skill he was getting paid a good deal more. It was obvious that this technical skill meant more money and Nunnally learned it quickly (unlike most New York writers, who were inclined to look down on this lowbrow literary form) and a year or so later, when he was loaned to Goldwyn for *Kid Millions,* he asked for and got six hundred dollars a week instead of three hundred, on the grounds that he was now dialogue man and continuity man all in one. "They were idiots—not for giving it to me, but for not knowing one man could have done it anyway . . . the triumph was that I was entrusted with the whole thing. I didn't have to depend on anybody for what seemed a childish bit of collaboration." His first solo script was a blizzard of Lap Dissolves, Wipes and Iris Outs—"I was going to let them know that I knew the whole business." He managed to make it stick—he, Robert Riskin and Dudley Nichols were the only writers in Hollywood in that period who consistently got solo credit. He knew collaboration wasn't for him in scriptwriting any more than it had been in newspaper or short-story writing.

Marc Connelly, who collaborated frequently with George Kaufman both for the Broadway stage and in Hollywood, says the ability to collaborate is "a matter of temperament. When you sit around that table your total attention is on the story and how to tell it. You may argue like hell but all personal rancor is put aside, the argument is strictly about what's going on on that page." When he and Kaufman collaborated one would write a scene and the other would rewrite it. Kaufman worked similarly with Nunnally when they collaborated on *Park Avenue,* a play produced for the Broadway stage in 1946 (an adaptation of an *SEP* article of Nunnally's called "Holy Matrimony"). The failure of the play might have had something to do with Nunnally's discomfort with companionate writing, though diagnosing a Broadway flop is far beyond my abilities. But for a writer like Nunnally, to whom control is everything, it must have been difficult to entrust part of a dramatic idea—fragile as a card house until it is on paper—even to the likes of George Kaufman. He saw it as being dependent on another person in a way he didn't like— you did it yourself, you stood or fell on your own product. He wanted his own failure or his own success, not somebody else's.

Bedtime Story was produced by Benjamin Glaser, who was "the inspiration for the Screenwriters' Guild." When the picture came out, the credits read: Screenplay by Waldemar Young, Nunnally Johnson and Benjamin Glaser. Glaser hadn't done any writing, but at that time the producer named the credits and abuses abounded. Glaser or any other producer could put his name up there or anybody else's he felt might be helped by a screen credit, while the actual writing might have been done by half a dozen writers who had worked without knowing they were working on the same thing. After the formation of the guilds there was more order, more fairness about the distribution of credits—now the Screenwriters' Guild names the credits, never the producer, who can only make recommendations. The

Guild protects writers from the kind of abuses that were common in the early days of sound, at the very time, ironically, when
they were most valuable. Now no scriptwriter writes a word—
ever—on speculation (unless he is, for his own satisfaction, trying an original). Once when I was anxious to start a script the
contract for which was not completely negotiated, my agent said,
"Don't you *touch* that typewriter until I say go."

At the end of a year at Paramount Nunnally went into the hospital with appendicitis and said to his friend Merritt Hulburd
when he visited, "I've been here for ten days and I'd like you to
know that if you suspend me during this time I will understand."
Hulburd said in some embarrassment, "I didn't tell you before
because you were so ill, but the minute the ambulance rolled
out, Hurley [the producer] chopped you off the payroll." Nunnally says "that was one of the few times in my life I ever hated
anybody." It wasn't as catastrophic as it sounds, because he was
hired the next day by Darryl Zanuck, who was leaving Warner's
to form the Twentieth Century Corporation with Joe Schenck
and Bill Goetz, L. B. Mayer's son-in-law. He never knew why
Zanuck wanted him—"I could hardly have impressed him in any
way because I hadn't done enough"—and it was characteristic of
him that, though he worked for Zanuck for twenty years, he never
asked. But Zanuck knew talent when he saw it. After the elegant
Paramount, it didn't look like much over at Twentieth Century,
with their rented typewriters and stage space on the Goldwyn
lot. "I don't think we owned one thing. You could have sold its
entire tangible assets for ten thousand dollars, but they made
pictures that were successful." As for working in cells, that
highly publicized form of writer torture, Nunnally didn't mind.
"Guys who had been working in the city room with a hundred
other people in the room would tell you how dreadful it was out
there in that little cell. What about *The New Yorker?* They're all
cells there. What do you need but a typewriter and a desk?" But
the relationship with Zanuck was to be the most crucial of his
career in pictures.

His first picture for Zanuck was *Moulin Rouge* (1934) with
Franchot Tone and Constance Bennett playing two look-alike
girls. The script is crude and frightfully sexist, but clever, and
would be funny if there hadn't been any woman's movement in

the meantime—girls are either nice or fast, are better off giving up careers and staying home, et cetera. The humor is broad—mistaken identity to a point where the males seem retarded, though I couldn't find a print anywhere and on film it might be more convincing. Nunnally collaborated (for the last time) with Henry Lehrman, who had worked with Chaplin for many years and claimed to have devised the Little Tramp outfit. (It was to Lehrman that Zanuck said, "Goddammit, don't say yes until I finish talking!") During the filming, Nunnally's writer-consciousness was further raised by overhearing Constance Bennett say to the director, "The hell with the writer."

The House of Rothschild, his next picture for Zanuck (George Arliss, Loretta Young, directed by Alfred Werker), is a serious and moving indictment of anti-Semitism. When Zanuck first presented him with the idea, Nunnally said, "Are you sure you want me to do this? I'm a writer of low comedy. My characters fall into flour barrels and things like that." Zanuck told him to go ahead and do it, and the result is one of his best scripts, tight and touching and powerful, complex issues (economic and political) turned into visual drama. It was the first picture to take up anti-Semitism, and at that sensitive time, (Jewish) Joe Schenck said he was "afraid people would cheer" at an anti-Semitic speech by Boris Karloff. It's hard to twist our minds into that 180-degree turn but "it was so pro-Semitic that many Jews were made uncomfortable by it." At any rate the passing of the years have made it work.

It is almost incredible that he learned so much so fast. Nunnally had a way of deprecating himself, of making everything sound easy. But learning to write scripts isn't the breeze he makes it sound like—there's more to it than scattering lap dissolves around. For one thing you have to know the mechanics of drama. A good screenwriter, Nunnally said once, "should have a slightly faulty memory"—one which allows room for your own contribution to the basic property. For him screenwriting was a complete reversal from newspaper writing, in which you tell it right away—ideally a newspaper story can be cut off at any paragraph and will still be complete. But in drama everything is held back until the last minute (which Scott Fitzgerald never learned, which is why his movie writing was so unsuccessful) as it is in short-story writing. The processes are analogous—you tell a situation, develop it as well as you can, and have a resolution at the end.

Possibly the most difficult thing for a fiction writer to learn about "cabinetmaking" is the switch from the verbal to the visual. "It's a visual art," says Phil Dunne, long-time writer and director for Fox, "an art of the reaction of the actor to what is being said, not what is being said. The perfect movie situation is —something happens; cut to the star, and the whole thing is told by her expression." "You have to know what your limits are," says George Seaton, Fox director and writer since the thirties, "and Nunnally was good because he quickly learned what's in the finder. The playwrights that came out rambled a lot because they found it hard to work with the camera in mind, they were still seeing the proscenium arch. Elliott Nugent never learned the trick, he always wrote for the stage. The camera can tell a lot more than dialogue." Faulkner was hopelessly long-winded, and Fitzgerald never learned it either. The problem still exists. "Neil Simon's *Murder by Death* is too broad," says Sol Siegel, producer since 1929. "It has a stage dialect. He doesn't know the medium yet." Some writers are suited to it and some aren't, and the art of writing dialogue like "night letters when you're paying for every word" seems impossible and infuriating to those who can't do it. But Nunnally's particular skills fitted it exactly—economy, good and funny dialogue, and the incessant push of the story, no room for rambling or rumination. Everything in a script, he told me once, should advance the action just a tiny bit, that pressure should never stop. And scenes shouldn't be more than three pages long, three minutes in screen time—after that attention begins to flag.

After *House of Rothschild* came *Bulldog Drummond Strikes Back* (Ronald Colman, Loretta Young, Charlie Butterworth and Una Merkel, directed by Roy Del Ruth), which he once told me was his favorite. "We pinched the 'missing room' plot, about the girl who returns to her hotel to find her mother gone, her room missing, they don't know her, they think she's gone crazy." It opens with Drummond walking along a foggy London street, he stops at a house to ask the way, the door is open, he goes in and there's a dead man in the living room. He calls a cop and when they get back to the house the dead man is gone, there's a drunk there instead. It goes cheerfully on in this manner, with nobody believing Drummond's reports of foul play, and the skeptical Scotland Yard detective says, "You found a body—it disappeared. You found a girl—she disappeared. Why does everything and everybody disappear but you?" It is all broad spoof and when I saw it I scratched down several dangling plot ends, about which I ceased to care because I was laughing too hard. I loved it, but then I love most of his pictures, and don't claim objectivity.

Next came a handful I haven't seen: *Baby Face Harrington,* a "small, quiet disaster" for MGM cooked up by Nunnally, Charlie Lederer and Charlie Butterworth, with Charlie Butterworth and Una Merkel; *Kid Millions* for MGM, directed by Roy Del Ruth; *Cardinal Richelieu* for Twentieth Century with George Arliss, directed by Rowland Lee, from which Nunnally asked Zanuck that his name be removed because "Mr. Arliss is rewriting stuff on the backs of menus and things, and I don't want to get credit if it's good and I don't want to be blamed if it's bad." Zanuck agreed and said he'd never been able to get either a writer or director to work twice with Mr. Arliss.

Then came *Thanks a Million* (Dick Powell, Ann Dvorak, Fred Allen, directed by Roy Del Ruth), the first picture made after Twentieth Century merged with Fox Films, which had "the biggest, newest lot, the greatest wealth, except that with the two biggest stars in the whole business, Will Rogers and Shirley Temple, at the end of the year they had made one half of one per cent on their investment, because they didn't have picture makers." The result of this merger for Nunnally was that Zanuck made him a producer. "They made thirty-five or forty pictures at that time . . . he named me and a couple of other fellows to be associate producers on pictures, hoping we would take responsibility for them . . . but I just couldn't do it. I suppose I took it because he asked me to and if he asked me to jump off the bridge I'd have done it. I had such a high regard for him and of course being a producer sounded as if I had more control." *The Man Who Broke the Bank at Monte Carlo* (Ronald Colman, Joan Bennett, directed by Stephen Roberts) was the last one he wrote without producing, which function started with *Prisoner of Shark Island* (Warner Baxter, John Carradine, Gloria Stuart, directed by John Ford, 1936).

I saw it and thought it was wonderful, though Gloria Stuart (wife of the late comedy writer Arthur Sheekman) says, "It was an absolutely perfect script but I'm not sure about the picture. Ford didn't get the script—something was missing. He sat on the set twisting, twisting, twisting a handkerchief and all he'd ever say was, 'All right, kids, believe it.' At no time did he ever give me any clue . . . but I think he had a great deal to do with the camera." James Whale, with whom she had worked in *The Old Dark House*, "was involved in every single aspect of the picture, every nuance of freezing and everything, he was *auteur*. And Nunnally was a very absent producer." For a picture with a non-directing director and a non-producing producer, it all came out looking right, except for Warner Baxter's unfortunate Southern accent, which John Ford refused to correct. Nunnally said to Ford, "Look, can't you get Warner to speak normally? Southerners don't know they've got any accent to begin with, and when they hear somebody mocking it, they get their backs up." Ford said he had spoken to him about it but "Baxter had an ego about equal to Ford's" and the accent stayed. After seeing the rushes, Zanuck and Nunnally went down to the set to see Ford, who was such a frightening fellow at that time that the executives at RKO had tossed coins to see who would have to endure watching the rushes with him. Zanuck told Ford the accent should go, and Ford replied that if he didn't like it he, Ford, would quit. Zanuck said, "Are you threatening me? Don't you ever threaten me. I throw fellas off this set. They don't quit on me." "I thought he was going to punch Ford in the nose," Nunnally said. "Ford had him outweighed by forty or fifty pounds. I was glad to get away from there, I just didn't want to witness this sort of thing." All of which explains a lot of his unhappiness about being a producer. Producing means confrontations (at which Zanuck excelled) and Nunnally hated them, shrank from arguments and was inclined to bury problems when they got too threatening.

Prisoner of Shark Island was one of the ones they "cooked up," which was the way most movies were made in the thirties and forties—a newspaper or magazine item would start someone's (frequently Zanuck's) mind clicking, and out of this bit of raw material they would, after much discussion, fashion a picture. Writers submitted ideas for pictures or else Zanuck called for them. (George Seaton recalls, "During the Berlin airlift Zanuck sent around a note saying that the airlift would be a good basis for a motion picture. I wrote back a rather sarcastic letter, 'Anybody who tries to write about the airlift from eight thousand miles away is an idiot. You ought to send somebody to Berlin to study the whole thing for a couple of months.' I got a note back saying, 'Pack your bags, you leave tomorrow.'" The result was *The Big Lift*.) Joel Sayre says that during Zanuck's years at Warner's he made pictures entirely from *Time* magazine. The germ for *Prisoner of Shark Island* was a *Time* reference to Dr. Samuel Mudd, who had been imprisoned for treason in the Dry Tortugas after administering medical aid to John Wilkes Booth on that fatal night. He was a Southern sympathizer and stood trial along with his acquaintance, Mrs. Surratt, who was hanged; but Mudd's treason was never really established and Nunnally, after doing some research, decided there was a case for his innocence. Mudd was the only doctor in the prison when an epidemic of yellow fever broke out, and as a reward for his medical services during this period he was finally released.

Though Nunnally once told me he had never written an original script, such "dramatic arrangements" as *Shark Island* are mostly original, put together from source material, certainly more so than the adaptations of plays and novels which dominated picture making in the fifties. "By then we were buying books for characters and we were actually buying the work and effort and the talent, and the man has already done a great deal of the work for you." Besides these two approaches, there was what George Seaton calls the "Briney" Foy school of films, of which Zanuck was also fond—one at a time or in a blend of several. "Briney had a library—I've never seen anything like it—it must have been thirty feet wide and about four shelves high. These were all just scripts—not just his, but everybody's. When I did *Song of Bernadette* he called me and said, 'Hey, kid, lemme see that script, will ya?' I said, 'What do you want it for, Briney?' 'What do I want it for? I want to steal it.'" And so evolved the art of the remake.

The Country Doctor, a story about the doctor who delivered
the Dionne quintuplets (played by Jean Hersholt), was the first
one Nunnally produced without writer credit, though according
to director Henry King he managed to write a few scenes in the
script anyway. It was another cook-up. The Hearst correspondent for the Dionne quints came from Canada and sold Fox
all the articles he had written about those five babies who, if
anyone has forgotten or wasn't around at the time, were headline
material for months in 1934. (I grew up hearing rapt reports
about what they ate, which one talked first, which one weighed
the most, et cetera.) King was signed along with Sonya Levien to
write the script, and together with Nunnally, says Henry King,
"we took these newspaper articles and we talked for ten consecu-
tive days, did nothing but talk, just thinking of this story." It was
approved immediately by Zanuck, who was in a great hurry to
get it made. "He talked to me about doing it and I said, 'Well,
I'll do it if we can make a story out of it that's good enough
without the quints.' He said, 'Without the quints? There's a
million-dollar project in the quintuplets.' I said, 'You don't understand what I'm talking about. If we can do a story that's good
enough without the quints, then think how good it will be with
them.'"

Nunnally wrote some of the sequences, including one intended
for Irvin Cobb which he persuaded King to let him do, of Dr.
Dafoe (Hersholt) at a city convention of affluent doctors asking
for money for his country clinic. King says, "It was the most
beautiful, sentimental, humorous piece of writing I ever saw in
my life. When Jean Hersholt read it, he said, 'I couldn't help it,
the tears came down,' it pained the man to say that tears came
out of his eyes—at the same time the next breath was a laugh
and the next was a tear—so it was just the most beautiful thing I
ever saw in my life." Given the undeniable fact that picture people are generous with superlatives, it is a lovely touching scene
in a very sentimental picture "full of corn," Nunnally said, "but it
did have, right at the nugget, a scene. This was one time when
there was a comedy scene that people knew in advance what
was going to happen. When Hersholt brought out that first baby,
and John Qualen, Papa Dionne, asked Hersholt, 'Another one?'
the audience rolled with this, because they knew it in advance

and you had to watch Qualen and he'd almost faint. The whole thing was one of the most wonderful sequences of comedy I've ever seen."

Dimples was the next cook-up (written by Arthur Sheekman, produced by Nunnally) and a less successful one. In it Dimples (Shirley Temple) endlessly tries to keep her reprobate music-teacher father (Frank Morgan) out of trouble, a touching but futile effort. It's the story of the good woman who loves a bastard, and Shirley, at seven or whatever she was, is doomed to disappointment. It is all rather forgettable, except that in it Stepin Fetchit says, "I was just restin' my eyes." Nunnally was a great admirer of Shirley, who was so professional she prompted Frank Morgan when he forgot his lines. "She was," he said, "a darling little girl, and by then was living the most extraordinary life. I got to know her mother and father pretty well. They lived in a little frame house in Santa Monica. They were completely unaware of the enormous celebrity that this child had become. They finally had to move when people began arriving in cars at their little house all day. They'd walk right up on the porch." At the beach Shirley would suddenly be surrounded by people, though she had nobody to play with. One day Mrs. Temple went to Harry Brand, head of Fox publicity, and asked him for a letter of introduction to someone in Honolulu, where they were going on vacation, to show them the sights. Harry thought she was kidding but promised her he'd send some cables and be sure they were taken care of. They arrived to find a hundred thousand people waiting to greet Shirley as she got off the boat—Honolulu had given its children a half-day holiday. They had never suspected such a thing would happen, it was almost beyond their comprehension. Mr. Temple, a bank teller, got promoted, because people came to do business with Shirley Temple's father. One day he told Nunnally he had gotten two letters from women who wanted him to father a child for them. "He was a big, dumpy man," Nunnally said. "I told him, 'That's good, but don't be unfaithful to her.'"

Road to Glory, in 1936, was a painful example of talent gone wrong. Starring Fredric March, Warner Baxter and Lionel Barrymore, it was produced by Nunnally, directed by Howard Hawkes and scripted by Joel Sayre and William Faulkner, so

says the credit—but Nunnally has said, and Joel agrees, that
Nunnally wrote most of it. "I put them together on this one,"
Nunnally said, "which resulted in two being drunk instead of
one. Bill was a real classy bottle man and Joel was not far
behind, and I don't suppose there were forty lines that Bill wrote
that we could use, and I don't think he cared much." The picture
was supposed to utilize footage from a French combat picture,
Les Croix du bois. In this case the war part is better than the
peace part, which features particularly execrable love scenes.
When Warner Baxter and his old father, Lionel Barrymore, are
both blinded in battle, what little credulity one had fades—or
dissolves. (I wrote in my notes, "There are too many dissolves."
About thirty-five years later Nunnally wrote me in a letter,
"Come to a dissolve reluctantly.") But there are two scenes that
work: the one in which Warner Baxter goes out into the gunfire
to shoot one of his own men who is hopelessly impaled on a
barbed wire fence, and the one in which troops hear the slow
tap-tap of German shovels digging toward their bunker.

Many tales have been told about Faulkner's unhappy Hollywood experience, including the one when, having asked if he
might work at home and being told he could, he was discovered
a week later in Mississippi. Stories about Nunnally, Joel Sayre
and Faulkner together all seem to be about getting drunk, like a
terrible caricature of writers who have sold their souls to Hollywood. During the writing of *Road to Glory*, Nunnally told,
"Came New Year's Day and the Rose Bowl and a lot of us arranged to get a bus over at the Brown Derby, put food and
booze in there, and go out to the Rose Bowl game. And Sayre
and Faulkner showed up at the Brown Derby, and Christ, they
were both plastered. This was about eleven in the morning. And
Bill had a newfangled zipper on his fly; and Sayre was trying to
help him. But anyway, I remember Faulkner sat down next to
the first Mrs. Thurber. Thurber wasn't there but she was. And
they'd never met. But out near Eagle Rock the bus stopped—
traffic jammed and there was silence. And then we hear Bill say,
'Ma'am, I can't hold my water!' and Mrs. Thurber says, 'Would
you please try, Mr. Faulkner.' And he says yes and went back to
sleep on her shoulder. Oh, it was awful. He lost his shoes at the
Rose Bowl, Gene Fowler managed to get them back, he was

about twice his size. . . . [In Hollywood] his contributions were
next to nothing but it made Hawkes feel good that he was
around. And as things went, he wasn't very expensive, a thousand or fifteen hundred a week, something like that. He was
doing it for the money, oh yes, that's all . . . he'd sell his short
stories to the *SEP*, but his novels were not big income. He'd
written some of his great novels by then. One day he left galleys
on my desk—I don't remember which one, something about wild
ponds. And there was a note that said, 'Dear Nunnally, this is
coming out in June and if you want it the price is $60,000. It is
about miscegenation.'"

Faulkner also worked on *Banjo on My Knee* and *Slave Ship*,
two Nunnally Johnson productions that I was unable to find. At
the same period Nunnally produced (but didn't write) *Nancy
Steele Is Missing*, *Cafe Metropole* and *Love Under Fire*.

By this time, around 1937, he knew being a producer wasn't
working. He was an "incurable writer" and unhappy dealing
with other people's scripts. Unlike Zanuck, he felt uncomfortable
telling other people how to write, and he told Zanuck this and
said he'd better quit. Zanuck asked him why he couldn't be like
Raymond Griffiths, who, when presented with a defective script,
simply handed it back to the writer and said, "Not right. Try
again." But Nunnally said he worried too much, and Zanuck
suggested a vacation. He went back to Miami Beach—"the only
place I have ever been homesick for"—to the house he and
Marion had built. After a month Zanuck called and asked him
how he would feel about producing only his own scripts, and
Nunnally was agreeable. He came back to write and produce the
remarkable *Jesse James*, an original and one of his best.

Not everyone can be a producer, especially one like Zanuck.
When Joe Mankiewicz left Fox (with four Oscars in his pocket
for writing and directing) to become an independent producer,
he assumed the offers would pour in. But, he told Nunnally, "the
stars I attracted were Michael Redgrave and Audie Murphy.
Those were the blockbusters I had for my pictures. Even when I
got Ava Gardner and Bogie for *Barefoot Contessa*, that failed
too. You and I are just not producers. Spiegel is. Sol Siegel is,
Zanuck is. There's a different talent involved. Look at their track
records." Only by his track record can a producer be judged.

Sam Spiegel, who made *African Queen, On the Waterfront, Suddenly, Last Summer* and *Bridge on the River Kwai,* is good because "he's picked subjects, he's stuck to them." He stuck to
Bridge on the River Kwai though five directors—including
Mankiewicz, Kazan and Huston—turned it down, and then made
that magnificent picture with the British director David Lean.

The main function of the producer is the decision to make the
picture, but with that decision goes enormous responsibility.
(Sol Siegel says, "Zanuck was able to take that responsibility. I
ran a coupla studios and you have to do that.") Besides you have
to have nerves of steel. Nunnally said, "It would scare the living
hell out of me to be responsible for the investment of that much
money [six or seven million] in a picture I was making or had
selected myself. I'm no gambler, it's not in my nature to do it."
Besides being a gambler, you have to have the nerve to do
what's right for the picture. Sol Siegel, who inherited the job of
producing *Ben Hur* when the previous producer died, fired
William Wyler, the director, because he refused to cut the two
hours out of it Siegel felt necessary (originally it ran five and a
half hours). "Wyler was the best cutter in the business, but I was
head of Metro and I had to protect the studio."

Selznick was the best producer of all, Nunnally said. He loved
the whole business of production, negotiating with actors, ma-
neuvering with other studios to get the ones he wanted, and
liked having his hand in every aspect of the picture. "Would I
try to tell Loretta Young how to make up? I wouldn't dream of it
. . . but those fellows, that's the joy of life to them. The late
Walter Wanger loved it. He would like to travel back and forth
three times a week to New York, or to travel to Dubuque and
open the picture, be interviewed, go on TV, help sell it. God, he
goes to jail, comes out, makes a picture about it. I go to jail and
the next thing you know I'd be down on Central Avenue, picking
up spikes in the gutter."

Jack Warner was not so good. In the late sixties he hired Nunnally to write a script. "For six months Jack Warner didn't have
to do a goddam thing, nothing," Nunnally said. "He didn't have to
make any decisions. He couldn't cast it because he didn't have a
script. When he finally got it, he made two or three foolish suggestions. The first one I remember. Somebody in the script

yawned, and he put a note by it, 'Never let anybody yawn in a picture.' It was his idea that, if somebody on the screen yawned, everybody in the audience would start yawning. That isn't very helpful, to tell the truth."

Jesse James ("Ah, that was my baby," said Nunnally) was another semi-original (Richard Corliss in *Talking Pictures* says *Prisoner of Shark Island* and *Jesse James* were Nunnally's only original screenplays) whose sources went back to matinees at the Springer in Columbus, where he first saw a production by the Jewel Kelly Stock Company. In a letter to an old family friend, he recalled:

"Those were the days when we were so caught up in the drama that we screamed warnings to Jesse on the stage. We of course knew the play by heart, and when that dirty little coward that they called Mr. Howard suggested to Jesse that the day was so warm he should take off his pistol and holster we screamed, Don't, Jesse, don't! And when Mr. Howard pointed out that the framed motto, God Bless Our Home, was a little crooked on the wall and Jesse drew up a kitchen chair to stand on to straighten it, with his back to Mr. Howard, every kid in the house screamed another warning. But it was no use. Mr. Howard poured it into him and Jesse twisted on the floor and, after making sure the rug was there for him to fall on, dived down dead. They don't hardly make them like that any more."

Nunnally said later, "I thought to myself, 'By God, anybody that arouses that much excitement, that much sympathy—' because we all talked about those outlaws in those days like you talk about ball players." He told Zanuck about all this and persuaded him to make the picture over the objections of the ever myopic New York office. Henry King directed, Tyrone Power and Henry Fonda were Jesse and Frank James and Randolph Scott was the man of the law, the marshal. The story was derived in part from articles by the editor of the Sedalia, Missouri, *Gazette,* who, writing at the time of the James boys, had been a fan of Jesse's, partly from books on Jesse James and partly from a play called *The Purple Mask,* from which he unself-consciously pinched the escape-from-jail situation. The story (like *Bonnie and Clyde*) is morally complex. The James boys only become train robbers after their land has been taken, their

house blown up and their mother killed by railroad robber
barons. Sympathy is strongly on Jesse's side, even the marshal
sympathizes. But the deep moral split in Jesse's life is bound to
destroy him. Righteous rage turns into a lust for violence, and he
becomes obsessed, neglecting his wife and child. "He's wild,"
says Zee, his wife, "like a horse you can't break." But as in many
Nunnally Johnson pictures the fact of a child is rebirth for the
father. Jesse retires to his family and we hold our breath and
pray that he'll get away with it—until Mr. Howard pumps him
full of lead and we know, sadly, that there must be retribution.

He took his script to Henry King, who wanted to do it immediately. Zanuck demurred, then finally said, "Oh, all right, go
ahead and do it. It might do well in Kentucky, Tennessee, southern Illinois, or even Kansas." (There are a lot of stories about
Zanuck grumpily giving in to a picture idea he doesn't really go
along with.) King found the locations in Missouri and shot it
there, a practice somewhat ahead of the times—in those days the
cheapie pictures were shot outside and the expensive ones were
done at the studio in front of a cyclorama. The locations look
very real, very right, and there are a couple of spectacular
scenes; one in which a horse jumps through a shopwindow, and
another in which several men on horseback jump off a cliff into
the river below (in which, Henry King says, only one horse was
lost).

The script was sent to Henry Fonda, who says in an interview,
"I recognized that Frank James would be a secondary role and I
wasn't sure at this point in my career whether it would be smart
for me to do it. I had Henry Hathaway advise me, and he said,
'Go, do it now, that's the part.'" They had eight weeks' location
in Noel, Missouri. "We'd had Big Bear for two or three weeks on
Trail of the Lonesome Pine," Fonda says, "except that I'd never
had a real location film until *Jesse James* in a little place as small
as Noel, Missouri. We lived in Noel and worked in Pineville.
Pineville was chosen to be the home of the James family—but
there wasn't enough room to house the company. So the natives
moved out of their homes to relatives up in the hills someplace
and made their homes available to the company. That's the way
we lived . . . we ate at the Shadow Lake restaurant behind a
rope to keep away the thousands of people who came from

Chicago, Texas, Tennessee, this was the first time an important movie location had been like that, and they publicized it too, the studio publicized it so people flocked by the ten thousands. We were never not being watched, while we worked, while we ate, while we brushed our teeth. It was a new experience for me. You'd be sitting at tables literally with people lined up at the rope watching you, staring . . . my part was a good part, Henry King let me be a character, they couldn't afford to let Tyrone Power be a character because he was Tyrone Power, had to keep an image. It didn't matter for me, I could chew tobacco and have a mustache, so it was fun. . . . I've gotten into a taxi in New York with a driver who hears my voice before he sees me and he says, 'Hey, Frank!' "

After the picture was finished Zanuck said to King and Nunnally, "We just cannot kill the hero." Nunnally said that was exactly what had happened to Jesse, but Zanuck was unhappy with it, so he manufactured one or two other endings, neither of which was strong enough. Finally Zanuck said, "Well, I've been thinking. We might as well commit suicide now as any other time. But I think if we ended up with a close-up of the mother and the boys, it would fit in with the rest." So Nunnally's original ending, a eulogy by Jesse's tombstone, was put back along with the close-up. It turned out to be an extremely successful picture, Ty Power's most successful to date and Fonda's most important part.

Henry King tells one curious story. While he was working on the script Nunnally said to him, "You know I'm writing the part of Frank James for me." He mentioned it two or three times, "in that easygoing, humorous way, he'd say, 'Do you think I could play Frank James?' " King thought he was joking and forgot about it. During a casting conference with Nunnally, King and Zanuck, after Ty Power had been cast, King said, " 'I've been thinking about this very carefully, and there's only one man in the world who could possibly look Frank James, be Frank James, play Frank James'—and Nunnally sort of sat up like this—and I said Hank Fonda . . . and Nunnally sort of said uuuhhh. When we got out in the hallway Nunnally said, 'You know I sort of hoped you'd want me to play the part.' I said, 'You're not serious.' He said, 'Well, I was serious then but not now.' I never

dreamed . . . and he had sort of patterned that part down so it'd
be a natural for him—of course he'd made a star of Hank
Fonda. I'd thought he was joking." The part of Frank James is
quietly strong—as the elder of the two brothers, you find your
gaze wandering to him from Jesse as though to confirm or deny
Jesse's behavior. Both Dorris, my stepmother, and Marion think
it had to be a joke but, like Henry King, I suspect there was a
moment when it was not. In 1971 he said, "I'm not sure I knew
that Henry was going to do the part, I may have, I can't
remember."

Hollywood 1932-1940

Since Nunnally went upward so quickly, he and Marion didn't stay long in their tiny Hollywood cabin. By the time I was born in January 1933 they had moved to Bedford Drive, in Beverly Hills, which is equivalent to moving from, say, the West Forties to the East Sixties. (It isn't really, but trying to draw parallels between Los Angeles and New York is almost hopeless.) They got Nana at the hospital and hired a couple. The house was one floor and very spread out, and I have a notion I have some ghostly memory of it, though this is probably from Nana saying, "Your mother and father were at one end and you and I were at the other, and I had to run back and forth for your bottles in the middle of the night."

After Marion had recovered from the caesarean birth I had been, she set about being a Hollywood wife (Rosa Mankiewicz, Joe's ex-wife, said, "The spouse of a successful Hollywood person is about as welcome at any gathering as venereal disease")— playing tennis and badminton, going to antique auctions or shopping with Gertrude Sayre and Gloria Stuart Sheekman, taking voice lessons because she had "seen too many beautiful women who opened their mouths and dreadful noises came out." In those days women usually stopped work when they were married and certainly after they'd had a baby, but Marion had a lot of energy and though it never occurred to her to get a job—I imagine it was tacitly assumed if anybody thought about it at all that such a thing would be emasculating to Nunnally—she filled the days as best she could. She was a natural athlete and worked off boredom and frustration in the surf at Malibu, on the tennis courts, and even batting a polo ball around. At first, anyway, life was more regular than it had been in New York, with more of the appurtenances of normality for a young family. Nunnally, an extremely systematic writer, worked from nine to five at the studio and then came home to his wife and the new (superb) baby. On weekends they played tennis, went on picnics with friends or to swim at a small beach club in Santa Monica.

It might have looked normal and some, mainly the men, claim that it was. Finley Peter Dunne, a newspaperman who spent time in early Hollywood, says, "We all lived a kind of suburban life really, the husbands went to work in the morning and came home at night, sometimes the hours were a little odd but not very, and we had a kind of social group of which Nunnally was the leader. . . . Joel [Sayre] and his wife, Evelyn and I, Ted Paramore and his wife and a few other people saw each other quite a lot, never talked shop. But it was a company town, everybody knew how much everybody else was making and you were rated on that scale, though this was something Nunnally never paid any attention to. It put a kind of pressure on people—like Hershey, Pennsylvania, or Bethlehem or somewhere."

But there was more than that. Men have never been expert at sensing those intangibles that make women miserable. Evie Dunne didn't like it, and Marian Spitzer Thompson, a free-lance writer from New York who went out with her husband Harlan in 1928, was "very ambivalent about early Hollywood—in the beginning I mooned and cried all the time. Women have no status out there—you were nothing if you weren't a star. Or maybe being the wife of a producer gave you a certain brief notice." Certainly very brief and nothing much. Eleanor Hempstead, wife of then producer and writer David Hempstead, says, "I sort of hated it out there . . . it was like Polish weddings. The women all got shoved in the back seat and the men up front . . . at dinner parties the men went one way to have their drinks and the women were left together to talk about their servants, their babies, their recipes, what the maid said yesterday . . . people could be as rude or difficult or impossible as they wanted, and you were supposed to accept it if you were the wife of a producer. Maybe I'd have liked Southern California if I was married to some man who was into Sunkist oranges or something." "Hollywood wives have no importance," Marion said. "I felt unfulfilled—shut out of Nunnally's life and yours, since Nana took you over completely and wouldn't let me near you."

On the other hand, Gloria Sheekman and Felice Paramore call thirties Hollywood "terrifically exciting," though Gloria was always a working actress and they, along with Amanda Dunne (Phil's wife, another enthusiast), are native Californians, which might have had something to do with it. Culture shock must have explained a lot of the pain, the jarring removal from the New York habitat. They had exchanged the privacy of New York for the high visibility of the fantastic village Hollywood was then, with its high-powered inhabitants. Felice Paramore tells, "It was a small community and everyone knew everyone, and there were very few places to go—no little theaters, and only a couple of restaurants. You knew everybody and they were mostly from New York. It was a fairly literate community. . . . Ted [Paramore] was the first editor of national affairs at *Time*, one of the editors of *Vanity Fair*, Mencken's fair-haired boy. . . . Wells Root, Scott, Zelda, Benchley, Don Stewart, Ogden Nash, who worked on *The Wizard of Oz* for a while before they threw him out, Nathanael West and the Perelmans—they hated Hollywood and saved like misers so they could go back East—Arthur Kober and Lillian [Hellman] and Marc Connelly and Dash Hammett, Elliott Nugent and the Hacketts. There was only Ciro's and the Trocadero and the Vendome on the Strip, all the writers congregated in the basement, one night at a big table there were fifteen of the brightest and wittiest of them, John O'Hara, Phil Dunne—we were all young and beautiful and life was very good though we didn't know it. I don't think there was a world-famous person in any department who didn't come in those years—musicians, composers, everything." It was fashionable then, as it is now, to regard Hollywood as a cultural wasteland. It was not a "saloon town" and some New Yorkers found adjustment difficult, though it depended on your point of view. Gloria Sheekman says, "Men like Arthur [Sheekman] and Nat Perrin and Irv Gleckler and Harry Tugend, the comedy writers I

knew, were poor boys from poor backgrounds who had worked
very hard and were terribly pleased and excited and stimulated
here. There was leisure time for tennis and partying and trips.
The theater people hated Hollywood but my gang liked it and all
of us were very untouched by New York's opinion of itself and of
us."

Another thing that made thirties Hollywood not quite like
Hershey, Pennsylvania, or Larchmont was that everyone got
richer and richer, while the rest of the country starved. "I'm always embarrassed when anybody asks me what I was doing during the depression," Marion said once. When Nunnally first arrived his salary was $300 a week, a year later it was $600, and by
1938 it was $2,000. Houses in Beverly Hills rented for $175 a
month, $200 with a pool. You earned a little more, you rented
another house. When I asked my mother what they talked about
then, she said, "They talked of what to do with their excess
money." Gloria Sheekman says when she married Arthur, "I went
down one day and bought the whole thing, service for eighteen,
sterling, Wedgwood, Baccarat crystal, and charged it—I collected everything, first editions, fine bindings, porcelains,
jade. . . . [Marion and Gertrude] and I bought a lot of Victorian
and French provincial antiques, had them done in cut velvet,
satins, French silks—it never occurred to us that this was anything special." For people who have grown up poor—and most
of these people were from simpler backgrounds—coping with
the accouterments of wealth can lead to strange problems. Gloria
said she and Arthur took trips to New York because they were
unable to fire incompetent servants. Sometimes their own ineptitude seemed hilarious. "We had a dinner party one night after
I'd been working on the set all day and we had a new couple
from the agency. We always had finger bowls with flowers in
them and service plates and lace doilies and all that . . . after
dinner we were all sitting in the living room and the new man
walked in with fourteen brandy snifters filled to the brim with
brandy. We fell off our chairs laughing."

In fact they laughed a great deal, as though the whole Hollywood experience was an enormous joke. It must have seemed so
incredible to be paid all this money to write these funny things,
to live in this fantastic place where even the trees looked like

something out of a cartoon. But only the guys shared in the joke, and a very, very few women like Gloria whose lives centered on the studios. The rest of the wives went along, as wives do, and laughed dutifully, but were not in on the joke at all. The newspaper-clubbiness of New York, the same gang that had met at Bleeck's and the Algonquin and the Dizzy Club, now regrouped and met at the Brown Derby for the Butterworth Athletic Club (Nunnally, Marc Connelly, Harry Ruby, Oscar Hammerstein, Dorothy Parker, and of course Charlie Butterworth) or at the Hillcrest Country Club for a sort of Hollywood round table headed by George Jessel (along with Jack Benny, George Burns, Mank and Groucho). In New York the women had been working too, and came along to the saloons, and were in on the jokes. But now the fun was all at the studios, at the writers' table in the commissary, or in the private dining room where Nunnally sat with Zanuck, Bill Perlberg, Lew Schreiber and Jessel ("he didn't sit at the writers' table because the writers were always moaning and groaning about their financial woes"); the wives remained each in her beautiful home and spent the day having massages, shopping at Magnin's, playing badminton and conferring with the gardener and the nurse. In a way it was a lot more restful—there was less drinking than in New York, says Marion, because "everything you did in Hollywood was so public," and there were only two or three parties a week. But there was an unmentioned feeling of impermanence. Contracts might not get renewed, or else people might simply get fed up—it might not last forever. So houses were rented instead of bought, and roots were sunk cautiously into the moving sands beneath the sprinkler systems.

Since there were no saloons, drinking was done either at Ciro's or the Troc or, most often, at somebody's house. Of all the "classy bottle men" around town Nunnally and Joel Sayre were among the most visible, though their drinking had different styles—Joel was inclined to break furniture and the mirrors over bars, while Nunnally, "old rubber legs," merely sank into a nearby sofa and went to sleep, and had to be taken home by somebody's chauffeur. Marion had never minded Nunnally's inability to hold booze (his speech started slurring at the end of one scotch and water), possibly because holding liquor was one of the few things at which she could outdo him, but the drinking here was different than in New York and not as much fun, as the parties divided up after dinner into male and female groups, and of these groups it was the guys who had the fun. "There was something larkish about the whole business," Nunnally said. "All that you heard or knew existed was pictures, the making of entertainment, and the makers of these pictures were just naturally extroverts and all of a sudden their pockets were full of greenbacks and the opportunities for fun were here and they weren't slow to take advantage of it."

If Marion had ever thought that the move to the Coast would solve their marital problems, she was wrong. She had never been so well off financially, her husband was going up like a skyrocket and now she had a remarkable daughter, and they were surrounded by charming and witty friends—the Sheekmans, Phil Wylie and his wife, Herbert and Helen Asbury, Charlie and Ethel Butterworth, Lyn and Nell Farnell, the Thompsons, the Sayres, the Hulburds. But Nunnally still disappeared for the night and never explained where he had been. She never asked him and he never told her. Why not? People didn't then, for one thing—it was long before the age of marriage counselors. Besides, says Marion, "there was a conspiracy of silence about Nunnally's weakness for women. Anyway, I had accepted his double standard from the beginning—I knew I couldn't change it" and "I was afraid I might hurt his feelings." Not only didn't they talk, they never admitted anything was wrong. They were, both of them, expert dissemblers. There wasn't anything unusual about this. "We didn't talk either," says Marian Thompson. "Nobody did." Besides, "it was the beginning of the era of what is now called open marriage, which didn't necessarily include 'going all the way.'" There were fewer affairs than one might suppose, and those that existed were kept very quiet, at least among married couples (which was why the Mary Astor-George Kaufman affair was so shocking), but married men and women went about with each other freely to lunch or to parties, very visibly, which might explain why the period has a reputation for being "fast," which it really wasn't at all.

Women were still "hurling themselves" at Nunnally—not only the starlets who wanted parts but the successful professional

women who were as important to him as friends as his male colleagues. Perhaps his closest friends were such women. Because
of the male tradition of don't-show-your-feelings-keep-'em
laughing-don't-get-involved it was easier for Nunnally, a tender
and sentimental man, to speak his feelings to a woman who had
both the brains and the unvarnished feminine sensibility to understand. Dorothy Parker was a good friend, as was Edith Haggard, a literary agent; Doris Vidor, a producer; Celia Agar, a *Variety* writer who used his letters in her columns; Marian
Thompson, a writer in Hollywood and New York; Helen Hayes,
Lauren Bacall, and all three of his wives, until he married them;
probably more I don't know of. Strong women, all of them. His
mother Onnie was the strong one, the doer, and Grandpa Jim was
the reader, the front-porch philosopher, the one whose eyes easily filled with tears, and Nunnally had a good deal of his father
in him. And women loved Nunnally, partly because he was
funny and charming, but also because he was at ease with some
of the feminine aspects of his own nature and was able to be unself-conscious about love and loyalty and kindness.

But, as far as Marion was concerned, Nunnally's magnetism
for women was mainly a source of anguish. What happened next
was almost inevitable—she had an affair with another man, who
happened to be a young novelist on the brink of what later became tremendous success. Such a relationship was doomed to
drown in its own complexity. Marion by then was hurt enough to
feel vengeful, and she had no illusions about the nature of O's
(the writer's) feelings. "It was vanity with O.—I was the wife of
a producer," which could be amended to read the most successful writer-producer in town, the wit, the darling, Zanuck's wonder boy, the guy everybody loved and admired and envied.
Producer—the town was crawling with producers. Nunnally was
very special, the sort of person whose jokes were repeated around
the studio within an hour after he made them. Success was written all over him, he had the magnetism of a person on his way
up. He worked hard and he was superbly talented in what he
did. Besides, he had an admirable kind of Southern, low-key way
of ignoring the caste system that everybody else felt bound by,
of paying no attention to the nasty little studio intrigues that
most people were afraid to ignore. He had enough personal secu-

rity to help other writers with their scripts without taking a credit, to give praise where it was due and to be modest and self-deprecating about what he did. It seems an unusual style out there in the land of superlatives and "those old pants pressers" as Joel Sayre calls the early studio heads, who traded, bought, sold and swiped ideas back and forth like Middle Eastern money-changers (though Celia Agar says, "Putting yourself down was the fashion then with the *good* writers. You couldn't boast or brag or take kudos, it wasn't done by Nunnally's friends, and they were all top-notch"). If all this seems blurred in daughterly affection, I've watched roomfuls of clever people go into immediate silence as he prepared to speak, I've heard him quoted and requoted for years, and have lived for months in a wash of affection from almost everyone who knew him. He was almost a legend in Hollywood, certainly a greatly loved and admired man.

O. must have been as affected by this as everybody else, being somewhat younger and newer in the writing profession. Nunnally on the other hand was doubly stung that Marion had chosen a writer and went into a rage that lasted for years. "But why can't you forgive me?" she asked. "I've forgiven you your other women." But she was Caesar's wife, it was different. Other women might do this sort of thing but he couldn't believe she would. "How could you do such a thing?" he asked her, and she said, "But why can't you forgive me?" After a miserable year and a half of non-forgiveness, she went to Europe for three months "to think things over"—another bit of pre-marriage-counselor behavior; thirty years later she would have gone into therapy for her unexpressed anger—at the end of which she came home and said she was going to get a divorce. Nunnally agreed, and they were divorced in 1938. Afterward they went home and to bed together, where Joel Sayre found them the next morning when he came by for coffee. Nunnally said, "Joel, Marion has left me." They all laughed hilariously, and then, I would like to think, sat around and had coffee and English muffins together. (But it contrasts strangely with a newspaper picture of Marion—under the headline "Nunnally Johnson Loses His Wife"—wearing a high Spanish hat with a veil and looking sad and lost. She testified, says the story, that "he would get mad at me for no reason at all. He would stay out late at night. He told me he didn't love me.")

Nobody questions that love makes us crazy, but in what we think of as the original plan we were only allowed one bout of madness before settling down, having children and leading more or less passionless lives until we died (at thirty-five or so, which, according to Margaret Mead, is the life span this plan was designed for). Now we live longer and sometimes we fall in love several times, producing children in between, and the juxtaposition can be weird and guilt-making. It seems almost impossible to be in love and be a good parent at the same time, unless you have a settled, secure kind of love. But the wild, blind, semi-psychosis that most of us go through at least once in our lives shuts the door in the face of children—love has to do with needs, and gratifying them, and a fierce concentration on those needs, a closed system that leaves no room for the patience and dailiness that make up being a parent. In the best of marriages the birth of children changes that sort of love, if it exists, rearranges it into something else; at worst it finishes it off, because love can't tolerate a third party. If they are our children, our blood, we try to recoup it somehow, make up for it later, make another home; if they are not ours, if they belong to the person we love, we can only bite the bullet and never say what we think, that we wish they had never been born. The quality of love between parent and nonparent always has this snag, the guilt of the parent and the placating unselfishness or grim tolerance of the non-parent, and that area of absolute disagreement behind whatever masks they are wearing. The non-parent has a sort of power—it is he or she who is going to put up with those kids, suffer the division of love and money and time, and accordingly demand a return —double devotion or (impossibly) absolute loyalty. "You sided with the children against me," cries the non-parent, and there is no answer, only more guilt, until, at worst, the parent must choose between divorce and rejection of his own children and, at best, a truce of gratitude.

When Nunnally and Marion were married, Marge was a seven-year-old child whose parents had done as badly as most people at working out what is legally called a "custodial arrangement." Alice worked, and the problem was what to do with Marge— Nunnally was unhappy with Alice's arrangements for her, which involved leaving her with Mrs. Mason. He approached Marion with guilt about his child, who didn't seem to fit into the current atmosphere of love in the city room. During the difficult period when Marion was in San Francisco, he wrote her, "I don't doubt you mean it about not minding Marjorie, but I still hesitate to be satisfied that you won't mind having her about." He goes on to suggest buying a house near the shore on Long Island to make a home for all of them and mentions putting Marge in a nearby boarding school. After they were married Marge came to the house in Great Neck for periods of time and later to Beverly Hills where she was taken to school in the Cadillac driven by Essex, the chauffeur. "I was a female Milquetoast," Marge says. "I could make friends with no one, never had a date, came home with the chauffeur, talked constantly with Essex and Roberta [the cook]. Essex taught me to drive behind Dad's back. Dad would come in, possibly prompted by Marion, and give me a lecture for being so familiar with the servants. . . . I didn't have anything else. I don't think I was ever aggressive or disobedient." I remember her as being rather wild, and so do others, but whichever, she was lonely and angry at having the door shut in her face—and my birth, when she was thirteen, didn't make her feel any better. ("He wasn't mine any more.") Nunnally's solution to the complex step-problem was always to side with Marion, as he later sided with Dorris, and Marion was doubtless exacting her price for Marge's existence by saying or implying that Marge was coming between them. She wasn't a nag, that wasn't her style, but when against the wall she could produce deadly silences, piercing stares and tiny killing sentences—and when it came to Marge I imagine Marion was a model of self-sacrificing forbearance, for which Nunnally was grateful and so sided with her always against his daughter. (Oh, for a marriage counselor! My mother said to me once, "I never nag people about their deeper emotions, it might embarrass them.") It was an unhappy situation but, interestingly enough, neither of my parents, when asked about their divorce, ever mentions Marge as having anything to do with it. They both blame Nunnally for his "drinking, wandering and inconsiderateness."

In 1937 Nunnally went to Florida to think things over about being a producer (after having told Zanuck he wanted to quit), taking Marge, but not Marion, along. He and Marge (now sev-

enteen) "had a ball," says Marge. "I drove the car and we went
fishing and did all the night clubs and I even sang in some," her
ambition at the time. "Pat ———— was around, she was in love
with Nunnally, but she married somebody else later. She had the
fantasy of all children of divorce—"for years I clung to the hope
my parents would get back together, and when he and Marion
split that was uppermost in my mind. Now I think, how could
they [Nunnally and Alice] have even lasted three years or five
years or whatever?" After years as part of a miserably unsuccessful family situation, she had her father all to herself. My mother
once said that Marge's problem was a father fixation, but if she
had one, then so did I, and so do my half sisters Christie and
Roxie, for the high points in my young life were being alone
somewhere with Nunnally, being gently courted, taken out on
the town, admired and listened to with no distractions, being introduced to glamorous people, being treated like a remarkable
female person. Without it we would all be lesser people. At any
rate the split between Nunnally and Marion must have been a
heady time for Marge, as it seemed to have been for half the female population of New York and Los Angeles, for prospective
wives appeared from all directions. Marge stoutly fought off the
unsuitable candidates—"I knew with most of these women that
my life with him was gone if this happened." A certain starlet
was "absolutely determined to marry him—we came practically
to blows one night when she told me she was going to get him
and get rid of me." It's always startling to hear of the sex appeal
of one's parent, and Nunnally was, as my mother said, "a plain-
looking man." He was tall and thin, with a loping walk, thinning
brown hair and sharp blue eyes, and not a single good feature—
small pouchy eyes and a largish nose and ears that stuck out. If,
as Marion said, he was self-conscious about his looks when he was
young, the amount of female attention he got later must have
abolished such an idea. His appeal was humor, gentleness, intelligence and, at this time in his life, enormous success.

Around the same time, Dorris Bowdon arrived in Hollywood.
She came up on the train from the South with Mary Healy and
Linda Darnell, three beauty-contest winners hoping to become
actresses (Dorris was "Miss Memphis"). Dorris was the youngest
daughter of a Memphis doctor who died when she was very

young, leaving her mother to support seven children. They lived on a farm and Dorris had worked since her teen-age years to support herself and help support the family. She got through college and became a speech major at Louisiana State, where she was seen in a school play by a talent scout. When she arrived in Hollywood she was only twenty-one, very small and pretty, and full of chutzpah—she went into the secretary's anteroom outside Nunnally's office and refused to move until she saw the big man. She wanted a part in *Jesse James*. No talk on the secretary's part of meetings with Zanuck and other crashingly important activities could induce her to move, and persistence paid off. She got through the door, where Nunnally immediately picked up the phone and called off the meeting with Zanuck. She didn't get the part, but he asked her to dinner—a portent for the future if there ever was one. "The attraction," Dorris says, "was instant and mutual." He spoiled her for all the other guys, though she and Mary Healy, who were "roomies," had plenty of them around. (Mary tells of a double date she and Dorris had with Franchot Tone and Burgess Meredith, during which Dorris talked incessantly about Mr. Johnson. At the end of the evening Meredith, instead of kissing her, said, "Get thee to a Nunnally.")

But the problem was Marion, and Nunnally's feelings about another marriage going on the rocks, and another child paying for what he felt were his sins and errors. They were, for a time, still in love. Nunnally's trips East and visits to the Sixty-sixth Street apartment Marion had taken in New York were all part of a long attempt to patch up what proved to be unpatchable—largely because neither of them really knew what was going on or else was unable to talk about it. Affairs in marriage are often metaphors, and since neither of them was inclined to self-examination they never looked past the fact of these affairs to the truth of whatever was going on behind them. I think Nunnally was guilty—the life he was leading was a far cry from Columbus and the values he grew up with, and he had begun to feel his personal life was a failure. Two divorces and two uprooted children before forty were hard to swallow for someone with the acute need and love for family life he had, and Marion, who as a personality is almost guilt-free, must have exacerbated this.

After trying to patch in New York, they tried it again in California. Marion, Nana and I lived in the house on Camden Drive and Nunnally lived nearby in an apartment and came for dinner every night. At the end of the summer he told her it was impossible, it would never work—"he still remembered my crime," Marion said. By then she had met another man, a dour commander in the navy. For some reason Nunnally was then able to forgive her—or was remotivated by a little competition—and he came to New York and took an apartment at 400 East Fifty-seventh for some serious courting. "He asked me to come back to him," Marion says, "but I stuck with Joe [the commander]. Nunnally never asked me to remarry him—I thought if I agreed to marry him it would turn him off." Marge, who had come along with Nunnally, was rooting for Dorris, who arrived shortly to join them in the apartment on Fifty-seventh Street. They were only three years apart in age and Marge loved her. The three of them kept house in a shambly way—Marge did the cooking, supposedly, but all she could make was strawberries Romanoff and roast beef. In the evening they played triple solitaire. They were clearly a good working trio, but still Nunnally held back—he was seventeen years older than Dorris. When she was born he was graduating from high school. When he grew old she would still be young. On the other hand he knew she had come up the hard way—Dorris didn't have a pair of shoes until she was thirteen. If hard times came she would stick by him (and he was always aware how quickly hard times could come). And Dorris was mad about him. She adored him, worshiped him to an extent that made his faults (women and booze) almost unbearable when they emerged.

It was a dreadful period for all of them. Nunnally went back and forth between Marion and Dorris, Marion tried to decide between Nunnally and the commander, Dorris was utterly miserable, and Marge ran around trying to solve it all (another specialty of children of divorce)—she wanted a home she would be happy in and thought Dorris was the one to provide it. It all culminated on a dreadful Christmas Eve, '39, when Nunnally didn't turn up at a certain theater where he was to meet Dorris, Marge and some others, because he was at Marion's apartment on Sixty-sixth Street trimming the Christmas tree. Dorris got drunk and sat in the theater and wept, long after the curtain was down and everyone had left, except a complete stranger on whose shoulder she had been crying. When she pulled herself together and looked at him, he said, "Merry Christmas." The next day she went back to California.

But Nunnally had already resigned from the project of getting Marion back, though nothing at that time seems to have been very final. In November he wrote her that the reason she could neither remarry him nor simply finish it off was that she didn't love him any more, she loved Joe, and the only emotion she felt for Nunnally was fondness and certain feelings of obligation about the marriage and me. Though he still loved her, he would bother her no longer. At the end he says he is "neither lost nor dead to another kind of affection." I suspect he was simply unable to end it himself—he had to put the responsibility on her, to attribute it to her changed feelings. To take the responsibility himself would have made the guilt even worse. At any rate it was over. Dorris came back and in February of 1940 they were married in Nyack, at the home of Helen Hayes and Charles MacArthur.

Kidnapped *1939*

We left Hollywood in 1939, when I was six, in the big black
Cadillac which was supposed to be Pop's. He had driven it to the
studio every day, and my mother had done whatever she did in
her Pontiac—mainly drive to the West Side Tennis Club. There
must have been some dreadful error in our having taken his car,
leaving him stranded—Harold, the chauffeur, my mother, Nana,
and me. Didn't he object? Nobody seemed to mention him, except Nana, who sat in the back seat with me. "Your poor father,"
she said occasionally. "My Lord." My mother and Harold sat in
the front seat, switching places every fifty miles because my
mother had read somewhere that such a procedure diminished
fatigue. Harold, impeccable servant that he was, of course never
argued with her. As I recall he wore his black uniform and
peaked cap for the whole trip, only asking permission to take off
his jacket in the worst stretches of the desert, but leaving his
black necktie in place. My mother took off her suit jacket and we
opened all the windows and panted as the hot sandy wind blew
in at us.

As much as a six-year-old ever has such thoughts, I imagine
that was the first time the notion crossed my mind that all adults
were crazy. My mother seemed to think this was fun. As we
groaned up narrow mountain roads crossing the Rockies, she admired the view as Nana and I, sick with terror, tried not to look
out the windows and Nana tried to pacify me. It was a withering

indictment of our characters—the sheep were being sorted out from the goats. To her it really was exciting, driving across her country. Vast mountains and great gashlike precipices turned her on, terrible hairpin turns between rocky red cliffs and bottomless canyons where we might all lie smashed like jelly beans made her smile with pleasure. If she worried about the desert, where our car might break down and where our whitened bones might be found weeks later after the vultures had left, she never showed it. I suppose she wanted us to experience our country. Or else she was trying to make the best of a bad job.

But our country was fearful. All I had ever known was Beverly Hills, which I learned some years later was not considered real, but it was my ordered universe. I had no way of knowing that the row of identical palm trees along our street hadn't grown that way naturally, or that the clean beauty of the village was a kind of national joke. I had crushed lemon leaves in my hands and lain on a great pile of eucalyptus leaves looking up into the vast trees that would be killed by the slightest frost. And I knew about the desert. In those days it was still everywhere, up in the hills above Sunset and even between the villages of Beverly Hills and Westwood, little arid stretches now paved over and covered with car washes and meditation centers, and all along Sepulveda when you drove to the Valley. If the water ever ran out, the whole place would go back to desert, all the green fragrance would disappear without a trace.

I knew that this was being prevented, for the time being at least, by Pop and all the other fathers who turned on the sprinklers when they came home from the studio, since it was better for the lawn to do it at dusk. It gave a great show for very little effort. Shortly after arriving home Pop would stride outside, me at his heels, pick up a sort of tonglike poker and turn a couple of little spigots lying flat on the edge of the grass, whereupon the entire lawn bloomed with geysers of water. Then with a smile of pleasure he would go back inside, while I followed him like a remora, and make himself a drink. We would sit and talk till it was time to turn off the sprinklers. In the car I asked Nana if she thought he would continue to do this even though we were gone, and she muttered, "Well, I dunno, the poor man, Lord knows *what* he'll do now." God—would he let the whole place turn back to sand? And what about his car, his poor car that had never gone anywhere but along Santa Monica to the Fox lot? Being a California child, I worried immensely about the car, I endowed it with a ghostly humanity. I even named it, I forget what, Panther or Cobra or Greyhound. Not that any glamorous identity I pasted on it would give it supernatural powers. It was clearly fallible, it clunked and wheezed and got a flat tire that Harold had to change, still wearing his cap and tie, while my mother admired whatever scenery we were in the middle of and Nana talked about snakes.

We even had to stop for sight-seeing. In the Painted Desert you went up in a tower and looked through a sort of periscope that made you feel as though you were falling upside down through space, which was worse than crossing the Rockies. The Grand Canyon . . . well. Awful. I don't recall going down to the bottom on a donkey, but probably my mother did, while the three of us sat glowering at the top. I wondered what Pop would have thought of all this. Nana implied that he would have hated every minute of it and that my mother was out of her mind, which didn't surprise me. It was clear who Nana was going to be sure I took after. The strange part was that my mother looked so cheerful all the time, so tidy and composed and in control. Whatever was going on in her mind didn't show. She was leading a gang of surly rebels back East where none of them wanted to go (but whose opinions didn't count) and somebody had to keep her head.

Of course part of the trouble, which I was too young to know, was that the whole trip was unnatural, you didn't go East, you went West. You stayed there and succeeded or failed and died. We were bucking a historic tide. What was back East, anyhow? Nana said it might not be so bad, she had come from Chicago herself. Mainly back East was dirty. And cold. Lord, she hated the cold. She was doing this for Mr. Johnson and for The Child, as she referred to me. She was there to protect my rights, like an attorney. If she thought we were driving too long after dusk, she said we had to stop soon because The Child had to eat, have her bath and sleep in a decent bed. We had to stop because The Child was about to be carsick, we had to get going so The Child could get settled in her new home. She invoked me more than the Lord, and of course nobody dared argue about The Child's welfare, though I knew my mother would have thought I was all right sleeping in the back seat, which I would have been, or going without a bath, which I prayed for.

We were irrevocably divided into pairs, as suited our stations and dispositions—Nana and I, being the least tractable, were in back where we belonged. Harold, on the other hand, richly deserved being in front. He was very good-looking and Nana said he was working with something called lucite and was going to start a lucite business someday. In the back were two little lamps made of lucite spirals that he was going to show to a manufacturer. It all kept him optimistic, as we trekked through the wilderness. Since he was Swedish and not polar about East and West, which the rest of us were or were rapidly becoming, and since he was well paid, his disposition, if not his spirit of adventure, matched my mother's. He was as pleasant and polite about Death Valley as he had been announcing dinner and wielding his butter paddles, activities which I thought were part of every normal home. Every evening in the butler's pantry, I had watched him take little bits of butter and roll them into butterballs. Their absence in New York was one of the signs that things had changed, whether from economic collapse or local ignorance I had no idea.

In Albuquerque Nana committed her first traitorous act—she gave my jar of sour balls to a suspicious Indian to induce him to uncover his head for a picture, a treachery I didn't discover till we were back on the road again. Of course I raised hell, mainly about the sour balls, but also about the whole spectrum of bizarre premises upon which adult behavior seemed to be based. Why did Indians cover their heads with blankets? Why should they take them off? And who wanted pictures of them anyway? Nana tried to rationalize her obvious guilt by saying those things wrecked The Child's teeth and Indians were ignorant anyway, my mother said we'd want the pictures as reminders of our lovely trip, and Nana said she hadn't really wanted the pictures herself but she thought Mr. Johnson would, a real silencer, at which I put a sweater on my head and kept it there until I almost passed out from the heat.

At dusk every day we would start to search for a place to stay.

If we didn't find one immediately an atmosphere of silent panic set in, from the dark, the strangeness, and from Nana's dread schedule, ticking away in our heads like an oven timer. We all became very quiet, like passengers in a plane that is in trouble. There wasn't much along the road then and places to stay were few and far between. There were no motels. We went from town to town. Once it went on quite far into the evening. I don't know what we were all imagining. The worst that could have happened was that we might have to sleep in the car. But Nana and I, at least, were primitive of mind, and we feared all the mythic perils of travelers, bandits and kidnappers and roadside thieves disguised as hitchhikers, as well as the change in the land. Now there was a palpable difference: the land was ominously flat and the air was different, strange earth and animal smells carried by damp gusts of wind. Tall grasses and trees rustled past in the darkness. Whatever was out there, it wasn't what we knew. I was going to be changed by it, turned into something I had never been before. It was so slow and sure, this process of division, this irrevocable pull into two parts. I could watch it happen without in the least understanding it. Since it was presented as inevitable it never occurred to me to resist. It only filtered through as an obscure bafflement, a muffled kind of pain which increased with every fifty-mile switch, every day we put between ourselves and California—for no one had said whether we would ever go back. Back—I was still half there. This ten-day march had only to do with what was in my mother's head, a land as uncharted as the one we were crossing. Such power she had, to be able to launch the four of us off without anybody understanding why, to do whatever she was doing to me, for I was the one who was truly being imprinted, it was my head scraping along the road and everybody knew it. Not that anybody worried about that sort of thing then, it was presumed children had remarkable powers of recovery. Of course they do, and I was lucky to be able to feel it happen, to watch the wound as it was made, to feel the immensity of that distance as I never would have in a plane, for air travel confuses the perceptions, sabotages the psychic clocking of miles. I was able to put in the time, to catch up, as well as I could, with what was happening. When we finally found a place to stay that evening, some switch had taken place, some change of direction. An old skin had been shed. And the next day we crossed the Mississippi.

It must have been quite painful after that, for the rest of the trip is pretty well gone. Briefly we seemed to be in a place called the Outskirts of Philly, and after that there is nothing till we surfaced on East Sixty-sixth Street, New York City, back East.

It was a penthouse apartment and Nana and I had the top floor, as we had had the back seat. We had a fireplace and a terrace that went all the way around outside where my mother planted flowers in boxes and watered them. From the terrace, which was on the tenth floor, you could see the whole city.

There was a whole confusing new life. Below on the living-room floor, grownups came and went, as they had in Beverly Hills. But it rained, and then it snowed, which I had never seen before. Nana shuttled me back and forth through the raw weather to my new school around the corner, which I hated, or rather hated my own strangeness. I was too big and brown and my dresses were too clean and starched, and I grinned too much. New York children were pale and intense and wore little woolly garments and they talked very fast. Everybody's knees had permanent gray stains.

Everything, the school, the streets, the whole place, was very small and cramped and dirty. Central Park was supposed to be a big deal, we were all herded off there every afternoon to play among the dirty rocks. Animosity filled the air. We played war and attacked each other with stones and snowballs. Back in the tiny school building with its little creaking stairways the air smelled of sweaters and mittens drying on radiators, of meatballs and steamed potatoes. Miss Carden, the head of the school, beat up the boys with rulers. I caused some excitement by peeing in my snowsuit in the back yard during play period. I got in dreadful fights in the park and came home with black eyes and bloody noses. At Christmas we put on biblical plays in which nobody ever seemed to be his own sex; big hulky boys were cast as angels and once I was God, a reward for being able to spell. It was a hard and crazy world, back East. Power was what it was all about, power and speed and indestructibility. Sex didn't matter. Being a girl was fine, boys got rulers broken over them daily.

Home at the apartment Nana and I sat by our fire and recharged ourselves, or at least I did, for the next day's battle. But downstairs was the stuff of life. It was all rather distant to me, since my mother could afford to buffer me from reality. Halls, stairways and pantries separated me from her and her life, which would have been fatal except for Nana, who was an accomplished eavesdropper. My mother had a new boy friend, for Lord's sake, an admiral or something in the navy. *Him*, Nana called him. *He's* here again. And then one night great excitement. The doorbell rang, and there was Mr. Johnson.

"Mae"—that was Nana's name—"can I come in?"

"Oh, Lord, Mr. Johnson, *He's* here. Come into the pantry." The pantry, the halls, arena of the Third Estate, the heart of the house. Mr. Johnson in the pantry. But Nana got out the scotch and fixed him a drink, which he was at that time not at all in need of.

"Mae," he said, "I'm better than him, aren't I?"

"Oh, sir, God knows you are. Not that it's any of my buisness."

"Have I got a chance?"

"Well, Mr. Johnson. If she had any sense. But I don't know. I swear I don't know."

Nana raged around the upstairs about that one, then settled down to soak her feet in Epsom salts.

"A good man like that. Nobody like your father, he's the best. Turn on the radio, darlin'."

Together we sighed and brooded. The truth was it disturbed me that my daddy had turned up in New York. He belonged in California, keeping up the lawn and whatever he kept up at the studio. I had begun to settle into the split in my life, to accommodate the tension necessary to keep the two halves apart but still in hand. It took a lot of energy and if anybody stepped out of place I was frightened. Change had caused only pain so far and it still didn't seem to be finished, it lurked everywhere. I see my father's back going into that living room on Sixty-sixth Street where my mother stood very straight and frightened, then the door was closed. I see the admiral, who was in fact a commander, standing in the hall in his uniform smiling grimly. Another time he and my mother kiss and then jump apart when they see me standing there. They both try to smile reassuringly.

Everything is suggestions, hints, possibilities, nothing is resolved, everything hangs in the air unfinished. Nana tells me, with satisfaction, that my mother is in her room crying her eyes out, but I don't hear her—I don't think I hear her. "She asked for it," Nana mutters grimly. "Imagine." Our lives are a puzzle that never gets solved.

At school I took up fighting seriously. I picked fights with the boys and they got punished for it. It was exciting and it seemed to work in that a fight made me feel simply wonderful. I was hooked on the attack, the rage in the face of some eight-year-old boy, the sting and thump of fists. It didn't really matter who won, it was the atmosphere of battle I needed, the explosion of feeling. There was as much triumph in his wounds as mine, it showed we had made vital contact. I got away with it for ages because nobody thought a girl would pick fights, it had to be the boys—and I had to fight the boys because the girls wouldn't fight with me, they cried and went to the teacher. I knew I had to fight to avoid being swallowed up by this East, this cold cramped little world where you had to run to stay in place and where the rules, if there were any, were beyond me. If I didn't I would lose that other part of myself that I so treasured, like some lost garden I never could get back to.

Beginnings: The Thirties

In that garden there were seven houses, each with its silent chapter on the end of a marriage. Each had its minutely increasing sense of doom, which I forgot in New York; I needed to preserve California as paradise.

In the beginning it was. I lay by the pool in whatever house we lived in, dreaming in the sun. My body felt alive and clean as it never did later in the East. Everything was sensation, the cool deep water, the heavy floral smells, roses or gardenias or jasmine, the grass like a tiny jungle I examined with one eye as I lay on it. The eucalyptus swayed and whispered miles above my head, the narrow pointed leaves spiraling slowly down on the dry earth of the flower bed. There were no weeds, it was really a desert; the desert air was soft and clear and kind. In the morning the cicadas sang in the haze that was burned off as the sun came up. I collected tiny symbols, little blood-purple bougainvillea blossoms and stiff shiny lime leaves and pieces of cactus with thick sap oozing out of them. I felt safe, even when the earth shook, when quivers made pictures sway on the walls and shot glasses to the edge of tables I didn't worry, I thought it was all part of some great benign natural rhythm.

But adults had a way of intruding with things they thought necessary. It had been considered vital to get me all done up, at four or five, in silk dress and enormous hair ribbon, to sit for a portrait. Or to go to Shirley Temple's birthday parties, great mass feedings held on one of the sets. Shirley, who was three or four years older than advertised, greeted all hundred and twenty of us by name as we came in and shook hands, after her mother had prompted her from a list. "Hello, Nora, I'm so glad you could come," she said, and handed me an autograph book with her name on the first page in curly little script. She didn't have to go to school, somebody came and tutored her on the set. She was in a picture of Pop's, *Dimples*, and I'd heard all about her and hated her because Pop thought she was so wonderful. I knew kids who were named after her, and occasionally Nana tried to roast my hair into those ringlets, a traitorous lapse in the person who was usually my friend. Shirley was what you had to be to get adult approval. Or the Dionne quintuplets, those five little faces that almost matched but didn't quite. If you couldn't make it as Shirley you might if you were split into five pieces, in five starched matching dresses.

And once all done up you had to be documented. The single memory I have of my mother in California is of her physically fighting me into a yellow silk dress because the studio photographer was coming again. Of course she won, they always did. They always got the blankets off the Indians. After a while you had to accept them. My mother always had a mirrored dressing table with organdy flounces on it, covered with pots and jars and silver-backed brushes. When I asked Pop years later if she had been beautiful, he said, "I wouldn't have married her if she wasn't." A dark-haired, round-faced pretty woman with a healthy, curvy body, she made it clear that prettiness was something you went after, you fought for and treasured if you had it. If it couldn't get you everything you wanted, it gave you a good start along the road. It could get you Mr. Johnson. But if you didn't have it, you didn't get to just give up—you kept at it, scrubbing and frizzing and smiling and squeezing your feet into shoes that hurt. And everything else hurt too. My older half sister Marge didn't have it. "Of course Marge isn't pretty," I heard someone saying. I would never have noticed, I thought she was wonderful. She was thirteen years older than I and she was angry, and wild, and she sang loudly in the shower and painted her nails green and ran away and was found and brought back by the police. Her life was one death-defying stunt after another.

It was what you had to go through if you weren't pretty, but to me it beat by a mile the constant struggle to be Shirley. Marge's life was too dangerous and remote for me to understand, her generational pains different. She wasn't always there, sometimes she was with her mother. When she was she expressed all the forbidden rage in the rest of the family. She was forever looking at herself in the mirror, putting wild and defiant colors on her face. She looked, as a matter of fact, exactly like Pop, puckish and wise-eyed. The older she got the more she looked and talked like him. She picked up all his gestures and mannerisms. She had nothing of Alice, it was all Pop. It made so much sense really. Somebody had to do it, she might as well be the one. I couldn't, I didn't look like him, and anyway I was too small and awful, in my perpetually starched pinafores. And it was a good way to get my mother, who handled everything wrong. Everybody fought over Pop, right from the start. Marge was right, she couldn't lose if she made herself exactly like him (he wasn't pretty either). She was the first one who did it, later on we all tried.

The best thing was to go to the studio with Pop. He always mentioned that the occasion was as special to him as it was to me. We would drive over together or else Harold would bring Nana and me over later on, depending on whether they thought I could be trusted to behave. We would have a tour of the lot and have lunch at the commissary and visit a set where some shooting was going on. We walked along those hot little paths lined with scrubby palms, with oleander bushes blowing against the long sheds that were called offices, Pop loping along in his open shirt and jacket, me pressed and stuffed and polished into presentability, the hair on top of my head yanked back by one of those mammoth hair bows. It was one of the few times when there seemed to be any point in it all, for people appeared from everywhere smiling widely and shaking hands and telling Pop how beautiful I was, which I liked and didn't like at the same time, since it had mainly to do with how submissive I had been that day to the forces of improvement and how effective Nana had been with matching ribbons and dresses.

The whole place was full of people looking like something they weren't—actors dressed as Indians eating potato salad, actresses dressed like Louis Quinze courtesans eating ham sandwiches, small men with lifts on their shoes, skies that turned out not to be skies, New York brownstones and Western saloons that had no backs, cars with no wheels, rooms with doors that led nowhere and stairways to nothing. There were tiny houses that burned up and halves of rubber balls that sounded like the clop-clop of horses, there was cellophane that sounded like crackling fire and white bits of something that looked like snow when it was blown around. And these people became something else, you stepped over the huge cables and were told to be quiet and not knock over the lights, and you stood and didn't dare breathe after you heard "Action," and a man who had been one thing at lunch or outside just a few minutes before turned into something else, his face changed, his body stiffened, his eyes refocused, he literally, before your eyes, transformed into a different person. Then when you heard "Cut" he would relax, blink, clear his throat, light a cigarette, and be whatever he had been before, except three people would run out and comb his hair and pat his face with Kleenex. It was frightening, all of it, and I didn't understand why they were doing it, why everything had to turn into something else. Pop told me it was to make a world of make-believe, but I didn't even understand why anybody would want to do that. I had a hard enough time trying to figure out which things I was supposed to believe and which I wasn't, and most of the time adults said one thing and did another, or else just did things that made no sense at all, and for a period there the whole thing just scrambled my head. It wasn't that he didn't try, he said that I made things up when I played, which was true, I made up little worlds and lived in them for short periods, and he said this was just the same thing on a bigger scale because adults wanted to get away from what was real too. He didn't understand that wasn't why I did it, because I had no idea what was real anyway, I just wanted to make up little worlds I could manage, where I knew what the rules were. The notion of adults making up some world to escape from what was supposed to be comprehensible was dreadful, there wasn't any end to the puzzlement, there weren't ever any answers, though you couldn't stop trying, you just went on and on forever through the maze while the man who said you were beautiful (which you only were because somebody else had made you that way) turned into something else before your eyes because somebody thought you would prefer him that way.

But Pop didn't turn into anything else. You could hang onto him. He looked more or less the same morning or night, his clothes didn't vary much, he always smelled of Knize Ten. He came down for breakfast, very clean, with his hair combed back, and said, "Ho hum," and put pepper on his cantaloupe, and ate sausages and grits, and read the paper. Sometimes he took out a large, monogrammed white handkerchief, flipped it out to its entire size, and blew his nose. Everything was very definite, very predictable. I liked to watch him, to see the things I expected happen. Whatever he did at the studio didn't seem to involve switching around. The only time he frightened me was when he asked me some question I was expected to answer, because I never knew what to say and I was afraid whatever I came up with would be wrong, or not as interesting as the things he said, or stupid. I didn't worry about this with anybody else, but Pop seemed to expect something better, whatever better was. He would look over the paper with those sharp blue eyes and ask me what I thought about something, and I was afraid if I told him what I really thought he'd think I was as screwy as I secretly suspected I was, since everything was so hard to understand. I would sit there in one of the seven breakfast rooms or dining rooms with the sun pouring in through the window, desperately scrabbling around for whatever I was supposed to say but, having nothing to go on, I never really found it. I didn't know what he wanted, and wanting very badly to know didn't help. When he asked me if I was going to play with So-and-so that day, I was afraid if I said yes he wouldn't approve because he didn't really like So-and-so, and if I said no, then neither of us would be able to think of anything else to say. I was fully aware that I was the most limited person he had contact with in the course of a day or week, the least glib, the most bewildered, and I doubted that he would have been interested in my small offerings of confusion or questions I was supposed to know the answer to. So I usually said nothing. I got the best and worst from him, I was sure he loved me (which I wasn't about anybody else) and I was also sure I bored him to death and made him angry for reasons I had no control over.

I also knew—or thought I knew—that he would have been pained to know this, that I had reached among the threads of his love and picked out the blackened strands, the impurities which didn't have anything to do with me anyway. It was unfair, really, when most of the time we were fine, we would sit down and read a book together or I would pull out one of my little collection of things that I knew would make him talk, or start one of our jokes.

"Daddy, what were you like when you were a little boy?"

"Oh, my." He would fold his hands and his eyes would float to the ceiling. "I was a little angel. My mama said to me every morning, 'Nunnally, every day I thank the good Lord for giving me such an angel child. But sometimes I wish you would do something just a little naughty, just for a change.' And I said, 'Oh no, Mama. I never could.'"

"What do angels do?"

"Oh, I jumped out of bed the minute mama called me, and rushed in and brushed my teeth fifty strokes, and got dressed, and tidied up my room and put my toys away, and washed my hands and ate every bite of my breakfast. Then I went to school where I never did less than perfect work."

"Did you ever get into fights?"

"Oh, never. Who would fight with me? And my teacher said, 'Nunnally, if all the children were like you, I would be the happiest teacher in Columbus.'" It was a great joke, we both knew damn well there weren't any angels—though if there had been they probably would have dwelled in Columbus, rustled their wings over all those kinfolk. It was the old dream, that place, the place you started from but had to leave, the place you could never go back to. It was where little boys played baseball in the spring and smoked behind the barn, where screen doors banged and mothers put pies out to cool, where you kissed a girl on the porch swing. It was where you knew the rules, a world that had worked. If you stayed there it would kill you, but leaving gave you a fighting chance, anyway, because you could keep the old dream in your head and make it into your lost garden.

I went there to visit my grandparents a couple of times before I was eight or nine. It was the first time anybody had thought of

doing anything about my religious life and my grandmother saw
to it that I was baptized Methodist Episcopal. I can hear her
saying it, "Nunnally, you got to baptize that child." She was a
round-faced little lady with rimless glasses and white hair,
Onnie, and she talked almost continually. Grandpa was tall and
craggy and sat on the porch reading. Johnnie Pearl Patrick and
James Nunnally Johnson. Early in the afternoon they sat down to
a vast amount of food, roasts and chickens and ham and sweet
potatoes and vegetables and biscuits. I had never seen so much
food in one place, I came from a world where a lamb chop for
dinner was fine. If I couldn't eat it they felt terrible, as though I
had personally affronted them. Once when I ate hardly anything
Onnie said, "Honey, you got to go tell Eula you're sorry." I went
around back to see Eula, the darky, where she sat incom-
prehensibly crying on the back stoop. She thought I didn't like
her cooking. There were five generations of her family alive at
once, her mother and grandmother and her daughter and granddaughter. Why did she care so what I thought, or what I ate? I
didn't know yet what food meant to people, particularly to
women. I told her I was sorry, up North we didn't eat very
much. I probably had a very small stomach. She found that
shocking, this congenital deformity of Northerners. My, the
world was strange. She put her black arms around me, her big
hands with their pink palms. She felt sorry for me—I would
never know such pleasures, and I would probably be sickly all
my life. Nunnally had gone up North and married a Northern
woman and produced this sad and sickly child.

The house seemed small and dark, with a screen porch in front
and overstuffed chairs in the living room with lace antimacassars
on them. To please Onnie and Grandpa I tramped around and
sang "Marching Through Georgia" which my teacher, Miss Carden, for some eccentric reason, had made us memorize along
with the "Marseillaise."

> "Hurrah! hurrah! we bring the jubilee!
> Hurrah! hurrah! the flag that makes you free!"
> So we sang the chorus from Atlanta to the sea,
> As we were marching through Georgia.

Mama grabbed me in the hall.

"Hush," she said. "You'll hurt their feelings, they were *here*, don't you see, when we marched on them."

"Burning and pillaging and slaughtering," added Nana. "They were on the other side, darlin'."

"What other side?"

"The Civil War, and it's not nice to bring it up here. You can sing it in New York if you want."

"But why did we slaughter them and burn them?"

"To free the Negroes," my mother said. "And don't ever say nigger."

Eula, who referred to herself as a nigger, earned three dollars a week and had something called "totin' privileges." Each evening she wrapped up the leftover food in paper bags and took it back to her daughter and granddaughter, her mother and grandmother. There was always a lot of it left, but if I had eaten more there would be less for all these people. In spite of this they seemed to like me, this chain of women. Sometimes they appeared in the evening as I sat in the back with Eula, which I liked to do when she wasn't crying. I couldn't tell which was whose mother, partly because the clues in their dark faces were unfamiliar to me, and partly because to a child all ages blur over twenty. At any rate they behaved as though they liked me. I remember sitting with them in some Georgia dusk, Eula's arm close around me, at the edge of what seems like a great grassy field, either behind my grandparents' house or behind some other house. A great many darky children were playing some game, tag or hide-and-seek, that I was too shy to join though they had asked me to. Beyond, the trees were high and dark, shifting and moving in a gentle evening breeze. The air was soft and fragrant. Sometimes they sang, spirituals, I suppose. It was so peaceful and complete, and God knows what I was doing there, Nana lurking around in the background to make sure they didn't turn on me and kill me. As darkness fell she whipped me off to bed— enough was enough. I wanted dreadfully to be part of them and knew I couldn't. Possibly it was better to be poor. Every stage up from the bottom seemed to tighten the adult gut. Their simplicity made even Nana seem like a nervous wreck (or caused her to be one) when ordinarily her essential value was that she wasn't. They disturbed her in some obscure way, and she made them obsequious, which they weren't with me. It was their ability to love that charmed me, their physical affection, their hands that touched, the quiet at the center of their natures. If it was only part of the story, it was the part I saw.

If Pop was along that time, I don't remember it. I don't remember ever seeing my parents together in that early time. I am always alone with one or the other of them, switching back and forth into different gears, trying to look through their disparate eyes. If I knew how they saw me, I would know what I was, even though I would be something different to each of them. But it was desperately hard to get a look. What was I to my daddy, who had grown up in this slow hot Southern town, among these endlessly chattering kinfolk? Though he hardly seemed part of this, all the calling back and forth, the coffee and cakes, the smiles and kisses and superlatives, the cousins and aunts, he had to be, he was made of it somehow, no matter how much you want to you never can change the material you came from, even if you think you have made yourself different the other is always there, you expect other people to supply it even more because you no longer do yourself. He was rather quiet, Pop was, but that was so the women could talk, chirp away like birds as they were supposed to. But I couldn't, and neither could my mother. As a trio we wouldn't have been much fun anyway, we probably wouldn't have worked. We would have had a lot of painful draggy silences. He couldn't sit back and relax among all that birdsong, his comfort and security, background music for his own sharp and funny words which could shoot through a room like some innocent-looking bullet, bringing that electric second of silence before the ripples of laughter and love. What power his words had, how seductive and compelling they were. If you would set him up, if you would supply the backdrop and feed him the lines, or if you played the clown a bit, he would do this for you, send you one of his gifts, for they were gifts really, they were like acts of love in their completeness and the pleasure they gave, even the tiny sting they sometimes had was part of it. He showed what happiness words could be, how total they were.

They could be the center of a life, the forgery and combining of words could be the most ultimate experience.

Eating our lunch on one of the seven patios in the midday stillness, Nana and I waited and watched. The vacuum we lived in was complete, all sound and trace of feeling were somehow sealed away. In those elegantly furnished, rented houses (or homes, as Nana called them) the noon sun filtered through tall curtains into the enormous silent rooms, flooded onto the acres of carpeting that flowed through halls and into rooms and out of other rooms—burgundy in the Beverly Drive house, a vast sunlit burgundy sea. I crept around in the silence listening for sounds I never heard, voices that never spoke. Daddy was at the studio, Mama was out somewhere—at the hairdresser, the tennis courts, or Robinson's buying me more starchy dresses. There was nothing but time and silence, long heavy empty days. When I followed the murmur of voices to the kitchen where Nana sat with the cook, they would glance up as I came in and stop talking abruptly.

"Go play, darlin'," Nana would say. "Go find Patty," referring to my best friend, who bit me whenever nobody was looking. "But stay away from that Jimmy Harris." Jimmy lived down the alley, and he and I had experienced heady excitement together the day we smeared Good Humors all over the leather upholstery of Louella Parsons' convertible. It had been Jimmy's inspiration, and curiosity about making Pop mad had overcome sheer terror.

"Good God," he said when he heard of it. "Of all people."

"Jimmy thought of it."

"You and Jimmy go and apologize to Miss Parsons."

"But you said you didn't like her," I said, stunned.

"Go," he shouted. "Never mind what I said."

God, they were all alike, I had thought he was an exception. I never played with Jimmy Harris again, he had been instrumental in revealing my father's feet of clay. I tried Pop another time, drawing pictures for him on a sun porch in one of the houses. On the other side of the closed door was trouble, something bad was happening, burning and pillaging and slaughtering. It was the

1. The Little Angel

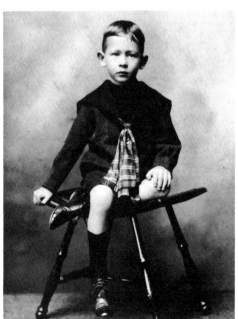

2. James Nunnally, Cecil, Onnie and Nunnally, around 1908

3. Nunnally at six

4. Columbus delivery boys (Nunnally front row, second from right)

5. Columbus High basketball team (Nunnally first row, on the left)

6. *Nunnally at high school graduation*

7. *Marion and Nunnally in Florida, probably around 1931*

8. *Marion and Nunnally, June 1936 (Nunnally always
identified this as "Gunman and His Moll.")*

9. *Marion*

10. Marion and Nora

11. Marge, Nunnally, Nora

first time I tried to fend off trouble by putting something on paper.

"Here," I said to Pop as he stormed out, his face dark. "I drew this for you." He stared at me as though he had never seen me before, or as though I had three heads—a way he had that was like a cold finger going into my heart. They were so inept, adults, at shifting from one thing to another. But I knew that, I was trying him out. He looked at the picture.

"It's very bad," he said. "It's messy and careless and not worth looking at." And he stormed out of the room. I relentlessly presented him with six more, in the next room where he was trying to sulk in peace, until he passed one of them, and I had my hollow victory.

"Daddy didn't like my pictures," I whined to Nana later.

"Your father's tired out."

"But he said they were bad and messy." They were good and I knew it.

"Good Lord," Nana muttered, stirring her coffee and exchanging a dark glance with the cook. "Your father's got a lot on his mind. Never you mind." I didn't really. What I knew was that his judgment of what I did could be wrong, and I knew it for good.

The last house, on Camden Drive, was less elegant than the others. It was closer to Santa Monica Boulevard, which, according to Nana, signified a certain decline in class, and as I recall it didn't have a pool. It was a small stucco house, rather dark, with round-topped arches between the rooms. It had a small front lawn and a wide straight little driveway, and Camden had the stuntiest trees anyway, it had that hot empty bleak look that things get out there when the camouflage of cultivation is weak or incomplete. An open car drove up one day and two pretty girls in tennis dresses got out. One of them crossed the lawn to where I was and said:

"Hi, there, honey, I'm Dorris." She smiled and touched me in some way, shook my hand or put her hand on my head, and so did her friend Mary Healy. Right out of the South they were, they chattered and laughed like the women of Columbus in those soft bright voices, the thing I never could do because I worried so much about what was coming out of my mouth.

The next thing I remember about Dorris was hearing on the radio, one night in New York when Nana and I were listening to the news, that Pop had married her. Nana sprang up, all five foot ten of her, gave me a terrified look and a kind of shake or hug, and ran out of the room, to return in a moment in one of her muttering rages, while I sat there on the floor feeling as though I had been shot in the stomach.

"Too late, too late, good Lord, she asked for it, imagine all this dilly-dallying, and *Him* around all the time, how long did she think he'd wait?" She grabbed me into her large lap, stared at me with her big long-jawed face surrounded by little permanented curls. "Don't worry, darlin', your daddy still loves you." This seemed unlikely, but there were times when you had to hang onto adult falsehoods and this was one of them. "Could of told her himself. Or she could have. Crying her eyes out, a lot of good it does now. Stay here now, I have to see your mother." She kept going back and forth since, characteristically, we were not in the same place nor did it apparently occur to anybody that we should be. Ah, he had gone with Dorris because she knew how to talk to him, he probably wouldn't ever come back from wherever he was (which was unclear), I was locked into the division now, the halves could never go back together, and if that weren't bad enough now *She* had him, now there was a *She*. The pain was very bad, I didn't tell anybody at school, it was like a death that I couldn't tell anybody about, a dreadful family secret.

Hollywood   1938–1945

Nunnally's next picture was *Wife, Husband and Friend* (Warner Baxter and Loretta Young). He was so fond of the idea that he remade it in 1949, with Paul Douglas, as *Everybody Does It,* "a real winking title" of Skouras'. It flopped both times. In 1939 he made the musical *Rose of Washington Square*, the original Fanny Brice-Nicky Arnstein story, with Alice Faye and Tyrone Power and Al Jolson, directed by Gregory Ratoff. It was another cook-up, based vaguely on twenties newspaper stories. There were some good songs in it ("I'm Just Wild About Harry," "My Man," "California, Here I Come," besides the title song) but it went only mildly, and the songs were better presented years later in *The Jolson Story*.

In 1939, just when his personal life was the worst, he made *The Grapes of Wrath*, probably his best picture. There was a lot of debate about doing the Steinbeck novel—it was too anti-Establishment, and some considered it dangerously left wing. Writing it was not an easy job. "It'd be about ten times easier now than it was then," Nunnally said in 1971. "Now I've learned to look for the backbone of a book, the skeleton, what this fellow was setting out to tell, so that he almost could have told it in a night letter. In this case he wanted to tell what an act of nature did to a great segment of helpless people and how they reacted . . . he created human beings, Ma and Pa and Grampa and

Preacher and Rosasharn . . . invoked in this act of nature that threw them out of their homes and filled them full of hope and drove them west to the land of Canaan and what they found there. That's a tremendously impressive thing to think of, but I had to read the book two or three times before it all came clear to me, like an X-ray photograph." In a big, sprawling book like *The Grapes of Wrath*, there is an abundance of material for the screenwriter to use, to take, to reshape. The trick is selection, and the hamburger stand scene, in which the woman clerk gives the kids candy for a penny, was, in the book, about some family other than the Joads. ("I never looked at the rushes of that scene without crying," Nunnally said.) The end is rearranged, Nunnally having put in the government camp scene because up to then it was too "relentlessly depressing." It is the first bit of hope for the family for whom nothing, up to that point, has come out right. It took a little nerve to tamper with the work of a novelist of Steinbeck's stature—he had never been given this big a book to adapt. But he did what he thought necessary to transform fiction into another medium, and Steinbeck was pleased with the result (he said, "My work still stands")—the only writer whose work Nunnally adapted for the screen who not only liked the result but spoke to him afterward, in fact became a close friend.

All the elements of making the picture worked right from the beginning. It was a big, successful book, one that every studio wanted. Both Zanuck and John Ford were dazzled by the script, as was Henry Fonda, who played Tom Joad (others in the cast were Jane Darwell, John Carradine, Charley Grapewin, and Dorris as Rosasharn, her best role). Henry Fonda says, "[*Grapes*] was probably the most memorable experience of my eighty or ninety films . . . one of the great experiences. The script was brilliant and Ford was at his peak in those days—and I just feel lucky to have been a part of the whole thing. It's one of the classics of the business. . . . Nunnally wasn't around much. I don't remember ever seeing him during the production. Ford was like that, he didn't want anybody around." It is doubtful that Nunnally would have been around anyway, even if Ford wanted him. Dorris (who calls "that hapless girl, Rosasharn, my best, most stimulating assignment") recalls, "On a date with Nunnally just before production shooting began, he suddenly told me he was going to take a leave of absence from the studio and go back to New York. He added that I was the kinda girl a fella marries and he was terrified he'd do just that. Having failed to make a go of two marriages, he couldn't risk a third where all the chips were stacked against its working. I was pretty stunned, more at his walking away from producing so important a picture than from me. But he did both. Zanuck took charge of production and Nunnally took a powder on me. Later, when I understood him better, I saw nothing out of character about his leaving the picture he was assigned to write and produce—once that script was finished and approved, he had little remaining interest in the project."

Fonda continues, "I'd been in love with the book before the movie was suggested to me. Zanuck wanted me to do Tom. I jumped at the idea—to the point that I signed the contract he'd been dangling for years that I wouldn't sign. I'd been very happy being free to choose. Tom Joad became the bait that got me to sign the seven-year contract." But the bait had a price. "After Tom Joad I was Alice Faye's husband in *Lillian Russell*. Now that meant Alice Faye and Don Ameche were the stars, I was the fourth most important character, a lackluster nothing. Now this was Darryl Francis Zanuck who said, 'I'm not going to give you Tom Joad if you're going to turn around and go over to MGM and do a picture with Joan Crawford.' [Banging the table.] He used those words! And I did a series of the most forgettable films you'll ever hear about after *Grapes of Wrath,* and the only other one at the studio I'm proud of was *Oxbow Incident* which he didn't want to have any part of. . . . I had nothing but fights; being under contract, I had to get out of doing some of these stinkers in order to do *Lady Eve* at Paramount or *Male Animal* at Warner's or *Big Street* at RKO. But the ones I didn't get out of, *Wild Geese Calling, Rings on Her Fingers, Lillian Russell* . . . I just don't think he tried. He tried with Tyrone, he knew he had a valuable property and wanted to keep him, but I don't think he ever felt that way about me so I just got shoved into anything. But the way he talked to me! Then the first picture after the war he put me into was one with Joan Crawford!"

The premiere, in New York, appeared to be a disaster. At nine-thirty in the evening a "collection of fat cats, caviar dribbling

down their chins, loaded with champagne," gathered after dinner at the Coronet Theater, where they belched and nodded or
fell asleep. In spite of this miserable bit of planning on the part
of Fox the reviews were excellent, though there was a storm of
complaint about its leftist sympathy for the common people,
which the Hearst papers called "Commie." Joel Sayre says that
Zanuck went to Hearst and said, "If you don't stop it I'll make a
picture about you and Marion Davies," at which the ranting
ceased immediately (but a year later *Citizen Kane* came out).
Grapes of Wrath was a huge success but lost the Oscar that year
to *Philadelphia Story*.

In spite of the distant sound of arms that was, ten years later,
to turn the industry into a political battleground, Nunnally was
apolitical to an almost eccentric degree—*Grapes of Wrath* is
the closest thing to a political picture he ever made (with the
possible exception of *The Senator Was Indiscreet*). Newspaper
writing had trained him not to let his feelings color a story and "it
became a part of me that I was an observer rather than a partici-
pant." He saw himself as a pure storyteller, "never aiming at anything beyond what I put down on paper, the characters and
what they did." But for a writer there is no such thing as complete detachment—some subjects attract and some don't, and
certain themes occur again and again in his pictures. Phil Dunne
says, "Zanuck, like Nunnally and me, was a Victorian moralist—
we liked the pictures in which grit, virtue, honor and decency
triumphed—*How Green Was My Valley, Pinky, Grapes of Wrath*,
not *Twelve o'Clock High*. We did pictures about the nobility of
the human spirit. I don't like anti-heroes—I want to look up to
the hero. *Midnight Cowboy* disgusted me though I know it's
beautifully made. Maybe that's the secret of Nunnally's approach
to the human condition. He really believed in these things though
he wouldn't admit it and he made a believer of you."

Most of Nunnally's pictures in that early period are men's pictures whose heroes are married to faithful, steadfast wives. By
his own admission he was more comfortable with married love
than the other, less secure kind. "Picking up the handkerchief
and meeting her and swinging through the wheat field and all
that kind of stuff—it just isn't in me," he said. His understanding
and sympathy lay with male problems and situations, and he

stuck to them, being disinclined to venture into areas where he
felt he might do badly.

Next came *Chad Hanna,* a circus picture with Henry Fonda
and Linda Darnell (who got the part over Dorris, who tested for
it). It featured a drunk scene with John Carradine that Henry
King said "was the funniest thing I ever saw in my life" but in
the picture "the story stopped and the sequence took over. Zanuck said, 'This is the first time in my life I ever saw a great scene
kill a picture.' And you know we had to take it out?" The reviews
were disappointing, and the picture became a kind of family joke
—Nunnally was "the man who gave you *Chad Hanna.*" Later
Garson Kanin suggested a remake called "the smallest show on
earth." Nunnally said, "That tickled Zanuck, tickled me. You
know, it's the old story. It hurts too much to laugh, and you're
too old to cry."

In 1940 he did *Tobacco Road,* another disappointment, and a
worse one. He had gone to New York to see the hit play, written
by Jack Kirkland and adapted from the book by Erskine Caldwell, and been puzzled by its popularity. People thought they
were going to see something dirty (incest and all that) but it
was really a superb piece of regional comedy. (But afterward,
when asked if *Tobacco Road's* South was his South, he said,
"Where I come from we call them the country club set.")

Ford, who had done so brilliantly on *Grapes of Wrath* and
Prisoner of Shark Island, not only didn't grasp the script but
wouldn't listen to comment from anybody else. "He was much
too powerful for me," Nunnally said, "and it was just as if I were
talking to him in Greek. To him a low, illiterate cracker and a
low, illiterate Irishman were identical. They reacted the same
way. Since he didn't know anything about crackers, except me,
and he did know about Irish, he simply changed them all into
Irishmen. The whole thing was a calamity, and Caldwell blamed
me, though I think if he'd been a little more thoughtful, he
would have read the script and found I was pretty faithful to
the play, but he never did. I insisted that the script was better
than the picture simply because of the way Ford directed these
people. You send the thing in red and it comes out green."

One of the hard lessons of picture making is that, once the
shooting has started, the director has complete control. If he

makes mistakes there is very little anybody can do about it, since nobody even finds out until the rushes are shown. If he makes an error early in the shooting, it might be possible to correct that error, but the odds are that he will make a dozen more before he is finished. If the director was Ford, everybody except Zanuck was frightened to death of him. "He was an arrogant director, and he humiliated actors out of this dreadful frustration of his that he was not responsible for the words," Nunnally explained him. "He had some strange delusion that the words weren't down there until his eyes went over the paper like some goddam chemical." The urge to be the author is so intense that directors have taken over the very word to describe their own interpretive function. A producer for whom I had written a script once said to me, regarding the agents, director and others involved in the project, "If the rest of us could do what you do we wouldn't be here today." It seems so evident that creativity is power that one can see why those with attendant skills envy it and try to claim it for themselves or else aggrandize their own functions, and why writers have always had such an unglamorous image.

Though picture making is (or used to be) teamwork, the writer-director struggle has been there since the thirties. Nunnally thought it was started by envious critics who remained on New York papers after their colleagues were in Hollywood earning five times as much money. Out of spite they credited the director with more than his due "since the director has a job which nobody can detect really—it's a kind of spiritual job. Now with this mystique I think the newspaper people were willing to credit him with all kinds of mystery and magic and so on." (A movie buff friend says, "What a charming idea.") The main reason things worked so well for Nunnally was that, as far as Zanuck was concerned, the screenplay was the thing. For *The Man Who Broke the Bank at Monte Carlo,* Nunnally told, a director named Steve Roberts had been brought over from Paramount "where the director, whether he could read or write, was the czar. Some of these guys were just incredible, they could have a script by William Shakespeare and the director would say, 'Well, I'll have to see what I can do with it.' And they'd whisper, 'Norman's going to see what he can do with it. He's going to try his best.' And these guys were never questioned. I

remember we talked—I had done this script, and Zanuck and
Roberts and I were talking in his office and everybody seemed
very pleased and Steve said, 'Well, I'll tell you what I'll do. Suppose I kick it around over the weekend.' And Zanuck said, 'Just a
minute there. What do you mean, kick it around?' And Steve
said, kind of surprised, 'You know, go over it.' And Zanuck said,
'Nobody kicks my scripts around. You read it, and if you have
some suggestions you bring them to Nunnally or to me. But don't
talk about kicking my script around.'"

Since directing is undetectable, "[directors who write books]
cannot find anything to write about themselves," Nunnally said
in an interview. "After they say, 'Try to get close to the actor,' all
that kind of stuff, they have nothing to tell you. I don't think that
means there's nothing to directing, but I think that directing a
musical comedy on the stage in New York is about five times
as hard as directing any movie because the things that Jerome
Robbins has done, Gower Champion, Fosse, you can see there's
something. But directing a movie—as Joe Mankiewicz said the
other day, 'A well-written script is already directed.' It's the
truth. I was with Fox for twenty-five years maybe. I would never
have dreamed of calling in the director until the script was
finished. And that doesn't mean that the director can't make a
contribution because he does. I'd say, let's say Henry Hathaway,
'Okay, Henry, let's go down to your office,' and we'd go over it.
He'd study the script and come back and say, 'I've got some
ideas.' But what he's doing is working on top of the bulk of the
thing. It would be foolish to reject his ideas, but their contribution becomes really very small. They can only do so much,
move from place to place, sit, stand . . . they follow the lines,
and if your head man has a good ear he can tell whether
they're saying them right or not. Now that's nine out of ten directors. The tenth is somebody like Hitchcock who dominates
the whole thing, who is part of the preparation of the script, the
story; Kubrick; these men are genuinely authors. But because
they call themselves authors Joe Blow thinks he's in with the big
ones and he calls himself an author when he can hardly write
'fade in.' So, many are riding on the coattails of these very able
directors who are not only directors but writers and producers."
Only with the true *auteurs* (Hitchcock, De Mille) who have

given a certain quality to a body of work is the style of a director detectable, but many directors have been credited by the critics for "directorial touches" ("a favorite cliché of critics who haven't the faintest idea what they're talking about") which were simply not there. In a *Vanity Fair* review of *Prisoner of Shark Island,* the critic attributed to "Ford's elliptical directing" certain cuts which happened to be cuts made by Zanuck against Ford's will.

Around the same time Nunnally wrote a piece which appeared in several papers around the country, including the New York *Herald Tribune.*

AUTHOR RIPS THE HALO OFF DIRECTORS' HEADS

Best known of "Men behind the Camera" merely Lucky Fellows, says Nunnally Johnson

Any intelligent person could direct a motion picture, says Nunnally Johnson . . . who believes the scenarist not only gets too little credit but too little money. . . . "This industry employs writing men of recognized reputations," Johnson pointed out, "and yet it virtually neglects to advertise the names of these men. Directors, with three or four notable exceptions, are local celebrities whose names mean absolutely nothing to the average person. . . . The success or failure of a director is, in my opinion, entirely dependent on the quality of the story he directs.

"The highest paid writer I know gets $3,500 a week. The highest paid director I know gets twice that much for reading something from a sheet of paper and telling his actors about it. The director is surrounded by experts and his players, generally, are people who have been in the business longer than he. The writer, on the other hand, creates something. . . . I say something should be done about it."

One of the first things that very likely will be done is that a committee of directors (Nunnally knows many and likes most of them personally) will call on him tomorrow to tell him he'd better keep quiet if he respects their friendship. . . .

Years later, Nunnally was quoted in *Time* and *Life* as saying that the principal use of a director is to see that the actors don't go home before six. He had meant it in reference only to one director (Stuart Heisler, who directed *Along Came Jones*) but in the magazines it appeared as a generality and, according to John Ford, led to the formation of the Directors' Guild—presumably as an organization of self-defense. At an early meeting of this group, Mervyn LeRoy proposed to the Guild that no member should ever work with Nunnally Johnson again.

Nunnally's stiletto wit ("you don't know you've been stabbed until you're bleeding to death") started another local furor when he let it loose on that fearful phenomenon Louella Parsons. In a 1939 *SEP* article (ostensibly written by Tom Wood, but rewritten, at the *SEP*'s request, by Nunnally) reference is made to Louella's "gay illiteracies."

"Even in her own field, where bad writing is as natural and as common as breathing, Louella's stands out like an asthmatic's gasps. Given any field at all, she is probably the most consistently inaccurate reporter who ever lived to draw $600 a week. . . . Louella is a familiar, easily identified figure. Plump and breathless, she has dark hair, hazel eyes, and an expression of blank bewilderment that no longer fools anybody . . . fluttering from group to group, eternally in search of those dainty morsels that her public gulps with its breakfast, she admits she hears more that is unprintable than any woman should . . . when she calls, Zanuck, Wanger, Warner, Cohn or any of the others drops whatever he is doing and gives her his undivided attention. With such cooperation it is hard to understand how she can be wrong so often."

On and on it went deliciously, no doubt to the extreme pleasure of anybody whose life she had ever ruined. When word got out that it was Nunnally who had done the actual writing, the enraged Louella asked Zanuck to throw Nunnally out, which of course he refused to do; at which point her rage fell upon Dorris. "Saw Dorris Bowdon Johnson the other night," Louella wrote shortly after their marriage. "My, how she's changed. She used to be such a pretty little thing." It hurt Dorris, but things like that escaped Nunnally—he functioned on a level above gossip and petty politics, they simply didn't affect him.

Roxie Hart, which came out in '41 (Ginger Rogers, Adolphe Menjou, directed by William Wellman), is a treasure, fast, funny and engaging. It falls squarely into one of our folklore traditions, the newspaperman movie, which evolved from the slick tough talk of the newspaper guys when they went West. Nunnally said, "It may be that Pauline Kael was quite right that this accidentally gave a real coloration to movies . . . that the kind of people [Mank] brought out were the kind of people who wrote things like *The Front Page.* There was nothing sacred about what they did and the result was that in the course of time there were enough of these rather sardonic comedies to give a little turn or twist to the way things were being told before."

At another time in history, tales were told by an old fellow sitting on a cracker barrel; now it's a reporter in a bar on a rainy night. We've seen it so often it's like Mom opening a book by the bedside—we settle back and purr in anticipation. This time the cub reporter is telling about lady murderesses who have gotten away with their crime, Roxie Hart in particular, who, it becomes obvious, has his heart no matter what kind of tramp she is. Roxie commits a *crime passionel,* melts the all-male jury and gets off, defended in a superb court scene by Menjou. At the end we are back in the bar and the reporter leaves and gets into a car outside driven by Roxie and inhabited by what looks like a dozen children. Home and hearth have won.

Nunnally found Wellman's direction too broad and corny. He let Ginger chew gum and say "Gee whiz" and Menjou rumple his hair. (These are directorial touches that Nunnally and the others who made the picture knew about, but an audience would have no way of knowing whether or not they were in the script.) But Wellman also put a mad black-bottom dance scene in the jail which is pure joyous craziness, which I found so enchanting I couldn't criticize the rest. There is a sort of reversal in this picture—usually the newspaper guy is the tough one, as in *Front Page,* but this time it's Roxie, and the reporter is all dumbfounded innocence. Doesn't matter, it still works.

In 1942 and '43 Nunnally did three comedies with Monty Woolley, *The Pied Piper, Life Begins at 8:30,* and *Holy Matrimony.* The first two were directed by Irving Pichel, "an extremely sensitive man," according to Nunnally, but Gene Fowler, Jr., Marge's husband and a director and film editor himself, calls him "a stumblebum. Nunnally liked him because he directed what he wrote." Wellman gave Roxie Hart the gum, Ford had let a tractor crash through a barn in *Grapes of Wrath* with what Nunnally thought unnecessary violence, but Pichel showed no signs of individuality whatever, in spite of certain oddities—"Irving would go around picking up matches and cigarette butts and all that sort of thing. I suppose he had forty-five different psychiatric problems. In addition to everything else he had Parkinson's disease and I didn't know anything about PD at the time. I remember I said, 'What is this? Is it a nerve thing?' 'Oh,' he says, 'I'm an ex-actor. I'm torn between wanting to autograph and hating to sign a check.'" Pichel was a relief to Nunnally after the first director on *Pied Piper,* who said to him, "'You know that night Woolley and the kids sleep in the barn?' I said, 'Yeah.' He said, 'We'll have Woolley be a pipe smoker, and as they wake up in the morning and as he gets his pipe out and fills it and lights it, he's filled it full of manure.' I said, 'Wait here.' This is God's truth. I went down the hall to Zanuck's office and told Zanuck. I said, 'This is the first idea that this man has offered the script, the only idea so far. I'd like to make it clear that if there's any shit in this picture, I'm going to put it in.'"

In *The Pied Piper,* it falls upon Monty Woolley to lead a pack of children (Roddy McDowall and Peggy Ann Garner among others) out of occupied France to England at the outbreak of the war. Otto Preminger, in his first movie role, plays a German general who persuades Woolley to add his Jewish niece to the group. Woolley, who wishes to God he were back at his club, has this exchange with Roddy about their latest member, a Dutch boy who Roddy claims has told him something or other:

Woolley: Do you speak Dutch?
Roddy: No, sir.
Woolley: Do you understand Dutch?
Roddy: No, sir.
Woolley: But he told you?
Roddy: Yes, sir.
Woolley: In what language did he tell you?
Roddy: In no language, sir—he just told me.

Life Begins at 8:30, from an Emlyn Williams play, is about an aging actor who can't keep away from the booze and his crippled (but steadfast) daughter Kathy, played by Ida Lupino, who encourages him to make a comeback as Lear. As in *Dimples*, which it resembles, the daughter tries to arrange her father's life to free her own. Woolley fails as an actor but marries a rich widow to free Kathy for her marriage to Cornel Wilde. I drew a picture for this movie, a picture of Woolley by Kathy as a child, and Marge claims her mark is there too—"There's a speech Monty Woolley makes and when I saw the show I was absolutely convinced Nunnally was saying it to me. And that drink, the Alabama Fog Cutter, I used to get it at this horrible place on the Strip and told Dad about it." We all cling to our little bits of immortality. At some point Woolley says, "Success is a straitjacket . . . a happy man has no obligations."

Holy Matrimony (directed by John Stahl) was adapted from Arnold Bennett's *Buried Alive* and was by far the best of the three. The delicious story is about Priam Farll, world-famous painter and recluse, who grasps an opportunity to fulfill his passion for privacy; the doctor who has treated his dying manservant mistakes him for Farll and so incorrectly fills out the death certificate. Farll attends his own funeral (at Westminster Abbey) and takes up life where the manservant left off—which includes a sort of mail-order bride in the form of Gracie Fields, a good, sensible, tea-brewing and particularly endearing steadfast wife. In an elegant French restaurant Gracie, in Mary Poppins garb, asks the waiter about a menu selection which, he informs her sneeringly, is the name of the song being played by the orchestra. "Well, " Gracie replies equably, "there's not much nourishment in that!" She and Farll settle down contentedly at her tiny house in Putney until Farll starts painting in secret and the truth comes out, Gracie having been selling the paintings for a few pounds apiece when money runs short. At a Dickensian trial Farll is identified by two moles. Nunnally liked the story so much that he adapted it for the stage in the late sixties, with disastrous results—it is better remembered as a lovely picture.

(Dorris says, "*Holy Matrimony* was the picture Nunnally most enjoyed . . . it was his favorite-size story, small, and the cockney wife that Gracie Fields played was Nunnally's dream wife. One that took charge and ordered her artist husband's life to suit his needs and provide full comfort. That's what Nunnally wanted.")

In 1942 he did another Steinbeck, *The Moon Is Down*, with

Cedric Hardwicke, Henry Travers, Lee Cobb and Dorris, who, as a Norwegian farm wife, stabs Peter Van Eyck (a Nazi officer) with a pair of scissors. It was the first of his war movies and features, as they all did, a sympathetic enemy officer. "I talked to Hardwicke about it," Nunnally said, "and I think he put it right. He said, 'I suppose it's like a Jesuit who doesn't really believe in the Church.' I said, 'That would do it. He was a soldier. He did his job. But he didn't believe in what he was doing.'"

The ponderous *Keys of the Kingdom* (directed by John Stahl) came next, with Gregory Peck (in his second Hollywood film) as a missionary in China. It was Nunnally's last film for Zanuck for six years, a period during which he "went independent." On *Keys of the Kingdom,* Nunnally shared writer credit with Joe Mankiewicz, possibly as a result of Zanuck's sulking over his departure, for Zanuck claimed Nunnally's script was unsatisfactory —which was by that time unheard of—and passed it on to Joe Mankiewicz. Co-credit was decided on by arbitration of the Screenwriters' Guild.

It was a blow to Zanuck to hear, after he got back from the war, that Nunnally had formed a partnership with Bill Goetz (one of the founders of Twentieth Century-Fox) and Leo Spitz, a well-known and wealthy lawyer, to make independent productions at International Pictures, which was then camping out on the Goldwyn lot. He thought Nunnally had been plotting behind his back with Goetz, but Nunnally wasn't a plotter. He wanted more money and he had been advised by his agent, Johnny Hyde, that he would never make it at Fox. As Nunnally put it, "At the end of three years it always seemed to me three men about four foot eight would come around: Abe Lastfogel, Johnny Hyde, and another little short fellow. These three little short-legged men would run back and forth between my office and Darryl's and then they'd say, 'It's all set. Three years. Four years.' Whatever the hell it was. Johnny was beyond being an agent, he'd become a good friend, and he was a very farsighted fellow. Johnny decided, 'You're not going to get any more dough here and it's all salary, so I think we ought to look around for another setup in which you will participate in the company and the production of the pictures.'" He turned down a staggering contract from Fox toward this end: five thousand dollars a week for five years, fifty-two weeks a year, six weeks off, paid vacation—in 1943 the biggest contract ever offered a writer. But he'd had enough of being on salary and wanted something more than Fox's equivalent of a gold watch or fitted weekend bag as a reward for his years of service.

At this point the whole subject turns into "impossible surrealism" as Pete Martin (who wrote two articles about Nunnally for the *SEP* in 1943) put it. Pete was referring to Onnie, who was afraid to tell the neighbors what her son was earning per week, but it's just as surrealistic for anybody who lives on a far lowlier scale. A couple of things are notable—one, that anybody making four thousand dollars a week in 1943 could feel pinched, and, two, that Nunnally really did think it was all brought about by short-legged gnomes. Joe Schenck, then head of Fox, once said, "Nunnally is a child with money. All he knows is that he wants more of it." As long as it came in by weekly pay check he could grasp it somewhat, but when he entered the complexities of incorporation at International, wrote Pete Martin, "a curtain seemed to descend between him and the financial facts of his life. After one or two singlehanded efforts had failed to clarify, for him, the processes by which his business was organized and the pictures financed, sold and distributed, Johnny Hyde set up an elaborate education expedition to make such matter crystal clear to his financially inept client. He brought up reinforcements in the shape of five lawyers, accountants and tax experts known for their ability to explain abstruse subjects in kindergarten language.

"Those present have since been quoted as saying, 'It was like trying to get the first communications through to Helen Keller.'

"After a sweaty session lasting well into the evening, the one who had come nearest to success was an accountant who hit on the device of persuading Johnson to think of his transaction as a deal in bananas, a twist which appeared to give the affair some semblance of reality for him. The try failed only because, just as all was beginning to go well, the accountant made the mistake of employing one of the innumerable mathematical terms which confuse and distress Nunnally. He spoke of a "gross" of the fruit.

"While trying to recollect whether a gross was 1,760 or 5,280, Johnson lost track of the explanation that followed, and was never again able to catch up with it. In the end, however, he smiled and nodded with the air of easy comprehension he has learned to assume when facing matters beyond his understanding. The delegation seized upon this nodding as a signal to adjourn, and in a matter of seconds had zipped up their briefcases, shaken hands all around, and were out of the building, mopping their brows and exchanging baffled looks."

Of this ineptitude Dorris says, "His interest span in business-of-living situations was about the equal of a small child's . . . in 1951 his contract with Fox came up for renewal. An important meeting was arranged with his agents and accountant. He asked me to be there. The next five years' work and terms had to be resolved. He was at a peak and very much in demand. Contract details were being discussed and I insisted he must have some participation in the returns from his pictures (few writers were in a position to make that kind of deal in those days). But TV sales were becoming possible and no matter how many sets of books the studio kept to keep picture profits hidden, when they sold to TV, I figured, they'd have to divvy up the percentage. (How I underestimated the studio's skill for fraud.) Talk was excited, decisions critical. In the middle of this Nunnally stood up and casually said, 'I'd better be getting back to the office. Let me know what you decide.' Everybody present was dumfounded. He calmly walked out of the restaurant after a coupla stops to have a few words with friends. He forgot the meeting and didn't ask for days what the terms of the contract would be."

The incredible sums of money earned by Hollywood people in the thirties and forties inevitably had strange effects on the mind. George Seaton says, "There were people here who thought it would never end." Those who knew it might provided against sparser times by incorporating or entering into any number of financial deals for tax shelters; those who thought the dream was real (an occupational hazard) are broke today. This is partly because of the huge taxes that had to be paid on straight salaried income, which phenomenon Hollywood people claim the rest of us can hardly understand. Possibly—but what glazes our eyes even more are their mansions, their Rollses, their nannies and gardeners and cooks, their matched shrubbery and mythic parties and epic jewels. (Dorris says, "It's like having lived through one

of the great courtly periods before they were all beheaded. I
have a feeling Hollywood was beheaded during my period.")
We can't help thinking, as they talk about tax bites, Then why do
they *spend* so much? There may be no answer—any of us might
do the same thing—but the fact is they do, or rather they did, for
things are different now; and when you are that rich, a pinch is
even having to think about cutting back somewhere. Rich or
poor, being pinched is when you can never come out ahead—
and in the Beverly Glen mansion, where Nunnally and Dorris
were living in 1943, they were ten thousand ahead one year,
ten thousand behind the next, but no *real* dough, real enough
to put away so they wouldn't have to worry so much. A way
of life that the rest of the country found unbelievable they
came to look upon as quite normal.

In leaving Fox, Nunnally was also leaving what had proved to
be the most important professional relationship he ever had. Zanuck, in spite of a raft of eccentricities, was a genius at that most
crucial of producer functions—the reading of a script. "Zanuck
had a Geiger counter in his head," said Nunnally. "He'd read a
script and the minute it got dull, or didn't move, or went off the
track, tick-tick-tick, he said, 'It stopped. Now where did this
start?' And he'd go back, two pages, three pages, and then he'd
figure out where the movement stopped, or the movement went
wrong. So when you came in to talk to him, he had exactly
where it wasn't moving right." Zanuck tested constantly, checking out his own judgment. He kept a handful of curious people
on the payroll to comment on scripts—Mike Romanoff, Aiden
Ruark, a polo player, and an old-time director named Al. "If a
script is clear to Al, it'll be clear to everybody in the United
States." Story conferences might take place at any hour of the
night, often after a preview at two or three in the morning. He
liked to think of himself as a writer, though he had no talent for
it at all, but it meant he always spoke in terms of the writer. His
flow of energy and ideas sometimes kept him up all night dictat-
ing a story outline or making notes on a script.

Unlike some producers, he valued and protected his writers.
"Zanuck was a shield between you and the unpleasant facts of
money, censorship and the New York office," says Phil Dunne.
"He took all that onto himself and left the creative people free to

create. If a picture didn't work he said, 'We made a mistake.'" He was happy as a lark with Nunnally because, having handed him the material, he could forget about it for ten or twelve weeks, at which time he could count on getting a pretty good script—not a perfect one, but one whose faults could be taken care of in one or two sessions. "I was almost like a contractor," said Nunnally. "After a while it became almost machinelike." During the writing of a script Nunnally sent him a weekly report, and there was never any reproach even if only two pages had been written during that week. When it was done they would sit down with the director. "He had this immense power of concentration," said Nunnally. "He couldn't pass the mark until he got it straightened out. I went along the lines that there's not one right thing and one wrong thing, but twenty rights and twenty wrongs. . . . I never worked for anybody I had the faith in I had in Zanuck." Compared to other producers, "perhaps Thalberg inspired this same faith in people who worked for him. A fellow was telling me the other day, 'You worked for Thalberg, and you come back from a sneak preview, and Thalberg would begin plying you with questions about everything. Suppose you're driving back with him in the car. "Do you think that came through?" "Do you think that was clear?" "Did you think that was effective?" If the director, or the writer, or one of the men whom he regarded, said, "I don't think the girl should have got up and walked out of the room. I think that gave a very bad impression. I don't think she would have done it," he said, "All right. Rewrite the scene the way you think it should be done." Or he said, "Tell me." The fellow would say, "If she stayed there, argued the point with him, and the man left the room, it would be more effective." He said, "All right. Bring the people back. We'll shoot it that way."'

"Now this could be a small thing, but his sole aim was to make a picture that was good and effective. You do that at Columbia, Harry Cohn would say, 'What do you think?' You say, 'I think the girl shouldn't have left the room.' 'Fuck you. The guy leaves the room, she's left, what do you think I'm going to do, bring back the whole company to keep this girl in the room—are you out of your mind?' It's the difference between their approaches to pictures. Zanuck wasn't like Thalberg in that sense. I never heard him do a thing like that. I've heard him say, 'The end is not good at all,' but he didn't let it go at that. We'd get back to the studio at one or one-thirty in the morning, maybe we'd been to Pomona. The day wasn't over. We went in and sat down, and there'd be an hour of preliminary discussion about either one scene, if that was it, the end, say, and he'd pace up and down and chew on that cigar. Finally he'd say, 'You're right. You're right. That son of a bitch ought to stay in there. Bring me something back. We'll do it again.' Thalberg did it quick; Darryl thought it over a long time. I never heard him talk about what it would cost, because I knew we'd be working on a picture, say, it's going to cost, those days, a million, a million and a half, and to do this extra thing would cost maybe five thousand, ten thousand dollars, and now those were big figures to me at the time, to me now, but they weren't to Darryl. They were little figures."

Zanuck's loss was real. Nunnally had become, by this time, one of the fastest, most dependable scriptwriters in the business. Few others could turn out (in ten weeks) a script that called for little or no revision, which was almost certain to turn into a picture that made money. Pete Martin told in his *SEP* article:

"Once, when the studio sought Johnson to adapt a story for its biggest star, Johnson's agent, Johnny Hyde, set a price that made the studio recoil as if kicked by a mule. But before it could answer, Hyde produced a set of figures on the writing costs of the star's five previous productions. In each case the story had been gone over and over and over again, each new writer adding another sum to the budget, until the total cost of the finished script appreciably exceeded the amount Hyde asked for Johnson. Assuming that the script done by Johnson would be final and satisfactory—and he seldom failed—Hyde pointed out that the studio would actually be saving money by paying him what he asked. The deal was made. The picture was a success. The studio did save money."

Since Nunnally's reputation as a money-making scriptwriter was so solid, there was no problem getting financial backing for his independent venture with International.

Crossings   *1940*

There was a period of hovering, of waiting until Pop and Dorris were settled somewhere, at which time I would be able to go and visit them. God—visit my own father? There was an atmosphere of warning as though someone, I don't know who, had told me to behave myself and not frighten Dorris, who after all had just acquired a couple of stepdaughters (one of whom was only three years younger than she was). In California I was supposed to be careful, when we were there Nana was forever shushing me and yanking my clothes back into place in a way she had long since given up in New York. California was where you had to look right, in New York you could look like a slob and say what you wanted.

We picked our way carefully into Pop and Dorris' new house on Beverly Glen, the most splendid so far. The flats of Beverly had been left behind for a high piece of ground in Holmby Hills, with rose trees lining the asphalt driveway that sloped steeply down to the street. Behind was a flat lawn and a pool, and a hedge of oleander against the fence of the tennis court next door. Across the lawn was a covered summerhouse that nobody used but me. Inside was that same carpeted sunny silence, those same quiet voices in the kitchen late in the afternoon and the smell of coffee as Nana, the cook and the maid sat there exchanging information on the entire gripping family situation. All I remember of Dorris in the beginning was that she cheerfully called herself

my cruel stepmother, a little joke I laughed at because it was evident it would help us both to laugh, but which puzzled me because it had never occurred to me that she might be cruel, but
rather that she would be so much better and kinder and more
beautiful than I that she would win the game effortlessly. Of
course she had won already. She was beautiful, small and golden
with graceful hands, and a slow, Southern voice. I remember
watching her, probably obsessively, to see what this person who
won was like, what tricks and qualities she had, what sort of
magic she was able to work.

But Dorris gave herself over to a startling and continuous production of babies, and so seemed to spend most of her life in
bed, exhausted by pregnancy or childbirth or breast feeding.
There were hardly that many—Christie was born when I was
nine and Roxie when I was twelve, but it was so clear, all of it,
so incredible, that Dorris remains forever in her lace bed jacket
in her enormous bed with a satin headboard, like a queen, holding a baby, her hair down in reddish-gold curls. The last baby,
Scott, wasn't born till 1948 but I have run it all together as
though Dorris had one a year without ever leaving her bed. She
lay in a movie bedroom, pink and gold and dusty green, with a
chaise longue and little upholstered chairs all about and a tiny,
elegant desk, at which I imagined she wrote thank-you notes and
regretted invitations to parties.

Most of the life of the house took place in that bedroom. Pop
arrived home in the evening, announcing himself by a certain familiar whistle (G-E on the piano) which brought me hurtling
out of wherever I was to fling myself upon him in an embrace
that was close to violence. Possibly I was trying to keep him
downstairs, but since that was destined not to work, after a few
minutes I trailed him upstairs to Dorris' bedroom where he sat
with his drink in a chair by the little unlit fireplace. Then Jane
Reilly, the nurse, would appear with whatever baby was around
and whatever children the previous baby or babies had grown
into, and there would be a general rollicking around and admir-
ing and muttering of admonitions from Jane, of an entirely familiar sort (Don't spill that, I just ironed that dress, be *careful*,
watch her little head, get your dirty feet off that quilt), a childhood litany, the running counterpoint of nurses and nannies

which intensified at the time of day when their authority was no longer absolute. This was when Pop seemed happiest, when his family eddied around him and Dorris presented him with all those babies, like gifts. She seemed very small and vulnerable, sitting there in the big bed with all those people milling around. I had seen her play Rosasharn in *The Grapes of Wrath*, a poor pregnant Okie girl, and sometimes she clowned around in Southern baby talk with the kids. "Honey, Mama's gonna fix yo' grits, put on yo' shoes and we'll go to town." Pop loved it. They always joked like that, and at the time I thought it had something to do with still being Rosasharn, because the ability of actors and actresses to snap in and out of personalities still puzzled me and I thought aspects of their parts still clung to them later like bits of magnetized paper. Later I knew they did it to remind themselves and each other what they had come from.

I felt as included as possible under the circumstances, because Pop implied that I was more mature and interesting than these babies, who were charming but limited. I didn't find them charming and was surprised that everybody else did. During the day the life of the house centered on them—they were either being brought to Dorris to be nursed (which I watched from behind the door, speechless with horror) or else, when they were a little older, they sat endlessly on the toilet, strapped into little white potty seats, talking and singing away like tiny inmates in straitjackets. At some point I saw the only decent thing to do was to occasionally let Christie off the toilet, which I did whenever Jane wasn't around. We never got into a real struggle about it since Jane held a full deck, it was only a gesture on my part, a message to Christie that she could and should fight the adult establishment. Jane's attitude was hard to detect. She was a strange, dour woman, tight and conscientious and as possessive of her charges as Nana was of me. She and Nana only co-existed (which they only had to do for a couple of summers, before Nana's illness started) by immediately carving out their territory and setting up strict limits—hands off each other's kids. It must have been almost impossible for them, two nannies in the same house. Nana called Jane "Reilly" and Jane called Nana "Miz . . . er . . . uh," and then Nana would snap, "Walker." They were like two prime ministers of the same country, but they worked

something out and at night I heard them talking together while
Jane did her fine sewing, for she made all the children's clothes
(which I sabotaged, letting Christie out when Jane said she had
to stay inside or inviting her to make mud pies in the summerhouse when she appeared in an immaculate sun suit). Nana
filled Jane in on anything she didn't already know, and Jane told
Nana about her Dodges, her previous family, who were so rich
and generous and had such perfect children. Jane had her
Dodges, Nana had her somebodies, I forget their name, that
other life that made the present one tolerable.

As I was to Christie, Marge was to me, though the age
difference was greater, and Marge's life resonated with things
beyond my comprehension. I see her in a rather small dark dining room, possibly in that house on Camden Drive where Dorris
crossed the lawn. It is during the war and the latest news from
Europe is on the radio. Nana is sitting there sewing. Marge
wears a jacket with padded shoulders and slacks and wedge-
heeled shoes, all very fashionable and admired by Nana. Her
long hair curls and flops over one eye like Veronica Lake's.
When the news is over and the music starts, Marge starts to sing
along with the radio, one of the war songs, "Comin' in on a Wing
and a Prayer." She sings as though she were really performing in
the movies or in a night club, or the way I imagine people perform in night clubs. She smiles, swings her arms, sways and
snaps her fingers. Nana is dazzled, I am again speechless at the
transformation. She closes her eyes, pantomimes a microphone.
Her voice grows low and husky, her long slender fingers splay
out. I wish the room were larger, it is all so overwhelming I want
to look away. When she is finished we all clap, Nana and I and
some other person, possibly Marge's mother Alice. She is devastating, she dips in and out of some other world. I am told she is
my sister, and in fact I call her Cissy, but she seems like a
breath-taking stranger. I have little or no experience with sisters
anyway, none of my friends has them nor brothers either. I live
in a world of only children, and I am not sure if Marge counts.
She is very confident, she has a lot of friends, mostly in uniforms,
who sing and dance to the radio. She calls them swell guys and
gals. They find me mildly amusing, I find them terrifying. No
one else seems to understand what I know in my bones, that

Marge would push me off a cliff if she got the chance (as later Christie doubtless knew about me).

On some occasion I was entrusted to Marge for delivery to Lake Arrowhead, a mountain resort some two or three hours' drive inland from Beverly Hills, where the family, or some section of it, had taken a cottage for a short period. Once I was in her power, she changed the plans at the last moment and handed me over to a friend named Jackie. Jackie sang mightily to the radio and drummed on the wheel as she sank the accelerator to the floor of her convertible, which was reasonable fun until we started up the mountains, where she took hairpin turns at fifty miles an hour and screeched along canyon edges as dust flew behind us in great clouds, occasionally yelling, "You okay, honey?" If I had an answer it disappeared into the screaming wind, but I was entirely taken up by the prospect of finally meeting the Lord as well as pretending I thought this was all just grand—the idea that Jackie might tell Marge I was scared was worse than hurtling over the edge miles down onto the rocks and rattlesnakes. When we got there I fell out of the car, gibbering and whimpering. Later I heard Marge had gotten scolded by Pop because everybody knew the way Jackie drove and she might have killed herself and The Child, though Marge drove exactly the same way. What puzzled me was why Marge hadn't done the job herself—had she lost her nerve (let Jackie go over the edge) or was it simply that she couldn't be bothered, I was too boring even to kill? Another unanswered question.

Another time I am in a kitchen, again in the Camden Drive house. There is a white table in the middle (the same table upon which at another time lay a map of the United States with a dark red line tracing out the coast-to-coast route). This time it is night and there is a young man in the kitchen, Ken. He is very drunk, he staggers and his speech slurs. Possibly he wears a uniform. He is angry and I know everyone in the other room is angry at him. Then he is gone and Marge is there, crying and being comforted by someone. It's no good, dear, he's a drunk. I don't know which of these images are real and which are emanations from my mind. Marge married a drunk, it didn't work, she's better off without him. But still she cries, great deep sobs in the kitchen at night.

It was partly because of the war, like everything else. They said the war was what was the matter with everything, they found it dreadful and startling, but as far as I was concerned there had always been a war, and it was hard to understand why they kept talking about how it would be when things were normal again. By normal Pop meant when he and Dorris had found a house and were settled in it, but that seemed a queer use of the word. To Marge it must have meant when your life stopped being messed up, but that was no more normal to me than to her. Pop talked about it most, I don't remember my mother ever mentioning it.

Because of the war you took whatever space you could get, which for Nana and me meant the Chief instead of the Super Chief. This didn't seem like any hardship except for that one moment, usually in New Mexico, when the Super Chief whipped by on the next track at twice our speed and disappeared into a point of silver on the horizon. But when that sting was past, I loved the Chief and those four days in suspension when I switched my gears, made all the tiny changes in my mental machinery necessary to cope with one parent or the other—four unself-conscious days when Nana and I walked nightly to the dining car for perfect meals (from the Fred Harvey Children's Menu) served on snowy cloths, or read away a gray morning in the observation lounge. I felt intensely secure in my upper berth with its tiny window and little net hammock while below Nana bantered with the porters and complained about the naïveté of some local paper. I don't remember ever being bored, though I must have been, for I was ordered out at every stop over five minutes and told to run up and down the platform. The trips were what ocean voyages were later, splendid, serious travel, a slow deliberate eating up of the terrain while the mind made its infinitesimal changes and Nana took the opportunity to pack in some advice.

Going west:

"Don't talk to your father about *Him* [the commander], it might make him feel bad."

"But why?"

"I dunno, just don't. And don't tell about your mother crying the other night."

"God, is she still crying, I didn't know she was *still* crying."

"Well, just a little, don't take the name of the Lord in vain, she was probably crying about your leaving." This was extremely doubtful. "All right, but she'll get used to *Her*."

"I like *Her*, she's pretty."

"Lord"—relenting—"that baby's almost bigger'n she is."

Or going east:

"Don't tell your mother about *Her*, she gets upset."

"But why *not?*" I got very tired of all this. How was I supposed to find anything out? "What am I supposed to talk about?"

"Tell about your boy friends." This would take about a minute and a half. Nana's advice was pleasant to hear—I liked being given advice—but misled. She was steering around my parents' fears, I was navigating my own. I had enough trouble trying to keep my own head in balance without worrying about theirs, let them do it. I never mentioned the commander to Pop simply because I didn't dare to. But one summer evening when he and I were playing double solitaire (which I found fascinating and he pretended to) he put down his cards and said in his abrupt way:

"Now, what about Joe?"

I turned to ice. "What do you mean?"

"Mama"—meaning Marion—"has told me she thinks you don't like him, and she asked me to talk to you about it." He lit an Old Gold. "Don't you like him?"

"No."

"Why not?"

"I don't know."

"I want you to think about something. You aren't going to like everybody you meet. It just isn't possible. Joe is somewhat . . . ah . . . taciturn."

"What's that?"

"He doesn't talk easily." Dreadful pause. "Your mama is still young and attractive, and it's perfectly possible she'll marry again."

"But she's forty."

"I'm forty-three and still devastating." He grinned and I laughed weakly. "And I was lucky enough to find Dorris. Your mama has found Joe and she's very fond of him. I'm sure you wouldn't want to spoil that."

I began bending the corners of cards until he told me to stop.

"But, Pop, he's awful," I whispered. "If she wants to get married, why doesn't she find somebody nice?"

He had been avoiding my eye, and for the first time he stared straight at me and crunched out the cigarette. He shouted:

"For God's sake, she deserves some happiness," and got up and left the room, while I sat there tearing up the cards. It turned out to be a kind of plot. Nana started telling me Joe wasn't so bad, a furious fib, and two or three of my mother's friends told me the same thing later in New York, to which I gave the same reply. Even Marge was part of it and gave me a similar speech as we roared along in a car. They were all on the same team, even Marge, who was supposed to be my sister, was one of them, they closed ranks like the Nazi army. None of them understood anyway, they kept talking about how my mother deserved love and one of them told me I was ruining her life, which wasn't what I meant to do at all.

Joe didn't like me any more than I liked him. The only thing we had in common was the mutual hatred that sprang into our eyes when he walked into the front hall in all his gold braid. There is no way to say who started it, we were like the snake and the mongoose meeting in a clearing. He did things like bringing a Christmas present for the dog and not for me, I did things like swiping the newspaper I knew he wanted to read. Somebody said (as though it would clear everything up) it was just that he didn't get along with children. It was a strange plot, but it didn't work and my mother didn't marry him, and years later all the people who had told me he wasn't so bad ate their words. Some even made a point of apologizing, which they needn't have, it was just that I was a child and not part of them.

Though I longed for California when I was not there, day-dreamed about it and tried to impress my friends with its boundless pleasures, the truth was that by nine or ten New York had invaded me. I was bigger and dirtier and more complicated, my knees were gray and I talked faster and my mind went in great jagged leaps and circles. Three years before we had stayed with my mother's sister and her family in Great Neck, on Long Island. Early one morning I had looked out of the bedroom window down into the yard where two strange little boys bounded around in great quantities of fluffy white stuff, which they made into little wads and threw up at me. I caught it and watched it melt on my red hand. They were my cousins, Bob and Jack, and they found my amazement very funny. They were further convulsed when I later came downstairs and said I wanted to go out on the patio. It had started to go at that moment, the whole pure California thing, because nobody, particularly a child, wants to be laughed at.

Back East   1941-1944

In 1941 we moved to a brownstone on East Sixty-second Street, which was my home until I was an adult. It was a strange sort of house, this brownstone, with its four floors and the kitchen in the basement and Nana's and my quarters up at the top, and a grubby little patch of a garden. Nana grumbled constantly about all the stairs and the floors that creaked and the first-floor toilet where you could hear everybody pee because it wasn't really a bathroom but only a kind of stall, and the basement that could only be arrived at by heaving up a great section of floor by an iron ring. I grumbled along with Nana and kept a cautious eye on my mother, who had proven to have a dangerous way about homes; she popped out of them as fast as she popped in, you never knew what she was going to do next, look what she had done in California, and I hoped to God this time she was going to settle down. At the penthouse she had shot the hose at the wall outside my room, round and round in great wet dripping spirals that I thought would saturate the walls until my room inside was a damp steamy cave, with great soggy strips of wallpaper curling onto the floor, no place was safe from her, my poor exposed room was like a great wound she kept shooting her hose at. Of course I had startled her when I began screaming and ran inside to hide, she had only been playing. But after we moved the nightmares about it stopped because the new place seemed safe and actually Nana and I had control, we could light our fire and crash it down on her head if she tried anything. But in fact she seemed careful about the brownstone, she wallpapered everything and put rugs down and put in beautiful furniture as though we were really going to stay there. It was the first root in the East, but I fought loving this smelly shaky old house with its radiators that banged in the morning and the view of passing feet from the dining room, which was below street level. The contrast with California was unmistakable, particularly the first two or three days off the train, it was all so dingy and dark and musty, we must have been terribly poor to have to live like this, and crappy old Third Avenue with the El roaring by overhead and all the drunks curled up in the doorways. I hoped Pop wouldn't ever see it, he'd feel terrible that his poor child lived in this slum while he was out there with the sprinklers and the matching rose trees.

But I felt safe there in a way I didn't in the West. In New York there was danger everywhere, you could freeze or get killed by trolley cars or flying Els or get shut in the basement or beaten up in the park or trampled by Shriners or die from all the germs or starve to death because we were so poor or bombed or shot by submarines in the East River, and a million other things they were always talking about, but somehow I knew I had my fists and I could fight. But in Beverly Hills, where it was always safe and warm and peaceful, I was the danger, I was the one who could do the damage, pee in the pool or kill Christie or disturb Dorris or talk during a take and ruin it or say something that made Pop mad, so I was never safe even in my room, which wasn't really my room, though I never told anybody this and for a long time I didn't understand it.

In New York the war was all of a piece with the natural state of siege we lived in, and it arrived the night of my mother's birthday. To a person who had seen as many war movies as I had (Nana took me to them all the time) the news that Pearl Harbor had been bombed—given to me over the phone by some grim adult voice, "Go tell your mother"—was no more startling than anything else, until I saw how frightened they were in the dining room when I told them. There was an immediate electric silence before they all started talking and yelling, and one of them grabbed me and asked me if I was sure, and two women

started to cry, and the commander and somebody else almost
fought over the phone trying to get Washington. We were in the
war, but who were *we,* anyway?

"The Americans," said my mother. "Our countrymen."

"But what's going to happen?"

"We're going to do our best and we're going to lick the bloody
bastards."

"Will we get bombed?"

"Well, dear, I hope not. If they come we'll hide in the basement." Then she announced that she was going to go all out for
the war effort. There was a chorus of similar resolutions, and the
phone kept ringing, and there were more tears and more wine.
Then Joe had to get back to his ship or the Brooklyn Navy Yard
or whatever and he and my mother spent an interminable
amount of time kissing each other good-by up in the vestibule,
and then he left and we were at war.

Pop wrote once or twice a week and tried to explain it all to
me, though I was fixed on Hitler as he was in *The Great Dictator*
and it was hard to see what harm that little man could cause. My
mother meant what she said. Once a week she went out in her
uniform to spot Japanese submarines in the East River and periodically she was an air-raid warden, patrolling the block outside
while inside Nana and I came racketing down the three flights
when the siren sounded, turning out lights on the way and
crouching in the dark kitchen whispering so spies wouldn't hear
us. My mother took up electronics and sat around in the evening
picking over a spaghetti of red and blue wires that eventually
turned into a radio. Probably the war was what we all needed, it
pulled us together. Now there were more people around, somebody was there for dinner almost every night and my mother
would shoot in after work and go down to the kitchen and turn
out another victory casserole.

If any doubts remained Miss Carden, dictator of my tiny
school, cleared them up.

"Children," she said, shortly after we were in the war, "the
Germans and the Japanese are perfectly dreadful people and
should be killed. Now be good children and do what Miss Carden says and you will help annihilate the enemy." We all
collected tinfoil and knitted khaki scarves and reminded our

mothers to save bacon grease to be used for making explosives. I
was happy then being her mindless slave, we all were, but it had
been startling two years before when I first arrived at the school
and she announced to everyone that Wendell Willkie was the
right man for President and Roosevelt was running the country
to the dogs. I had never heard anything but adoration expressed
for Mr. Roosevelt, as he was called in my family, and I was further impressed when Miss Carden got away with it, nobody
came to haul her off to jail. The next day most of the children
came to school either partially or entirely covered with Willkie
buttons. I tried to brazen it out with my four or five FDR buttons, but they disappeared during recess. I was new at the school
and thought Miss Carden would make quick work of this thiev-
ery, but of course she didn't. I was different from the rest of
them and I might as well know it right off. Miss Carden was
quick to let us know who had it and who didn't, there was none
of this nonsense about everybody being equal. Roger the son of
the shoe repairman didn't have it, he got beaten up with rulers.
Vicky the daughter of Bankers Trust Company did, Annie the
daughter of something else did, Natalie didn't because her father
was a poor artist and her mother taught at the school. In general
girls passed and boys didn't, though Tony Perkins passed, as I
did, he and I were in a separate category because our fathers
were in show business. Making it at Carden's meant being bright
and fawning over Miss Carden, which Tony and Vicky and I
did; at Christmas we got to be the Three Kings. But Vicky's parents were still married and her father worked for a bank and the
entire front of Vicky's dress had been covered with Willkie buttons, Tony's father was dead but he had been a famous actor
named Osgood Perkins, and my father was Nunnally Johnson,
who made movies.

Just how he did this wasn't clear. He said he wrote them and
produced them, but I didn't know what producing meant, and
those bare scripts were only pale reflections of what came out on
the screen. It didn't sound so wonderful to me, at least Tony had
been able to see his father on a stage or screen doing something,
unless he had been too young to remember. But in the fine social
shadings of Miss Carden's mind neither of these things was quite
like being a banker or lawyer or anybody who went to some de-

cent respectable office. Charming, fun, but on the light side.
Tony and I had something to make up for which Vicky didn't. If
we were Roger we could just not bother, repair shoes or sell
newspapers or drop into the gutter and be carted off to potter's
field. But Tony and I had talent and promise, precious commodi-
ties which were sinful to waste, and besides we had to run faster
to keep in place.

"Tony, Miss Carden wants you to be Nebuchadnezzar this
year," she would say, shoving a twelve-page speech into his
hand, or, "Nora, Miss Carden wants you to stay home from the
park today and draw her a great, big, wonderful picture."

My talent and promise were considered to be artistic, and I
hated them, all I wanted to do was go to the park and fight. All
Tony wanted to do was escape into fantasyland. He liked to
create little worlds and take his friends into them, little worlds of
doctors and missionaries and cruel uncles and lost children and
dogs with dread diseases, poverty-stricken slaves, rich society
women, kings and cripples. He wore knickers and long brown
socks and he was double-jointed, he could bend his fingers back
until they almost reached his wrist and his knees bent backward
instead of forward. He had lovely smooth olive skin and bright
brown eyes, and he was the only one of the boys I never fought
with. If anyone ever attacked him I would have rushed to his defense, he was so vulnerable, and nobody had ever told him there
was anything wrong with crying. Of course he was going to be
an actor, we all knew it, he already was. It was such a natural
process to him, popping in and out of roles all the time, that I
lost my fear of it, because in time I saw that no matter what
series of masks he put on he would always end up being Tony
again. Presently he got Vicky and me to do it too and then we
were always trios of something else, a king and two cowering
servants; missionary, cannibal and great white hunter; mad doctor, dying patient, terrified nurse; cruel kidnapper, child, dis-
traught mother; rich lady, robber, faithful servant. It was better
than fighting, and since we were constantly on stage besides—
Miss Carden had a fondness for interminable biblical plays at
Christmas—it became a very natural and even necessary thing to
do, since being ourselves all the time had obvious limitations.

All we ever really studied at Carden's was English, French

and piano, Miss Carden being rather uninterested in anything
else. What we really studied was Miss Carden, her enormous
confidence filled that little school building like *son et lumière*.
Not a parent could stand up to her. After she told us she disapproved of comic books, I went home and dumped waist-high
stacks of *Wonder Woman* into the garbage (there was only one
Wonder Woman). We ate what she said was good for us and
scrubbed our knees with brushes when she said we were *sale*.
We never flinched when she beat up the bad and the poor, when
she broke rulers over Roger the shoe repairman's son and Carl,
nobody's son. There was an aristocracy of blood and money and
talent and that was all there was to it. Anybody who didn't see it
was a fool. She was the only adult who was perfectly sure of herself, who told us exactly what to do and who answered all the
questions.

Tony and Vicky left a year before I did and during that last
year I felt lost and began falling in love with other show-
business children, probably to connect myself with my other
world. John Kerr went to Carden and so did Bill Erwin, Stuart
Erwin's son. John's mother was June Walker, an actress; his father, it was revealed many years later to John, was Franchot
Tone. I adored them both, John one week, Bill the next, and controlling my feelings (which I suspected would startle them as
much as they did me) was a real problem. I wrote them yearning little notes which surprised and pleased John and caused Bill
to chase me into the coatroom for a little clumsy nuzzling, which
I pretended to object to. It was all a very strange business for
nine and I had no idea what to make of it. I had never been in
love with anybody before and now these two rather unfamiliar
little boys had taken over not only my head but everything else
too, for I trembled and sweated and gulped in their presence,
dropped books and tripped over my feet. Miss Carden accepted
it all with equanimity (there were no secrets in her tiny school)
but somebody gave me the idea it was all rather dirty and dreadful, possibly the teacher who knew I picked fights with boys that
they were later punished for.

The next year I went into the sixth grade at Brearley.

Sandwiched in between the two distinct worlds in which I
lived was a third one, rather ghostly and sad and lavender-

scented—Nana's home in Chicago where we always stayed for a couple of days between the Chief and the Commodore Vanderbilt. In half a house near the lake lived a small enclave of O'Neill women, a mother and the two middle-aged daughters who hadn't left home. Into this world of bleeding Jesuses on every wall and the incessant click of rosary beads came Nana (who became Mae upon crossing the threshold) and I for twenty-four hours of inquisition and boiled potatoes. Shortly after we arrived Win, the skinny friendly sister, took me into the front room (reserved for state occasions) and tried to wring out the truth about Mae's churchgoing habits, which in fact were spotty.

"Well, we went to mass about a month ago, and the priest made us promise not to ever go to the movies."

"And before that?"

"Oh, I think Christmas Eve."

"Not *Easter*, darlin'?"

"Oh, that's right, Easter too, I had to wear this crummy hat."

Then later from Nana:

"I told you to say I went every Sunday, now they're raggin' me to death."

"But I can't tell a lie." They had effectively gotten that one into my head.

"Just a little white lie, they don't count. Well, never mind, on the way back we'll say I went all summer with Reilly."

Old Mother O'Neill sat in the dining room dying, which she did by incessantly rocking and saying Hail Marys. The rest of them sighed and shook their heads— "Mother won't be with us much longer." Anne, the popeyed sister who ran everything, went to work every day and did the shopping and came home and cooked dinner, she didn't even trust Win to boil the corned beef and potatoes. Another sister, Peg, was a corset buyer in Detroit ("a fine figger of a woman," Nana called her) and then there was Mae, who swept in trailing New York and Hollywood glamor. It was considered she had done very well. Walker had left her, nothing surprising about that, and her baby had been born dead. Now I was her baby. Late at night in our shared room with its dark woodwork and crucifixes over the beds she would mutter, "Lord, can't wait to get on the Chief and get to the Coast." The place made her guilty and made me guilty too for unnamed sins, you breathed guilt as soon as you walked through the door. And the old woman rocking to her death in the dining room, clicking her beads and staring out the window as though at her own extinction. In front of all the houses on the street were little patches of lawns surrounded by fine wire tied to stakes; every time I was there I tripped over one of them and cut myself though somebody was always calling, "Be careful of the wire." But nobody ever took the wire down. We were always very glad to leave. When I thought of the place later it was with puzzlement, as though there was something I should feel bad about, repentant, though I didn't know what it was. Those women's faces I saw in my mind never spoke, only looked at me in sad reprimand.

Since Nana came from a house of death, I knew, and she knew, that she had to die; and that I knew this was embarrassing to her. One by one all of them died, except for Peg, who for all I know is still alive, because she left and went to Detroit. But Nana had to return and then she had to die.

I sensed this and began to hate her for it. I could sense impending separation like a bad smell—I already knew what that was like and I prepared for it like an animal readying its defenses. Possibly I overheard my mother—"I don't know what to do about Mae, Nora's too old for a nurse now she's at Brearley." I pulled away from Nana and fought her so the bonds wouldn't all have to be broken at once, this time I wasn't going to be so dumb. I was growing out of her anyway, I had found I was smarter than she was, I could think rings around her any time. She was big and dumb and boring and I didn't need her any more, if she needed me, which she clearly did, that was her problem.

Anyway I had all I could handle with Brearley, the place was making me crazy. Nothing from Carden worked there. The show-biz children (Linda Berlin and Sidney Howard and Nora Sayre) didn't seem to suffer from the stigma of having fathers who were not bankers or stockbrokers. Nobody ever pretended to be what they were not, and physical violence was no longer the province of adults (I wasn't sorry to see that go, Miss Carden's exhibitionistic beatings of little boys was starting to make my head hurt) but rerouted among the girls in a sadistic game called prison ball. Instead there were Ins and Outs and I was an Out—I lacked an apartment with an elevator, a doorman, a resident father in a dark business suit, and a highly visible mother who picked me up in a Lincoln to go to the country (we went to our country, when we got one, either on the train or in a Jeep station wagon). The only subjects I grasped even minimally were English, French and music, and the rest were disasters; though I had braces, a social plus, I also had to wear glasses all the time, which more or less canceled out the braces. I had not yet learned that what you had mattered less than how you presented it, and I wore myself out in an intense, daily comparison of myself with everybody else in which failure rang like gloomy bells, over and over again. In this context (and everything was) Nana was becoming a liability—by the sixth grade nannies were pretty well phased out ("Mummy and I drove over to see my old Nanny, she lives with her sister in New Jersey, and they were so *darling*, they made this huge chocolate cake," et cetera) and so it was time for Nana to go on the block. My mother told me I was cruel, that Nana would give me the shirt off her back. But it was my neck or Nana's, and I did what I thought I had to to survive.

Nana's illness accordingly started at our country home, which was at Center Island, near Oyster Bay, the summer I was eleven. For the first time I didn't go to California, I believe by choice. Possibly I knew I was going to have to confront my mother sooner or later and wanted to get started on this difficult project; and I was grateful to her for getting another house and behaving as though she was going to keep it, though she frightened me to death again by spattering the floors, a decorating trick where you take a paintbrush full of paint and whack it with a stick, it was almost as bad as the hose business, I thought she was going to ruin everything, mess up this little house she had bought that was going to be so pretty with her goddam spattering, and she wouldn't stop, she thought I was funny, and I ran out in the woods and stayed there till it was all over. But afterward it looked all right, the whole place did, and it was as though we had survived something. I didn't want to leave it and go out there with all those babies and nothing to do, if I stayed here I could help with the house, which I was frantic to do—paint things or hang curtains or weed the victory garden, anything that would help it root and be ours forever.

Then everything began to go wrong.

First Nana got an infection in her leg and wouldn't go to the doctor because she was afraid he'd put her into the hospital and cut her leg off, and she limped around and gave off fear like static electricity, with a big red sore on her leg that wouldn't heal. Then I found blood in my pants and it was as though we were all getting hurt and my mother and Nana were astonished at this and put me to bed, for some reason, and there wasn't any Kotex or anything in the house and we didn't have a car because of the war and the nearest town was two miles away and my mother got on her bicycle and went to Bayville for a box of Kotex. Meanwhile I lay in bed while Nana told me not to worry.

Then Nana went to town on a series of buses and trains and taxis and came back at the end of the day and said the doctor was going to put her in the hospital, just like she said, though he hadn't mentioned cutting her leg off yet. She was pale with fear and I was too, and I was still bleeding anyway with one of my endless menstrual periods that went on that summer for two weeks out of every four. My mother tried to cheer us all up by making her best war casseroles with vegetables from the garden and occasionally smiling upon me and saying, "Dear, now you are a woman," which at that point seemed a hell of a doubtful blessing, which I expressed by refusing to take baths and wearing my hair in two mangy pigtails with rubber bands on the ends which I never combed out and rebraided, and Nana was too frightened to make me shape up and my mother, never having tried, didn't know how.

Then Mama, who was trying to run this little house and two acres of land and grow half an acre of fruit and vegetables and bicycle to town for food and cook and placate two miserable people, also tried to remove all the poison ivy from the property and ended up swathed in bandages in the local hospital. When she was better she took me to three doctors to find out why my periods were two weeks long and none of them seemed to know or to think there was anything wrong with it, so then she decided I should go daily to a place called the Seawanhaka Junior Yacht Club to learn to sail. I fought for my rights, all I wanted

to do was stay home and take care of the dog (who was pregnant) and dig in the garden or paint something or build something with wood and nails, frantically sinking roots, but since she
had lost on the bath-and-hair front she was determined to make
it on this one.

"But why do I have to go?" I wailed.

"To be with other children and to have something to do every
day."

"But I have things to do and they're all horrible."

I lost, or most days I lost. I would go to the Junior Club, a
small clubhouse for children of Yacht Club members (which we
weren't, not being exclusive enough) where a group of young
Roosevelts and Couderts and Rockefellers sat around and said
shit and fuck and fart and endlessly made peanut butter and
jelly sandwiches and drank bottles of Pepsi-Cola. Some of them
owned their own Seabirds and when it was discovered I knew
nothing about sailing they either left me behind with the shit-
fuck group or said, "Oh, we'll take Nora along for ballast." I had
never really known boredom till the Junior Club, boredom in-
terspersed with horror when I was trusted with the main sheet
and let the boom jibe or when somebody threw me into the
jellyfish-infested Sound while I was wearing my Kotex, which
was most of the time (I doubt my mother had ever heard of
tampons, and anyway, I was only eleven, and anyway, they
might have wrecked my virginity).

Every night Nana limped down to the guest cottage (there
were only two bedrooms in the tiny house) and every morning
she limped back. Finally she went into the hospital in New York.
When this happened I felt a guilty relief that her haunting presence was gone, she had become one of those silent Chicago
faces. And she was right, they did cut off her leg, but not till the
middle of winter.

Then we got a maid named Alma who came out to help but
she lit a match in the basement where gas had been escaping
and the basement blew up and she blew out of the side of the
house and ran screaming through the strawberry patch, with the
flesh burned off her face . . . but that might have been the following spring, as well as the hurricane that cut off the electricity
(which included the plumbing) so for days we crept out in the

woods, sitting on fallen sumac logs to empty our bowels. It couldn't have all happened in one summer. But this was how it was here, if you survived it made you strong. Nana had probably reached her capacity for hardship, it was too much for her, children have a way of leaving adults and I was all she had. Nobody ever tells you that total devotion is never rewarded, but even if they do you don't believe it.

Hollywood   1940-1950

Dorris' screen credits are: *Down on the Farm, Young Mr. Lincoln* (with Henry Fonda), *Drums Along the Mohawk, The Grapes of Wrath* and *The Moon Is Down*. In the first four she played a barefoot country girl, and though she got first-rate reviews for *The Grapes of Wrath*, she wanted to get out of Fox's type casting. After the release of the picture and her marriage to Nunnally in 1940, she went to the William Morris office, her agency, where she was ushered in to see one of the partners, Johnny Hyde. "I was a lowly actress and usually I saw someone who handled lowly actresses," Dorris says. "Because I was Nunnally's wife, I was ushered in in a VIP way, but it was clear it was more like a social call than a professional one, and Johnny's whole attitude was, Why, Dorris, you don't want to work now that you're married to Nunnally. It was a very ego-bruising experience and I felt I was losing my chance at important assignments or further work even. That's exactly the way it developed. I don't like to blame things on other causes, but I do believe if they had tried to sell my services shortly after that I would have got work. Which I didn't do." In a story in her home-town paper, the Memphis *Commercial Appeal*, around that time Dorris is quoted as saying, "I was supposed to have taken the feminine lead in *Brigadoon* but that would have interfered with our honeymoon, so we talked the studio out of it . . . but there's a role in Nunnally's play for me if they'll let me take it" (*Stag at Bay*, a collaboration with Charles MacArthur). Around the same time she tested for *Chad Hanna* and lost the part to Linda Darnell (Nunnally said, "There was a certain coolness around the house at that time"). In *The Moon Is Down* she plays a farm wife in Nazi-occupied Norway. (In this she is no longer barefoot but still has braids, as she did in at least two other pictures.) But before she was cast in that Zanuck called Nunnally into his office and said, "Look, you don't want your wife to work, do you?" to which he replied, "Oh, it doesn't make any difference to me, if she wants to, but I'd rather she didn't"—which exchange he laughingly reported to Dorris, having no idea how painful it was to her. Christie was born in 1942, and Roxie in 1945, which effectively filled her life, though for years she thought about working again. "It hurt like a toothache." By the time Scott was born in 1948 it seemed too late to start again, and it injured her because her only two good credits were on Nunnally's pictures.

Documenting Nunnally's sexism is like shooting fish in a barrel. It came along with his Southern background and a concept of marriage which was not only unquestioned but simply not subject to question. But sexism must have as many varieties as the men who wear it. Nunnally had no objection to a woman having a career as long as she wasn't married to him, but one wonders if it was the career he objected to in principle or the inability of most women to manage a successful career, kids and the sort of highpowered household management called for by the life they led. There are men who smile with dreadful pleasure at the sight of a woman toiling away in the kitchen, but Nunnally wasn't one of them—as far as he was concerned the cook belonged in the kitchen and the woman in the living room with him. Later on, when times changed and certain cutbacks came, he hated seeing Dorris out there chopping onions; that by then she enjoyed it bewildered him. The problem was more his aggravating male blindness about what went into creating the good life he saw as his due. He simply didn't see what all the fuss was about—didn't he earn enough money? And how could he do what he did without somebody to take care of all that other stuff, which apparently had to be taken care of?

Dorris, as much a product of her time as he was, agreed that he couldn't, that somebody had to step back and that his was the greater talent. She said to me once, "I learned early that you writers need a wife. . . . I recognized very early that a successful career actually demanded a partnership operation. I never belittled or diminished my contribution or my need in Nunnally's career nor did he. And I made it clear from the beginning that I recognized I had a real heavy work assignment to maintain a life that was right for him professionally . . . my attitude about wifing has always been that a wife is an equal partner in effort, not only the business of earning . . . they just come in different forms." Dorris—in spite of her "toothache"—took her end of the partnership seriously, and it wasn't easy. Besides illness and the difficult pregnancies which laid her up for long periods of time, she had some other things to handle—Nunnally's drinking, which continued as before, and her own anxieties about the new role she had to fill; now she was a producer's wife (as welcome as venereal disease). Besides, she felt for years the ghostly presence of Marion, who she thought had done everything better, including please Nunnally. Their marriage had happened quickly after two or three years of wavering on his part, and she could hardly believe the wavering was over—in many ways it wasn't. "Marion was the only woman I was ever jealous of," Dorris said once. "All the starlets . . ." a shrug. She said later she thought Marion might have been better for him—made him more "independent." All these things, along with her own rather driven perfectionism about anything she put her hand to, were the other side of what was really a good marriage—for "where it counted, in our private partnership, it was understood that there was no Second-class Citizen."

Sometimes, in the houses of the rich, there is a sort of built-in watchdog in the form of the nanny, for whose substitute mothering a psychic price must be paid. Strong women can handle it, but insecure ones have trouble with the whole triple relationship. My mother simply relinquished responsibility—"Nana wouldn't let me near you." Nana became the boss, and my mother and I the children, which worked until Nana died, and then I paid the price. But Dorris fought Jane Reilly every inch of the way. Jane was a dour, wizened little woman whom, Dorris once said desperately, "we have to keep because she's the only one who knows where everything is." It was true—only Jane had control of that big house on Mountain Drive, with its pantries and servants' quarters and upstairs sitting room and closets and bathhouse by the pool. She operated out of the nursery with its adjoining bedrooms and tiny kitchenette, where she would sit until two or three in the morning doing that delicate needlework which was her genius, finishing up a pinafore for Roxie or a skirt for Christie. Those things would have been hard enough to get rid of, but worse still she was completely dependable—she would have crawled miles through mortar fire on her white-stockinged knees for any of the children, nothing was too hard for her, nothing too tedious, and nothing ever forgotten. Since she took up the kind of slack we love to have taken up, she stayed, needed and tolerated by all and hated by Dorris.

The silent struggle reached a breaking point when Scott was born, in 1948. Jane had been widowed at twenty-one and had to give her son to her mother-in-law, because she couldn't afford to keep him; Scott, the first boy, was going to be his replacement. In traditional nanny fashion Jane zeroed in on the breast feeding, which Dorris had been unable to do with the girls. She refused to leave Dorris alone with the baby for a minute, and during the night, when he cried, she would say, "You'll never be able to get the baby quiet because you're inadequate to feed him." This was really twisting the knife, since Dorris felt inadequate anyway, about practically everything. Nunnally was no help—it was one of his blind spots. "That's typical new-mother talk, they always blame the nurse." By the time Scott was a month old and the breast feeding had been successfully sabotaged, Dorris was having dreadful crying fits, locked in the bathroom. When the hatred became unbearable she told Nunnally she couldn't take it any longer, but he only said, "Honey, it'll be all right, go away for a while."

Things smoothed out a little as Scott got older, but since they couldn't bring themselves to fire Jane, she was there until the entire family moved to Rome in early 1959—and possibly was one of the reasons they moved to Rome. After that, really for the first time, Dorris was on her own, in control of her home and her life.

The first picture Nunnally did for International was *Casanova Brown* (with Gary Cooper, directed by Sam Wood), a mild

comedy about a man who, on the eve of his wedding, discovers
that his ex-wife is about to deliver his child. In the course of
many events he steals the baby and takes care of it in a hotel
room. I couldn't find a print and am unable to comment. But the
next one, *Woman in the Window* (Edward G. Robinson, Joan
Bennett, directed by Fritz Lang, who left "a trail of hate"), was
a real gripper, a murder with what everybody admits is a cheat
ending. (Marge was the cutter, the first time she worked on a
picture with her father.) Robinson, professor and family man, is
alone in the city during the summer. After dinner at his club, as
he muses upon a portrait of a beautiful woman in a gallery window, the actual woman appears beside him, and Robinson, fascinated, follows her home. They are having a drink together
when her jealous lover appears and Robinson kills him in self-
defense. He dumps the body in the woods, but the victim turns
out to have been a well-known public figure and there is a serious man hunt. One of Eddie's friends at the club is the detective
on the case and keeps his cronies informed over the port. Will
Eddie get caught? The net closes in and Eddie in despair takes
sleeping pills. He could be saved by a certain phone call, and as
it rings and rings the camera closes in on Eddie as we pray for
him to *answer the phone!* But the camera pulls back and there's
Eddie, asleep in his chair at the club—it was all a dream. (This
was done in one shot, with Eddie's breakaway clothes whipped
off him while the camera stayed on his face.) The doorman and
other club attendants turn out to be the victim, a blackmailer, et
cetera.

Though a preview audience gave a "low animal moan" at the
trick ending, the picture was very successful. Probably the comedy ending (Eddie, after seeing his dream characters as doormen, et cetera, again passes by the window with the portrait. A
woman comes along and says, as Joan Bennett did, "Have you
got a match?" Eddie flees in horror) made up for the cheat,
which Bill Goetz had insisted on rather against Nunnally's
wishes. When I looked at this picture at a viewing table at
UCLA, several film students gathered around to watch the last
ten minutes of what seemed to be a favorite. One student said,
"Fritz Lang was entirely against this ending but the studio forced
it on him." Nunnally didn't remember what Lang thought, but it

hardly matters—film students will make heroes of directors and villains of studios.

The last picture Nunnally made with International as such (before it merged with Universal) was *Along Came Jones* (1945), a comedy Western with Gary Cooper, directed by Stuart Heisler, and produced by Cooper, who "wasn't about to do much producing," Nunnally said. When he suggested that Loretta Young's $175-apiece costumes be bought at Sears, to look authentically farm-girl, Nunnally (who was doing most of the producing) said, "Would you like to tell Loretta?" "Okay, okay," said Coop. "That was the last producing effort he made," Nunnally said. It fell to him to tell Cooper, the producer, that Cooper, the actor, was causing the production to be run behind because he had not memorized his lines. He said, "Do you know we're running in the red, all on account of one actor?" Coop tried to think who it was. "He's not ready with his stuff and he's having to have more takes," said Nunnally. "Who is he?" asked Cooper. "You," said Nunnally, and walked out. After that there was no more problem.

The Dark Mirror, in 1946 (directed by Robert Siodmak), was the first of three released by Universal-International, a merger which took place for the same reasons Fox took Twentieth Century. Universal needed good producers making money-making pictures, and all it meant for Nunnally was that now he was working on the Universal lot in the Valley. Olivia de Havilland plays twins (a good one and a bad one), one of whom has killed a man—but which one? Lew Ayres is a sort of all-purpose boy friend-psychologist who tries to find out. Olivia switches wonderfully back and forth between sweetness and light and well-defended psychosis which gradually peels away to reveal the soul of a murderess (when Lew Ayres shows signs of falling in love with Ruth, the good twin). Scenes with both twins were done with a "traveling matte." "I hadn't the faintest idea what a traveling matte was," Nunnally said. "I still to this day don't, but I always suggest it if some problem like this comes up."

Olivia set about playing a crazy lady with seriousness. Nunnally was gone during most of the production. "Most of the time he spent off in Tennessee, I thought it must be the bad twin in me that had driven him off. He even kept his address secret, can

you imagine?" In fact it was Georgia, where he spent three
months with Onnie, who was dying of cancer; but Olivia, striv-
ing for a paranoid mentality, had already begun to get into the
part. "I made him kind of nervous because I took everything so
seriously," she says. "And I said, 'We can't do this movie
unless we meet with a psychiatrist, all of us, and we did . . . and
it made your father *very* nervous, but of course it paid off in the
end, it always does. May Romm [the psychiatrist] explained a lot
of things about the character of the bad twin, paranoid schizoid,
I think she said. She explained the whole personality to us, because after all I think your father had adapted the material, he
had dramatized material which was original with somebody else
so he hadn't wanted to do all that sort of thing. I wanted to do a
good job." She did a splendid job, but there is a price for playing
madness. "I didn't enjoy making *Dark Mirror* at all—too disturb-
ing. I enjoyed the idea of it . . . you enter the skin of the person,
that is a very unhappy skin, it's a whole dark world you exist in
and explore and start being inventive about . . . the only reason
I survived it was because there was Ruth [the good twin] to
play." Besides there was a little director trouble. "I found that
Siodmak would go for an effect whether it was logical or not and
he underestimated the intelligence of the audience, who if you
could get their interest would be following every single nuance
of the development of this story, and you jar them by something
being out of rhythm and illogical and imposed, you wreck the
material as a whole, you destroy your success, and that was hard
on me, I had to watch Mr. Siodmak all the time."

Years later, in 1964, Robert Aldrich sent Olivia the script of
Hush . . . Hush, Sweet Charlotte, "a Gothic anecdote." Joan
Crawford had started out in the part but had gotten ill. "When I
read *Hush . . . Hush* I thought, Oh, it's Terry [the bad twin] all
over again. I became absolutely mentally ill doing that, it's such a
dark part, I suffered a lot, a real black kind of depression when I
was playing her, I thought, I can't go through that again even
eighteen years later. I met with Bob Aldrich and explained that I
had driven Nunnally straight to Mississippi and said, 'We don't
want that happening to you.' I said, 'The character is entirely
black, like Terry,' and Aldrich said, 'I'm surprised you don't see
the ambiguity.' I said, 'Mr. Aldrich, I never change my mind,'

but I read the script again. I still didn't see it, not only was the murderess wicked but she was rude and she was going to lose the audience. The way to solve it was to make her manners impeccable—that's the way your father would have written it, keep the suspense until the last minute. The part as written had made Joan Crawford sick. Your father was very much on my mind in 1964—very much influencing a decision. I was so thrilled I had this creative idea. I think if I'd suggested it to your father he would have sneered at it."

Dark Mirror was the last of what the family refers to as Nunnally's "scissors period." In *The Moon Is Down*, Dorris stabs Peter Van Eyck with scissors; in *Woman in the Window*, Eddie Robinson does likewise with his victim, and in *Dark Mirror,* it is a pair of scissors that Terry grabs in her most demented state. ("And that's why they won't let me have any scissors," said Nunnally.)

The Senator Was Indiscreet and *Mr. Peabody and the Mermaid,* both with William Powell, were the last two Nunnally did for Universal-International before returning to Fox. *Senator* was Nunnally's only screen collaboration since the early thirties, this time with Charles MacArthur. "Charlie was a man who sparkled with ideas," Nunnally said, "but, my God, we would have been forever. He said, 'why don't we change them to rabbits?' He came in one morning and said, 'Why don't we make it a lady senator?' My God, rewrite the whole bloody thing. Like always, I wrote the final draft. That's why writers, authors and playwrights don't care much for the screenwriter." George Kaufman directed, his only directing job in Hollywood, apparently with good reason. Asked what he thought of directing movies after directing for the stage, he said, "The only problem is staying awake." Gene Fowler, Jr., Marge's husband and Kaufman's badly needed assistant, says, "He sat with his back to the actors and listened to what they said. He didn't give a damn where the camera was."

Senator was a disappointment, partly because it came out at a time "when everybody who didn't wrap the flag around himself was a Commie," Nunnally said. "The shrillest one of course was Hedda Hopper. Louella hadn't ever heard of Communism, but Hedda was saving the country, and that was just about the time they begot that Duke Wayne-Ward Bond outfit that passed on everybody." Though there was nothing new about show business clowning about the government. Will Rogers had done it, as had the Gershwin musical *Of Thee I Sing*. *Senator* was about a man who figured he had no talent doing anything else but be President of the United States, which notion seemed unpatriotic. One night Bill Goetz ran the picture at his house and Clare Luce was there. In the middle of it she stood up and said, "Don't tell me an American made this picture." Goetz tried to kid her, but she meant it, this was subversive. After she made her feelings known, *Life* contradicted its own three-page, favorable spread on the movie in a column called "On Second Thought," which said on reconsideration this movie was rather un-American. Other super-patriotic organizations condemned the picture before it was released. Nunnally had thought humor overrode everything, but *Senator* failed because of its subject matter, politics used at the wrong time and in the wrong way.

Nunnally's non-political nature was hard for late-forties Hollywood to grasp. When one potential investigator came to his office (the story goes) and asked him was he or had he ever been a member, et cetera, he leaned across the desk and hissed, "We're not allowed to tell." It was the time when the most innocent group could find itself on the list of subversive organizations, when actors couldn't get jobs for no reason that anybody would put into words, nothing that could be pinned down, just that "he isn't right for the part." (On the other hand the incompetent actors were proud of being turned down because they were Communists.) "So many outrageous things went on," Nunnally said, "that made me ashamed of the whole industry . . . think of John Huston having to go and debase himself to an oaf like Ward Bond and promise never to be a bad boy again, and Ward Bond would say, 'All right then, we clear you, but we've got our eye on you.' Some actors wouldn't do it. Harry Kurnitz, a very good writer, just left because he would not go to this Ku Klux Klan and ask them for permission to write, even though Harry was about as political as I was. Irving Pichel . . . there was a strike here, there was a fund being raised for the wives and children, and Irving, who was almost Christlike in his sympathy for the unfortunate, made a contribution of more than he could afford. Boy, no more work for him. He finally went crawling out to Duke Wayne and Ward Bond and a number of them. Gary wasn't far from it, and Jimmy Stewart, a very good friend of mine."

Mr. Peabody and the Mermaid (directed by Irving Pichel) is exactly what it sounds like, which is exactly what's wrong with it. It was too fey for Nunnally—one senses his disbelief, though it was about a man turning fifty, written when Nunnally was turning fifty. It is a trifle, though William Powell performs capably. Nunnally said to him once, "You know, Bill, I have never yet talked to an actor speaking of how he became an actor that he didn't reply in what really was a slight apology. You know the French have a saying that an actress is a little more than a woman, an actor is a little less than a man. They all say, 'Oh, I just happened to be on the set,' or 'a fellow saw me somewhere.'" Powell said, "You are now talking to a fellow who never wanted to be anything else but an actor and who said so from the time I could pronounce the word." There is one lovely exchange in *Peabody*. Peabody (Powell) is in a shop buying a sweater for his mermaid love, who he thinks might get cold. He admires one and asks the salesgirl what colors it comes in.

Salesgirl: We have green, white, puce and licorice.

Peabody: What's licorice?

Salesgirl: It's a kind of light black.

These two financial losers ended Nunnally's period of independent producing. Somehow or other "I suddenly was aware I wasn't even employed there. My company was gone or sold or bankrupt or whatever the hell it was." Who knows? Whatever it was, gnomes or little short-legged men solved it all, and he became available for other employment. L. B. Mayer invited him for lunch, trying to entice him to MGM with talk of "firmaments of stars." But Fox wanted him back, and he returned to Zanuck and picked up "as though I had never left."

In 1949 he did *Everybody Does It,* a remake of his *Wife, Husband and Friend,* with Paul Douglas, which didn't work any better the second time around than it had the first. It was directed by Edmund Goulding unnotably except that Goulding had one nicety about shooting—he would not let anybody walk "off the frame." That was Gower Street (the Hollywood street where the "potchky" studios were, Columbia and others now long gone). If somebody was leaving the room, he panned him to the door, or cut to somebody who was still there. It was graceful use of the screen, but *Everybody Does It* seems to have needed more than that. I didn't see it, though the script seemed sexist to a degree that set my teeth on edge, with funny/not funny lines like, "There's an ugly streak of music running through the women in this family like the green cracks in Roquefort cheese."

Three Came Home (directed by Jean Negulesco) is a tense and moving tale of a British woman (Claudette Colbert) in a Japanese concentration camp in Borneo. The story was true, but Agnes Newton Keith, the author of the original book, didn't like Nunnally's adaptation, which she thought too sentimental. It didn't seem that way to me. My notes say, "A gripper right from the start, who says there's more violence now?" Mrs. Keith objected to the end where husband and wife, separated for months in different prison camps, are finally united. They meet and weep, falling to the ground in a clumsy embrace. "She [Mrs. Keith] is English, I suppose she felt they should go forward and shake hands," Nunnally said. Sessue Hayakawa plays the Japanese officer in an early role.

Pop told me once that *The Gunfighter* was his favorite script, certainly the tightest. Though Bill Bowers and William Sellers have screen credit, Nunnally expanded the pages brought him by Bowers into a full-length script, which he put in the hands of Henry King, who put it in the hands of Gregory Peck. King, with a passion for authenticity, strove for a Frederic Remington effect. Greg Peck says:

"We started *Gunfighter* when Zanuck and Skouras were out of the country, dressed me up in a mustache, an old frock coat like the old photos of the West, for they didn't wear Western costumes, they wore hand-me-downs from the East. Some tucked their trousers into boots, some let them hang out, some wore civilian coats and ties with Western pants and dirty hats, so we decided I would dress like someone out of an old daguerreotype, short cereal-bowl fifteen-cent haircut. Skouras looked at film in New York and bellowed and screamed, you could hear it clear out on the Coast. 'Goddammit, this is a romantic leading man, what you try to do to my leading man? He's a-sex-appeal, you got him looking like an old man, women don't like kissing a man with hair on his face.' I loved the character, I was thirty-one and no longer the smooth-faced American kid, Henry King and I were determined not to give it up." When Zanuck saw the picture he said, "I'd give fifty thousand dollars of my own money if I could take the mustache off that guy," but King said he thought women really did like mustaches on men. Skouras, the head of Fox, wanted to shoot the first two weeks (at which point he saw the rushes) over again at a cost of a hundred and fifty thousand dollars. Greg Peck and King went to the production manager and said, "Can't you up that a little? For one-fifty he might just do it." They managed to get it up to three hundred thousand, which was enough to deter Skouras, and it was left. The picture wasn't a hit, not because of the mustache, but because it was a new sort of shoot-'em-upless Western, one which has now been put in a category with *High Noon* by the film historians. "*The Gunfighter* just played itself. On those rare occasions when you get a perfect script, it's like taking money for nothing . . . it was lean and sparse and understated. The violence was mostly held back and only broke out two or three times in the picture. The sheriff beat up the little weasel who shot me in the back, dragged him off in the barn and beat him up something terrible . . . the potential for violence was over it and it played out against the clock. That saloon was like a time bomb there, ticking away. It was really almost like a play and in fact several people suggested turning it into a play."

Jimmy Ringo, the retired gunfighter, was a first for Peck, but he turned down the lead in *High Noon* a year or so later because he thought it was too similar. He had "the mistaken notion that versatility is important . . . the public doesn't mind if you play the same role over and over if you play it with finesse and depth and insight, which is really the secret of the success of Bogart, Spencer Tracy, Cagney, Cooper, Gable, they played the same role with slight variations, the audience recognizes them as real people up there. It's a special kind of acting, not easy to do. Some of the best stage actors in the world can't accomplish this rapport with the film audience because their acting is play acting rather than behaving, they aren't able to shift gears and reveal themselves, which a good screen actor does completely. What you're seeing is what he *is*, underrated by amateur critics and ac-

ademic types who say he's just a personality . . . it requires a lot
of courage and honesty to be so revealing of oneself, and that's
what the audience reaches out and attaches itself to more than
they would to a classic stage actor of versatility, projection,
semaphore-type acting. Good screen acting is just as difficult, the
feelings must be there, you can't be deadpan . . . the audience
can't read what's behind it unless it's there. Bogart thinks his
way through a part with a very keen intelligence, the emotions
are there, the audience reads it from his eyes and subtle changes
in his face and body and finds itself living the part with you. An
agent said [about *Gunfighter*], 'You've got a prototype here in
this beleaguered, tired cynical gunfighter who would like to settle down and be normal, an appealing character, the criminal
who wants to go straight but can't. Not dumb, under different
circumstances he might have become governor of the state but
he got off on the wrong foot. He's trying to make up for it, but
it's too late.' *The Gunfighter* was a new kind of Western character, it gave me a kind of credibility and it was gratifying to get
wonderful notices. People still like it twenty-five years later."

The Mudlark (directed by Jean Negulesco) was an adaptation
of a book by Theodore Bonnet, who correctly described every
detail of the interior of Windsor Castle, without ever having seen
it. He wrote it when he was a soldier in the South Pacific, with
information from guidebooks and histories sent by his wife. The
story is about a small boy, a "mudlark," who sneaks into the castle in hopes of getting a look at the forbidding Victoria (Irene
Dunne, in a rubber mask), who has been in isolation since her
husband's death. At the discovery of the boy the Queen suspects
some sort of plot and withdraws still further; and the film
climaxes when Disraeli (Alec Guinness), who has long been trying to persuade her to go out to her people, delivers a public
reproach to his Queen in the House of Commons. The yearning
of the child is what happens when "children beg for their
mother"—will the Queen serve the living or the dead? The
speech was filmed in one long (seven- or eight-minute) approach shot, done in only one take, a breath-taking bit of filming.
At one point Guinness paused, looked left and right as though
moved to silence by his own emotions. Asked later what had
made him think of such a dramatic pause, he said, "I forgot my

lines." Both Guinness and Irene Dunne are magnificent. Guinness had wanted the part very badly—"All actors want to play Disraeli, except fat ones," Nunnally said. "It's such a showy part —half Satan, half Don Juan, man of so many talents, he could write novels, flatter a Queen, dig the Suez Canal, present her with India. You can't beat that, it's better than Wyatt Earp." Guinness complained during the filming of Negulesco's lack of direction, though most directors might well have been in awe of such a superb actor. Both the family quarters of Windsor Castle and an entire House of Commons had to be built, at great expense, because filming wasn't allowed anywhere around them. (I spent a couple of afternoons in that made-up House of Commons as well as the real one and there was simply no difference, except that one was a set. They even had the same feel.)

When the picture was released, it was selected for the Royal Command Film Performance of the year, after some struggle— the British hadn't anything to compete with it, so they tried to persuade Fox to withdraw the picture from the race. *Mudlark* might have been technically a British picture, but there were so many Americans connected with it, it just didn't look like one. "The only way I can see to beat this situation is to change my name to Noel Johnson," Pop wrote me. When the committee unanimously voted for *The Mudlark*, "many people around the lot now address me as Sir Nunnally."

Changes 1941-1947

When I was about eight or nine Pop and I went to Seattle together, just the two of us, to visit my uncle (his brother Cecil) and aunt and cousins. It was rather extraordinary to be alone with him and he called it our honeymoon. I went on a plane for the first time and so flying became part of the Western Cluster (along with light, peace, boredom, flowers, cars, sets and artifice, babies; the Eastern Cluster was dirty trains and buses, dark, disaster, noise, pain, struggle, work). I remember very little about the trip, probably because Pop didn't know what to do with me for hours on end, and I didn't know what to do with him either. Afterward he talked as though we'd had a very good time, and probably we did. But something happened to him when he was off his home turf—discomfort, impatience, irritation—and I sensed it. He was deeply, intensely rooted to that quiet perfect home that Dorris made, those even predictable days that were his prime reward. Dorris said years later, "You don't know the work that went into all that perfection." I didn't, I thought in California it grew like oranges, or like a finished film, when you were still ignorant of what had gone into making it.

He made me nervous when he turned up in New York, which he did occasionally. I was afraid he simply wasn't up to it, it would break him or send him into fits whenever he ventured away from the Plaza or 21. He stiffened in taxis on the way to the theater, darkened in the Oak Room over an imperfect steak,

spoke sharply about dirty fingernails, as though there was anything you could do about them. When he came to our house for
a drink I was as nervous as a bride, polishing table tops and
pitching all the comic books behind the sofa, even rebraiding my
hair. When he arrived I winced as the house shivered and rat-
tled, the dog covered his dark suit with golden spaniel hair, the
roar of the El drowned out his funniest remark, or my mother
did something wrong, served some dip he turned out to hate or
said something awkward in her nervousness.

Once he came to the house on Center Island, for reasons I can
only begin to guess. He stayed in the guest cottage, which was
either frigid or hot as an oven, depending on the season, and
which had no toilet, you either walked fifty yards up to the
house or went out in the asparagus bed to pee. In the morning
he appeared, gray-faced but still good-humored. He was holding
what appeared to be an old cleaning rag. "I unfolded the towel
and it fell apart in four pieces," he said. I don't believe he had
ever had such an experience before, our lives were such that
towels were sometimes in four pieces and things often fell apart
in your hands. My mother laughed, and it seemed incredible that
they had been able to live together for five minutes. She had a
startling tolerance for chaos and almost no embarrassment
(though I had enough for three people), which was the natural
complement to my father's discomfort. It was almost impossible
to faze her, which must have been intolerable for a man who expected women to rush around and create perfection (which even
I tried to do in a clumsy way); nor did she have any visible
guilt, which must have been hard on somebody who got such
pleasure out of consoling the people he loved. If she burned the
eggs, never did she flinch, she served them up as *oeufs au beurre
noir*. If a chair broke when somebody sat in it she said that was
the risk with antiques, if the electricity went out she said we all
looked better by candlelight. When I refused to shave under my
arms she said in other cultures underarm hair was a sign of great
beauty. So where were you, anyway? Pop didn't stay long, he
beat it back to the Plaza, or to Beverly Hills, or wherever he had
come from, and I felt the two terrible pulls of relief and abandonment, left in this East that I was now part of.

Late in the war we crossed the country together, Pop and I

and Nippy the dog. (It might have been the summer after
Nana's leg was amputated, when they sent her back to Chicago.)
I was terribly excited, Pop and I were going to be together for
days and days, for the only space we could get was on a Union
Pacific train whose route brushed the Mexican border. "Just
Nora and I and a hundred and fifty cans of dog food," Pop said.
I stuffed them all under the lower berth in our compartment,
where they periodically rolled out and Pop tripped over them.
One day out of Los Angeles the air conditioning, a generic term,
broke down and the temperature inside the train went up to
about 120. The dog panted, black tears streaming down her
golden cheeks, we panted, the cans of dog food rolled, the air
grew rich with all of our smells. The hours crept painfully by.
"Oh, good God," Pop barked periodically, "Oh, for God's sake."
At least it was nobody's fault, we weren't in New York, I didn't
feel guilty. We could blame Hitler, couldn't we—but Pop
blamed the dog and spent longer and longer periods in the
lounge while I agonized over whether or not to put the dog in
the baggage compartment to bring back Pop, though it might
have been too late anyway, the whole place was covered with
dog hair, half-eaten dog biscuits, little spilled cups of hairy water
and one or two of what we called "Nippy's accidents." On the
third day out of L.A. (somewhere in Texas) the train limped to
a stop in the middle of the desert, while I sat and worried about
death and vultures. When it started up again, an hour later, Pop
appeared in the doorway and said:

"The cook just took off across the desert."

I giggled. "Is he going to come back?"

"Not if he has any sense."

"But now what are we going to do?"

"Well, we could open some of the cans of dog food. Or we
could go with the cook." He looked tempted. "He went to Mexico."

"Where's that?"

"Right out that window."

We looked out. It was tempting, we could find some cool patio
with a tinkling fountain and stay there forever, eating tacos and
listening to mariachis. (But what would we talk about?) I could
have wept, it was all turning out so badly—and it had started so

well, that festive first night in the dining car, Pop in his Knize Ten and me in a clean Wright & Ditson shirt, ordering a Horse's Neck. Now it was hard to say which of us smelled worse, the water having run short too, and though I was used to being dirty he suffered from not being clean, and I suffered because he did.

"Someday we'll go to Paris," Pop said. "We'll go to Maxim's and the Tour d'Argent."

For the rest of the trip we ate Spam and canned vegetables, dished out by the exhausted sweaty porters, and Pop sank into a depression so profound I began to wish one of us had gone off with the cook. I made periodic hysterical efforts to get him to speak, smile, or do anything except stare gloomily into space. I asked him questions he couldn't refuse to answer and tried to entrance him with riddles and word games. I pretended it was all fun (just as my mother would have done) until it was obvious he was making a tremendous effort not to tell me to shut up and get lost, at which time I left him in the smoker and retired back to the compartment and what I called the dog-doo. I had learned about simply giving up, about leaving somebody alone. There were times when you couldn't do a damn thing.

When finally we got to Chicago we spent hours washing and cleaning up at a hotel, and then we went to the Pump Room for dinner, wearing our best clothes. We were elegantly served by waiters and little black boys in turbans and silken knickers, and I ordered an entire meal of flaming food, which delighted Pop, who taught me a new word—pyromaniac. Now he was in splendid spirits, the whole dreadful train trip was a joke. "Halfway across," he told people later, "it was so hot the cook took off across the desert." I began to laugh when he told about it, and for years I forgot how terrible it was. There were times when I felt very funny about his jokes, they complicated everything so, half the time I didn't know whether I was supposed to laugh or not. I accepted the complexity of humor only when I was old enough to have some notion of what I was, around fourteen or fifteen, when there were firm enough things for jokes to bounce off. Before that they simply got lost, sank in and disappeared without meaning like arrows into a cloud.

The curious pains and ambivalences of his world were hard to see in the bright sunlight. In 1941 he had made *The Pied Piper,* with Roddy McDowall, a young English boy who had been evacuated from England during the war and then went on to stagger ten- to twelve-year-old America in 1943 with *My Friend Flicka* and *Lassie Come Home*. Roddy wore his fame gracefully. His fondness for Mr. Johnson was such that he could be induced to take me riding with him and his sister and his mother, who drove us back and forth to the stable on Beverly Glen (now gone, the proprietress murdered, the horses dead, all cleaned out and covered with the green turf of somebody's front lawn). Mrs. McDowall, a hefty British lady, would wait at the stable while the three of us went out on the trail. We rode in the mountains of Bel Air, very wild at that time, narrow dry trails where yuccas grew and great sheets of rock rose high behind us, the air hot and heavy with the smell of wild fennel, the horses stumbling and tripping over rocks, even snakes occasionally darting out and slithering through the dust. At some high point we looked down on UCLA like a little pink city below us.

Afterward we got into the car with Mrs. McDowall (Roddy was about fourteen then and his sister a year older, and if they were bored with having a ten-year-old along they were too polite to say so) and went to the studio to pick up Roddy's bags of fan mail, which we all helped carry to the car. Then we drove to their rather modest house, not in Beverly Hills but in some less fashionable district. Then we took the bags and boxes inside and drank ginger ale while Roddy opened them. The house was rather small and dark, the shades usually being drawn, and we all sat around the dining-room table, our ripe stable odors filling the room, while Roddy read letters from people who told him how much they loved and admired him and opened meticulously handmade gifts. The whole house, in fact, was largely furnished with gifts—on the sideboard was a Yankee clipper ship made entirely of toothpicks, on the wall hung art works of various sorts and degrees of talent, on bureaus and over backs of chairs lay pieces of needlepoint; I had the feeling that if all these things were removed there wouldn't be much left in the house, only a few pieces of brown furniture.

It seems now that the McDowalls regarded all this with a sort of awe—that they had determined not to let all this change their lives, but the sheer quantity of it, the numbers of strangers who were moved to spend hours or days of their time weaving or making ceramics or doing charcoal likenesses or writing poetry to Roddy, a little boy they had seen in a movie, was a phenomenon they had no idea how to respond to. If it was serious it couldn't be respected, if it was ridiculous it couldn't be laughed at, but its abundance demanded something—what nobody knew. Whatever it was, it was overwhelming, and the McDowalls with their sensible brown furniture seemed in danger of being buried under thousands of torn-open envelopes and toothpick clipper ships.

We sat there for a long time opening mail and boxes, which I got bored with very quickly, but the McDowalls of course didn't, or else didn't feel they could without being impolite or ungrateful to a hundred unknown people (as I couldn't leave without being impolite or ungrateful to the McDowalls). Perhaps they were simply hooked, as most people would have been, as I certainly would have been.

The summer days were slow and lazy, the heat almost like a brace that held your body in one position. Dragonflies flashed and hovered over the pool, at night the air smelled of jasmine, which was one of the things I missed in the East without knowing what it was. Christie, at two, had a pet duck that followed her around. She had crossed its path at the right moment, it was explained to me, and the duck thought she was its mother. Pop and Dorris had a butler, Ludwig, who turned out to be a Nazi spy, and a Doberman pinscher so crazy it leaped off a ten-foot wall that dropped down to the driveway. The wall had replaced a steep slope and the empty area was filled in with sod and covered with lawn that came in rolls like a carpet. Years later you could still see the seams where the rolls met. Someone had given them the dog, possibly the saturnine Jed Harris, that was the sort of gift he gave. He was Christie's godfather and he had given her a tree with a silver tag on it saying, "Christie's tree." Nobody really cared about the dog, whose name was Heidi. The dog had been some sort of joke, but now it shivered and ran around the yard in circles and cried like a child, then sailed off the wall and broke its legs.

Sex was starting to appear everywhere, more than in New

York (women in hot climates develop faster, my mother explained). The boy next door left a note in the secret passage through the hedge: "I know you love Roddy McDoll but I love you anyway." I rode slowly up the canyon on my bicycle waiting to be whistled at by a boy up above in a tennis court. Every day he was there, every day he whistled through the mesh fence high above my head. When it got too steep I walked until I was up above the houses, on a dusty, rocky cliff high over the city. I sat in the shade of a scrubby tree looking down on Hollywood, a handful of glitter down in the flats. When the bugs got too bad, or I got too nervous about snakes, I got back on the bike and coasted down and the boy whistled from his tennis court again.

As New York children went to the country, Los Angeles children went up to the lake. My friend Patty, the one who had bitten me, had become a water-ski champion and took me along to her family's cabin at Lake Elsinore. They were a muscular, rowdy, cheerful bunch, stamping about the little wooden cabin in bathing suits, slinging wet towels at each other, endlessly opening bottles of beer and Coke and pouring them into paper cups. Meals were casual, somebody would boil up a pot of hot dogs and put it on the table with a package of rolls, and everybody grabbed, occasionally spilling mustard on one another. The business of maintaining a home—to Dorris a way of life—never seemed to have entered the head of Patty's mother, the house sort of ran itself anyway, you kicked the shoes aside and found the driest towel and stuck a piece of Wonder bread in the toaster for breakfast.

At twelve, Patty had a gang, they water-skied all day—consoling me and then immediately forgetting about me after I fell off for the third time—and at night they put on white pants and clean shirts and came over to dance on the patio and drink more Cokes while I feigned headaches, stomachaches, muscle cramps, anything to escape to my room. Patty would creep in in the middle of the night. "They all think I'm fifteen, don't you dare tell Biff (or Buck or Chuck) how old I really am. Gee, you missed all the fun," adjusting her bra, which was half off. "Biff and I were making out in the car. Which one did you think was the cutest?" We had once shared every secret—between bites—now it turned out we were from different cultures. Cuteness was beyond me, so was wanting to be fifteen—I had enough trouble handling being twelve. She had made some terrible leap it would take me years to make, but then she had dimples, too.

When I was in the East the home in California became almost more real than it was when I was there, warmer and noisier and smaller, with fewer cool distances and impenetrable silences. (It remained an anchor as my mother sold the little house in Center Island and bought another, and then sold that and bought another, and then sold that and bought a fourth, so that by the end of the way I knew none of them had been homes anyway, only investments.) I took its image along to Brearley when I went there, and tried to use it to make an impression, which failed— only the brownstone counted. The house on Beverly Glen was for my mind's eye only.

Also fixed in my mind like a tiny, obscure pain was Nana, who had been sent back to Chicago with her artificial leg. I had been horrified when they cut it off (which I heard about in New York by picking up another phone extension) but hardly less horrified than I had been watching that leg become infected and then green and black with gangrene, which was picked off in bits by a woman doctor who conducted her treatment (while Nana screamed in pain) on the top floor of the brownstone, while I crept down to the back porch and tried not to hear. I could hardly go upstairs later, the whole place smelled of sweet dead flesh and Nana's poor eyes were wide and glazed with the fear of death that had come upon her so suddenly that summer on Center Island when everything went wrong; the gods were after one of us then, and Nana had been picked. She wanted me to save her, I was all she had, but I could hardly save myself, and I was furious as children are when strengths are demanded that they don't have. After Nana was gone (crying, she didn't want to go back to those gloomy sisters) I spent a great deal of energy— more than I or anybody else was aware of—trying to forget she existed, which I managed to do most of the time, but the huge gap where she had once been was like a break in a wall, now the invading armies could enter. Worse, the apparent insanity of the adult world was harder to take than it had been a few years before when it was a safer distance away; it bothered me more to

be scolded for never writing to Nana, for being told I was ungrateful after all she had done for me, for not wanting to see her,
concepts of obligation and gratitude which became meaningless
compared to my fearsome feelings. I could no longer sigh and
shrug off their interpretations, now I began to feel I was dreadfully wrong.

After the war the Johnsons moved from Beverly Glen to
Mountain Drive, north of Sunset. That last summer before they
left, Dorris, who was pregnant with Roxie, fainted in a taxi (I
am at a loss to say what we were doing in a taxi) when I was
with her, and had to be carried into the house by Jane Reilly,
while I followed in terror, never having seen anyone faint before,
and having some notion Dorris would never revive. It was explained to me later that Dorris did faint sometimes when she
was pregnant, and that was why she felt bad so much and was so
sick to her stomach. They were very matter-of-fact about the
dreadful bondage of the body, which in my mind was tied up
with this doubtful pleasure of being a woman—something that in
truth no woman seemed to look very pleased about, except
possibly my mother.

Nana came for a visit at the new house with her artificial leg,
which I watched her take off at night in the other bed of our
shared room. The stump, which rose up at an angle, was silhou-
etted in the moonlight that came through the window; I couldn't
take my eyes off it, nor could I sleep, though Nana did. When
she left after a few days' stay it was as though my head was
released from a clamp. In letters written to Pop at the time I said
that I looked forward to her visit, wouldn't it be fun to see Nana
(just as when I was younger I had written endlessly about doll
tea parties and how cute the dog looked with a bow on her neck,
femininity and cheer being encouraged by my mother). Those
letters are by some Goody Two-shoes child I hardly know, I had
not yet learned you didn't have to be polite on paper. A year or
so later, when I went away to school, I began writing things to
ease the pain rather than the comic dialogue (illustrated) I had
done for years to amuse myself.

The new house had a driveway which looped around a
planted island, a fenced pool, a rose garden, chickens (in case
the Japs stole our eggs) which cackled around on the Hollywood

lawn and the elegant patio, and a cool green living room with a shaggy rug, a marble fireplace, curved sofas, a section of bookcase (with false-front books) which swung out to reveal a movie projector, and doorknobs plated with—and chair upholstery threaded with—pure gold.

There was an elegant dining room with black and white mural wallpaper being slowly, meticulously painted by a butler named Alex. Every day he colored a few more verdant fields and towering elms and another bit of wilderness sky. Upstairs was Dorris' pink and gold and green bedroom, and several other bedrooms variously occupied at different periods. Part of it was nursery territory where Jane did her best to barricade herself and the children against outside influences. The rest of us had various styles of intrusion through this wall of Jane's mind. I came and went rather freely, since I was neither adult nor child; if she objected to me she didn't show it. Dorris braced herself before entering (while Jane festered and muttered against Mother, the real threat), her jaw set, her speech slowed and hardened. Pop didn't know there was a wall, he walked in and sent everyone into frenzies of joy.

Having begged to be allowed to bring something with me to California (my dog, a girl friend) and been refused—I wanted to fill Nana's place, I suppose, or else to buffer myself from real or fancied rejection from a family I didn't feel part of—I went off one day with my friend Avery to buy a dog. The whole excursion was rather bizarre—nobody ever took a taxi anywhere, which we did, nor did anyone ever go to downtown L.A. except for some dire emergency. Of course nobody had given us permission to do this, and we sat in the hot, butt-strewn taxi for an hour, which was how long it took in those days before freeways, had the driver wait while we went to the pound and Avery bought a cat (fifty cents) and I bought George (two dollars). Then we rode back home with our pets and waited to see what would happen. That evening after dinner George began to howl from the garage where he was tied up.

"What the hell's that?" asked Pop.

"It must be coyotes," I said.

"That isn't any coyote, I'm going down to see."

"Pop," I moaned, "it's George, please don't be mad, I got him at the pound, I love him, and Avery got a cat."

"Oh, God."

"Please," I said, "please, may I keep him?"

After some discussion it was decided that George could stay. He was the next natural force, after the chickens, to threaten the lawn; the war was over, we were back to normal things. George was black and mangy, forever scratching his stomach with his hind foot. Unlike almost everyone else in my life, he lacked charm completely. A few years ago I would have loved him for this but I no longer could, now I had changed. Now Christie loved him. I was touched that Pop and Dorris had let him stay, that they accepted his tackiness, the commonness of his nature. Kids were tacky, they liked dirt and mangy dogs and garden slugs and dead bugs, they didn't understand quality. Later that fall George was hit by a car during a period when some painters were working around the house. Before anyone had worked up the nerve to tell Christie, a new white dog wandered up the driveway. "Look," Christie said, "the painters painted George white."

The forces of growing up were experienced differently in New York and California. Painful daily encounters with strange new selves, obsessive measuring against other people, the specific miseries of wearing glasses and being ignored at dances, of suddenly finding that success called for an entirely strange group of skills seemingly impossible to acquire, the whole exhausting conglomerate, all this had a becalmed quality in California. In New York I lived the battle, fought it, withdrew from it to hover on the edge and study it before another attack, hated it, dreamed of it and longed to win it; in Beverly Hills I forgot there was a battle or, if I remembered, I didn't know what it was about.

It was nice; it was peaceful. Misery was muted, atomized in the sunlight. Avery and I had floated through many summers together on a layer of fantasy thick as her fat or my spectacles, sitting in the Beverly watching *Gilda* or *Now, Voyager* over and over again, fueling the long journey home with a pint or so of peach ice cream from Will Wright's. Back at her house on Roxbury or mine wherever-it-was, we would spend hours drawing pictures of ourselves done up in Adrian gowns and Rita Hayworth hairdos, reshaped with perfect legs and vast breasts, and mapping production numbers of ourselves dancing at the head of a long line of men in tuxedos. We painfully longed for—something; not sex, which frightened us, or even the kind of lives we fantasied, which we knew we would never be able to manage. I imagine it was power, of which we had none, or else being necessary for something to somebody.

We were so afunctional, Avery and I, so expendable. Avery's father was a writer and producer who had gone to the top very fast and was going down even faster, a descent which caused him to rage at everybody around him, particularly Avery. Why? Because she wasn't perfect. (Her little brother wasn't either, but he was a boy and didn't have to be.) The more he told her how awful she was (which he did, frequently and explicitly) the more she made for the refrigerator and the fatter she got. Why were all those goodies in the fridge at all? Because her mother, Eleanor, had been brought up in Grosse Point where you had to have silk blanket covers and a well-stocked icebox or else God would get you. However, when her father wasn't home it was a lot more fun at Avery's. They all wandered around unceremoniously in the nude, for one thing, which nobody would have been caught dead doing at the Johnsons', and it was smaller and messier and nicer, and I liked Eleanor because she was so funny (which treachery of course I never told Avery).

I was expendable because Dorris didn't know what to do with me, though the truth was she didn't know what to do with a lot of other things either—the enormous house she lived in, the servants (particularly Jane), the children, the cars, the shopping, the closets of clothes and shoes, the high-powered dinner parties, the whole frustration of trying to be something she didn't think she could be. I didn't know all this at the time, and didn't understand why she always seemed so harassed—didn't she have everything? And wasn't she doing everything perfectly? Around ten or eleven Dorris would emerge from the house to where Avery and I lay like two sponges by the pool, Avery in some bag from the Chubby department and me in my faded Sub-Deb. With her pink linen dress and golden hair, she made both of us feel larger and worse than ever, like a couple of sea monsters washed up on some perfect jewellike beach. She would talk about domestic frustrations—a car that wouldn't start, a cook who wouldn't cook, a child's earache that wasn't responding to treatment. We were both uncomprehending and sympathetic— we thought creating perfection was easy and we found Dorris' anxiety puzzling and sad. If Dorris wasn't happy, could anybody be?

Dorris orchestrated parties, two kinds in glaring contrast: the ones with Olivia or Bogey and Betty or Coop, and the ones with a handful of woebegone adolescent boys rounded up for Avery and me. She did them both equally well, with an enthusiasm that made Avery and me believe, every time, that life might touch fantasy. Of course it never did. At our parties, the stage set overwhelmed the players. None of us, thirteen and bumbling, could muster up the sort of personal style that seemed to be demanded by moonlight swims or dinner served by the butler in white gloves, during which self-conscious silences were punctuated by loud burps from the boys or crosseyed faces behind the butler's back and storms of giggles. It was all too grand for us, particularly since most of the other children were, for some reason, non-movie children, or else movie children whose parents were not at the top. Since my father was, I should be some sort of example of something, though all I wanted was for somebody to be an example for me. When we chose my house for the parties, for its elegance, I had thought it would make me less vulnerable than Avery, who often ended up weeping in the bathhouse when faced with appearing in her vast bathing suit; on the contrary I was more so, when they giggled at the butler serving the hot dogs it was me they were laughing at, when they crept around the elegant living room in silence it was some fearsome quality of mine that held them speechless. When Frank, whose father was a Communist, stroked the telltale doorknobs and breathed in horror, "Holy moley, *gold*," I knew what agony was. If I'd been more brash, I would have ducked it and told them my real home was New York, where I lived in a miserable old dump. But I couldn't do that. I had to claim it, all of it, every gold thread in the upholstery was part of me too. You had to take responsibility for your parents, disassociating yourself from them and their ways was worse, then you had nothing. Whether you liked it or not you sprang from them.

Avery and I were, like everybody around us, fixated on physical beauty. Dorris' other parties, the real ones, were festivals of dazzling women and homely men, or so it seems now—for some reason I have strained out the actors. The men, who didn't look like much, were producers and all named things like Goetz and Spitz and Mankiewicz; they gathered near the bar and talked business with Pop, whom they treated with a certain deference, a certain expectancy—it was he who was going to put whatever-it-was into words. The women, in ravishing evening dress and perfect silken hair, gathered in the center of the room and talked rather like Dorris; the Nanny had quit, the dressmaker had lost her touch, the Japanese gardener had gone mad.

There were not many of these parties—Pop and Dorris led a relatively quiet life—and they have all run together, a frieze through which I wandered while trying to be—and I think succeeding fairly well—invisible. On one occasion Judy Garland suddenly appeared, wearing black and diabolically drunk, in the nursery, causing Jane, me and the children to reel back from the force of such a personality magnified and distorted from the booze. At another time a beautiful actress wept unaccountably in the powder room, thinking she was alone; at yet another, Ginger Rogers swept in as stars do, sending out confidence like radiation, embracing Pop as Dorris—what?—tightened, possibly, gave a tiny gasp, made an extra little effort at control? I may be imagining it, their world was closed to me, I was utterly unable to comprehend such confidence, such size. This was no longer home, New York had become home. Though I had to claim this place as mine, it was too much for me in its constant example of what I never could be, I simply tuned most of it out. It was a race I was getting ready to drop out of and had never been much in anyway—Pop was too hard to get at, there were too many other people in the way. I exasperated Avery because I no longer cared what Ginger had worn, whereas she could report on every inch of Jennifer Jones after seeing her on an RKO set, and how Eleanor had asked Rita Hayworth to leave her dinner party. The idleness and frustration seemed endless; Avery and I began to have dreadful fights, beating on each other with coat hangers, out of sheer boredom with each other, for there was so little else in our lives—and I was sick of fantasy, of hanging around movie sets, of being a spectator, fed to death with all of it. The juices were starting, an insane restlessness was setting in.

To amuse me, Marge took me flying, a sport she had taken up with her new husband, Gene. They put me in the back seat of a tandem stunt plane, strapped me in and put goggles on me, then Marge waved good-by and we took off. There was an earphone arrangement through which the pilot (Gene) could talk to me but I couldn't reply (an arrangement, Pop said later, intolerable for any daughter of his) and through which he would occasionally announce what he was about to do—snap roll, barrel roll, or upside-down glide—as I shook my head wildly, to which he would merely grin. Again and again the landscape whirled around, again and again I stared death in the face while Gene got his jollies from jumping the plane around in the air. After I was delivered home and they had left, I staggered into the bathroom and vomited. Later I told Pop about it and would like to think he scolded Marge, but there was nothing surprising about what she had done, there never had been. The rage was all too clear, but in my case it remained aborted, choked down under a fantasia of supposedly delightful babies, a pale and wan Dorris (don't bother Dorris, she isn't feeling well) and an adored father whose life was taken up with everything but me, and whom I wasn't supposed to get mad at anyway. Besides, anger wasn't nice, it wasn't charming, you swallowed it and endured, you pretended it didn't exist.

One afternoon in the summer of '47, in the green and gold living room, I picked up an extension of the phone (did I learn nothing directly?) and heard that Nana, finally, was dead in Chicago. She had had a stroke that morning in the brown bedroom, half her face had collapsed, and she died later in the hospital. That day I was finally cut loose, thrown out the door; after that there was no more rescue. The pain was dreadful, and I could no longer cry or scream because it was ugly, it cracked the surface too badly, and I sensed that it would threaten all the rest of them, make them feel they'd done something wrong—and now I had to deal directly with them, there was no other appeal. They were all I had left, and if I mishandled them I might lose them too. I grieved, but not enough. Later Pop told me my mother had said, on the phone, that she was surprised I still cared anything about old Mae.

Abbot Academy 1947-1950

That fall I went away to Abbot Academy in Andover, Massachusetts, a very strict, straight girls' school of a sort that doesn't
exist any more—rules like that have been laughed out of existence. We were expected to work hard, behave like ladies and
lead Christian lives. Church and chapel were compulsory, along
with stockings, oxfords, vigorous athletics and the development
of a working conscience. Character counted—honesty, loyalty,
integrity, co-operation, charity, consideration for the feelings of
others. Looks didn't count, dress was strictly secondary, and as
for fantasy, there just wasn't much of it around. I had never been
in such an atmosphere before and I simply didn't know what to
make of it. At Brearley it had been simple—if you were an Out
you were treated like one. Here all the Ins were of rather a missionary turn of mind and spent a lot of time trying to make the
Outs feel In, which clouded the caste distinctions. Boys were allowed in once a week for an hour and a half of closely
chaperoned dancing in the recreation room, before which the
housemother went around checking our necklines, which could
not be lower than an inch below the collarbone.

Most of the girls came from nearby and were equipped with
the dun-colored dresses and sensible shoes that went so well
with bricks and autumn leaves, but my roommate, a high-
spirited English girl who lived in Mexico City, was indignant
about Abbot's obvious social limitations—she and Mummy had

thought it was a sort of finishing school, a place where she could find a husband, learn to pour tea, deal with the servants and that sort of thing. This was absurd, she wasn't even supposed to look pretty (no lipstick during the week). I pretended to agree with her, though Shirley was on a more rarefied plane than the rest of us, she had already received two proposals of marriage and was considering accepting one of them. But secretly I loved being told what to do every minute of the day, loved the New England sense of the past, and loved being counted for how I used my head rather than how I looked in the mirror. Not that I used it much at first, my lungs were too full of Christian air and my stomach too knotted by the haunting presence of boys, for Phillips Andover was just down the street like a forbidden window display. After the initial novelty wore off and the cold set in, Shirley and I spent a lot of time mourning our imprisonment and devising ways to escape. She really wanted to leave, and eventually did, but all I wanted was to keep things stirred up. If I settled down and accepted Abbot, Shirley would lose, the Establishment would win and I would be vulnerable in some unpredictable way. In the early spring Shirley and I decided to put on an original musical comedy, which we would toss off after classes. Miss Hearsey, the principal, wisely neither laughed at us nor expressed skepticism, but encouraged us to go ahead. I was to write, produce and direct (if Pop could do it, so could I) and Shirley was to star, organize the costumes and generally boss everybody around—we would bring light and art to this dark corner of the world. Pop wrote:

"[The plan for the show] delighted me very much. Don't try to make it too ambitious. A simple act done well is about fifty times as good as an elaborate one done poorly. Don't ask too much of your cast, keep them well within the range of their talents . . . a lot of group singing is always effective . . . save your best stuff for just before the final curtain . . . don't be bothered particularly about the originality of the plot of your show. Just adapt any situation you think you can stage and never mind about its source."

The project was very ambitious. I wrote the book, shaky plot line and all, and other friends wrote original music and lyrics. It really wasn't bad. In retrospect I am staggered at what we

12. *Nora, Nunnally and Marion on board ship*

13. *Nunnally in Hollywood in the early days, still looking like a New York newspaperman*

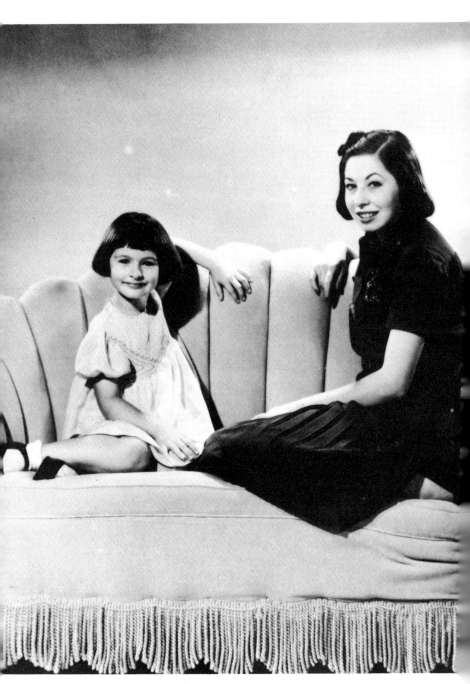

14. *Nora and Marge*

15. Nora, Nunnally and Marge in California, circa 1938

16. *Boulder Dam, 1938: Nana,*
Nora and Harold en route
back East

17. *Nana, Nora and Nunnally*
on the roof of the Empire
State Building

18. *Nunnally and Nora*
on a visit to Cecil in
Seattle, around 1941

19. *In the study of the Beverly Glen house (bound film scripts by Nunnally's elbow)*

20. *Dorris and Nunnally in the early forties*

21. Dorris, Nora, Christie, Nunnally, Scott at Mountain Drive, 1948

22. *Nunnally and Nora o a movie set, around 1950*

23. *Lauren Bacall, Johnr Mercer, Dorris*

pulled off—costumes, props, rehearsals, even a couple of production numbers, and hardly anybody forgot her lines. It was a backstage romance peopled with every imaginable stock character—a dumb but handsome hero, a wisecracking but warmhearted second lead, a vapid but sweet heroine, a beaded and babbling mother-in-law, and a crusty but lovable director. I suppose it was original in that never had so many secondhand ideas been put together in one show. We thought it sparkled with wit and originality, which in fact was a thick layer of show-biz jargon picked up from movie magazines and eavesdropping in powder rooms.

It supplied, for one evening, the quality so notably absent at Abbot—glamor; or it did until afterward, when everybody cuddled around Miss Hearsey's feet and begged her to read from *Winnie-the-Pooh*. It was exactly this sort of thing that made Abbot occasionally exasperating—when its nice solid coziness turned to infantile regression. Then I felt as though I were trapped in some awful playpen.

Pop came for a visit at least once a year for the three years I was at Abbot, visits both wonderful and terrible. We were unused to being alone together and conversation was strained; besides I still felt nervously responsible for him whenever he was off his home ground, and the Andover Inn had a way of putting him in a basement room full of pipes. There wasn't much to do, marching around in the snow or sitting in the Victorian reception room with Miss Hearsey. A sense of the dullness and worthlessness of my own life was so oppressive when I was with him (and I was guiltily convinced that it came from me, not him) that I half dreaded seeing him. It would have been easier really if he hadn't been so nice, if he'd been a cigar-chewing immigrant producer (Skouras or Harry Cohn) so I could go into simple, normal rebellion; but he was far too likable. He even jumped the walls of his golden ghetto to fit into my little hair-shirt world for a weekend, and everybody thought he was great—including Miss Hearsey, a good sturdy soul with a hair net, who carried on an intermittent correspondence with him for years. In retrospect it must have been just as difficult for him (now I have marched in the snow with tongue-tied children) trying to get through our wall of mutual bafflement, trying to draw parallels between our disparate lives—for my life at fifteen was light-years from what his had been in Columbus (where you only put on shoes to go uptown) and, God knows, what went on in my head must have been different. Except for a certain kind of pain and fear, and a certain way of handling it.

The following year, when he came, it was to see me play Ellen in *The Male Animal* at Brooks, a nearby boys' school. This plum had dropped into my lap for some reason known only to Miss Hearsey but which, I suspect, had to do with using up excess energy and providing me with a little glamor—or to make up for *Winnie-the-Pooh,* for Miss Hearsey was very astute. I had never thought of acting until it happened and being on a stage was galvanizing—as it almost never fails to be with sixteen-year-olds —as was falling in love with the two male leads. Besides, I lost my voice in the middle of the third act and had to carry on in a throaty whisper. Afterward Pop wrote:

"I couldn't have been more pleased with the play. I saw Elliott Nugent, who wrote it with Jim Thurber, and told him about it yesterday. His eyes lighted up at the report of the success you and the company enjoyed. He told me that your part was played in the original production by a woman named Ruth Matteson, whom I had in *Park Avenue* [a 1946 musical for which he wrote the book]. Gene Tierney played your sister."

Part of this success, as far as Abbot was concerned, was that I was "well rounded"—like "a sense of proportion," a favorite term in those days, meaning not getting too interested in any one thing or, if you do, you must pay by doing something you hate. You can be in a play as long as you pass biology. You can write poetry but you have to take math. You can enjoy the company of young men but you can't screw. Maturity was learning to adjust your dreams to your certain fate (wife and motherhood) without actually giving them up—you might need them when you had nothing else, insurance against despair or madness.

That spring I began to write stories. I had written little comic essays and stories since I was ten or eleven, which everybody thought were cute, but this was the first serious effort. The first one was about Nana and I wrote it partly because the pain of her death had now, two years later, been transformed into something that could be put into words and also because I was giving off sparks during that period, I had to try everything, I was still a little drunk over my own ability to be effective. I sent it to Pop and he wrote:

"Your story is first-rate. It is understanding and eloquently told . . . don't be concerned about the autobiographical character of what you write. All writers are autobiographical at some time or another throughout their lives. Some of them never do anything else. Scott Fitzgerald never wrote about anything else but himself and his wife and his child . . . the biggest mistake young writers make is to try to detach themselves from what they are writing, and write reflections of other writing or of the movies or the radio. The truest thing you can do is to try and figure out what your emotions would be . . . my guess is that Conrad is a little cloudy for the guidance of a writer at your stage. Maugham is the person to read about writing. He tells about the three kinds of writers (a) the one who writes in the first person and tells only what he has observed with his own eyes and offers you only his own reflections, (b) the writer who writes in the third person but puts himself into the mind of one of the characters, generally the principal character, and speculates through that one intelligence, and (c) the omniscient writer who puts himself into the mind of each character and tells you what they all think about what's going on. Maugham's favorite way of telling a story is the first person as an observer, but occasionally he uses the second . . . all three are recognized patterns and the writer can make his choice according to his material.

"The reason I don't recommend newspaper work very strongly for a girl is that she's not often given a very fair shake in the city room. Only infrequently does she get a good hard-hitting assignment . . . mostly she's on nonsense. Generally the most she learns in the way of actual writing is facility, and you already have facility. Being able to write is of great value for human expression, one of the greatest needs that a person has, regardless of his or her other vocation. Keep at it. Write what interests you. Just for the fun of it, you might do a story first in the first person and then do it again in the third, which would make it recognized as fiction. And don't wince at rewriting. When Oscar Hammerstein has to rewrite *South Pacific* four complete times, to say nothing of the dozen times he rewrote individual scenes, you can see how hopeless it is to try to get away with the first draft. All writers rewrite. Except Maugham. He told Moss Hart once that he just sat down at nine o'clock in the morning and wrote steadily until 1 P.M. without ever having to rewrite or go over his stuff. Moss went out and tried to hang himself."

He wrote to my mother as often as to me, and sections of their letters were forwarded to each other. They obviously got on better divorced than they had married and I couldn't get between them, play one against the other, one of the usual prerogatives of children of divorce. Together they chorused approval and disapproval. Whatever the sources of this co-operation, it freed me from a tension that had, for most of my life, used up vast stores of energy—as though their differences were my responsibility, and if I couldn't solve them, I was supposed at least to brood about them. That pull is exhausting: it explains why children of divorce often look tense and guarded, or else sad and tired—they are endlessly engaged in some great adult project whose purpose they don't understand. My parents had, by that time, been able to close ranks, to get me out of their game. And for me, the difference between being away from them and being with them, or going back and forth between, was the difference between function and non-function (for at Brearley I had done very badly) and it was a pleasure to be able to lump them together even in their sins, without wondering who was right and who was wrong.

"Marion dear, I read Nora's stories with immense interest. She is still far from able to tell these stories perfectly, but her instinct recognized the makings of a story and she was groping in the right direction in her telling of them. I don't want her to get too analytical about her stuff, that makes for self-consciousness in writing. It might be better just to let her go ahead using her own head, her own judgment . . . her principal fault is carelessness . . . I want her stuff to look professional. I want everything she does to look professional. Amateur is a tiresome state to me; it's an apologetic word, asking indulgence, etc. To hell with that. Be a pro, or drop out. Amateur is for Junior Leaguers and the Triangle Club of Princeton. Get it over with. Leave it to the dickey-bird characters. Without pressing her, I want Nora to have her eye on professional standards, not cocktail party people. . . ."

Notes on stories:

"COMMUNISM: Apparently Nora is inclined to be calm about this problem and she is very sensible to demand a little thought before branding somebody with the epithet Communist. I just don't want her to be too calm about it.

"ON NOT DOING HOMEWORK: This composition is a very superior form of comedy. Indeed it is quite intellectual. The idea of assuming an outrageous point of view and then defending it in solemn terms is first-rate stuff.

"ENCOUNTER ON BROADWAY: This is the only story of the group which has an actual fictional construction, and both in form and in the idea, it is very sound . . . it is in legitimate fiction terms and constructed very properly, with dialogue rightly told and the clinch-point held back very skillfully until the proper time for it to come. And I like its spirit, the anger and indignation over injustice.

"FEAR: This has a good ring to it. She put herself into a young boy's mind and managed to be very persuasive about it, understanding and sympathetic . . . it is one of the superior pieces.

"THE GREAT WHITE WAY: I object to such writing as 'Before I started this, I was undecided on what to write about,' which is of no interest to the reader, but once she got into her theme she did it well enough. Her view of Broadway is not quite as penetrating as her view of individuals.

"ON SEX: This reads like an argument and I, for one, am not inclined to get into it with her. What she has to say is sensible enough, but I suggest she put it away for ten years and then read it again."

But he couldn't resist getting into the argument, for I had spoken out against the double standard. "I believe you neglected, in a sense, the one overwhelming quality in sex, which is emotion. It is an odd fact that emotion can make a monkey out of the most sensitive and intellectual rationalization ever heard of. There was never an intelligent view in the world that emotion couldn't dispose of in the first round. . . . You suggest in your essay that a wedding night of two completely inexperienced people could be genuinely tragic. I think it could be, too, with fools. But tragedy will overtake fools anyway. . . . I'll take the suggestion that this night would be completely beautiful and satisfying if the bride as well as the groom had prepared herself with preliminary adventures. Technically I suppose it would be true. But what about the groom's emotions . . . never mind his bold broadness of mind, his tolerance, his intelligence and modern views of life and love. No young man worth his salt is going to admit anything else. But at bottom he always excludes himself and the girl who is going to be his wife. She's the one he loves, she's his, all his. And his wedding night is the opening of the glories of love for him and her together. There is truly no tenderer moment in life . . . examine his emotions as he learns that the privilege of the groom is not his after all. It went to some man somewhere in the past. She is more experienced and technically the occasion would have a better grace for it. But there would be a certain emptiness, a certain despair that might also pass for tragedy. It might not be logical or intelligent or civilized, but neither are emotions. Put yourself in the bride's heart when she sees in his eyes this emptiness and despair, on this their first night, their first union, this tragic loss that he will never be able to forget, never be able to understand completely. I don't think he'd leave you. I don't think he'd stop loving you. I only think that his heart would bear a scar as long as he lived, a wound inflicted by the one he loved. Do you imagine he would be comforted by a certain added facility that night? The reverse of the situation does not exist . . . life has taught women that men do not come virginally to the bridal bed. Nor do I think for one moment that women would have it so. It is never spoken of, never mentioned, but this is the moment when the bride looks trustingly to the husband for guidance, without bothering to know how he became qualified to guide. He must be prepared or lose the respect of his bride."

God knows it seems strange now but in the fifties this was very much an issue and I swallowed what he said, every word—"on his heart would be a scar as long as he lived." Going to bed with somebody now (though I was not exactly overwhelmed with opportunities) would be actively hurtful to some other man (perhaps Nunnally) whose opinion was more important than these temporary chaps from Andover and Brooks—to one of whom I had just returned a class ring when he revealed to me he had

"behaved like an animal" with his previous girl friend. He had
been apologetic about it (he was as brainwashed as I was) and I
think I threw him over because I couldn't bear the fantasy of
him and the girl behaving like animals, which I longed to do and
couldn't. The message was simple and old-fashioned and very
much tied up with quality—nice girls don't until they're married.
At the same time I was—somehow—supposed to be professional,
which meant doing things well, except not sex, so it was clearly
to be a double life. My mother handled this one, characteristically, by keeping her mouth shut, as well she might, since
none of these considerations had ever bothered her. But when it
came to her daughter she worried about what people might
think and about horrid infections and of course pregnancy—
which meant in those days either marriage or else back-street
abortion and possible death. Sex, in a sense, meant death; to
marry someone you didn't love was a kind of death (both parents had told me that), and pregnancy could mean death, you
could be gotten by your own body. We all knew condoms didn't
work and getting a diaphragm was almost impossible—it called
for a level of competence and deception far beyond what most of
us were capable of, certainly than I was. But sex, my mother also
said, was beautiful with the man you loved, as she and Nunnally
had loved each other; and since I never knew whether I was in
love or not (how could you tell?) the message was, you can't
fuck the way we can (did, could); and since non-quality fucking
could kill you, the safest thing was not to do it at all. So the result was that for years I had a series of—well, sort of romances,
where I endlessly tried to figure out if I was in love or not, and
never went to bed with anybody, which indicated to the boys
that I was a nice girl and then they would come forth with a proposal of marriage, which they assumed I wanted, but I didn't because I was going to be a professional; which in turn made them
feel misled (understandably) and they would move on to someone more anxious to be imprisoned behind the white picket
fence. What did I want, anyway?

To find out if it was to be the theater, I worked as an appren-
tice, the summer I was sixteen, at the Cape Playhouse at Dennis.
It was a curious period. My mother, having spent some months
with her leg in traction (broken during a skiing accident), was

now hobbling about on crutches. She rented a tiny house near the theater, to which I commuted daily on a bicycle, brooding about the boy whose ring I had sent back, for I knew I had done something wrong, though I didn't know what. At the theater I slaved, like the rest of the apprentices, painting sets, running errands, cleaning up after actors, selling Cokes in the lobby during intermission. I was the youngest one there and terrified—what dash I had at Abbot turned into quaking insecurity. The other apprentices were frightening in both their experience and their confidence, and if anybody was going to get a walk-on, it wasn't going to be me. I understood that you had to start at the bottom, but the bottom in show business was terribly far down.

"What you get out of apprenticeship is what you see and hear, not what you do . . . the show itself is in the hands of actors and actresses who have been through the mill already. The theatre itself has to be operated by commercial people qualified for their various jobs . . . none of this can be entrusted to apprentices. . . . Listen to everything. Watch what they do and how to do it. Marion tells me you are alternately pleased and bored which is as normal as breathing . . . by the end of the summer you will have picked up, in addition to all those cigarette butts, a fat lot of knowledge of what goes on in the staging of a show. You will have seen the various vexing little problems, the things that make stage managers and directors irritable and ulcerous. You will have a pretty clear conception of a part of show business . . . where the percentage of boredom is less than in any other commercial activity. Most businesses are a continual and uninterrupted bore. But at least in show business you have something to look forward to, that thrilling moment when the curtain goes up the first night. Now you have a show! You have an audience and people and excitement and bright lights, and a demonstration and a justification for the niggling work that has gone on before."

He took my little whispery desire to be an actress quite seriously, and wrote my mother: "Explain to Nora I didn't base my judgment on her performance in *The Male Animal.* The fact is, no untrained voice is right. All of our voices are conditioned by a lifetime to address someone between six and twenty feet from us. That calls for about one third of our vocal capacity. An

actress has to address another actor six feet away and have it
heard clearly in a gallery two hundred feet away, and still not
shout. Tell her it's the difference between saying a word at the
top of her register and singing a note at the top of her register.
Let her try that once and see the difference . . . if she's genuine
in this effort she should by all means have this training." But I
was so ill equipped for all this, perfect voice projection and blaz-
ing first nights seemed unlikely to visit my life. Here I sat in a
hut on Cape Cod with my crippled mother, with no electricity
(there had been a hurricane), writing letters by candlelight to
somebody I had got rid of but still wanted. My arena was so narrow, compared to his, my wants and needs so common, my store
of confidence so small. The scale of his life seemed unreachable.
He wrote, for instance, of a visit, with his friends Dave Chasen
and Harold Ross (the editor of *The New Yorker*, who financed
Chasen's restaurant), to Lucius Beebe's railroad car in Virginia
City, Nevada.

"Beebe is a particularly elegant writer who was on the *Herald
Tribune* with me. He is loaded with dough, inherited, not
earned, and one of his tastes is for a private railroad car. It is
decorated in the style of the old West, a long living room with a
fireplace and comfortable chairs gathered around it, a bedroom,
a guest bedroom, a dining room, and galley, or kitchen. It is all
very 1890, old-fashioned chandeliers, red plush, etc., and this is
where he lives with another fellow and a kind of manservant
who calls himself a steward. Every time Mr. Beebe hitches his
car on a train for a trip he has to buy 22 tickets. At the moment
he is writing some kind of history of something in the West and
finds it convenient to live in this car on a siding in Nevada. I
would like to add that he always dresses for dinner . . . in the
middle of this ghost town we found a restaurant which was practically like 21. Mr. Beebe does not care who has the atom bomb
as long as he knows where there's a good restaurant . . . while
everybody else in town was eating foot-long hot dogs, we dined
on a very elaborate Swedish smorgasbord, and very expensive.

"We stayed one night in Reno, which consists of one hundred
thousand slot machines. I was told that there are only seven laws
in Nevada. One of course is against murder. One seems to be
against burning down orphanages. You are not supposed to shoot

policemen with dumdum bullets. One or two other rights of society are protected but after that every man seems to be on his own. No traffic laws, no speed laws . . . slot machines in the airport, in the railroad station, in every other store in town, in the outer offices of dentists, and in all toilets. Between the slot machines are roulette wheels and dice tables. The place is packed with women getting rid of their husbands and men getting rid of their money. Nevada has no income tax, no corporation tax, no inheritance tax, no sales tax. Its whole government is operated by a tax on gambling. When you have to pay anything your change is given to you entirely in silver, slot machine money. If you buy a pack of cigarettes and hand the fellow a ten-dollar bill you can hardly tote what you get in change. To relieve yourself of this backbreaking burden you drop it all in slot machines. It is a remarkable sight and someday we must go up there and take a good look at this Paris of the West."

Oh, promises, promises! But it was hard to be really jealous of him because he always deprecated himself. "I am going on a very high-class radio program on Sunday, the 'Invitation to Learning' program on CBS. Two other intellectuals and I will discuss Sinclair Lewis' *Babbitt*. You will be able to distinguish me by the fact that I am the only one not addressed as Doctor (the other two are college professors) and also by the fact that I won't know what I'm talking about. (This may hold true, of course, with the pedagogues.) This is a desperate attempt on the part of radio to ward off television.

"I will continue my series of lectures at our next meeting. The girls will kindly put their books away and file out quietly. If they wish to consult me later I will be in the saloon."

"How did you like Mr. [Jules] Glaenzer? I met and knew him slightly a number of years ago when he was married to a wife whose name was Kendall, but my relationship with him seemed to grow more and more distant with every meeting. I couldn't understand his coolness, since I am notoriously an attractive man, until it was called to my attention that I was addressing him as Kendall. Attractive, that is, but confused. I suppose he was no happier with this recognition than I would have been if he had hailed me as Alice or Marion or Dorris."

And how could I be angry when he was so concerned with my

love life, or so understanding about money? "I tried to follow
your account of your expenses and use of allowances, etc., but
you use what might be described as the Robert Benchley system
of reporting on finances. He used to give a Treasurer's Report, a
young man reading the annual financial statement to the committee, and while he enunciated clearly on the happier items, his
voice always fell into an unintelligible mumble on the more depressing details. Not being in a position to voice these facts, you
have found a splendid substitute in the form of garbled hand-
writing. That's the way, kid! Always confuse 'em!"

The truth was, as I cleaned out actors' dressing rooms and sold
Cokes during intermission and painted flats, it was becoming
clear that I had been, at most, only mildly stage-struck, and it
was already ebbing away. It was too hard, all of it, and I found
nothing rewarding about working till 2 A.M. the night a set had
to be struck. The other apprentices frightened me with their ag-
gression and drive, their willingness to work till they dropped, or
their daring and even seductiveness in approaching visiting stars
in hopes of making a permanent impression. The Cape Playhouse had a package show system—Basil Rathbone was there
that summer, John Lund, Ann Harding, Edward Everett Horton, the great Gertrude Lawrence (her husband, Richard Aldrich, ran the theater) and Helen Hayes in a show called *Good
Housekeeping;* in fact the first time I emerged from invisibility
was when Helen Hayes greeted me warmly because she was a
friend of Pop's. After that the apprentices became terribly
friendly, which made me even more nervous because I knew it
had nothing to do with me. At the end of the season I did get on-
stage, as part of a group singing Welsh songs in *The Corn Is
Green.* Then it all began to be fun, and I even followed that
band of traveling players to their next stop or two. Later I wrote
Pop about my new and somewhat bizarre friends.

"I want you to use your head about people. I want you to pay
attention to your instincts about them. I don't want you to be a
chump or a sucker. Don't run girlishly into all kinds of situations.
I want you to be grown up, intelligent, and give a cool look at
some of the human oddities you come up against in show business . . . the sooner you try to put some kind of measurement on
them the sooner you will be an adult in every way. The time

grows close when you will be your own responsibility. Marion and I will always be present but a little more in the background. Nor will you want to fall back on us. Have a good heart for [flaky] people but he careful they don't engulf you in their own misfortunes, which they are nearly always anxious to do. Don't be too impulsive. Take a good look at these human oddities and remember that the important thing for you is to avoid situations that may become uncomfortable and to steer clear of people who are living invitations to trouble."

Sometime that summer I asked Pop the haunting question—why he and my mother had divorced.

"There is no shameful secret why Mom divorced me . . . beyond the fact that any divorce is a matter for regret and embarrassment and sorrow. My behavior became more than she could tolerate. I drank too much and I was too given to life after dark. As I look back at it now, I don't see what else she could have done. Life with such an irresponsible, undependable, unattractive husband couldn't have been anything more than miserable. She put up with it for quite a long time but obviously it couldn't go on forever. Presently she didn't love me any more. She hated my drinking, my wandering, my inconsiderateness. And why did I behave so? I don't know. I'm not enough of a psychiatrist to explain it either to you or to myself. Perhaps I had too much money for my own good or for my own previous impecuniousness. Perhaps there was something about the kind of success I had or the movies that might account for it. I just don't know. You were quite small and we made an effort to weather it for your sake, certainly to hide our feelings from you, but that is rarely successful. The situation reached a point finally where we agreed that a divorce, bad as a divorce is, was still better than to continue in such tension."

He went on to say that they had discussed remarriage but hadn't the courage; and that they had both decided that a friendly divorce was better than a bad marriage. Presently they had both fallen in love with other people, Dorris and "a less ungovernable man," though their affection for each other remained. My mother, who had referred me to his opinion when I first brought this up, confirmed what he said. It was hard to swallow all this—hadn't she done anything wrong? Besides, the notion of my father chasing starlets (I assumed they were starlets) was a strange one. He simply didn't seem the type, and anyway, what did he see in those dumb blondes? I had been under the impression he had some respect for female intelligence—he was always dealing with my head and what went on in it, but then I seemed to be for another purpose. There were women and then there were women.

Back at Abbot that fall, I captured the lead in the senior play, a Victorian antique called *Fanny and the Servant Problem.* "The report of the new Lady Bantock is wonderful. I take it that you will skip Broadway and go directly to London and possibly Paris. I see no sense in your wasting any time on the Theatre Guild, Gilbert Miller, or any of those pushcart peddlers. Be polite but don't allow them to get familiar."

The story was about a high-spirited and rather flashy young woman (me, Fanny) who marries, along with her nice new husband, Bennett, a tribe of impossible servants who have always gone with the house. Somehow she must accept them or lose Bennett, whom she loves. I sent it to Pop and he found cutting irresistible. "Back in the old Jerome K. Jerome (author) days there were touches of cuteness which might have been effective then but they are just silly now . . . there are certain obscurities, clear at the time but not now, that have no place in the play . . . the reason for the cuts, taken as a whole, is that the plot is thin and much too trivial for modern tempo and unless the play is speeded up you are likely to have your audience yawning and fumbling for cigarettes and so on.

"Much of it puzzles me. Is it comedy or drama? What did the author intend? I must say I can't make out. The minute I hear that there are 23 relatives working in one place it's comedy to me. But the dialogue between Fanny and these relatives is evidently set down in all seriousness . . . the only way I can see to keep the matter as I think it should be is to gloom up the servants."

Miss Hale, the drama teacher and something of a Victorian antique herself, was thrilled at the cuts and Pop continued his long-distance direction. "Don't let him be the standard English butler, proper and all that. Make him a long-faced, deep-sighing religious type. Let him moan at the thought of his niece an actress, let him sigh deeply at the marriage, let him lift his eyes to heaven, and all that sort of thing. Make him very, very sanctimonious, in fact let all the servants be gloomy religious people . . . sympathy will go immediately to Fanny and the audience will be pulling for her to defeat them. All the servants should be gloomily dressed, melancholy characters, like a dark cloud over the heroine, who is a normal, pleasant, attractive type . . . let the servants play their sanctimoniousness very broad, as though Fanny had fallen into a pack of Holy Rollers . . . as one after the other of these Lord-have-mercy-on-her servants show up on the stage the audience will be whole-heartedly with Fanny—and that's always what you need in a play—somebody you are rooting for . . . a piece of business: when one of these servants exits, make a long face in imitation of her (or him). . . . There must be some progression or dramatic climb in your attitude, so that in the climax the audience takes your situation seriously . . . a sort of fear must come into your character, the fear that you will lose your husband. It should be like playing a game until you become aware that the other person is no longer playing but is actually going to try to kill you. These ghouls of servants, whom you tried to laugh off, become dreadful zombies closing in on you. If you and the director could bring it off like that you would have achieved something very good and interesting.

"I hope you noticed that no matter how awkward the situation the finale of each act was contrived to leave the leading lady, the star, on stage at the curtain. That was the Victorian idea of stardom. The most awkward example of it is the curtain at the end of the third act, where about ten people are made to exit just so Fanny can remain there, when modern dramatic construction would be for her to exit after her big speech and leave all those people on stage gaping at each other as the curtain falls. It gives more point and importance to her speech . . . rewrite the lines when they are too awkward to speak and have no hesitation about fitting the dialogue to your characters and the dimensions of your stage. For example, some lines are long just to get a character across a wide stage, so if your stage is narrow, or if you don't want this character to cross at this point, cut the line down or rewrite it—you are not dealing with Shakespeare here.

"You may be tempted to move too much, which would make

the play look artificial, so try to figure out how you would behave say in our living room or yours. Try to make the move-
ments as natural as possible. Try to have a reason for each cross.
And never move on a very important line. If there's a movement
involved in this particular moment, try to move first and then
speak. Casual lines can be spoken almost any way and anywhere
but if it is a punch line the actor or actress should be poised in
one position when it is spoken . . . remember always that this is
comedy you are playing. Even your anger should have a sort of
coloration of comedy in it. Play it straight, but not Eugene
O'Neillish. Do you know how Helen Hayes gets the most attention? She lowers her voice. If there is a commotion out front she
doesn't try to lift her voice above it. She deliberately drops it.
Then people become still so they can hear her. The same could
just as well be true in such a speech as that long one about the
servants. Begin it very low, contained, and you'll have people listening closely. Then you won't have to lift your voice."

Pop hadn't been sure if he could be there for the December
performance though "you can depend on it that if it's at all possible you will find me waiting at the stage door afterward, hat in
hand, with an invitation to a charming little supper at Rector's
with a cold bottle and a hot bird." As it turned out he didn't
make it to see what turned out to be my theatrical swan song. I
still told everybody I was going to conquer Broadway, to hide
my fickle-heartedness, but it had been gone really since the Cape
Playhouse. I didn't really want to read somebody else's lines—I
wanted to write my own.

London 1950
Hollywood to 1953

I spent the summer of 1950 with Pop in London, where he was making *The Mudlark*. I was terribly excited when he proposed it. Fathers, for most of my friends, went with mothers—half a unit as familiar as the living-room furniture. But mine was distant, glamorous, and wrote letters that all my friends wanted to read.

Though he praised ocean travel ("always travel first class when you can . . . you can always say later that you wish you had traveled third") and gave tips on how to cross the ocean gracefully ("see the dining-room steward immediately, don't tip till just before you get off at Southampton, reserve a deck chair and rug—blanket—on the deck of the ship, not boat") I spent most of the first two days on the *Queen Mary* crying in my cabin —I think from change, sea change, parent change, school change, changes in myself that were going to make me different. Besides, I was afraid Pop was going to find me dreadfully wanting over a long period of time, a dreary girl who was better on paper than in person. (It was so safe, writing—it was the human contacts that were dangerous.) And what was I doing on this boat (ship)? I was fairly provincial, New York child that I was, and I was frightened—I would have given anything to be back home in the brownstone.

After a couple of days of this I got a note from Jack Benny, whom Pop had asked to look me up, at which I cried harder

than ever. That's what the trouble was, it was sheer panic at trying to be interesting all summer, and it was already starting. I
was already wit-weary, unnerved at the prospect of struggling to
be clever rather than saying what I felt. It seemed to be expected of me—Pop liked to be amused back at his own level,
and probably Jack Benny did too. I knew I couldn't stay in my
cabin the whole time (a conclusion neither rational nor courageous, but because I wouldn't have been able to face my
friends) and I told Mr. Benny I would be happy to have cocktails in the captain's cabin. I had to start sometime, but it wasn't
easy—the struggle for verbal overdrive wore me out, though the
struggle was largely unnecessary, I know now, because it was
doubtful if either of these two essentially kind people, Benny or
my father, expected much in *mots* from a shy seventeen-year-old,
nor would any fond parent fail to try to respond to what there
was. But I didn't know those things, and instead I always felt on
stage, or on scene, writing my own lines for some production my
life depended on, for some harsh critic who could cut me down
with one perfectly chosen word.

Cocktails with the Bennys were not as bad as I had thought
(things never were). To distract from my other deficiencies, during those years, I dressed to kill, strapless tulle, dangling earrings, blood-red lipstick—armor which, I thought, would relieve
me of the necessity of being intelligent. In 1950 it pretty well
did, except I often ended up with the wrong people, a distinction
I usually failed to detect until too late. The Bennys were pleasant and friendly, though as usual I felt something was expected
of me I couldn't produce; and I thanked them very much and
spent the rest of the trip with Rochester, who was the most popular person aboard, a group of touring Brearley girls, and four
insurance salesmen from Cleveland who laughed at my jokes.
Given the choice of feeling drab and frustrated with the Bennys
or devastating and worldly with the Cleveland Elks, I of course
chose the Elks, and scolded myself at the end of the trip for having missed the good stuff—a little drama I have acted out
around a thousand times before and since.

Arriving in England was like being in touch with reality at
last, finally connecting with my cultural origins after a lifetime in
a crass, plastic society. (We all felt that way so strongly, I was

surprised to realize, ten or fifteen years ago, how fascinating my
own country had become.) Everything took on a marijuana intensity—the green of the grass was the essence of green, the pub
by the road was the essence of pub. I even did it with people
that summer—Peter Bishop was essence of Oxford under-
graduate, Nunnally essence of Hollywood producer, Denis, a
friend, essence of British queer (I was a Jamesian heroine). It
was really a way of simplifying all the newness and anxiety
about spending the summer alone with Pop—for when I got
there Dorris was packing to go home to the children. On one
hand, it was oedipal triumph, and on the other I was frightened
to death—Pop with his foibles was all mine for two months,
Dorris mentioned as she left for the airport.

London was still visibly war-torn, its inhabitants down at the
heels. Food rationing was in force, and one of my first chores
after the first excited sight-seeing was to try to feed Pop. The
comfortable flat on Grosvenor Square had service, which meant
if you rang they would send up meals, which I found satisfactory, a chop and two veg (you didn't come to England to
eat), but which Pop found inedible. This was too bad, it all
seemed so easy, but he had a way of sulking if he hadn't been
properly fed; and so I got the ration cards and went about shopping and cooking. It was reasonable in theory ("When Nora
comes she won't mind doing a little home cooking") and even
sounded like fun, except that I didn't know how to cook anything but cheesecake and zabaglione and something called kedg-
eree, and faced with a long queue with a butcher at the end of
it and a lot of people waiting behind, I had no idea what to get
for my meat ration. The chicken was at the poulterer's, the milk
and eggs at the dairy, the veg somewhere else, and I didn't even
know what to do with the chicken when I got it; and after a few
disastrous dinners (which Pop hardly touched, picking pin
feathers out of his teeth with a pained look) we gave up and
went to restaurants every night. There weren't too many, but we
found two or three and went to them over and over, the Ward-
room, La Rue's, the Screenwriters' Club, and one or two others
that are probably long gone. After dinner we would stroll to
Hyde Park Corner, to Marble Arch, to Piccadilly Circus, or along
Bond Street and we would talk.

Him: Now, what about that boy, what's his name, Ed?

Me: Oh, him.

Him: Isn't that the one you've been seeing a lot?

Me: Well, I was. Now it's over. I mean, we're taking the summer to think things over. He's a very unrealistic person.

Him: How's that?

Me: He wants to get married.

Him: What's so unrealistic about that?

Me: What would happen to my intellectual life, stuck in the kitchen?

Him: (a sigh) Oh my.

Me: That's boring.

Him: Well, honey, how do you feel about him?

Me: I dunno.

Him: It all comes down to that, you know. But I think this one's out. When you meet a fella that makes you crazy about that kitchen, I'll put my money on him.

Sometimes he would tell me about London as it had been in the twenties when he first came, or else stories of the British he had encountered—Mr. Cleverly the bootmaker, Alec Guinness, the char, the barber. I hung on his arm and listened while he interpreted Britain, and then later on, home in bed, either wrote a long letter to a friend or else lay in the dark and talked to myself until I had said all the things I wanted to say before. When we went farther afield, to Oxford or Broadway or Maidenhead, we traveled about, like the rich Americans we were, in a Rolls with a driver named Atkins. At first I liked such protection, but as I began to make friends in London I felt bad about the Rolls because my British friends were so poor, so shabby from the war which had battered their land. Pop had long since finished this argument with himself and decided on first class, but my head was just starting to be jarred by travel and the questions travel was causing me to ask myself. Pop was—in a kind way—dogmatic; he thought his own answers would help my puzzlement, but of course they didn't, though for a long time I accepted them.

My British friends were—as American college students now are—educated beyond a limited job market. They spent summers lugging crates about the basements of grocery stores or selling cars or picking hops—the boys did, and the girls couldn't get anything. They were all broke and for the most part cheerful about it, more cheerful than I would have been, though when I first met Peter, in a boat on the Thames with him and Florence, his mother, and Pop, Florence whispered to me, "Peter's depressed about the bloody job at Cooper's" (a Gristede-like chain where he sold cheese). I had the feeling that she was whispering to protect Pop rather than Peter, in case we felt bad about the Rolls and Grosvenor Square. I wondered why Peter and his friends were so hospitable to me, particularly when I was so American and crass, but possibly I was a novelty, or a relief— here was somebody free from the grime and stress of being poor. But we did manage to go to pubs or dancing or to somebody's flat for spaghetti. When Peter came to our flat (often in top hat and furled umbrella) he mumbled, and Pop couldn't understand anything he said. In time my ear adjusted to his sound, and anyway, I cared, so I got most of it. But Pop's eyes glazed over and he looked agonized as Peter's speech got softer, faster and less coherent. What should have been pleasant became painful, so I kept them away from each other, which I hated—there was so little time with both of them.

After the cooking was over I knew I had to have a project, so I spent two hours a day playing the piano in a practice room, the most conspicuously non-verbal thing I knew how to do. The practice room was in Dickens' house, a few minutes' walk from the flat, and there I drove myself mercilessly through pieces which were far beyond me technically, slapping myself in the face if I failed to master some phrase (which, twelve years later, my analyst wrote down and underlined).

> *Him:* Now, honey, you've got to be more professional about your work. Why don't you do what I do [he was writing the script of *The Desert Fox*], sit down in the morning after breakfast, in the other room, and work till lunch-time?
>
> *Me:* But I don't have an idea.
>
> *Him:* Now look. Ideas don't just come, I've told you that. You have to keep pressing for them. You have to keep saying, "What if—" What if she were older, what if she lived in London, if her mother were dead, if she was a whiz at Latin? [Family joke: "I don't like to say what my

daughter got in Latin this term, but if Julius Caesar came along and started talking to her, she'd only understand forty-five per cent of what he had to say."]

Me: It's not funny.

Him: Perish the thought. It was just an illustration, to show you the possibilities. You should take your work seriously.

Me: I do, but I'm not a machine. [This sounds sharper than I meant.] I can't work this summer, I don't know why. I think it's being seventeen. Don't you remember what it's like to be seventeen?

Him: I was always a little angel.

We were both surprised that I didn't do any writing—it had been mentioned as one of the possible benefits of this trip, me writing and Pop criticizing. But it was impossible with him writing in the next room, I couldn't produce a word. When I wasn't in the practice room I wandered around London, still enchanted by everything I saw. I found I closed off certain parts of myself from Pop, protected my own space, which I felt bad about. I blamed it on my inability, never his—he had a curious quality of fragility which made people want to protect him, as Florence had in the boat. I worried about all sorts of things I usually never thought twice about—that he wouldn't like his dinner, that his shirts wouldn't be done correctly, that the Abbey or Knightsbridge or the potted shrimps would suddenly bore him, and I resented it—ordinarily these were Dorris' problems, and I didn't want the unasked-for responsibility; though at the time all this came through only as an edgy feeling of annoyance, an urge to pull my privacy around me like a cloak, which in turn made him wonder what he was doing wrong. Of course we never discussed any of this, it was in neither his nature nor mine to do so.

In July we went to Paris, very elegantly. We stayed at the Georges V and had our first lunch at Fouquet's, where we ate *truite bleue* boned before our eyes by the waiter. We had dinner at Maxim's, and the Tour d'Argent, we had peaches in champagne at the Coq Hardi (on the way to Versailles, where I threw up). He taught me about food for the first time in my life, and wine, which I had never thought twice about. We laughed a lot —about "darks" for instance, which Pop said were what went on when you pushed the switch by the door in France, or mashed it, in his language. Before we had gone he had made it sound like one of our honeymoons, but in fact we were not alone— American cronies joined us in our suite and in the cafés, and Celia Agar, an old friend, came everywhere with us. I would have picked Celia over a lot of people, but I kept wishing she weren't there—though without her we might have had a hard time, and perhaps Pop knew that. The only off note was the shadow that non-English-speaking countries cast over Pop. To him foreign tongues were a plot, almost a personal insult. When I, or anybody else, chattered in bad French, he darkened at the loss of his most vital social instrument—sulked, in fact, until whoever had been doing it hastily knocked it off.

The day before we were to leave—me for Switzerland to stay with Peter's family at their chalet, Pop to Germany to see Frau Rommel—Celia and I went to the flea market and bought two small birds in a cage, which, as the saying goes, seemed like a good idea at the time. I had no end of trouble getting them to Switzerland, where they immediately escaped, and I must have wanted them to, for I was rather pleased about it. A week or so later Pop, now back in London, phoned to tell me that if I brought the birds back the British customs would impound them and quarantine me for parrot disease. He was shocked when I told him they were gone—he had gone to a great deal of trouble to get this information. I felt dreadful, ready to go out and catch the birds, which still hung about the chalet in a tree, and deliver them to British authorities, so his time might not have been wasted. What made me feel so guilty was the pleasure I took in telling him the birds were free, a curious feeling of triumph, as though I had outwitted him.

After I got back from Switzerland the flat had to be given up and we moved into a suite at the Dorchester. Now I didn't even have to shake a box of corn flakes, everything could be ordered from downstairs. (I could—I still could—live that way forever.) The Dorchester was for Americans, and the appointments almost made up for its not being Claridge's. Peter was still in Switzerland, and during the last part of the summer I went here and there with Denis, who was, in my father's language, a pansy. He was in his mid-twenties, as broke as everybody else; he

loved film people (as he called them) and got very excited
around Pop, who loathed him, partly because he (Pop) usually
ended up picking up the check. But I found Denis delightful. I
would come into the living room where the two of them were
having a cocktail—Denis chattering about things he considered
interesting, Pop sinking lower and lower into his chair—and
Denis would look at me, clap his hands and chirp, "Darling, it's
almost perfect, now let's make it just right, run back and get
your jewelry box." I would get it and Denis would pick through
my Bloomingdale's costume jewelry (both of us pretending it
was the crown jewels) till he found just the right earrings, which
he would put on me and clap his hands with joy. Then, while
Pop looked as though he was about to throw up, we would go
out. Often the three of us went places together—I was very innocent about people's machinations, but I think it was because
Denis so often managed to come by for a drink at around the
right time. Once we went to the Royal Film something-or-other
Awards, a very grand black-tie affair, and Denis almost fell out
of the box pointing out celebrities from the Queen on down,
while Pop sat in black silence. I had unloaded a lot of guilt in
the course of the summer, and decided that if my friends made
Pop suffer I simply couldn't help it. Of course we went to some
very elegant club to eat afterward, the Ambassador or the 400,
and of course Pop picked up the check while Denis sparkled
thank-yous and oh-Mr.-Johnsons and reached futilely for his
wallet. It is hard, twenty-eight years later, to say who was right
and who was wrong, and by how much; but I do know Denis
was embarrassed by a situation he was almost helpless to do anything about (if the fun was to keep up) and Pop, I suppose,
didn't have to invite him; it seems now they were simply stuck
with each other. Pop made little attempt to hide his feelings—it
was simply beyond him that I found anything interesting or attractive about Denis; that I found him amusing, a good dancer,
and easy to talk to were quite enough for me at the time, and the
absence of the sexual element was a relief—with Peter it had
made me tongue-tied and heavy-headed at a time when I
wanted to be alert and alive.

Shortly before I left, Denis announced that there would be *one*
evening when we went out alone, that *he* would pay for—he had

saved up enough money. (I obviously didn't appear to be a cheap date.) But it wasn't easy to find a place to go. The Dorchester was one of the few places with affordable dancing, and so we ended up in the whatever-it-was room. Denis ordered champagne and an elaborate dinner, at the end of which Pop came in with Celia. He had not expected to find us there (we were supposed to be Out) and was none too sober, and when they walked in we all stared at each other in horror. There didn't seem to be any way they could avoid joining us, or none of us could think of one fast enough, so they sat down at our table. Denis mentioned that it was his birthday, which was part of the reason for the celebration, and so when the check came, guess who reached for it? Poor Denis tried to protest, but Pop was drunk and definite, and Denis never had his moment. But when I left he introduced me to a young man ("his name is Wills, darling—Wills tobacco") who, on the *Queen Elizabeth* going home, introduced me to Elizabeth Taylor and Nicky Hilton.

This time I didn't cry. Pop and I had accomplished quite a lot —put in the time together, for one thing, and more important, I had found that he refused to give up on me. I had, rather delicately, tried to push him, to see if he would simply lose interest in me, turn his back and not bother any more. But he never did. He kept asking me what I thought, what I was going to do, where I was going. I think now I was rather surprised—after all, he had left me once. It took that long to find out that his doing so had nothing to do with me, it always takes children that long. I kept trying that summer, kept going back to see if he would be there when I got back, or shutting myself in my room to see if he was still there when I came out. And he was, he was.

The Desert Fox, an adaptation of the best-selling book by Desmond Young (directed by Henry Hathaway), had germinated in a magazine story about what was called the June 20 plot—an attempt on Hitler's life. Nunnally did careful research, with Desmond Young's help, talking to Frau Rommel and her son and to British officers and soldiers, for he knew he was in charge of high-level material and wanted to do the job properly—in spite of interference by Skouras, who invited himself to the hotel room during an interview obtained with difficulty with Field

Marshal Auchinleck. "Auchinleck was about as big as a middle linebacker," Nunnally said, "two hundred and twenty or forty pounds, all muscle, wore a bowler absolutely horizontal, and very clipped . . . like a character in a picture, he had come in and sat down and I'd tried to take his hat and he said, 'No, no, not at all,' and he put it down beside his chair. I guess he thought, Well, I want to be ready to leave here. Maybe he had some kind of premonition. There was a half hour of continuous talk by Skouras about how he had saved the war by sending Greek ships full of food or something. I could only get in a word or two to get some kind of expression from Auchinleck on his view of Rommel as a soldier. Suddenly, in the middle of what Skouras was saying, he just reached over and got his bowler and put it on and said, 'Good day,' and ran out of the room. He didn't even wait for the elevator. He ran all the way down three flights of stairs."

In London that summer James Mason had approached him about playing Rommel, and Zanuck liked Mason, though Mason was at the bottom at that time. "As so often happens, you get this ex cathedra word from New York, 'Mason is through. Can't have Mason.' Zanuck called them or cabled them or something and said, 'Either give us somebody who's right and acceptable or we're going ahead with Mason.'"

The story takes up Rommel at the height of his career when he is starting to doubt the wisdom of his boss (Hitler) at ordering a raid he considers suicidal. He is sympathetic—though not actively involved with—the July 20 plot, and we watch the noose slowly tighten around him as Germany is losing the war and the Fuehrer becomes increasingly desperate. Finally the SS presents him with a choice: a hoked-up public court-martial for treason with no guarantee of protection for his wife and son, or immediate suicide by poison, with honors, a fine funeral, and a lifetime pension for the widow. He chooses suicide and tells his wife and son good-by before he gets in the car to go to his death.

The story is told in flashback, with an episode with Desmond Young (who served as narrator, to give the picture a documentary flavor) preceding the titles in what was probably the first pre-credit footage. His care in handling what was then sensitive material (it was only five years after the end of the war) paid off, and the picture was a success in Germany as well as here, for he had depicted Rommel as a great hero, a general who had almost magical powers for both sides (to such an extent that the British reminded their North Africa troops that Rommel was in fact an enemy, not a magician).

Except for Bosley Crowther and *The New Yorker*, the picture got an excellent reception, though some reviewers reacted nervously to its surprising position. But Nunnally as usual was unbothered. "Give me a combination of big grosses and a carping review and I am breath-taking in my quiet, grave dignity and tolerance."

In *Phone Call from a Stranger* (directed by Jean Negulesco), Shelley Winters, Gary Merrill, Michael Rennie and Keenan Wynn are all aboard a plane. Gary is leaving his wife for an adultery he can't make himself forget, Michael Rennie is running away from an auto accident and Shelley from a mother-in-law. The plane crashes and Gary, the only survivor of the four, makes the three phone calls to tell the news but, having become more forgiving himself, pads a little here and there to make the memories of the dead more palatable. The Keenan Wynn story was Nunnally's favorite. Wallet pictures of Keenan's wife (Bette Davis) caused the others to wonder why she had married a nerd like him. But years before Bette had run off with another man, who deserted her after a swimming accident which paralyzed her completely—but Keenan had come in when she was in the iron lung and smiled his forgiveness, saying, "Hi ya, beautiful." "Every time I looked at it I cried," Nunnally said.

Dealing with Bette Davis had not been easy. She had volunteered to do the part because of her husband, Gary Merrill, but after the first day or two of rushes Nunnally found something wrong with the way she was using her voice, and as the producer it fell to him to speak to this formidable woman, who flew into a rage. She said, "You certainly don't expect me to use the same voice or manner as Margo Channing?" while Nunnally, terrified, wondered who she was talking about, only realizing later that Margo Channing had been her name in her last big hit, *All About Eve*. Gary Merrill tried to mediate this row, but Miss Davis screamed herself into four days of laryngitis, emerging with a low contralto which fortunately fitted the part. They finished the picture only on the condition that Nunnally not go on the set.

The picture got an award for screenplay at the Venice Film Festival. "Now don't ask me what this prize is or where it is," he wrote me at the time, "for I don't know and probably never will. It will probably be taken back to our headquarters in Paris and hung there and every now and then someone will say to someone else, 'I wonder if perhaps we hadn't better drop Johnson a line about this thing. Might buck him up a bit, you know.' But somebody else will say, 'Why don't you do it, *mon vieux?*' And the first fellow will say, 'The *enfer* with it.'"

In *We're Not Married* (directed by Eddie Goulding) a justice of the peace marries six couples before he has the legal right to do so, and must inform them that their marriages are not worth the paper they're written on. The six couples receive this news with highly varying degrees of pain and pleasure. One couple, Fred Allen and Ginger Rogers, have a cheery radio breakfast show that contrasts sharply with the utter loathing they feel for each other, and in another skit Marilyn Monroe ineffectually portrays motherhood.

In 1952 he did the marvelous *My Cousin Rachel* (directed by Henry Koster) from Daphne du Maurier's best-selling Gothic novel, with Olivia de Havilland as the is-she-bad or is-she-good Rachel and Richard Burton, brought over from England for his first important part in an American film. The picture never really answers the questions it asks. Did Rachel kill her husband with a poisoned tisane? Is she trying to kill Philip (Burton) the same way? Has she plotted it all to get her hands on Philip's fortune? It all takes place in an old mansion on the Cornish coast, with howling winds and flickering candles and ambiguity, which probably hurt the commercial success of the film because "movie audiences don't want to go home with questions . . . in the old Lou Holtz line, you've paid your money and you're entitled to know what's going on up there. I would never do a thing like that again."

Burton was brought over at the suggestion of Betty Bacall and Bogey, who had seen him performing at Stratford. After he had signed and shortly after he and Nunnally met, he startled Nunnally by asking him how you went about finding a hooker in

New York. Nunnally said he knew there were call girls, but he hadn't the faintest idea how to find one. "I nearly went crazy," Burton said. "I was there three days." But "he was wonderful in the picture," Nunnally said, "and he's the kind of man you look at and you know this is quality, this is passion." During the filming Olivia told Nunnally, "The first time he grabbed me on that staircase, that was no stage kiss. He had his tongue down my mouth right there in front of the camera." "He was smart enough to have his face angled off from the camera," Nunnally said, "but I think it absolutely startled the hell out of Olivia, who wasn't easily startled. She didn't expect this kind of attack in front of the camera. But he was so good."

There was some difficulty in getting it all lined up. Carol Reed had been one possibility for director, and then George Cukor. Olivia says, "I couldn't wait to work with him, he'd done the first scenes in *Gone With the Wind* and he'd been responsible for my being chosen as Melanie, I'd made a read for Melanie with George playing Scarlett so George was all wound and bound into my destiny." But Cukor objected to a string of possibilities for Rachel, including Olivia. He had wanted Garbo, who got as far as reading the script and then lost her nerve. She told Nunnally, "No, I don't look like the actress I was any more. There would be difficulty photographing me. And my arms, upper arms, are flabby." Nunnally tried to reassure her as much as he could, and "she was very polite, very sweet." But in the end she said no. "I haven't got the courage. I like the part, but I've always said that I wouldn't get back into pictures and I won't." When Cukor objected to Olivia ("I can see through her") he and Nunnally agreed that it would be better if he withdrew from the picture, with no ill feeling but sighs of relief from Nunnally. He wrote me at the time:

"I move steadily backward with *My Cousin Rachel*. Now my director, George Cukor, has bowed out. I'm not altogether displeased. He's very impressive to female stars in this business, what with his feminine sympathies and bewildering aestheticism, but I finally came to the conclusion that he sounded a little more like a fashionable interior decorator than anything else, and interior decorators operate in such a rarefied atmosphere of nonsense and snobbery that it is difficult to have much patience with them. Anyway, he's gone. And we still haven't signed a star, though Miss Olivia de H. looks quite likely. She doesn't suggest Rachel to me any more than Roxie does, but I don't know who else."

There was a great deal of discussion about the ambiguous ending. Olivia says, "I don't know if it was the right decision [to leave Rachel's innocence a question]. The main thing, I suppose, was to be faithful to the book and since the book didn't reveal what she was . . . in fact I had to read it three times before I knew. *I* had to know which she was and never discussed it with your father at all—or maybe I did. The third reading it couldn't have been clearer, she was absolutely innocent. I had to play it that way but everything she did appearing to be guilty, though she was innocent of what she was doing. All of it had to be ambiguous, every act, every reaction. But once you know which she is, that you can do, can't do if you don't know." After the film was released she met Carol Reed, who told her he was very close to Daphne du Maurier. "I asked if she had ever confided in him which Rachel was. He said, 'Yes, I'll tell if you promise not to tell' I've kept the secret for twenty years, but now I'll say it. She was absolutely innocent. Isn't that delicious? Isn't that grand?"

Unlike others who worked with him, Olivia didn't have an easy time with Nunnally. "He had this caustic wit, you know. I think he was fond of me. I was always in terror of him, because he had annihilating wit and he could destroy your confidence for maybe a year with a single remark and I was always afraid of being the butt of some such remark, it would just shatter me. He took me out to lunch once at Romanoff's and I was trying to work out some figure of speech, and he said, 'Oh, you're not going to try that are you?' as if it were really far beyond my capacities, and I sort of stopped in the middle and I didn't try, and I thought, Why, that's ridiculous, with someone else I might have charged ahead and come out quite well." She continues: "I think your father was afraid of ideas from women, afraid of intelligence in women. Maybe actresses. I think he needed to feel that actresses weren't very bright. He wanted to like them and there was this deep mistrust . . . one whole sequence in *My Cousin Rachel* I saw playing it one way, Koster was fascinated by this interpretation. There was one scene where Rachel could

really extend herself. Nunnally came down on the set. It seemed
to be true feeling being revealed, he felt no, it all had to be
much more restrained and mysterious. It was a perfectly good
way to do it, I accepted the discipline of his opinion. The
producer's word usually prevails. It has to. Koster bowed to superior authority and your father's intellect and taste was something to take extremely seriously whether you were weak-willed
or not."

How to Marry a Millionaire (1953, directed by Jean Negulesco), which starred Lauren Bacall, Betty Grable and Marilyn
Monroe, was the first CinemaScope picture ever made, though
The Robe, which was actually made afterward, was used instead
to introduce Fox's super new technique because "it had some
sort of majestic sound to it," Nunnally said, "and you had to
open up this new glimpse of wonderland with an epic." There is
a long sequence of a full orchestra before the titles of *Millionaire*
to show off the incredible *width,* and many shots of the New
York sky line, et cetera, scattered throughout—and of course
those three ladies are marvelous to look at. The picture is very
funny and did well. CinemaScope probably saved Fox and indirectly the motion picture industry, which was just beginning to
sag. It also made money for Skouras, who required that all theaters showing CinemaScope pictures had to have CinemaScope
equipment. "That sounds pretty suspicious to me," Nunnally
said, "unless there was a brother-in-law who just happened to
make that kind of equipment." (When first asked how he would
adjust to writing for the wide screen, Nunnally replied: "Very
simple, I'll just put the paper in sideways.")

In this very fifties tale of husband-snaring, Marilyn is dumb
and nearsighted (an idea claimed by Sol Siegel), Betty Grable is
semi-literate, and Betty Bacall is their butchy, wisecracking ring-
leader. (They snare, respectively, David Wayne, Rory Calhoun
and Cameron Mitchell.) After his experience with Negulesco on
The Mudlark (when Alec Guinness complained of his lack of direction) Nunnally asked Jean if he might rehearse the actors before each scene, which he did. "The picture turned out about five
times as good as anything Jean had done before, simply because
somebody had taken the trouble," Nunnally said. Betty Bacall
says, "He was very firm about his words and I was rather sur-

prised at that. He was quite inflexible and I thought, Ho, ho, ho, this is an area I'm certainly not going to get into any *crise* with Nunnally about. If I'd really felt strongly about it I would have discussed it with Negulesco. But if I said, 'Do you think this is okay?' he'd say, 'Just try it this way.' And you have to try it if someone says try it. But I was interested that he was as tough as he was, he was not all sweetness and light. . . . I think he had very definite ideas about what an actress should be. I think he was somewhat of the school that you shouldn't have too many opinions. Actors always get in the way of writers, actors are a pain in the ass because they have ideas, there's always a momentary clash."

She and Bogey were close friends of Dorris and Nunnally. "We had dinner two or three times a week, we'd sit in front of the fire with trays and Nunnally would say, 'Put another log on the fire, Dorris.' He and Bogey were known to bend an elbow together while Dorris and I raised our eyes skyward . . . he would kill for anyone he loved, there were no boundaries." When Nunnally called her about *How to Marry a Millionaire*, he had to ask her to do a screen test, which was close to an insult to the actress who had made screen history with *To Have and Have Not* (not to mention marrying the star). Nunnally was infinitely tactful and explained that it was only because she hadn't played comedy before. "He said, 'I know you can do it, honey, but *they* don't, they just have to see it on the screen, it will make Zanuck feel better.' I said to myself, Jesus, I made it eight years ago, I have to test? I always resented testing, it's very much the Hollywood syndrome, they'd still test now, still wouldn't be sure I could do anything, you're judged on that and that alone. Nunnally knew it was a sensitive point, he didn't want to hurt my feelings and yet he wanted to make his point. Bogey was standing right there and he said, 'Just remember, you will probably never have as good a friend as that.' I was fascinated by Bogey's reaction, he knew that extra something that was there, because he had a far greater perception than I had about that sort of thing."

In those days Marilyn Monroe was no myth but rather a distressed, neurotic girl who drove directors crazy. Nunnally had met her first with Johnny Hyde. "I'd see her sometimes at lunch

with him. She never said anything. I can't remember her saying a
word. And I wasn't bowled over by her beauty, either. I thought,
She's another of Johnny's little girl friends." (This has a similar
ring to a story Nunnally told on himself, of being offered *Gone
With the Wind* and turning it down because he didn't believe
people named Scarlett and Rhett could possibly interest anybody. "And that," he said, "is why they call me Deadeye Johnson.") Betty Bacall says of Marilyn, "She was really terrified—
shaky—she was late all the time. During *Millionaire*, Nunnally
was very sweet to her, he made all those jokes about him and
Marilyn, but she didn't have tremendous humor. She wasn't easy
to act with because she never looked at you, she didn't react to
what you'd say. She'd rehearse, she had a coach, she'd gone
through the scene with the coach and the coach had told her
how to do it and screw what anyone else did, which was great
for her because she had a magic on film, but it wasn't terrific for
the rest of us poor slobs. And then at the end she would never
look at Negulesco, she would look right past him at the coach
. . . she was really very selfish but she was so sad you couldn't
dislike her. You just had to feel sorry for her, her whole life was
a fuck-up. She just happened to have this great thing and she
made a connection with the camera . . . she ended up being
very good in the movie, though she was not an actress." But
Betty Grable "would do very funny things when we were re-
hearsing, then in front of the camera something changed, she
turned into that little Kewpie doll again. If she had really done
what she did in rehearsal she would have been a wonderful co-
medienne."

At the opening Marilyn was of course the star. Pop wrote me
at the time: "When I broke the news to the children (that
Marilyn was going with the Bogarts and us to the opening)
Scotty immediately began to chant a line he had got from his
sisters, 'Best undressed woman in town!' The two girls began to
writhe like belly dancers, both of them dropped their waists off
their shoulders, and Roxie showed me a knee full of small cuts
and bruises. It was necessary to inform them then and there that
if they made one crack in the presence of the young woman I
would not bother to say anything, I would simply grab the guilty
one by the neck and rush him or her out of the room . . . what

this girl does to people is almost unbelievable. She was late, of course, and when she rang the bell the door was opened by three children, two in Oriental kimonos and a small boy in his finest dressing gown. We let them serve the hors d'oeuvres and they did this with such gaping awe that she was lucky not to have got most of the stuff in her lap, which would have been a major disaster, for the studio wardrobe and make-up department had been at work on her since shortly after noon. She owned nothing that she wore. She told a girl reporter at the studio that the only thing she wore that she owned were her underpants. I was informed later by Dorris that she wasn't wearing any. That's all I know about that."

Smith and Berlin   1950–1953

I was outwardly scornful of Smith (they all wore Bermuda shorts and knee socks) and inwardly terrified. My old friend June and I shared a small room at the end of the hall, far from the In group, by whom we were immediately pronounced weird —a word used a lot around Smith that fall, along with "strange," "nuts," "peculiar," applied to anything not—well, normal, at that time an unexamined concept. We did everything we could to promote this image, passing the word around that we were Communists, bohemians, and members of a strange pagan cult for which we performed unspeakable rituals behind our closed door. It didn't last long. We were avoided and stared at, and shortly we dropped the whole thing, for we were as desperately conventional as everybody else. We learned quickly that there wasn't to be that sort of fun at Smith, that there was nothing amusing about being out of step. Nunnally wrote:

"I'm sorry you find any difficulty whatever in any of your studies. It might interest you to know that in my time I was an excellent scholar, being particularly proficient at short division. As unnecessary as it was, I studied early, hard and late, never allowed myself to be diverted by temptations, and was a particular favorite of all my teachers and instructors. One and all they pronounced it a sad day when eventually I left school. Please be good enough not to spoil this family record."

Besides advising me about scholarship, he kept an eye on my

love life, now at a hectic pace. "I can hardly keep up with your romances. But I suffer no loss at the extinction of B. I doubted that he would last long anyway. He looked too good. [B. committed suicide at thirty-eight.] I'm saving my money to put on a psychotic. You're at a stage when a man with faults that you think you can correct would be way out in front of the flawless candidate. You're in a fixer-upper stage. The ideal boy gives you nothing to work on. Phooey to him." This was a self-fulfilling prophecy if there ever was one, and I obliged by falling in love with D., whom nobody could stand. D. was poor and didn't go to an Ivy League school, so he (and I) could feel misunderstood and oppressed by a conventional society. Pop, fired by what must have been desperate accounts by my mother, wrote:

"I can't quite see what pleasure or satisfaction you can get out of buying too many meals for a bum. At first, when I heard about him, I was fascinated. Anybody who could be blackballed from a fraternity at NYU for being Jewish, when there can't be more than eight Gentiles in the whole school, seemed to me to deserve a niche in Huber's Museum. I wanted to see such a fellow. Now it's all clear. He wasn't blackballed for being Jewish; he was blackballed simply because he wasn't what you might call admired. Long ago George Kaufman told a sad story about a girl who used Listerine and still wasn't popular . . . if you don't mind, I might point out to you that you are an extremely good-looking, even beautiful girl with intelligence and attractiveness, and you don't really have to take up with every lad who looks in your direction. You're quite in a position to pick and choose. If I were you I wouldn't let myself be a soft touch. They're not going to close down the show Saturday night or anything like that. You'll have plenty of time and plenty of opportunities. Study the candidates a little more closely. Think of yourself as the Cub Room, not Schrafft's. You have the style and quality. Use it. Keep it in mind. One lad of quality is worth 150 D.'s. And you're worth 3000 of him. Stop slumming."

That one made me cry. I was in love with D. and it took months to get over it, a hair-raising trip over the rapids of my feelings, D.'s problems (which abounded), meetings, renunciations, tears and frustration. And that quality stuff didn't help, I knew I didn't think of myself that way and I didn't know why.

The D.s of the world were chalked into my future and I knew it
—the nervous grace, the dark desperate eyes, the slender hands,
the fast crazy voice. How could I love somebody who didn't understand pain?

"You haven't even got near the fat part of life," Pop wrote.
"Things will get better and better for you from now on. You may
not believe it, but you are only approaching the big times. With
all you've got in the way of looks and taste and intelligence,
you've got a really glorious future to look forward to. You can't
miss. Just take it easy—and call on me if ever you think I can be
of help in any way whatsoever."

How could I ever find anybody who thought as much of me
as this, even if I didn't believe it? And why the hell did he set
himself up for disappointment when I was so much less than
glorious?

Pop's solutions for a husband were not helpful: "Thornton
Delahanty telephoned the other night and said he'd seen you
and wanted to marry you. Wanted to know if I was rich. I told
him not now but would come into money upon the death of my
uncle, J. Pierpont Johnson. He said he loved you but couldn't
afford to marry unless there was a tremendous *dot* in sight. This
must be true, for after a moment or two he kept referring to you
as Dot."

But then my taste didn't seem to be trustworthy. "The girls in
Morris House are a hundred per cent right about me. The fact
that you are only able to see me in terms of whether I've got hair
on my head or not has no bearing on my sexual combustibility.
The truth is, it depends on the angle. Naturally if you want to
look straight down on the top of my head you'll find a suggestion
of thinness in my hair, but that's true of everybody. But from a
low angle shooting up for a three-quarter profile, you'll be
amazed at the thickness and silkiness of my locks. From that
angle I've got as much hair on my head as Hemingway has on
his face, and that's enough for me, brother! And besides, what
has hair got to do with it? Did you never hear that Don Juan,
Cassanova (Charlie Cassanova), Romeo, Valentino and Peter
Lawford were all as bald as peeled eggs?"

Other letters brought assorted love. Milton Berle's ex-wife,
Joyce Something, put on rather a show of trying to destroy her-

self in Billy Rose's apartment in the Ziegfeld Theater last Sunday afternoon but, happily for all, was 100% unsuccessful. According to the papers, she locked herself in his bathroom and cut her wrist very delicately with a razor blade. The only really interesting point in this is that Billy Rose has a steel door on his bathroom, which couldn't be battered down with a fire axe. . . . Most people feel sorry for Joyce Something but the delight over Billy Rose's plight is deep and universal. . . .

". . . While trying to cross a mountain pass during a snowstorm several years ago, [Harold] Ross's car was stalled and he and the other fellow had to put chains on the tires. Ross pitched right in on this duty, but paused every four minutes to massage his hands with Elizabeth Arden's skin lotion." (This sounds like revenge for Ross's 1947 comment about him: "Johnson is one of the six humorists in the country, but he's also sickening, for he's been sucking around the diamond merchants of Hollywood for the past fifteen years and hasn't written anything. There is a misspent life.")

About a one-act play he wrote:

"There are a few rules for dialogue too. One is that each line should advance the audience's information at least an inch or two, even the jokes. Smuggle your information across in it. Another is to figure out precisely where your scene is headed, the exact line you want to take and the exact culmination, and never let your dialogue get far off that line and point. If you succumb to the temptation to make jokes just for laughs, it's vaudeville . . . never hesitate to cut. No matter how good it is, the audience has never heard it, knows nothing about it, and will never miss it."

About a couple of stories:

"You must remember that when you tackle satire you tackle the aristocracy of writing, and comedy may be only a cut or two below. Just as a satirical dancer must have first mastered the classical steps before he can lampoon them, a writer has got to have a pretty good mastery of primary writing before he can begin to have fun with it. A satirist is like a sprinter. No satirist ever goes out for the marathon run. . . . [In your story] I'm sure you found that the satirical situation began to fade out and you hurried melodrama in to support it, which many more experienced writers than you have done time and time again. But only on very rare occasions does it work. The drop from satire down into broad comedy is too quickly detected."

I must say, his restraint was admirable. At that stage, when in doubt, I piled on the production numbers and Communist plots and mind-bending coincidences or whatever else would seem to shore up my sagging ending. All my stories ended rather like the film *Casino Royale,* in which Indians, bands, cowboys and parachuters appear in batches to help Woody Allen through the monstrous finale. It is a method born of high enthusiasm and low skill, and was an error Pop made himself in some of his short stories and even some of his pictures—I think of the young man who sits on his girl's dog and kills it and the one who blows up his future father-in-law's house, and *Casanova Brown,* whose frantic search for an ashtray dissolves to a shot of the house he has just burned to a charred heap. I must have gotten it from him, for though I had never read any of his stories then I had read his scripts often.

". . . you will have to learn to work everything out in your mind before you start a story, so that you can discover for yourself the mood in which you want to tell it . . . you should have it shaken down into your consciousness before getting to the typewriter. You will never be able to get it precisely set in your mind but the main structure should be there. When you leave New York it is essential that you know whether you want to drive through Philadelphia or Cleveland en route . . . in this story you enjoyed yourself more than you permitted your characters to appreciate their experiences . . . what you might do next time you use a similar incident would be to try to put yourself in the place of, say, the governness and see everything through her eyes. That's often what Maugham does. He tells the story through the eyes and thoughts often of a very commonplace person. Incidentally, it is next to impossible for even an experienced writer to use a living character intact. A fictional character is much easier to handle. Never bother to try to be true to the original inspiration. That's just reporting. The artist creates his own character from a suggestion. That's the difference between a painter and a photographer."

In general, he said, I was doing better at drama than comedy and whether because of that (oh well, it probably was) or for some other reason I then wrote a series of no-beginning, no-ending stories about a boy and a girl in a bar having an intense discussion of their relationship. They were both dull and incoherent, but they were the first things I wrote in which I wasn't trying to ape my father.

Occasionally he sent me a plot. One was about an aging old-days movie star who tells of her three marriages; the first to an older, very rich and extremely kind but unromantic producer, who died and left her a great deal of money; the second to a comedian, and the third to a romantic and sexy scalawag. At the end she says, "I made only one mistake—I married them in the wrong order." I couldn't ever write that story, and Pop should have done it himself. At that time it was too cynical for me, and now I never could get into that woman's head (and I'm not even so sure she married them in the wrong order).

By 1952 my mother had married a professor at the Columbia Business School, Rogers Flynn. Pop wrote: "I am of course delighted about Mom's engagement. Mr. O'Flynn is a fortunate man, and to judge by Marion's pleasure, she herself feels that life has treated her well. It's an additional satisfaction, I'm sure, that you like and approve of the groom. I remember how savage you were when you disapproved of a candidate—and with very good reason, in my opinion, but nobody asked me. Nobody asks me now, of course, but your opinion is good enough for me." At this time I was in love with a young man everybody would have approved of, had he only known I was alive. He worked for the Eisenhower campaign, which I immediately joined and devoted the summer to, even though I was a secret Democrat, though I didn't know it at the time. Pop kept me up on politics in Beverly Hills:

"The truth is, politics is so fervent and articulate out here that it is often very hard to bear. We had a few people in for dinner last night and the gathering was scarcely five minutes old before it was sounding like a meeting of idiots. There were two Ike people present against about seven Stevensonians. (James and Pamela Mason are for Churchill. Negulesco is a Rumanian and hasn't been able to figure out yet who is running or for what.) The din was terrific. The only quieting influence in the room was

Roxie in a Korean outfit moving from debater to debater showing an autographed picture of Richard Burton expressing his
love for her." Pop liked Ike but, like anybody who thought twice
about it, liked Stevenson almost as well (or a lot better). "We
are still loyal Ike People of course, but there is a new satisfaction
in knowing he is not necessary to save us from brother Kefauver.
If we should lose, we could still feel that our fate was not in the
hands of a man so racially prejudiced that he hasn't the decency
to describe his trademark as a colored-folks-skin hat." He was
afraid Stevenson's ignorance about baseball might cost him the
presidency, even though Betty Bogart was working for him.
"Bogey claims that Betty wants to be the First Lady of the Land
but that while the country may accept one divorced person in
the White House, it certainly wouldn't stand for two, so he feels
that the only honorable, patriotic thing for him to do is to knock
himself off. Betty says that the only indication of a personal interest that she has been able to detect in Adlai so far was that
during one conversation he carelessly rested his hand on her
knee and let it remain there for an hour or so. This, she says,
gives her hope."

Ike did better than I did in trying to win Tip, the eminently
respectable young lawyer-politician I had followed to the Chicago convention and back. Unlike D., Tip was Eisenhower-
years normal, from his affluent-suburbs upbringing to his fondness for Ebbets Field (where I pretended I enjoyed going), and
disapproved of anything oddball, which I think was me. I tried
harder than ever to be something I wasn't, and Tip saw right
through me—I would never stay behind the white picket fence.
It was obvious to the adults, anyway, that the style of my generation was, to say the least, contradictory. Wrote Pop: "I received a letter from your mother last week [which] said that
Nora Sayre's garb was almost monastic in style and added that
Smith girls, by your report, were just as modest—long sleeves,
turtleneck sweaters, ankle-length dresses, and Oriental veils
across the nose. I don't know what you can get with a presentation like that but a fellow straight out of a psychiatric clinic, a
fellow with a fetish for acres and acres of tweed. Still, I daresay
you girls know what you are doing."

I'm not so sure we did. My mind of twenty-five years ago now appears a Gordian knot, a tangle of rationalizations which attempted to make the unworkable work. What would happen if I—or any of us of the same turn of mind—peeled away our tweed and came on sexy? We would not be thought of as nice girls, that's what, which meant we would be loved and left, raped possibly, toyed with and cast aside. We would not be respected, nobody would marry us. But did I want to get married? Yes/no. What the hell did I want, anyway? It wasn't any clearer now than it had been five years before (it still isn't). I wanted it all, work, love affairs, success, marriage, children, travel, a classy and unforgettable life. There was beginning to be the tiniest possibility that I might not be able to have all this and there was nothing in the list that I could eliminate. Sexiness meant vulnerability somehow, a sort of powerlessness that worked against the challenging project of getting everything. We sensed—in a way I doubt children do now—the power of sex, that the violence of its rhythms could rattle the mind and mark the soul, that its complexities would stun us and rip us loose from our systems if we let it—why else were we warned to approach it so carefully?

But in the darker hours, in bed or drunk or locked in the frenetic grip of an Amherst boy who knew he was going to have to stop, the real stuff bubbled up. There were only two things really—I wanted to write and I wanted to love deeply, desperately, cosmically, and be loved back in the same way. I wanted to walk the thin edge, put everything I had on one number. I was tired to tears of my generation's obsession with safety, and I was so much a part of that generation that I hardly knew the way out any longer.

With *Night People* (1954) Nunnally started directing, the only picture-making function he had not yet set his hand to. It was to be made in Berlin, and he said he had been so bored during the making of *Mudlark* that he decided to direct so he wouldn't have to spend the days in Germany sitting around his hotel room. This explanation has more to do with Nunnally's dread of appearing high-minded than anything else, and he did have other reasons: that ambitious people want to keep moving up and trying new things, and that he wanted to protect his lines —he had been unhappy for years over misdirection of his scripts, from Roxie Hart's gum to the tractor crashing through the house in *Grapes of Wrath*. It certainly had nothing to do with directorial mystique or auteurism, which he called "arrogant nonsense." Since he found nothing mysterious about the process, he saw no reason he couldn't do it as well as somebody else.

"In the old days, a fellow wrote a script, they hired a director. Now, quite often, unless they can get somebody like Willie Wyler or Billy Wilder or somebody like that, the writer directs it. This all goes to prove, to me anyway, that the old-time directors were a real collection of frauds." (The great Lubitsch was an exception, and in the early days Nunnally had studied his pictures intensively.) He was bored and exasperated by critics who told how the director "bores his camera right into the vitals of the changing social order," he said. "Maybe it had deeper meaning to the critic but I rather doubt it did to the writer or even the director, who is doing his best to tell a story." He believed that broader interpretations came later, that they were never intended by the writer. (How I wish I'd argued that with him.) Betty Bacall says, "He was so all wet about directors—so, Oh, it's the easiest thing in the world to do. Bogey and I used to talk about it. He was due for a shock, it ain't that easy."

Though Henry Hathaway told him he would never make it as a director because he wasn't enough of a bastard, Nunnally asked Zanuck if he might direct *Night People*, which was derived from a story by Jed Harris. Zanuck replied that it was all right with him as long as Gregory Peck, the star, agreed. Peck says, "I didn't have any doubt about it because of his experience and his talent, his character and personality. A director doesn't really tell actors how to act, he reacts to what they do and he fine-tunes it. He says, 'A little too much,' or 'Not quite enough,' or 'Give this an extra shaving'—very few directors go right down to the roots and psychoanalyze the character and get into all of that. And it's a good thing they don't because what you really want there is a good mind, a good character, and a friend you can trust, someone with taste who can maintain his objectivity. While you're in front of the camera and your emotions are involved, very often you kind of lose perspective and you lose the thread of the story. In each scene you're retelling another bit of the story so it will all piece together . . . because actors do involve their emotions, it's very important that they do, and certainly the audience isn't going to unless the actors do, it's impossible to watch yourself and to maintain objectivity."

Nunnally was "surprisingly grateful and even a little humble about it," says Peck. He was also nervous and looked to Peck for guidance. On the first day of shooting, on a Berlin roof just before the first take, he looked up and saw Greg staring at him, as though wondering if he had entrusted the direction to a fool who didn't know what he was doing. "We both realized what the other was thinking and bust out laughing." As Greg Peck tells it, the shooting went like a dream. He is a colonel with the American provost marshal's office in Berlin and Brod Crawford is the axle-grease tycoon from Toledo who comes blustering over when his son is kidnapped by the Russians. He bangs on the desk and gives orders, he thinks the Russians can be bought off, he is willing to start World War III to get his son back. Peck tells him off for eight or ten pages, dialogue he had memorized as he always does before shooting starts. It went perfectly the first time. "I think Nunnally was grateful to me because it got him off to a terrific start," Greg says. "The dialogue was so well written . . . a lot of it was verbal battles, there wasn't that much action, we were able to bite off enormous chunks of dialogue. We made the whole thing in about five and a half weeks from a schedule of seven or eight weeks, Nunnally was a hero with the studio." Peck gave him little bits of help throughout, such as making sure the camera was on his back when he was slugging (supposedly) Anita Bjork, which Nunnally had forgotten about. "To some extent he would watch me rehearse to find out how much directing he needed to give," Greg Peck says. "Any good professional would come prepared to give a performance without any direction . . . maybe I was helpful in giving him clues about how the scene should be played."

Since movies are not shot in chronological order, Peck finds it necessary to be meticulous about continuity. "I always discuss it with the director . . . she said so-and-so, we haven't played that scene, would he still have that on his mind about what she said two scenes ago? Would he give her a special kind of look so she understands what's he's saying? That kind of intricacy is very important and Nunnally, having written it, had it all at his fingertips. There's an extra bonus in having a director who has written the script as well. He's in total control of the material."

The story is about Van Dyke (Peck) conducting delicate negotiations with the Russians for the return of the kidnapped boy. He operates through Hoffy (Anita Bjork), girl friend and double agent who eventually betrays him. When Van Dyke learns of her treachery he tries to give her poisoned absinthe. She doesn't drink, but he does; and at the end the Russian ambulance returns the boy and Van Dyke puts the unconscious Hoffy (he has clipped her one) inside, instead of a promised hostage, and goes off to have his stomach pumped. (Also in the cast are Buddy Ebsen, Rita Gam, Walter Abel and Casey Adams.) It is a good, tight thriller (though to my surprise it seemed a little dull and talky when I saw it recently) which was not pushed much by the studio—there was some feeling that people were tired of hearing about Russians and Communism at that time. But as usual there was something here for everybody. Hedda Hopper tried to make it a patriotic tract, and the *Daily Worker* called Nunnally a Fascist for making *Night People* and *The Desert Fox*. Pauline Kael, in *I Lost It at the Movies*, calls *Night People* anti-Communist propaganda because Peck refers to the Russians as "cannibals."

But Nunnally was no propagandist. In this picture, along with *Three Came Home, The Moon Is Down, Desert Fox* and several other pictures, nobody is all bad or all good—instead there is moral ambiguity. The bad guy, rather than being a villain, is just a fellow doing his job. Nunnally said, "When I've done pictures which involve conflicting forces, I have tried to imagine all of them doing exactly what Americans would do, and I remember once I was very much impressed by something Ludwig Bemelmans said—'There are no bad people, just bad governments.' . . . People in general are about the same. There are so many bastards, so many cowards, so many brutes, so many decent guys . . . the last thing I want to do is a picture in which they are all Preminger or Peter Lorre . . . we've got bastards to equal any bastards the Germans ever had."

Nunnally's bad guys frequently become sympathetic because of parenthood. Sessue Hayakawa, as the Japanese concentration camp general in *Three Came Home*, tells the frightened Claudette Colbert about his children; in *Night People*, when Peck's

Russian opposite number dies, our sympathy is aroused when we hear that he shot his children and wife before shooting himself. Rommel's farewell to his son—just before he goes off to take the poison—is touching, and Otto Preminger as a Nazi officer in *The Pied Piper* becomes human when he asks Monty Woolley to take his Jewish niece out of the country. The Gunfighter and Jesse James both melt over their children, and Fredric March, the corporation executive in *Man in the Gray Flannel Suit*, sees himself through his failure as a parent. It is, to Nunnally, what makes us all the same size—and by that time he himself had been "reading *Little Black Sambo* for thirty-five years."

His children supplied some of his best material. He wrote me: "Scotty . . . now has about six people in charge of him. Not that he cares. He is so happy that he is completely bewildered by the least harsh word. Last night when I spoke rather sharply to him about something, he looked at me for a long time very solemnly and then said, 'You are not good.' Naturally I burst out laughing (knowing how wrong he was) and that was the end of that . . . he gets more and more loquacious but within a rather narrow field. At the barber the other day,

Barber: What's your name?

Scotty: Scotty.

Barber: How old are you?

Scotty: (after some thought) Tuesday.

". . . The one time when I begin to doubt Roxie's complete mental balance is when she asks Christie to sing for her. The current favorite is 'Mockingbird Hill.' Christie is always pleased by this tribute to her voice and favors us with a rendition in which she not only never hits one note right but is never within 45 miles of the general tune. . . ." Escorting Christie to a school dance ". . . there was one father-daughter dance, in which I fancied I was doing well enough until I noticed that Christie was doing a little shoving to get me to some other area of the floor. Then I saw that Fred Astaire was dancing with his daughter right next to us and so naturally I fell in with Christie's impulse to remove me from what could not but be an unhappy comparison. . . ."

On more solemn subjects: "Christie has been what might be called a non-attending, non-recognized, unofficial Catholic, with a Methodist coloration. Just before Christmas Christie's affection for Judy Rosenson reached a point where she decided to become Jewish. Dorris, who on that day had reached the don't-give-a-damn stage, said it was okay with her. Then Christie's cool, mercenary mind recovered its possession and she turned to Judy and asked her if she got many presents on Chanukah . . . Judy regretfully replied that she didn't get many. This gave the incipient convert pause. She reflected on the situation for a moment or two and then announced that she would defer making up her mind until after Christmas. . . . When I came down to breakfast this morning Scotty was wailing that Roxie had punched him. Roxie said that Scotty had started it by pushing her under the breakfast table and that it was all his fault. I asked Scotty if this was true. 'Certainly,' he replied. He has now taken to introducing Tippy, the dog, as his brother. The family is growing in all directions."

I was in Berlin with them the summer they were making *Night People,* and everybody was nervous about the Russians. It was before the Wall had been built, but the atmosphere was that of a delicately balanced powder keg. There were border incidents, like the one in the movie, all the time, and all along the boundaries of the Western sector, where the Wall stands, were Russians with tommy guns. You could go into the Russian sector on a tour bus, embarking only at permitted show places—monuments and memorials of great muscular workers, and Stalin Allee, a dreary stretch of Moscow-modern apartment buildings. There were few stores and little life in the streets, it all contrasted glaringly with the lively, tacky American sector.

It was a strange period, the month I was there. Those of us who were not directly involved with the making of the picture—wives, children, sisters, ex-husbands—had to fill our days somehow, and we were all, in our various ways, endlessly on the prowl. Dorris and Jerry Oswald, wife of production manager Gerd Oswald, were after bargains in Meissen and antiques, Rita Gam (who played Peck's secretary) was after the name of a good psychiatrist in New York, Brod Crawford was after booze and a good fight, and everybody was after some evidence that the Germans didn't hate us, which wasn't easy to find. We all sniffed around this ragged and complex joining of East and West with our American guilts and fears and the deep sense of shock that is as natural to us as optimism. We sat around a lot at the sidewalk café in front of the Kempinski Hotel, where we were all staying, and I remember Walter Abel, Buddy Ebsen, the cameraman Charlie Clarke and one or two others saying that they'd been on some tour where it was assumed that everybody hated the Russians but in the middle the whole thing twisted around, and it turned out the real hate was what the Germans had for us. We had bombed them, we had killed their people. Hitler or no Hitler, we had conquered them. The Russians hadn't done any of these things. It was Jamesian, our innocent contemplation of the devious European mind. It did shock us—didn't they know right from wrong? One evening at some sort of songfest led by Casey Adams, an actor in the picture who was also a pianist and composer, everybody was startled when all the Germans, who were sitting together, got up and began singing *"Deutschland über alles."* The Fatherland was not dead. The blinders had not been ripped from German eyes, they did not regard us as saviors. They hardly even had any regrets. As Americans we are baffled when there is no process of guilt and retribution, as Nixon baffles us. Our national conscience is such a source of pain to us, we can't imagine others being without that pain.

Looking for answers like everybody else, I prowled the city, the part I was allowed to go to, for the Russian zone surrounds Berlin like a sea. As in London, I found the ruins hypnotic, more so this time because I knew we had been the ones who did it. I didn't know at the time why I was so fascinated by acres of rubble or so drawn to places like the Potsdamer Platz, where all four sectors came together in uneasy truce; but I do know that my youngest son has looked up from a battleground of toys he has created on the floor and asked me if the war was over between Daddy and me, and who won, anyway? The endless pacing was my own metaphor, the silence, the eyes across the border, the lack of explanation, the slowly building arsenals. I understood this tension, it had become a fell alley of my mind, one that was all too easy to keep taking refuge in—a place where nothing was ever resolved, where love and rage and pain were covered over

by fragile shells of dailiness and where one waited, forever, for
something to happen.

Sometimes I trailed around after Dorris or some of the other
women as they looked for Meissen to buy from people who
could no longer afford to keep it, or gold as an "investment" or
strange brassieres with holes cut out of the middle, a Berlin odd-
ity that made us shriek with laughter. When we had exhausted
the Kurfürstendamm, we went on the bus tour to East Berlin, to
glide through those silent empty streets and tell ourselves how
much happier we were than the people who lived in them. We
were only allowed to get off the bus at certain places, usually
those war memorials guarded by Russians with tommy guns.
Once when the bus stopped at a red light Dorris suddenly got off
it and stood outside handing out candy to a group of children.
She had moved with astonishing speed and it took me a moment
to realize that the elegant little blonde lady out there in Forbid-
denplatz was Dorris. After a stunned moment she was escorted
back aboard by an ashen driver and two heavily armed VOPOs.
I thought she had lost her mind (as Pop did when he heard of
it) but now I think it was simply her way of saying, fuck it all.

She had gotten to a point where she needed to say that. Years
later, she told me that was the summer when she got the money,
which was what she got to replace other things that seemed
unattainable. "Nobody," she said once to the Bogarts, "knows
who I am. I always have to say, 'I'm Mrs. Nunnally Johnson.' I
want to be me." Bogey said, "What does that mean, 'I want to be
me'? You should be happy you're married to this dazzling, funny,
wonderful man. If that's your identity, what's wrong with it?" I
doubt that consoled her much. She had to have something of her
own, which had not turned up in any of the therapies or hypno-
sis or clinics which were her way of searching. She was really
looking for a certain vision she had expected to find in her husband—and felt she had every right to expect—which turned out
not to exist, certain antennae were missing. He had turned out to
have clay feet. He was unused and disinclined to self-examination, he saved his best powers for his work, his strength for story-
telling. In other areas of his life he was blind to the point of cruelty, and more cruelly so because it was so unintentional. Marge
told me that once in New York during the war, shortly after she

and Gene were married, "I had been promised a job on the Coast, but till then I was living on one meal a day, a hot dog and an orange drink at Nedick's. Gene got twenty-one dollars a month from the army and his ex-wife got seven dollars of it and I had no job. Dad was staying at the Savoy Plaza and he invited me up and we ordered dinner in the room. He just picks at food, so I ate my dinner first and then I ate his. He said, 'How the hell do you keep your shape, you eat like a goddam truck driver.' Ten years after the war Gene told him the story and he was simply stunned that we didn't have any money. He was a very Olympian fellow and he couldn't imagine anybody not having enough money to eat on. Having been poor didn't stay in his mind."

Similarly—though he was not alone among husbands—it never occurred to him that Dorris might not have enough money, or that it might be difficult for her to ask for it. Since he had no feeling about it himself it didn't enter his head that she might need it. In the beginning she was shy about handling money in amounts larger than she had ever had experience with, and assumed that Nunnally knew what he was doing. But, she says, "I presently learned to my distress and dismay that he didn't know about it, didn't care about it, he always thought he could just earn more, and he knew so little, he hated always to be confronted with money matters and would either immediately dismiss it or change the subject or indicate he had more important things to do. You can't operate a home and a family on the scale we operated without knowing money matters and somebody had to handle the exchequer, and it had to be somebody concerned with family matters."

In Germany it came to a head. "I wanted to buy things for the house. I had no money. It didn't occur to Nunnally that two hundred dollars wasn't enough, to say, 'Take five thousand dollars,' he had it, but he thought in terms of small money, it was the only money Nunnally understood because he left off understanding money when he left off a Saturday check from the newspaper . . . it became an embarrassment to him when he earned big money. When we went to Venice"—a trip Dorris and I and Jerry Oswald took after Munich—"I got the money to make that trip by doing something that still embarrasses me. I had bought a gold necklace in Munich and Greg Peck admired it ·

on me and said I should get Veronique one, so I took that necklace and put it in a box, put the price tag on it and put it in
Greg's mailbox and said, "Here it is, it's yours." He sent me the
check for it. I still think how I closed in on Greg that way and it
embarrasses the hell out of me."

Shortly afterward she and Nunnally had a "confrontation." She
wanted to get rid of the business manager ("I still think we were
fleeced to a degree that would be grand larceny") and take over
herself, which she did. "I went about it very studiously . . . I
studied daily. I told the business manager I was going to handle
the money and the decisions were going to be made by me. Nunnally was pleased. . . . I started to make investments that would
improve our income position and I distrusted Hollywood money
—I had seen people make big money, lose it fast and have no
seats in their pants any more, they were down-and-outers. . . . I
started first in the farm business, cattle business, that was quite
unsuccessful, I lost a lot. Land investment eventually made
money."

While we were in Munich (where the interiors were filmed) I
had done two days' work as an extra, in a shot of a smoke-filled
Berlin bar. Pop wrote later: "As for your big role, you'll have to
look fast to see yourself as the camera pans with Brod Crawford
past you. I was much disappointed about this and informed
Charlie Clarke [the cameraman] that if I had been behind the
camera and if it had been his daughter out there I would have
stopped for a few beats. . . . I'm tremendously pleased that you
had a good time over here. Your visit made me very happy too.
We must have more of these little location trips. We may get
things shaped up so that we'll only see each other in foreign
parts, near a camera. Love to you, darling."

We had not shared Berlin as we had shared London, but it
might have been that that sort of thing was over by then anyway.
But now there was something I could do about communication
gaps of this sort, and back at Smith I wrote a novel about Berlin.

Hollywood 1954–1957

The next picture written, produced and directed by Nunnally was *Black Widow* (1954), a so-so mystery melodrama with Van Heflin, Peggy Ann Garner, Ginger Rogers, Gene Tierney and George Raft. Some of these were second choices—he had wanted Maggie McNamara for the Peggy Ann Garner part—but the loss of Tallulah Bankhead (for the Ginger Rogers part) was more fortunate. Asked to do the part, she talked to him on the phone for twenty-five minutes about how she was a star, while Nunnally thought, If at the end of this she says yes, I'll cut my throat. He said, "I could just see myself, day after day, arguing with Tallulah about every bloody detail in the thing. Finally when she said, 'I couldn't possibly—' I said, 'I'm terribly sorry, Tallulah' and hung up."

Peggy Ann Garner lacks charm in a role that demands charm —she sends a group of high-powered people into a flurry and one doesn't understand why. Her progress as a climber is marked by street signs—she moves upward into better and better neighborhoods, which Nunnally got from Onnie, who had similarly moved her family upward in Columbus. There are two of Nunnally's thematic characters in *Black Widow*—the steadfast wife (Gene Tierney) who stands by her wronged husband (Van Heflin, accused of murder) as in *Prisoner of Shark Island, Desert Fox,* and *Jesse James;* and the ambiguous woman in baffling shades of black and white (*Rachel, Dark Mirror, Woman in the*

Window, and the ultimate one, *Three Faces of Eve*). Peggy Ann
Garner is supposed to be a sweet innocent, but she is really a
black widow spinning a net. And Van Heflin is the good man
who gets screwed, like Dr. Mudd in *Prisoner of Shark Island,
The Country Doctor,* Greg Peck in *Keys of the Kingdom,* and
Edward G. Robinson in *Woman in the Window.* Even a writer
who adapts other people's material must be attracted to certain
kinds of people and problems, his mind is going to start showing
(especially in a body of work the size of Nunnally's) whether he
likes it or not. There are a few things that hang out, spill around
the edges of the cabinetmaking.

How to Be Very, Very Popular (1955; an all-around Nunnally
Johnson production) is a dreadful comedy (he called it "a
piddling little picture") with Betty Grable and Sheree North
(who was "amazingly untalented") in a part written for Marilyn
Monroe. Two koochy dancers (or something) witness a murder
and must hide away so they won't have to testify, a procedure
they see as not only a nuisance but downright dangerous. They
hide out on the campus of a sort of joke college where students
hide for years in the basement and adult male students are
shooed off to bed by a housemother. The incredibly complicated
plot has to do with bald men being confused with other bald
men (trustees, murderers, fathers, deans) and the graduating
class doing high kicks and throwing their diplomas around. If
any of it sounds familiar, Billy Wilder swiped the plot and made
a much better picture with *Some Like It Hot* (as he swiped the
plot of *Night People* and made *One, Two, Three*). Nunnally had
no ill feeling about this, he was amused and saw this intra-
industry theft as a sort of compliment. It was done all the time—
Warner's *Sudden Death,* for instance, was Hitchcock's *Stranger
on a Train,* with a golf player instead of a tennis player. Said
Nunnally, "There was one guy at Warner Brothers in the old
days who made a career of it. He'd go and see *The Good Earth.*
The next morning he'd call a writer and say, 'Take a look at this
picture and see if we can't make it in Kansas.' But he was very
happy to admit it. He certainly never made any bones about it."

The direction of *How to Be Very, Very Popular* and *Black
Widow* (or what I think of as the direction) seems slow and

soggy—people do a lot of standing around, and reactions are molasses-slow.

The Man in the Gray Flannel Suit was based on the best-selling novel by Sloan Wilson, one of the two or three original authors who liked Nunnally's adaptation. In it Greg Peck plays the advertising executive whose life almost goes out from under him, and Jennifer Jones plays his wife. It is all very fifties. There are stresses and strains about money, and flashbacks to Tom Rath's (Peck's) wartime affair with an Italian girl, which his wife comes painfully to accept. The story is about the struggle up the corporate ladder, the setting suburban. There were the usual starting pains. Nunnally wrote me at the time: "This is show business. We sent a copy of the script of *The Man in the Gray Flannel Suit* to Keenan Wynn and asked him to play Hawthorne. He sent back word that he didn't want to play Hawthorne, he wanted to play Gardella. We sent a copy of the script to Ernest Borgnine and asked him to play Gardella. He sent back word that he didn't want to play Gardella but would be very happy to play Tom Rath. We sent a copy of the script to Lee Cobb and asked him to play Judge Bernstein and he replied that he would much prefer to play Hopkins. We sent a copy to Jennifer Jones and she didn't want to have anything to do with any part of it. She finally said she would play Betsy Rath but yesterday, four days before we start to shoot, she backed out of that."

Greg Peck says: "I recall that Nunnally did not have too high an opinion of that book. I once said to him, 'I hope it turns out to be *The Best Years of Our Lives* ten years later. . . .' The picture was successful but didn't have that kind of size or stature. I got the impression it was something Darryl asked him to do, a hard book to lick. I liked the war scenes the best, but I thought Nunnally was at his best poking fun at Madison Avenue. I don't think he was terribly involved with suburbanite problems." If suburbia is not Nunnally's milieu, the family is, and the family scenes have a lot to do with making the picture work. One of the most moving scenes is between Fredric March and his daughter, who has grown to hate him for his super-corporation values. He sees that if he has failed as a parent the rest doesn't count for much, one of life's hard lessons that Nunnally was painfully aware of. March gives a superb performance and Nunnally wrote me: "The picture goes along with no more than the customary troubles. Peck does a good deal of deep thinking, which slows up progress while we discuss the psychology of a scene, and Jennifer Jones often wants to know if she isn't concealing a feeling of guilt when she says "hello." On the other hand, Freddie March, about five times as good an actor as both of the others put together, simply wants to know what suit he is wearing and where he should be standing when I call Action."

Shooting around New York caused a little excitement. The Fox public relations department hoped that Peck being filmed on Madison Avenue would tie up traffic for miles around—"they forget that having Gregory Peck stand over a grating and blowing a blast of wind up his trousers is not exactly like doing same with Marilyn Monroe." The picture was too long, "my worst error in determining the length of a picture." Usually the scripts he wrote for his own direction were very short, about a hundred and twenty pages.

Greg Peck's concern with minutiae "scared me to death," said Nunnally. "He had a copy of the book and you know how many times you get a book from the library and on the side it says, 'How true!' Things like that. Well, Greg had all kinds of notes and little pieces of paper sticking out of the book. Most of them were minor, but you had to listen to them . . . he's a stubborn man, and I think he's afraid of comedy." Though Nunnally joked about Greg's compulsive psychologizing, Greg says, "I don't like a lot of detailed analytic chatter from directors, it tends to confuse you. But there's another kind of actor's director, he waits for extra values, extra insights, and he knows when you capture something special, a new shred of illumination. . . . Wyler is this kind of director, he isn't terribly articulate, doesn't talk a lot, but he knows it could be deeper, could have more life in it, could have more edginess or more comedy or more sentiment, he knows it could be better and he'll say so over and over again . . . once in a while it's something very slight, doesn't sound at all like high-class direction, he'll say 'Get mad this time,' and you do it, and he says, 'Not quite like that,' not fancy things, direct things. It may be that Nunnally didn't develop that appreciation of the acting craft . . . it may be that if he heard his own words played back in a lively way he thought, That's as good as they can do it. It may be that if he'd gone on a little more, he could have gotten more of a personal contribution from the actors, to shed a little more light on his lines. I think it's fair to say that. It's not a matter of a lot of talk, it's an instinctive understanding of acting. Wyler, Robert Mulligan, some directors have that extra depth and insight. I don't think Nunnally was greatly gifted in that way. But in every other way he was an ideal director, patient, wise, he kept a good mood on the set, never blew his top, always dealt with things in terms of humor. He could always set us straight on the meaning of lines and continuity." Nunnally's direction was—not surprisingly—merely competent. Others have put it more harshly than Greg—"He only directed to protect his lines." Though he wrote, produced and directed eight pictures, he was, first, last and always, a writer, "a compulsive, dedicated storyteller," as Dorris described him. Nothing else— professionally or personally—interested him as much, and producing and directing were, to him, afterthoughts.

Jennifer Jones caused certain problems. Nunnally found her hard to deal with—"her eyes were rather out of focus, I couldn't tell whether she was hearing what I was saying or not." One scene was close to catastrophic. Shooting on the lawn of a house rented for the purpose on Long Island, Jennifer was supposed to run out of the house after a fight with Greg, who then catches her and kisses her as they fall on the ground. "She came out like an impala," Nunnally told. "God, she's a big, leggy girl, you know, and Greg has a gimp anyway, so she forgot all about that spot and was leading him by about eight lengths when she passed it. I said, 'Cut.' I said, 'You must have forgotten, honey, we've got to get you in the camera.' She said, 'Well, I thought I was supposed to be real.'" The next take seemed to be perfect, except that this time Jennifer had gone wild—"She just opened up my face," says Greg. "There were big claw marks there." "By this time," said Nunnally, "eight doctors and nine make-up men were surrounding him. He said, 'I don't call that acting. I call it personal. Can't you get her to do the scene right?' I said, 'I don't know. You worked with her in *Duel in the Sun*. I thought you'd know how to cope with this particular thing.'" They had to do it again, for a close shot, and "this time," Nunnally told, "she but-

ted him. You never saw a madder actor. He said, 'Have we got to
do it again?' I said, 'Well, if we do it again, you wear your cup,
because I don't know what's going to happen.' I talked to her
. . . what do you say to a woman who is fighting savagely when
they're supposed to be make-believe? She listened to me, looking
past me, and then walked back to her dressing room. She didn't
answer. . . . One time she did a kind of emotion scene, and
much to everybody's astonishment, she suddenly made a gesture
and knocked everything off the dressing table." It looked right,
so it stayed in. "Oh, Jennifer Jones," Betty Grable said about her.
"She thinks that doing knee bends makes you an actress."

It was worth all the aggravation, for the picture was a financial success and Zanuck made it his "personal" production for the
year. Said Nunnally, "This suits me from the ground up, for I
will have a percentage in the profits of my pictures from now
on."

Oh, Men! Oh, Women! (1957; Dan Dailey, Ginger Rogers,
David Niven, Tony Randall in his first film, Barbara Rush,
Natalie Schafer) was a strange picture, described by Nunnally
as a comedy. It was an adaptation of the play by the same name
by Edward Chodorov, but what had worked on the stage failed
commercially on the screen. Nunnally said only, "The material
interested me, but it didn't interest anybody else . . . mine was a
minority report." It is about a psychiatrist (David Niven) whose
patient (Tony Randall) is still in love with—or inflamed by—
Barbara Rush, Niven's fiancée. Another patient is Ginger Rogers,
unfulfilled wife of Dan Dailey, famous actor, who also was involved with Miss Rush in the past. Old desires and jealousies fly
about as Niven wonders what he's gotten into—not only are Barbara's ex-boy friends screwy, but Barbara appears to be a little
screwy herself; her handbag is a garbage can, her apartment is
stacked with dolls, and she believes strongly in repressing the
past, which upsets the good doctor. For a while it's all funny, but
about halfway through a strange intensity appears, almost like
pain. (I wrote in my notes, "Maybe by '56 N. felt too much pain,
people hurt in this picture, it throws off the comedy.") Dailey, in
whom is invested the voice of the author, says, "Suppose a guy is
just a husband—and *that* makes her mad?" and—along with a
reference to Ibsen's *Doll's House*—"There must be something

they want out there. Can you tell me what it is, Doc?" and "Can I help it if I'm the kind of guy who does the home and family business—can I help it if it isn't very interesting?" We are told, and shown, how women go to analysts to complain about their husbands, and since the analysts agree when they say the husbands are nuts, the women fall in love with them (the analysts). What, the men keep asking, as Freud did, does a woman want?

Ginger tells Dailey he dominates her and overwhelms her, that if she dropped dead tomorrow she would never be missed—the children have gone away to school and they have a cook. She is no longer needed. Is it because they have so much, do women only feel useful if they are poor? Her husband tells her emphatically, "I cannot make you feel necessary." Niven suggests Dailey treat his wife as a sweetheart, not a squaw. When Niven asks Rush what women want, she says they want to be manipulated, outsmarted—and some cave-man stuff too. Nunnally must have had some trouble with this. There are two endings in the script I read, and a third one (the cave-man one) in the finished picture. From him the issues are irreconcilable, these questions men and women ask each other. This picture, along with *The Man Who Understood Women,* reminded me of some of his late short stories, when the male-female enigma with its attendant high feeling stained the comic surface. It is a second breaking-up period, of both marriage and work. The marriage to Dorris lasted, but all these things came up in their marriage, and Dorris struggled for her identity in her marriage to a man she felt "dominated and overwhelmed" her.

Marge cut *Oh, Men! Oh, Women!* She had cut *Woman in the Window,* but this was the first time she had worked closely with Nunnally (since he was director). Marge and Gene were by then highly successful film editors, at that time still in their own arenas (though years afterward they worked together on TV's "The Waltons"). In 1944, the year they were married, they had both started out on *Woman in the Window.* Gene was editor, Marge was assistant editor. At that time the top editorial salary was a hundred and sixty-five dollars a week, the assistant's salary eighty dollars, though Nunnally got Marge a hundred dollars a week. When Gene was drafted, Fritz Lang, the director, made Marge the editor. Encouraged by what seemed like a tiny bit of extra help from her father, she asked Nunnally for a hundred and sixty-five dollars a week. He said, "You're so lucky to be the editor on this picture you'll take whatever they decide to give you." Marge says, "Justice in his mind was that I'd gotten a tremendous break. Nunnally didn't help his children unless they could perform. At the end of the picture Fritz went to Nunnally and said, 'We need more time and Marjie's a little slow.' Nunnally said, 'Fire her.' I loved it because it made me feel so clean." This remarkable leap, on both their parts, from father-daughter into a professional relationship that really worked, came partly out of a daring and willingness to fight her father that I never had (none of the three younger children ever tried to work with him). She had him first, and in spite of other problems she was probably more secure in her feeling that he loved her than any of the rest of us. He was only twenty-one when she was born, and in a sense they grew up together. She could influence him in a way nobody else could—she had known him when he was malleable. Besides she had always been feisty. Once he wrote me, "Back in 1937 Marjorie wanted to make a trip through Europe on what was called a hostel tour, and when I objected on the grounds that the Nazis were being particularly nasty to Americans, insulting them with slaps and kicks and jailing them on the smallest provocation, Marjorie drew herself up to her full seventeen years and replied, 'I cannot imagine a situation with which I could not cope.' This filled me with pride and I trembled for Hitler, but in the end I was compelled to say no. In such a mood she might have touched off World War II two years earlier." Later on during the war Marge got thrown out of Nunnally's house. "I had gotten some notion early in the war that it was ridiculous to fight," she said, "and if Hitler took over we would simply be under a different economic situation. I spouted this out at some gathering up at Holmby, and Nunnally took me in the other room and said, 'Look, I will not have this spoken in front of my friends, as long as you have this attitude you will not be welcome at this house.' He wouldn't even discuss it—it was radical surgery."

She had been working around town as a cutter for twelve years when Nunnally called her and asked her to work on *Oh, Men! Oh, Women!* at Fox as an assistant cutter. "I was shocked," she says. "I'd cut two pictures for him [*Woman in the Window* and *Mr. Peabody and the Mermaid*]. I was a full editor. He didn't even know I was a member of A.C.E. [the film editors' union]." Recovering from the fact that he had totally forgotten her hard-won professional status, she invited him to a preview of a picture she had done and the next morning he asked her to be editor on *Oh, Men! Oh, Women!* She went home to Gene that night and said, "What am I going to call him? I can't just walk on that set and say, 'Hey, Dad.'" But how could she call him Nunnally or Mr. Johnson? "After two hours of agony she settled on Nunnally," Gene says.

She loved making the picture but was under a good deal of stress. During the first cut run, which took place in the evening after a rather boozy dinner, Nunnally sat by Marge giving her endless notes on what she had done wrong, convincing her she had utterly failed. She spent a large part of the next day writing Nunnally a nine-page letter because she couldn't talk to him. Somewhere along the line Nunnally called and said, "Honey, dis-regard all those notes I gave you, that was Jack Daniels talking." "I didn't know yet how to deal with him," she says. "I did later, I got in violent arguments and discussions with him by the time we got to *Three Faces of Eve*. All my life I'd worked with direc-tors who didn't want to cut one goddam frame of anything, and he as a writer was cutting his own words and script far more deeply than I thought was proper. We kidded about this, some-times I'd win."

The influence of the cutter (film editor, as they are more ele-gantly called by cinema students) is largely unrecognized by any-body outside the industry. Badly shot sequences can be saved, well-shot ones heightened by intelligent editing. In *Oh, Men! Oh, Women!* Marge decided to try a trick. Nunnally wanted to drop a good deal out of the middle of a scene with the four prin-cipals in a ship's cabin. "Gene had experimented in some wagon train thing, he put two black frames in and jumped two hundred feet, which made you blink your eye, and then went on with the scene. I did the same thing, I found a place where they were all in approximately the same position. You couldn't see anything. In those days we used hot splicers and if you wanted a close shot or something you had to fill in that frame—we used to cut in the middle of a frame and fill it with a piece of black [to keep six-

teen frames per foot]. A lay person can't see that—time after
time the director wouldn't know, wouldn't see the black frame
even if it extended two or three feet. Working on this premise, I
found the spot, put two black frames in, jumped out a hundred
and fifty feet, ran it a couple of times to be sure I could get away
with it and then ran it for Nunnally. He thought it was marvelous
and I told him what I had done." Though Nunnally liked it,
higher-ups objected because "it went against studio training."
"You can't do it," Marge was told. "You and your cheap Republic
tricks." A much more awkward method was used.

Both Marge and Gene were "kinda treated like mavericks" because they were the first to experiment with subliminal cutting,
which is fascinating to the point of being frightening. The brain,
it seems, moves faster than the eye, and up to four or five frames
of other material can be spliced into a film without our being
able to see it but *somehow we know it's there.* (The eye starts to
catch it at about six frames.) In an experimental film Gene did,
the father of a retarded child is talking to a psychiatrist about
the best thing to do with his son. Gene cut in shots of the child,
only one frame, from other parts of the picture. Says Gene: "I invited people in to look at it but you couldn't ask them, 'Did you
see this?' . . . Stanley Kramer said, 'I kept thinking of this poor
sad kid.' I told him what it was and he didn't have guts enough
to allow it to be. He was afraid." The eight-frame cut is one third
of a second, which is minimum for consciously seeing it. Ten or
fifteen years ago a test was run at the Directors' Guild, during
which film was shown and the viewers were told to push a button when they saw anything that shouldn't have been there. The
film had been marked with red crosses, grease pencil, and one or
two frames at a time blacked out. They didn't start getting the
buzzes until six frames of black went by, and they didn't see the
red Xs until there were twelve in a row. Possibly because the
implications are so chilling and 1984-ish, subliminal cuts are not
used much at the moment, though eight- or ten-frame cuts (such
as those quick flashes of the Devil's face in *The Exorcist*) are
somewhat in fashion.

The largely unrecognized possibilities of film are what make
up the cutters' art. Gene says: "What I drum into these kids [ap-
prentice cutters] working for me is, when you get film, always

look for a third dimension in that film. Maybe you can find something in that film that even the director doesn't know he shot—many times you can do that with byplay, double cutting, presenting it in a slightly different light which accentuates the dramatic meaning. An old experiment done in 1920 demonstrated the time relationship. A boy walks right to left in front of the Kremlin, a girl walks left to right in front of the White House, they meet in front of the Eiffel Tower. Because of the juxtaposition of the film they were both within eyeshot of each other—you can do that with films, bend it around. Unfortunately there are as few of those kinds of editors as there are Nunnally Johnsons."

Nunnally came to depend on Marge in the pictures they did together partly because she is so good and partly because he was so uninterested in the technical side of movie making. In *Mr. Peabody and the Mermaid* Marge said to him, "Let's have a wipe here," and he replied, "Fine, I'm sure we have a lot of wipers around." "It was one reason he wasn't a good director," Marge says, "though he was the first to admit it. A director should know about lenses for visual effects. A wide-angled lens will give you a distorted foreground and great distance in the background. When you shoot at close-up you should never use more than a 75 millimeter, if you go less than 75 the nose gets large and the ears get far away. The director should know his craft as writers do. When people run and run endlessly toward the camera, that's a 500- or 1000-millimeter lens. Nunnally said, 'I know it's necessary but I don't want to know about it.'"

Smith, New York, Arabia
1954-1956

I read the Berlin novel aloud, a chapter a week, by the fire at our evening writing seminar. It was a kind of scrapbag of the Berlin summer. Since not enough time had passed for me to know what any of it meant, the flavors had not married and the book was full of undigested material—people and places and profound theories which had nothing to do with each other, but which, like a thrifty housewife, I threw in because they couldn't be wasted. The class seemed to like it, and I felt as though I had never done anything so wonderful before. Being mid-novel was security blanket, status symbol, and reason for living. In a sense it mattered less what it was like than the fact that I was doing it. I had done something, Pop wrote, that he had never been able to do—"there is nothing else in the whole realm of writing that could be a substitute for that achievement, no matter what its success or lack of it when and if published. You will know that you can make the distance."

I had already got an agent. I had sent several stories to Edith Haggard, Pop's old friend who worked for Curtis Brown. Edith read them all and sent a couple around to magazines for editorial comment. "The writer labors in a kind of vacuum," wrote Pop, "so the least word of encouragement is like a hypodermic shot to him. He doesn't even have to believe the word. It might even come from someone for whom he has little or no respect. But after such a word he feels a lift that is worth its weight in gold in his work. From that minute on he'll do better stuff. It's like souping up a car and many agents know and understand this."

But in spite of my novel and my agent, adulthood and the outside world hung just outside the gate and, from what I could gather, neither looked friendly. "Without meaning to be too morose about it," Nunnally wrote, "I still can't help a feeling of sadness that the law is transmuting you next Monday from my child to a free and independent adult with the legal right not only to sign contracts but to tell me to go to hell if you wish to. I'm afraid I'm going to miss the kid, but I can't think of anyone who seemed readier or more qualified for the new role." There were a few of us, that spring, who had no prospective husbands. It was characteristic of the time that the ones who did shut down whatever ambitions or interests they might have had, at least for the time being—marriage was expected to take care of everything. Among the rest there was a great rush for the Northampton secretarial school. We started wearing our graduation robes early in the spring, and I remember the group of nervous seniors in their flapping black robes, riding off in the dusk on their bicycles to learn to type and take shorthand. Our educations were sweeping, patchy and impractical. The science majors had been offered jobs, but the rest of us, who considered ourselves literary, faced the yawning gap between a Rona Jaffe fantasy of life in New York and the economic realities of being an English major. Sylvia Plath, who had started out in my class, had been the star, the one who was obviously going to make it—but Sylvia had taken sleeping pills and crawled under the porch after her summer on *Mademoiselle*. It got her out of the running (she graduated a year later, in '55) but it was strange and startling commentary on what might happen to you in that glittering magazine world we all longed for.

I hadn't the slightest notion how I was going to go about leading a successful life, beyond an idea of going to Europe on a cattle boat and writing in a Roman garret, which I thought sounded romantic. In June I hung around the brownstone in a kind of postgraduate stupor until Pop suggested I spend a month or so in Caifornia rewriting the Berlin novel under his tutelage.

In California I worked the way Pop did. He was on the set every day, shooting *How to Be Very, Very Popular,* and I used

his office at Fox. Sometimes we drove over together and if I
finished before he did I would go home and then go back and
pick him up later. We usually had lunch at the commissary together. In between I sat in his elegant office and rewrote, and
Betty Baldwin, his secretary, sat in the outer office and typed up
whatever I had done. It was all a little hard to believe, and I had
never been so painfully aware of my inexperience. In the eve-
nings, after dinner, we would go over my manuscript (which
seemed worse every day) and Pop would make suggestions for
change. Most of the time I had no idea how angry all this made
me, except when he called the book a script, the ultimate Hollywood takeover. Then I was guilty about being so ungrateful for
his well-meant and loving help. It all clouded what literary judgment I had—on one hand, I resented his changes but, on the
other, my own work wasn't so hot either. We were doing our
best with a sow's ear.

When I was back in New York he wrote: "The question may
rise in your mind as to whether such editing and revision is
proper or ethical. I can only tell you that it has been done literally thousands of times. To cite Max Perkins again, he made far
greater alterations in Thomas Wolfe's work than I have here, and
wrote the transitions to bring the book together again . . . no
one thinks of taking any credit from Wolfe for that reason. . . .
People have said that Wolfe was a very lucky fellow to have
such an able and conscientious friend and editor as Perkins. I
hope they can say the same of you and me . . . do not go
around, with unnecessary modesty, and tell everyone that your
father 'practically rewrote' the book. That is not true. I feel I
must admonish you about this because of your intense honesty
and reluctance to accept what you think is not properly your
credit. (As a matter of fact, who can say for sure that what I
have done is right!)" He told me to use either version, his or
mine, or parts of both, and then warned, "I wish you the best of
luck, darling, but the publication of a first effort can only be described as a miracle . . . if it doesn't happen, don't let it get you
down. Just blame it on me. It wouldn't be my first flop."

The novel, pared down to little more than half its original size,
was submitted to and rejected by the best publishers in New
York and Boston. I knew more than to blame Pop for this, but I

had the feeling that his work, rather than mine, had been judged, and that it had been turned down for the wrong reasons. It was true, though not in the way I thought; most of the ideas in the book had been taken from his originally, the setting was copied from his movie, one of the characters was a version of him, and another two or three were lifted from *Night People*. It wasn't really my voice, which I hadn't found yet; and when I realized that I put it in the drawer with a certain relief.

That fall I got a job on *The New Yorker* as a sixty-dollar-a-week receptionist. Of the three gloomy floors that made up the offices, I was on the gloomiest and dullest of all and writing on the job was not only accepted but encouraged. Along the hall were half a dozen attractive but strangely withdrawn young reporters and behind me were Lois Long ("Lipstick") and Sheila Hibben representing Fashion and Food. My job was to answer the dozen or so phone calls a day and try to fend off Mrs. Hibben, who seemed to think I had a switchboard, besides typing Edmund Wilson manuscripts and wondering what Lipstick meant when she told me what an adorable bastard Nunnally was. Otherwise I was free to write stories and ship them upstairs to the editorial department, an approved activity for receptionists. It was a pleasant period and it would seem, in retrospect, that I had got it together for the time being. I still lived at home, which I talked about leaving as soon as I found a suitable roommate. My stepfather Rogers, who wanted to get rid of me, encouraged this move by taking over more and more bits of the house until the elegant, peacock-walled living room had become an office resounding with the deafening zonk-biddle-biddle-zonk of something called a Friden Calculator, which he turned on whenever the conversation bored him. But I couldn't take an apartment yet—what about the Roman garret? What about tinkling oriental music and jungle sounds, would I ever hear them or were they being drowned out by Mrs. Hibben nattering on about bechamel sauce and the clatter of the Friden Calculator? How could I write if I never did anything, what was there to write about? As the road seemed to narrow, as alternative after alternative faded away, I found myself, as a lot of other women have said afterward (because that is really how it happens), getting married early in 1955.

Everybody approved, more or less, or they said they did. Pop liked Len because, "Thank God, he is an adult. Boyish charm is a thing that is pretty well lost on me. If I never see any of it again, that's soon enough for me . . . the spectacle of an eager and promising youth scrabbling for a foothold in life depresses me. Len suggests neither . . . you will be spared the frantic hopes and despairs of a husband still wildly groping for a rope to climb up the side of life. That may be a dramatic and stimulating thing in retrospect, but you may take it from an old groper that it is nothing but unhappiness at the time. God help the poor bride who has to go through it." This was very game of him considering that Len proposed to take me to Saudi Arabia, where he worked for Aramco. Besides, Len was Catholic and we were to be married in the Catholic Church, during which arrangements I was constantly referred to as a non-Catholic—probably the most negative thing I have ever been called. Pop wrote: "Under this Catholic-Unaffiliated arrangement, am I to understand that you will have to be married in some kind of Jim Crow section of the church? All I can think of when things like this come up is of the time in Great Neck when Groucho's little son Arthur came back from the Kensington pool with the word that he was not permitted to go in it because he was Jewish. 'Go back and tell 'em your mother is Gentile,' Groucho ordered him, 'and go in only up to your waist.'"

In arranging the wedding, which was to be rather a production, the suggestion came up—I forget how, or who said it—that Fox might be called in to help. Nunnally wrote: "I must admit that you hurt me by a certain loftiness of attitude toward the company I work for, and indirectly Hollywood and my business. . . . When you say that Fox might be called on for assistance if it is able to remember its place, there was a suggestion that the colored folks would be permitted to pitch in and help provided they understood that they were not to mingle with the white guests . . . a suggestion of contempt which is common enough but which I hope my family will never share.

"Intellectually, the movies compare favorably with books, magazines, etc. Good people turn out good books, movies, music, paintings, bad people turn out bad ones. Most people understand this now, and the snobbism in that field is limited these days to a few precious ones, the dickeybird aesthetes. But a good deal of this desiccated snobbishness remains here and there and I wouldn't like you to become infected with it, for one, because it is a stupid form of stuffiness, and two, because, after all, you have benefited from it. Besides I have a certain pride in my business, and I shouldn't dare to see you, like S., ashamed of her father because he is neither Dylan Thomas nor a rich stockbroker. In any case Fox wouldn't have the slightest interest in such an affair. . . . I doubt that I am so celebrated that you will be troubled or embarrassed by anything more than a mild identification of me, your father, as a musical director of Hollywood, California, but I'm sure you wouldn't want me to present myself as a manufacturer of plastic webbing. This would be a lie and might leave us all open to charges of perjury.

"Just keep your head. Remain balanced. In dusty corners of the world it is still fashionable to be politely contemptuous of American movies, but I'm sure that as you grow older you will find such affectations to be no more worth while than S.'s adolescent airs and superiority.

"I love you."

After a couple of months in New York, Len and I left for the Middle East. On our last night we stood on the steps of the brownstone while the last El train—full of city officials—went by, the last clattering note of my childhood. I would, Len had promised, hear the tinkle of oriental music instead, and breathe the incense in Arab bazaars. But whatever I was—and I had not quite found it—I left behind, like a story that ended up in the drawer because I had not found the ending.

Arabia was . . . Something in my brain falls apart when I try to write about it. One tiny story still rings in my head. At the end of two years, when I was leaving to come home for the first time, I was having coffee (we were always having coffee) with a woman I had come to know somewhat while I was there. I liked her because she was one of the infinitesimally few people in the compound who admitted that her life wasn't perfect. She was intellectually a cut above most of the other women—an anthropologist like her husband, with whom she had spent some time digging at ancient Sumer, which was not far north of where we were. At the end of her "call"—we called on each other at coffee time or tea time—during which I had talked excitedly about how I couldn't wait to get back to civilization, to shops and restaurants and theaters, the woman, whose name was Charlotte, looked me straight in the eye and said, "Oh, Nora, grow up." Then she turned and left.

On the way home with my daughter, then less than a year old, I stopped in Cairo to stay with friends in the State Department. I was very fond of these people and the first evening (while the slaves took care of the children and served us dinner) I told them what Charlotte had said, that it was grinding away like an uncorrectable false note, and how exasperated I was at having been left speechless.

"You should have kicked her in the groin," said Chuck, "wherever it hurts most, and when she was lying on the floor crying, you say, 'Oh, Charlotte, grow up.'"

The false notes of Dhahran, the American colony of 2,000 on the Persian Gulf, only presented themselves as oriental music, which had a pattern if you were smart enough to figure out what it was. Not only was I unable to do so, but I hardly knew what the problem was, and nobody else seemed to know of its existence. Even when, among the coffee cups and bridge hands, I found a Charlotte, whom I wanted to shake and say, "Look here, you understand what I mean, you must understand," she turned away. The place made me feel nuts—paranoid, hallucinating stresses and strains nobody else felt. It was terribly strange, for one thing, to be a housewife. I had spent my entire life, nine months a year, in the daily use of my mind and now there were no classes to go to, no papers to write or tests to take. It had all been, apparently, some sort of caper, and now my days were spent going to the commissary, playing bridge, cooking, and telling the houseboy what to do. I had lived with competition, which now was transformed into who could make the fluffiest cake or the suavest marchand de vin. "Dorris laughed [wrote Pop] when you reflected on the subject of conversation among the wives. It was the laugh of a wife who has found that no matter where she goes or with whom she associates the talk of wives is just about the same, which is to say, about the fundamentals of life, babies, food, and how to be comfortable. This may be a little startling after the intellectuality of college life, but I imagine that in time these subjects will become the meat and potatoes of conversation. Other subjects will be the sauces and salads. But this isn't too bad a balance. Don't forget, people can be bores on intellectual subjects just as quickly as they can on housekeeping problems, and often a great deal quicker."

It was baffling how so many other people in this place, including Len, didn't seem to mind the things I did; the heat, the confinement, the Islamic laws (no booze, women not allowed to drive outside of town, et cetera), the dullness, the homogenized population (no old people, no aunts and uncles, no whores, beggars or thieves, no blacks or Jews) and the blatant anti-Semitism —people sat around after dinner telling anti-Jewish jokes, thinking they could offend nobody. It was the first time I had run into this enraging behavior in people I otherwise liked, and I had no idea how to handle it. Wrote Pop around that time:

"One other incident on the boat may interest you. With us at the captain's table at the big gala was a young Frenchman, a Count, and his Countess, from Danville, Va., who looked like L. [a friend] but acted like a female Boob McNutt. While they were throwing these little white balls around at the height of the festivities, she whispered in my ear, 'I'm throwing at Jews.' So I said, 'Then throw at me.' She gaped at me for a moment and said, 'But you're not one!' I said, 'Half Jewish, my mother was Jewish, throw half a ball at me.' Then she said, 'But you can't be, because I can tell 'em like that!' She said, 'I like you and so does my husband'—which, as you can imagine, was a great relief to me. But I insisted very coldly that I was half Jewish, implied that I was insulted, and continued to order her to throw a ball at me. At this she got up and moved and we never spoke again during the trip, thank God.

"P.S. Dorris didn't think it was very funny when I told her I was going into the ship's library and sing, 'I'm a rambling wreck from bibliotheque.'"

When I complained about Dhahran Pop, who had about given up telling me of the glories of small-town life, wrote: "It seems more imperative to me than ever that you should set yourself a very strict schedule of writing . . . have your breakfast, do your housework, and then, in your nice air-conditioned home, get to the typewriter. It doesn't matter whether you actually write or not. Stick at it the way Len sticks at his job. . . . I should certainly give it two or three hours, or perhaps a couple of hours before lunch and a couple of hours afterwards. Once you can get yourself into a routine like that, I promise that you will have obtained a very satisfactory balance of life. . . . My mind automatically resumes its consideration of the story the moment I stop reading or talking or doing whatever I'm doing. Just as automatically, and as politely as you please, it comes back to the business at hand . . . nobody ever knows or notices it, and it doesn't bother me. It keeps me at times from boredom. But no rush, no pushing, no straining. Just like marriage, easy is the way to do it."

I began to work very hard, turning out several short stories and the beginning of a novel, a project well suited to pregnancy. The novel was *The World of Henry Orient,* which was about an old friend of mine from Brearley and based on something that had happened to both of us when we were thirteen and in love—at a distance—with Oscar Levant. I wrote Pop of the idea, and he replied, "My belief about the idea of June and Oscar Levant is that it doesn't seem to have enough body for a whole book. It sounds more like a short story." Besides, he was afraid I couldn't handle the problem of removing a real incident to the realm of fiction. "The more I think of it, the less I like the idea of your tackling such a job. It usually takes an old experienced hand to manage it. Use bits and pieces if you want to, everybody does that, but to aim at a whole person is a formidable proposition. But don't discard the idea of June definitely and permanently. Wait a year or so and think about it again." But the story haunted me, and he began to come around. "If June has no objections, I see no reason why you shouldn't write the story about her, particularly as you have such an urge to do it. As for a plot, it might be enough to take her through five years, if you can justify the changes that took place in her during that time. She begins the story as one person and emerges as another, and what you are telling is the circumstances that brought them about." When I couldn't get it going—"lay it aside for six months. You'll be surprised at the new view you'll have when you go over it then. Meanwhile, either fiddle around with something else or just throw up periodically . . . it rarely comes easily or quickly to anybody. Quick success is a miracle. Just be pleased you are not having to depend on your pen for a livelihood."

I put the novel aside and continued to send short stories to Edith, who sent them around to magazines. Then the word came that *The New Yorker* was considering one of them. "I am now holding my breath. I haven't done this for a long time, but I still know how to do it. Back in the twenties, I did it constantly . . . it will happen every time. Conscientious writers, even when they are independently wealthy, never get over that sweating-it-out experience . . . there is another eternal truth about writers. A young man went to someone like Molière and told him he wanted to be a writer. 'Very well then,' Molière told him, 'but there is one thing that you must be prepared to face when you become a writer. You will never laugh but you will say to yourself, I am laughing, and you will never cry but you will say to yourself, I am crying.' So say goodbye to all simple emotions. . . . The truth is, once you have ambition, you'll never more have any peace of mind. Only the vegetables are happy and contented. And you'll be sorry a million times that you didn't decide to be a vegetable."

When the word came (by cable from Edith) that they had bought it, Dhahran had never seemed so frustrating. Though Len and I celebrated as best we could, it infuriated me that I was there where my first splash could hardly be heard. It made no sense, being in this place, that I had married someone who worked here, which didn't seem to have anything to do with it. We began, slowly, to talk about leaving, though it was beginning to seem that this correction was too late, the real mistake had been in leaving New York and now something had gone that I would never catch up with. I hadn't grown up, it was true, I had dropped out of some life process before it had finished, one I was hardly aware of even being in; that I was now married, and giving elegant little dinner parties, and about to have a child, seemed to be a kind of second life imposed on top of another more painful rhythm, one which never let up.

The story came out in *The New Yorker* three days before Marion was born, and a copy flashed through the mails while I was still in the hospital. The woman in the other bed had never heard of *The New Yorker*, and said that if she had a daughter, like me, rather than a son, like her, she would have killed herself. Pop's concern remained with the father. "It began with you in the Hollywood Hospital here and by the time Scotty came around I was pretty well resigned to this role of extra with no lines. I don't think fathers are really as nervous as they pretend to be . . . the night Dorris went into the hospital for Scotty, I think I shook this tradition a bit in the waiting room. After sitting there for an hour or so and watching the other fathers and fat female relatives enacting their parts, I got up and said, 'Oh, to hell with all this!' and walked out."

It was remarked early that Marion was the only grandchild who didn't look exactly like Nunnally. "Your mother's genes are even stronger than mine," he wrote. "All of my other children bear a dismaying resemblance to me—all of them! you're the only one who bears no resemblance to me whatever. You're all Marion."

I took it as prophecy, this double success—maybe I could have it all. For a while it felt as though I could, and for a period, when Marion was a baby, there was peace.

24. *Producer and star*

25. *Dorris, Betty Bacall and Nunnally, early fifties*

26. *At the crest*

27. *George Raft, Ginger Rogers and Nunnally on the set of* Black Widow

28. Nunnally in his Fellini period

29. On the set of The Angel Wore Red *in Italy: Scott, Nunnally, Ava Gardner, Roxie, Christie*

30. Big Marion, Paula and little Marion, around 1965

31. Nora and Anne Gartner planning Smith benefit of Henry, Sweet Henry in 1966

32. Nunnally and Roxie on her wedding day

33. *A scene from* Night People, *Nora in background, Brod Crawford in foreground*

34. *Darryl Zanuck around 1976*

35. *The Patriarch: Christie, Scott, Marge, Roxie, Nunnally and Nora, summer of 1975*

Arabia—New York *1956-1958*

Always Pop kept me informed about Stateside life.

"Ike has never been more popular and Eddie and Debbie have settled down into an engagement that everybody hopes will be permanent. . . .

"N. [the son of a friend] arrived for a few days and nearly ran me nuts. Never says anything simply or briefly. For instance, he couldn't just say no. He's got to say something like, 'I would not be entirely averse to that idea.' Talk, talk, talk. The kids loved him. But he made me into the damnedest TV addict you ever saw. The instant I heard his footsteps, on went the TV. I looked at everything from old Westerns to Sheriff John's Animal Circus for Kittikins.

"The whole town's talking about a garden hose whose nozzle keeps going deeper and deeper into the earth. Nobody knows why. Just keeps going down about a foot a day. Nineteen feet gone already. Thousands of people tramping over the poor guy's lawn to look at a piece of hose stuck in the ground. . . .

"We had some people in for dinner for the Otis Wieses last night, Joe Sayre, the Milton MacKayes, the Dolans, the Bogarts, and the Masons. No fights. Bogart always makes me nervous, and so does Dorothy MacKaye. Dorothy gets a few drinks aboard and denounces me for taking her to lunch at Romanoff's and says she is not impressed. The last time she was at the house she denounced me for having some celebrated people as my guests also. Not impressed, she stated. I asked her if she would like me to round up some bit players for her next time. But she wasn't impressed by that either. So last night when I saw her and Bogart tête-à-tête, I looked for trouble, and for the moment my sympathies would have been with Bogart. I flipped an ear in their direction and she was off on some silliness about "an actor giving so much of himself" to which Bogart was replying that he didn't give a God-damned thing of himself, he sold it."

He was soothing about what I felt to be a cool reception to my first published work (*The New Yorker* story).

"You are getting what all writers, composers, painters and such must come to expect throughout life. That is, most people are inarticulate in the face of a composition that is out of their sphere. 99% of the appreciation that a writer ever gets (and it will always be astonishingly less than he expected) will be only from other writers or people who have been exposed to writing. They are the only ones who know what went into it . . . others are not sure of the proper way to express [their feeling or appreciation] and are reluctant to risk themselves in a matter as alien to them as painting, say, is to me. And the more intelligent they are otherwise, the less likely they will take this risk . . . long ago I gave up looking for even a light acknowledgment of anything of mine that appeared, except from members of my own profession . . . the only kind of writing that is likely at all to get some kind of non-professional response is comedy writing . . . a story like yours, which was dramatic, I can understand what we call private people being a little uncertain how to tell you this. Moreover private people rarely like to admit that they were moved emotionally. They feel this to be some sort of weakness . . . the world of a writer, or any other artist, is largely a private world, and a lonely one . . . only a few people should have any importance to what you do. The first is yourself. The second is the editor, who represents the public that you and he are appealing to . . . then there are your colleagues, other writers, members of your profession . . . after that it really doesn't matter.

He continued to talk about writing, but during the next two years, as I continued to publish stories, his tone changed. He had started out in a comparison of my first sale and his.

"I would say that it is about a standoff between *The New Yorker* and the *Smart Set* of that day. Both had the highest short-story standards in the business, and a sale to the *Smart Set* had as much glory to it in those days as one to *The New Yorker* has today . . . *The New Yorker* is and always has been the toughest market anywhere, and with the highest standards. And it plays no favorites. The temperish Mr. John O'Hara has not appeared in *The New Yorker* for a good many years [because] they turned down four of his short stories in succession and he swore then that he would never offer it another. Well, hardly ever, anyway . . . you are three or four years younger than I was when I sold my first. During that year, 1924, I sold about 6 stories to the *Smart Set*. Then it folded. This shows you what one man can do. Mr. Mencken and Mr. Nathan invited me to write for their new magazine, the *American Mercury*. . . . I had to alter completely my way of writing short stories, for the *Smart Set* story was a highly specialized affair, sardonic or mordant or both, and there was no other magazine that was interested in such stuff. [To switch to *SEP*] was as radical a change as it would be for a right-handed batter to switch to a lefty. . . . I would study short stories in the bigger circulation magazines. This is not to say that you should alter your style or approach to a story, but a professional must try to get a line on every market, and it will be only a question of time before you'll get the hang of the kind of stories favored in other magazines."

But as my stories kept appearing the nature of his advice changed.

"I think the story is first-rate and you told it with excellent effect . . . but I should guard myself against too much advice to you. You have developed, or are developing, your own way of telling a story, which so far as I can see is in no way imitative of anybody else. It seems to be your own. In which case you should be very guarded against anybody else's suggestions, even mine. Go right ahead as you are going. [The story] is not stylistic. You are completely intent on the story that you are telling, and that is the way it should be."

"The one most valuable element in 'The Day of Miss Durbin's' [a story] was your compassion, your refusal to condemn anyone in the story. Implicitly there was a deep sympathy for the least of them. This is a rare position for any writer to take, particularly a beginner of your age, and quite aside from its literary or artistic value, it has a genuine commercial worth. You don't mind my being crude about it, do you? Such sympathy, unless it's pressed to the point of being maudlin, is worth its weight in gold. It lifts every story above its ordinary worth."

"You are an independent writer. You don't have to make a living at it . . . take advantage of it. I know that I have urged you to consider other courses but I am convinced now that this was not wise on my part. All I urge you to do now is think of the story first and the publication second . . . it may take time but success is inevitable. If I didn't believe this I wouldn't put it to you in such positive terms. But I know something about writing and I can tell real writing from imitation writing. Yours is real."

"Yours is real" . . . something else seemed to be emerging, something nobody had planned on. I never heard any more about studying the magazine market. We were peeling off, he and I, our talents were different, comparisons between our careers had to be done with caution. Not that I really took in what he was telling me, it was far too frightening, and I was far too used to looking to him for advice. At his suggestion I wrote a story called "The Gift Horse" whose idea had germinated in an incident with Christie. It was one of the rare times when someone has presented me with a usable fiction idea and this one came out well. Since it was about his family I sent him a copy at the same time I sent one to Edith.

"Actually, we come off very well, so far as I can see. It's a truly wonderful picture of Christie, and hardly less so, in brilliantly brief fashions, of Roxie and Scott. God knows I have nothing to complain of about myself, and as you will see from the notes, my only concern is the rather haggard picture of Dorris and the somewhat snotty allusions to, for God's sake, our graceful living! If only it were like that! . . . Hollywood people are hypersensitive about criticism or a critical attitude that seems to be based on no more than that they try to live pleasantly. This is particularly true of Dorris. I guess it's some sort of sense of guilt out of her poor and almost penniless childhood. Myself, having been brought up in the lap of luxury, with tutors and French gov-

ernesses to protect me against the world, I take the present elegance more in stride. Doesn't everybody live like this?"

He requested several changes in the character based on
Dorris. "I can see no harm being done to the story if Louise were
less fretful, easier and pleasanter, more sympathetic and understanding . . ." and to remove "a strain of disdain for the Hollywood house. I would try to avoid that. It's a kind of inverted
snobbism, out of place here so far as I can see, and its loss would
be no loss to the story, while it might prickle Dorris, to put it
frankly. As you say, it is a bit of walking on eggs to write about a
house and a family where you have visited, and the wisest thing
would be to make sure that you do not unnecessarily hurt anyone's feelings."

Well—sure. I would have been afraid to offend Dorris or any
of them, since visitors can so easily not be invited back. (No
matter that I was now around nine thousand miles away, it was
still the other home.) His suggestions were precise and only God
can say whether they made the story better or worse. "[Dorris] is
still touchy about our Southland. Like Jews and Jewish jokes, it's
all right for us to tell them, but we don't want to hear any of
them from you gentiles."

But when Roger Angell, *The New Yorker* editor, liked the story
and asked for revisions, Nunnally immediately called off the
hounds.

". . . you must now feel free to make your characterizations
exactly as you see fit, in any way that is dramatically effective,
without regard for me or Dorris or the children. You have paid
your respects to the family and that is all over and done with.
This is now a work of fiction and it must be shaped by the
writer, not the daughter. From now on I recognize it as fiction
and promise not to make any identification of any of the characters with any of my family . . . when an editor as smart as Angell thinks of the story as being close to a "very touching and
powerful piece of fiction," by far the best you have done, nothing
must stand in the way of its proper polishing."

"The Gift Horse" was the third and last story I sold to *The
New Yorker*, which was painful—it's hard to start at the top—
and though other magazines were buying I rather felt I'd been
thrown out of paradise. Pop had no patience with such market

loyalties and told me that the *Smart Set* bought Maugham's "Miss Thompson" ["Rain"] for two hundred dollars only after every other magazine in New York had turned it down.

"Don't take *The New Yorker* too seriously . . . it's really a parochial affair, consisting largely of urban and exurbanite New York, but there is more to the world than that. If you doubt this, ask yourself how many of the world's great writers would have been acceptable to *The New Yorker*. I shudder to think of what would have happened to something sent in by Dickens. . . . *Vogue* or *Harper's Bazaar* at one time would publish no story about people who worked for a living."

In '61 he wrote that both Thurber and John Cheever found the editorial climate at *The New Yorker* "too lofty and capricious" and had turned their faces in other directions—Thurber, who helped make the magazine, was now receiving rejection letters from Roger Angell with "juvenile lectures on comedy and humor."

Because of the success with short stories I had been able to go back and finish *The World of Henry Orient*, which, after a few turndowns, was accepted by Atlantic-Little, Brown for publication in the spring of '58—by which time we would be back in the States. I was pleased by the novel. It seemed to express an intense, difficult period of my life in a way I'd hoped and to evoke the New York I had left and missed so badly.

"Marion sent me your letter in which you described that gloomy reaction to the story ["Bird of Paradise"] in Dhahran . . . it's like the time I gave my mother a Grant Wood print of a woman holding a potted plant in her hands. She may have been a little dubious about this herself, but she hung it nevertheless in the living room. After a few months, she took it down and put it away . . . it puzzled her friends. They asked if the woman was a friend of hers. When Mamma told them it wasn't a portrait in particular, but simply a painting of a woman who appealed to the painter, they just didn't get that at all. When Mamma told me this, I guess it was the first time I ever realized the revolutionary nature of modern art."

I had lost track of myself in Arabia somehow, had never been able to pick up the threads I had left in New York and picked up other ones instead, ones I didn't like much but felt helpless to change. I didn't like the sort of person I was in Arabia. I was always beating at my walls, either depressed or restlessly hyped up, longing for what I called civilization but what I was beginning to suspect was only a receding, rosy memory of something I had once wanted but never got. Would nothing satisfy me? At twenty-five I had marriage and a baby I adored; I had traveled to places most people never saw in a lifetime, I had friends I valued and a strong start on professional success; and besides all this Len had pretty well agreed that Dhahran was not the place for us (I imagine he got tired of seeing me standing at the window crying) and was to look for work elsewhere, which I felt guilty about.

But the worst thing I had done in Arabia was to stop being honest with myself about most of the things in my life. In some ways I never had been, but when the alternatives were still open, at Smith, self-deception had a certain usefulness in the constant effort to eliminate some of the endless choices life seemed to offer. Now that some of the doors were closed off I never questioned that I had done the right thing, never even dangled some of those lost possibilities around in my mind like Christmas toys. It seemed too dangerous—like a child, I had never really got past magic thinking. I was afraid if I even considered the (now obvious) fact that I never should have gotten married when I did, I would be struck by lightning; if I pondered life in some walk-up in the village, or the lost Roman garret, or a love affair with another man, or a rapid rise from receptionist to reporter at *The New Yorker,* or any number of things that might have happened, Len—a gentle man—would sense my treacherous thoughts and take out a gun and shoot me. Since all these other ghostly possibilities were as much me as living in Arabia and having a baby, I closed off large parts of myself and would, a few years later, pay the price of self-deception. The thought of having made such a dreadful mistake so early was simply too much to face, and I buried it beneath hard work, motherhood, gourmet cooking and housewife-glow; and blamed the nagging unhappiness on Dhahran, which would soon be solved by arriving in New York.

But of course my New York had gone. Marion and Rogers had given up the brownstone and taken an apartment on Morningside Heights, to be near Columbia, where Rogers taught at the Business School. I came back a month or so before Len and stayed there with the baby, then ten months old. I wandered around, trying to find my old landscape. Its tenants had scattered and regrouped, its light had shifted and refocused. Without the brownstone or any other home, it had no central force, things kept flying off the edge, there was too much that was unaccountable. I had simply lost its beat. Of course everybody knows you can't go home again, everybody goes back and finds the population has changed and the children have grown up and the old places have closed. But it gave me an undue amount of pain and threatened my work. I had lost the sense of community out of which I knew I had to write, those silver wires which, if I had only followed them, would have led to artistic consciousness, that mighty ability to clamp onto self and place and wrest the meaning out of them that makes writers great. Joyce had his Dublin, Faulkner had his Mississippi, Jane Austen had her Sussex. Even Nunnally had his Riverside, but I had lost my Manhattan. I didn't know this at the time, particularly since I was still writing and selling. But I was going on momentum. The fix that produced *Henry Orient* (which with all its awkwardness did spring from a profound sense of location) had a freshness and urgency that I was able to manage less and less. Was it simply that since thirteen (the age of the two girls in the novel) everything had gotten too hopelessly complicated, that cosmic consciousness had come and gone by the time I was out of Brearley bloomers? If that were so I was worthless as a writer anyway, by the ambitious standards I was beginning to hold for myself.

"I've enjoyed movie writing, though I don't regard it as anything more than a third-class endeavor. (There is next to no creation in it, even by the most generous interpretation. All you can do is polish other people's efforts. Not that their efforts are often much more than trash.) My satisfaction, such as it is, is in the fact that I have lived well and comfortably and have been able to help a number of others to live comfortably. I have few illusions about writing or about my own. I have never been a man to live in a garret if I can get into the Plaza. . . . I must let others write the literature of our time, just as I must let others work out a rocket to the moon. Both undertakings are clearly beyond my capacities."

The implication was that they were not necessarily beyond mine. Carrying the torch onward would have been difficult enough, but it was more frightening to be on my own, out where he had never flown before, entrusted with another quality product and expected to deliver. It was the sort of thing that had sent Sylvia Plath under the porch with her sleeping pills, that terrible dread of failure. It was a fraud, this notion that you could always retreat into your family (for now there was another baby coming) for rest or solace or completion—a fraud if you were a woman, anyway. You had to keep running.

After reading the novel, Pop wrote: ". . . three-fourths of *The World of Henry Orient* is first-rate. To me, that is. One fourth of the book, in spots here and there, I felt that you had lagged a bit, either through not giving it enough thought or from weariness. Beginning about the middle you picked up tremendous pace . . . at the end you got a little foggy . . . you took a challenging subject, one that is fresh and heretofore unused so far as I can remember, and you handled that with life and warmth and sympathy . . . all the way through there are splashes of writing that are brilliant, with the same simple, unefforted strength that is throughout 'The Gift Horse.' Oh, you have it all right. . . . Never drop into simple narrative. Approach every scene as if it were a little drama. Examine the point you want to make and sneak up on it . . . never tread water . . . never, never, never be satisfied. No real writer is. And you're a real writer, while I never really was. You have depth and quality, which I regret to say I have never been able to find in what I've done. Amusing, yes; pleasant, at times; ingenious, often; but never really tops . . . all writers must always be measured by their best, not their lesser stuff. And all good writers fluctuate between wonderful and not so wonderful. Consistence is the mark of mediocrity. . . . I know of few first novels that should command the respect that *Henry Orient* should. You tackled a tough one . . . and you continually get better. There is nothing in the world more important than that.

"Congratulations, darling. There is no question about it any longer. You've got it made."

Hollywood to London
1956–1964

The Three Faces of Eve, in which Joanne Woodward played a woman with a multiple personality, was one of Nunnally's best pictures and certainly his best work as director. The story was a true one, based on a case history written up by two Georgia psychiatrists, Corbell Thigpen and Hervey Cleckley. Nunnally talked at length to the doctors and watched films they had made of this woman who transformed to another person before their eyes. To give it a documentary air he got Alistair Cooke (who was then big on "Omnibus") to introduce it on camera, a function his effectiveness has since turned into a sort of Good Housekeeping seal of approval—if Alistair Cooke introduces it you've got to believe it. When Nunnally asked Alistair to do it, he says, "of course I was terribly excited, the idea of being in a real movie." After quickly acquiring an agent for the occasion who—over his protests—got him five thousand dollars for the job, Alistair flew to California.

"I arrived, it was a hot day, Nunnally was leaning against the stanchions of a truck talking to a couple of the crew. He never asked to look at anything [a script]. We went in this little theatre—the idea was it started with me up against a screen— and they put the lights on, and they said to the cameraman okay, so I did it once, and then we stopped and he said, 'Perfect.' I said, 'This is ridiculous.' He said, 'Now we have to do it again for a close shot.' I said, 'It'll be slightly different though it will end

the same way.' He said, 'That's all right.' I said, 'I think I can
remember,' so I did it again, and he said, 'Well, that's it. Shall we
go to lunch?' On the way to the commissary I said to Nunnally,
'I feel like an awful thief, it only took ten minutes.' I didn't want
him to get in bad with the studio. He said, 'Look, you're one of
the very rare people they call flesh, like Robert Benchley, who
rolls his own.' I said, 'What's the alternative?' He said, 'The alternative is you get two writers, you employ them for two weeks,
then you hire James Mason, and you have rehearsals and then
you shoot it. It costs $20,000, so relax.'"

Casting was painfully slow. Nunnally said in '56, "It takes a
long and irritating time to cast anybody these days. In the middle of the worst slump the movies have had in years, everybody
wants more money than ever before." The part of Eve was
offered to Susan Hayward, Doris Day, Jennifer Jones, June
Allyson and July Garland, all of whom turned it down. "They
were in analysis, all of our leading ladies, and they were afraid
this would in some way conflict." In a way he greeted each turn-
down with sighs of relief. He felt Hayward wasn't right for it
and Nunnally wrote me that Doris Day was "a little spooky herself . . . when she made *Love Me or Leave Me* she became convinced that Jimmy Cagney had either raped her or attempted to,
because that was what he did in the picture, and was so terrified
of him that she would run off stage whenever he showed
up. . . . Now we're after Judy Garland, the queen of all the psy-
chopathic cases around her. In addition to drink, junk, and any
other pills she can find around the house, she's also a little loony
otherwise. She would give a great performance but . . . if she
says yes, God only knows what my future will be."

At any rate the role went to Joanne, who played the part of
Eve White (the drab and prissy good girl), Eve Black (the
swinging, partygoing bad girl) and Jane (the integration of the
two, except that she had no memory). David Wayne played her
rather klutzy unsympathetic husband and Lee J. Cobb was the
psychiatrist. When Joanne first read the script she found it "so
complex—I could certainly understand why all those stars
turned it down." She was twenty-six at the time and this was her
third film and first major role, and the Georgia accent she
brought to it was real. They started off by showing her and Lee

Cobb the psychiatric film made of the original Eve Black during her treatment in which she snaps back and forth between personalities. Joanne said in an interview, "I was mesmerized. I said, 'There's no way anybody realistically can make those transitions that fast—like lightning.' Lee's comment after we walked out was, 'I don't believe it, she's a fake.' I told Nunnally I didn't know what to do about those transitions and Nunnally, who was nothing if not succinct, said, 'Just do them slower,' I believe that was the only piece of directing he gave me. I can't remember his saying anything else but he gave me the greatest gift a director can give an actor and that is the total freedom to try anything and feel good about it, and not to feel criticized or anything but just to go full out in any direction. We shot that film in thirty-one days, mostly in continuity, and that was good, it gave me a relaxation so that by the time I came to the more theatrical parts I felt good about it and very secure."

Nunnally claimed no credit for the Oscar she won for her performance. "She could have almost directed herself," he said. "She's very, very knowledgeable. She had an awful lot of mannerisms, mannerisms that really I think was what stopped her career, or made it drop down. She has a habit of pointing at somebody when she addresses them . . . she'd studied at the Actors' Studio, and she knew what reality was. I remember once she had to fall and she didn't fall in a position that seemed right or natural to me. But she insisted on it because, she said, 'That's the way I fell.' You can't teach an actor anything on the [sound] stage once they get started anyway. You have to use what you've got. And she had it."

Though Nunnally was the most genial non-director, "he'd sit propped up in that chair with that half smile," Joanne says, "puffing his cigarette and dropping ashes all over, it was like having the best possible father who was just sitting smiling at you approvingly whatever you did and letting you alone." He refused certain requests she made for line changes and was very firm about it. The script was right and he knew it.

Joanne says, "I didn't understand it then—I would get very irritated and think, He doesn't understand, he's not a director, if he really were a director he'd understand. But he forced me into making what was there work and that I learned many years later from Laurence Olivier. That is after all the job of an actor, right? Unlike the Actor's Studio where we said, 'Well, it's our right to change so-and-so.' It is not your right, the words are there for you, you make it work." Though working with Joanne went well, the picture was difficult to shoot because it took place almost entirely in Dr. Thigpen's office. Marge (who cut the picture) says, "Stanley [Cortez, the cameraman] was getting desperate about different ways of setting it up or lighting it or something. I remember the twentieth or thirtieth day of shooting, still in the office, Stanley said, 'Now let's just lie back and drink the set in.' Some grip on the side said, 'We're drunk.'" Nunnally, uninterested in technicalities, left these problems up to Stanley and Marge. He would direct the people in the scene "as if there were no fourth wall" and, when it seemed to be going all right, checked it out with them to be sure it was being done in the most economical and effective way. She would tell him the number of setups she would need to cut it, and he would say, "All right, but don't come to me tomorrow and say, 'I can't get the guy out of the room.'" She did the job successfully, even taking a bad sequence and turning it into an acceptable one. "I remember one scene, probably the worst cut scene in the world, which really doesn't matter to me. It was a scene in the psychiatrist's office with David Wayne and Nunnally had let Wayne get out of hand. He was miserable with the scene and cut as per script and as it should have played it was so broad, so bad, Wayne was camping and being cutesy. I fooled around with this, cut it backwards, playing practically everything off Wayne, finally I said to him, 'Look, cut the script pages up, put the lines where you wanted them to be, reconstruct it and let's see what we can do.' He said, 'Can you do something like this?' Dialogue-wise and filmwise it's backward, it doesn't look very good, but it got across what he wanted. Nunnally said, 'Marjie's gonna make magic.'"

Gene Fowler, a director himself, says, "Nunnally as a director would be concentrating on their getting their lines right, but if there was a crap game in the background he'd never see it. He concentrated on performances and relied on the cameraman, in my opinion the worst guy to rely on because the cameraman has been trained to shoot scene to scene. He may set up a marvelous master but he has no idea where you cut into that scene. And one thing you shouldn't do is, in the middle of a camera move, be forced into a close-up. A director who knows what he's doing will settle the camera in order to make your cuts and then come back perhaps and finish the scene. The cameraman doesn't have any concept of the thing as a whole nor does he know how the beginning or the end of any scene connects with the next scene . . . writers think in words, directors think in pictures. That's why screenwriters shouldn't direct. When you're reading an action sequence written by a writer, unless the thing is really structured well, you have to restructure the whole thing, reinvent it almost." (Nunnally: "When a man writes a script, he directs it at the same time. That whole picture was directed while I was writing it." Henry King: "It's impossible for a writer to sit at a desk and tell you what to do with certain things. The translation from the script to the screen is a job on its own.")

Marge says, "The pendulum has swung to the director so everything is visual . . . directors would just as soon improvise the dialogue and their stories have gone to hell because of what the writer was contributing . . . the desperate need is for the combination of these two truly creative approaches."

And Gene adds, "You've gotten to a point now where the goddam *auteur* bullshit, the director, the fellow who was not there when the page was blank and who did not think up the words, suddenly is given the whole credit. . . . If that were truly the case he should have written the goddam thing, directed, acted in it, cut it, written the music for it. Like Chaplin, even Chaplin needed help. Nunnally was as close to *auteur* as there is and there is an unevenness, he wasn't that good a director even of his own material."

To protect their scripts from the whims of directors, writers are now asking for contracts saying that not a word can be changed without their approval. What was once teamwork has become a struggle of egos, which might be one of the things that has happened to Hollywood. Director George Roy Hill (*The World of Henry Orient, The Sting, Slapshot*) says, "There's all this profound silliness about the *auteur* theory and more old writers and old directors are making horses' asses out of themselves. It's utter nonsense, I've never seen so many raw egos on display, and it's sad to see Frank Capra scrounging for credit after all these years. It's so silly because nobody can tell where the writer ends and the director begins. Now obviously there are great combinations, people who feed and build on each other, and this was the case of Frank Capra and his writer, their personalities were such that they formed a single unit, and it's perfectly true that the director's stamp is very positive on a piece of material. But I've never seen a director take a bad piece of material and make something good out of it."

Under the old studio system there was a kind of forced cooperation, since everybody who worked on a picture was a peon working for a Zanuck or a Thalberg, who took both praise and blame. Everybody was on salary, nobody got a percentage; dozens of pictures were made a year, and a few flops could be easily absorbed. It must partly account for the casual confidence that those thirties and early forties movies had in pre-blockbuster days.

By 1956 the whole industry was into a downward spiral from which it hasn't recovered, and probably never will. Zanuck left Fox that year (*Three Faces of Eve* was the last picture Nunnally did with him) and after that nothing was the same, for Nunnally and a lot of others too. After the dreaded consent decree which made it illegal for studios to own their own theaters, the old studio system, with all its implications, slowly broke up, like an iceberg. Now, for each picture maker, success is survival in a way it wasn't before, there is no protection against the financial buffeting and shocks that were previously absorbed by the studio. The *auteur* is on his own, staggering along in a medium whose tradition is teamwork, like one man trying to play all four instruments in a string quartet.

The Man Who Understood Women (1959), from *The Colors of the Day* by Romain Gary, starred Henry Fonda and Leslie Caron, never more beautiful. "Nobody understood it," says Henry Fonda. "Certainly the critics didn't." Nunnally blamed it on the casting—Fonda had begged for the part. He tells, "The assistant director, who had been on another picture, smuggled the script to me and said, 'I think you should read this.' And I read it and loved it because this was more your dad for me than *Jesse James* or *Grapes of Wrath*. They were adaptations of Americana, but this had Nunnally's real humor, his own. I read it

and thought, Wow, what a marvelous part, but I knew he'd
never think of me for it. So I memorized a scene that had a long
speech and I came in to see him at the office and went right into
the scene. And he was just sitting there, watching me, and I sold
myself playing that guy, because it was very flamboyant, unlike
anything I'd ever done before, and I got the part and I had a
ball. I think Nunnally meant Willie to be a cross between John
Huston and Orson Welles and maybe two or three other directors. I wore a sort of flat Panama and funny cream-colored slacks
with a long thin cigar and that was Huston. And I was in that
clown suit and tails and frock coat and every kind of wardrobe
you could think of. . . . I never saw the film either. You can't
not love this man [Nunnally] and he was so inventive with the
script and so ready for somebody to come in and play it like I
tried to do in that office scene, and he enjoyed hearing his words
come out like that."

But Nunnally said, "That picture, for all of my real admiration
and affection for Henry Fonda, was just not for him. It was supposed to be Orson Welles, and written with Orson in mind, and
the studio wouldn't even think of letting Orson play the lead.
That was at the low point of his career, or one of the low points,
anyway. When Henry begged to play it, I just couldn't resist it,
though I didn't think he was able to do it. He just didn't
have the formation of body and mind. After all, Hank Fonda is
old Hank Fonda. The fluctuation of behavior that was necessary
in *The Man Who Understood Women,* you could accept that
from Welles. He was an eccentric, when he walks out with two
or three Oscars and salutes with some double-talk Latin, you
would have had them, but when Henry did that they know that's
good old Henry, true blue."

Marge was the cutter and as usual Nunnally "seemed to
depend a lot on her," Fonda says. "He obviously had a great deal
of respect for her, he was leaning on her gladly and proudly."

The story is about Willie Bauche, Wellesian actor/producer,
who marries the beautiful actress Ann Garantier, makes her into
a legend but doesn't make love to her. After a wedding night
which he spends making deals to secure her professional future,
she closes the door on him for six months; after an unexpectedly
successful premiere, they do seem to make it, but he runs off im-

mediately to organize the party at Chasen's. Ann then has a
French idyl with a soldier who leaves her to go back to war, but
only (I think) because he knows that she is still in love with
Willie, to whom she returns at the end, when Willie says, "Will
you marry me again? I apologize for such a long courtship." This
is not the usual Nunnally—why on earth did he do it? "I wanted
to see if great tragedy couldn't properly mix, or be used with
broad comedy," he said. "It can be done, but I couldn't do it, or
didn't do it. [Besides I wanted to show that], unlike most standard pictures at that time, the wife who has gone off with another
man doesn't necessarily become lost, or that it isn't obligatory on
a husband's part to say, 'Go. Leave me.' I wanted him to be just
as much in love with his wife when she came back. . . .
Infidelity in certain circumstances is not the final horror that can
befall a man or a woman. At that time it wasn't often used as it
befalls a woman, and that I wanted to show."

One of the problems is that the pivotal information—when
and whether Ann and Willie are making it—is never clear,
whether because of Nunnally's delicacy or because this was 1958.
Has Willie some problem? We know he isn't dumb—he says,
"When the wife sins, the husband is never innocent," and another time Ann says to her *militaire* lover, "I have the feeling
that Willie knew I was going to do this or something like it. He
used to arrange for me to go away by myself—even before I
knew I needed it." Ann's scenes with her lover are unconvincing
—this was the sort of "swinging through the wheatfield" Nunnally wasn't comfortable with. The two dance clingingly and late
in smoky cafés and go through the market holding hands and
laze about in the *militaire's* bountiful supply of bathrobes, but
somehow there isn't much electricity. It is the arrogant self-
deceiver, Willy, whom we watch (though part of the fascination
is watching Fonda in this unlikely guise), Willy who is in love
but can't show it, the clown who can't stop clowning. If the
difference between good writing and bad could be boiled down
to one simple sentence, it's that good writing holds back and bad
writing tells all, denying us the pleasure of supplying our own
fantasies. The tension of what is only implied excites us, and
Willy captivates by the fact of passion that almost never shows.
This might all be my romantic nature, for Fonda saw the part as

straight comedy—probably another reason why it all seemed so out of sync.

"It became a love story with Leslie Caron and then became a sad story," he says. "To me it was a burlesque or satire or broadly drawn picture of what it's like to make movies, broadly drawn character of a director . . . so much of it was funny. I loved playing some of this, that's why I'm an actor, because I'm not that way and I enjoy so having a writer give me a character to play what I can't be. I can't write and in my own life I'm not funny or anything else. I just had a ball being this flamboyant person, which I'm not, and being funny, which I'm not. I've enjoyed not being typecast. *The Man Who Understood Women* is probably as different as anything I've ever done in eighty or ninety plays. . . . I just loved the way Willie talked, I loved to be that guy."

Like *Oh, Men! Oh, Women!* this picture is full of Nunnally's old values coming into conflict with change—and in 1959 nobody suspected how great the changes would be in the next decade. The double standard is gone, women can be forgiven. If he is not always on target about their needs, he knows they have them, and *The Man Who Understood Women* has a sensitivity to women throughout that I found endearing and more fitting to a man who was never happier than in a roomful of women.

It was the last picture he made in Hollywood and the last three-way NJ production. He ended up with grave reservations about the triple function. "A man ought not to be all three of those things," he said. "There ought to be somebody else so that you didn't have the whole responsibility. At least I can't take that responsibility. Other guys can, but I have never felt that confident or that arrogant about what I'm doing."

Mel Frank, a producer-writer-director (*A Touch of Class*) and one of the few who has survived the transition from old to new Hollywood ("by sheer luck"), says, "Nunnally was the first independent writer-producer-director, he was the one we all tried to follow. He must have had to learn what I did. You're faced with the problem of knowing your script absolutely cold because you've written it. . . . The trick is to get the actor to do precisely what you intended him to do in the first place. Another thing you have to learn is that after going over the script and the lines for eighteen months there may be another way of doing it that's better."

But the trouble is, as George Hill trenchantly puts it, "It's very hard to direct your own stuff because your first creative flush is when you first approach the material. And if you've already had your creative jollies out of it, it's hard to get it up again."

The culminative act of the real wordsmith is to get the words on paper. Turning them into another medium—and a visual one at that—is another talent which he may or may not have. It is fascinating—and no less an art—to tell a story by means of images. But that talent not only isn't endemic to writers, it implies quite a different creative style, and a style that might to some extent grow out of the frustration of not being the original creator.

By 1958 change lay heavy over the whole industry. At Fox, Zanuck, the life force, had left to go to Paris and produce pictures. Buddy Adler was appointed his successor. "Nunnally had no respect for Buddy Alder at all," says Dorris, "a very unimaginative man, a poor superior for a storyteller." After Nunnally had done four of the six pictures under his 1953 contract he had the right to make a picture off the lot. "He had seen the trend, people were going everywhere (to avoid U.S. income taxes), if a picture came along for Europe he was willing to do it." The offer came for *The Angel Wore Red* in Rome. "The auspices were so good, Ava Gardner and Dirk Bogarde, and some kind of minimal profit participation . . . all expenses paid for the family. We planned to rent a house for eight or ten months. We rented our [Mountain Drive] house to Judy Holliday and moved." It was a serious wrench for all of them. Christie had finished high school and was about to start at Pembroke, Roxie was going away to boarding school for the first time, Scott to elementary school. Dorris was "a little fearful, never having lived abroad." But it would solve the problem of Jane Reilly, which demanded nothing less than a move halfway around the world. "One of my main interests was to get the kids away from the Nanny, to get the Nanny out of our lives. I couldn't fire Jane, she had been with us too long. I had endured so much, it seemed foolish. I now look back and realize it was good for us to make the break."

They rented a house in Rome, "a lovely marble villa," says Roxie, who was thirteen at the time. "There were tall madonnas everywhere and tapestries hanging on the walls, and servants to go into the bowels of the house and do things for us, meals and clean sheets and laundry and all that. I think everything was difficult for Mama then, and I don't think she looked forward to it—there's an attitude you can take with you." "There was a formal fountain with little squirting dolphins and that sort of thing," says Scott, "and a mysterious catacomb kitchen where various people slept and voices came from. Dad aged during that period, started growing old. Suddenly playing catch was quite a chore. He started to get more remote."

The Angel Wore Red (1960), filmed in Rome, was the last picture Nunnally directed. It takes place during the Spanish Civil War and the rather unlikely story is about a love affair between a priest and a prostitute. "It was nothing but misfortune," Nunnally said. It was dogged with trouble from the start. Working with the Italians was difficult, and being called upon to deal with the constantly shifting balance between Communists and Catholics. "The whole thing is so distressing to me," he said, "I never saw the final cut. I've never seen the picture. The day I finished the photography I was given a ticket to leave town." Vittorio De Sica, "a wonderful actor, charming man," played the part of a general, collecting, daily, a thousand dollars in cash before going on the stage—"he doesn't trust anybody." The story was based on a book called *The Fair Bride* and there was a part in it Nunnally hoped to persuade Hemingway to play, but Hemingway, speaking from a saloon, only said, "You tell Nunnally that book is full of shit"—it was far too Fascist for him.

It wasn't exactly like directing a picture at Fox. He found himself among things that might have seemed like high adventure at thirty but at sixty-one were merely huge nuisances. In Sicily permission money had to be ante-ed up before the Vatican would allow them to shoot in a certain cathedral, and the Mafia, it turned out, was in charge of the six hundred extras and the assistants in charge of them—one of whom suddenly flew back to Rome when he found a picture of himself drawn on his dressing-room wall with a slash across the throat.

This was his swan song as a director. The terminal moment came in Sicily, on a slippery rock at two in the morning, when he suddenly said to himself, "What the hell am I doing here? Two in the morning. In Sicily. At the age of sixty. On a slippery rock. On a cold night. Saying, 'Put the camera here.' I should be home in bed." At the end of the picture, he resumed his role as writer. But if it felt like relief it had to be mixed with regret, the first giving up of a function because of age. Besides, he and Dorris had no idea what they were going to do or where they were going. They considered Geneva, to qualify for certain tax benefits and to make something of his Swiss corporation, which would produce pictures backed by financing from one of the big companies. Then, for one reason and another, the decision was made for London.

Nunnally moved to a hotel room there in late '59, leaving Dorris to wrap up the house in Rome. While she was doing this, their Beverly Hills real estate agent phoned and said an offer had been made on the Mountain Drive house for immediate sale at a good price, and every cent in cash. The purchaser wanted a decision in an hour. She phoned Nunnally in London and they decided to do it, cut the last tie. The house had become an albatross, too expensive to maintain and too full of associations better forgotten. "We thought we'd only stay two or three years. We'd never miss the company town atmosphere, the gossip, the trade papers, the rumors, the studio politics." They took the offer and moved into a house in London, on Elsworthy Road, "a magnificent Victorian" where Nunnally kept tripping the burglar alarm and the maid made up the bed with Christie in it. As usual Nunnally picked up his Olivetti and moved from desk to desk, while Dorris accomplished the multiple move and set about immediately looking for permanent quarters, which turned out to be two flats on Grosvenor Square—one for family living and one for Nunnally's working quarters. While she set about furnishing the flats, from scratch—"When I went into that place the building wasn't even finished, everything gray concrete, very strange to Americans, you have to supply lights, wiring, fireplace, kitchen"—Nunnally moved between desk and typewriter, drawing room, or out to the square for a stroll. Alistair Cooke, a good friend during that period, says, "After six months or a year in London Dorris was still having trouble getting the faucets right and was reveling in the fact of England being primitive. But

Nunnally said, 'I like it. I can't get over going out in the morning into Grosvenor Square and I pause on a corner and a cop comes up and I'm terrified, and the cop says, "Are you in any trouble, can I help you?" And they say good morning, and thank you, it's very weird, but I like it.' I think if it hadn't been for *Buried Alive* [called *Darling of the Day*, an adaptation for the stage of his own *Holy Matrimony*] and *Henry Sweet Henry* [the stage musical made from the movie of *The World of Henry Orient*] when he found himself ridiculously living in London and not able to work in the United States, they might have stayed. He told me one place he'd never go back to was Hollywood. New York had lost his old cronies, it obviously was not his New York. Of course, with Nunnally, you never sensed that he knew one tree from another, he didn't care about landscape, he didn't know where he was."

Every writer has a drawerful of the manuscripts that never made it—but Nunnally's batting average had been so high that when the aborted projects began to pile up, which started around this time, he took it hard. Twenty-eight years of working under Zanuck's protection—on that weekly salary they all complained of so—had made him forget that writing and financial insecurity go together like gin and tonic. If you don't have the stomach for the bad times you're better off doing something else and writing on weekends. But tremendous amounts of money can addle the brain, and just as the best-selling novelist with paperback and movie contracts in his pockets can easily start to believe he will never fail again, so can a scriptwriter making a hundred and fifty thousand dollars per script (in the fifties) start to believe he is foolproof. Those of us in lowlier brackets—with higher piles of unsold material—are more aware that we are, always, living on the precarious edge of security and constantly try to provide against the bad periods, besides "keeping the overhead down." But, as Marge said, being poor didn't stay in Nunnally's mind—or else it did and he hated it so he resolved never to be that way again. The flats on Grosvenor Square were as attractive and comfortable as Dorris could make them ("California right," Roxie says. "They didn't look English at all") and certainly helped atone for the fact that Nunnally was, in a sense, unemployed, or rather self-employed, which can lead to unemployed very quickly. (When Len and I visited there in 1961 the flats appeared to be comfortable and well run, a miracle of American ease and efficiency, just as the California houses had been—a notion which, when I told her later, brought an anguished laugh from Dorris.) There was no thought of financial difficulty then, since Nunnally was working on one or another of three successful Jimmy Stewart scripts; and Dorris' investments were paying off by then and she would, like Scarlett, never be hungry again. But later in the sixties, when he struggled for work (though none of us had much sense of this struggle or, even if he mentioned it, we didn't believe it), they were both frightened and slightly indignant that Nunnally's magic with a script was getting less marketable than it once was. The industry was changing drastically, and by the late sixties, so was everything else—the world and the way picture makers or writers or artists depicted it. The fact that Nunnally had fitted so well into previous times made it inevitable he wasn't going to fit into a world that was turning inside out, whose upheavals affected so many people.

He had worked for a long time on *The Wandering Jew,* a big, exhaustively researched project which would justify a large budget. But Skouras thought it was anti-Semitic (he had also thought *The Diary of Anne Frank* was anti-Semitic) though Nunnally had had the script okayed by half a dozen local rabbis. "There are people," said a friend of Nunnally's about Skouras' obsession with anti-Semitism, "who carry the ghetto around with them." Nunnally said, "I thought this script had a dramatic understanding of the wandering Jew from the time he spat in Christ's face, popping up all over history. There were people who thought Disraeli was the wandering Jew. It was wonderful, dramatic stuff." He sent it to Sam Goldwyn, who told him Skouras was a coward, there was nothing to take exception to in the story. But it was shelved, scratched in 1957. In 1955 he did an adaptation of *The Visit,* the Dürrenmatt play. It was rejected, and he revised it in 1960 and tried to interest Ingrid Bergman in it. He had set it in a Western town in the period of *High Noon.* He told her she would have to play a bitch, but after she read the script she found that particular bitch too unlovable. Even the inducement of a *Saratoga Trunk* wardrobe wasn't enough, and she turned it down.

In August of '61 he wrote me, "Getting through this script I'm working on is like trudging through deep sand. There always comes a time when I envy everybody in the world who doesn't have to write for a living. This one, I feel, I'll never finish. Just too hard. I keep trying to remember that I've been through the same ordeal before, over and over again," and in November: "My run of hard luck continues unbroken. After stringing me along for nearly a year, Mitchum dropped out of *Stranger in Galah* [a story with an African background]. Other plans, etc. I have no idea what the real reason is, except that he may have been advised not to go into a picture with a racial situation. If that's true and others feel the same, I may have had nearly a year's working for nothing—as with Miss Bergman."

Before leaving Hollywood he had written *Flaming Star*, a Western with Elvis Presley, produced in 1960. When it turned up on TV I approached it a little nervously, but it turned out to be quite good. Elvis is the half-breed brother with loyalties torn between whites and Indians. I wrote, "Again moral ambiguity and as always decency triumphs." Elvis is first rate, and sings only one hoedown song.

By 1961 Twentieth Century-Fox was embedded in the disaster that was *Cleopatra*, the final, monstrous convulsion of the old Hollywood. Since Zanuck's departure in 1956 (to become an independent producer in Paris), Spyros Skouras had been head of the studio. Skouras was squarely in the tradition of the "old-pants guys" with thick accent and notable lack of taste. Under his hand Fox had been losing money rapidly and was in danger of going bankrupt. *Cleopatra*, which was supposed to save the studio, was so fraught with problems right from the beginning that it sounds as though somebody up there didn't like Fox. The exorbitant demands of Elizabeth Taylor (a flat million), including the stipulation that *Cleopatra* be filmed abroad (to lighten her taxes), started the trail of woe, then came labor problems in England, where Fox was attempting to make the shambly Pinewood studios look like Egypt, strikes, Taylor's near-fatal illness, and the disastrous and belated discovery that even Skouras couldn't control British weather. The whole production was moved to Rome; Rouben Mamoulian, who had been directing (what little had taken place), was replaced by Joe Mankiewicz; Fox, twenty-two million in the red in 1961, sold its back lot in a last desperate gamble to save the picture and itself, and Taylor (in case anyone was dead or in a coma at the time) fell in love with Richard Burton, who played Mark Antony.

Nunnally was working on the script of *Mr. Hobbs Takes a Vacation* for Jimmy Stewart. Walter Wanger, the producer, and Bob Goldstein (Buddy Adler's replacement as head of Fox) insisted he drop everything and go to work on *Cleopatra,* which he did. But shortly he saw that Mamoulian didn't like him. "I knew that," Nunnally said, "because he began all his speeches to me with, 'Nunnally, I have the highest regard for you.'" But Mamoulian was "more of a show-off than Anatole Litvak. He had only directed one picture in about fourteen years, *Silk Stockings* over at Metro, and he was scared to death of such a project." Nunnally bet Walter Wanger a pound that Mamoulian would somehow get out of directing *Cleopatra,* and a month later received an envelope containing a single pound note. Nunnally was only on the picture for a month or so, at the end of which time Mamoulian was replaced by Joe Mankiewicz, who, according to Roxie, who was very much around at the time, "was pulling out his pages on the set and writing them himself. The whole *Cleopatra* ordeal was miserable, people trailed in and out of the flat twelve hours a day, Wanger, Joe Mankiewicz, and they had all these heated discussions. Dad's fingers bled from the amount of typing he did, they were in such a hurry and the whole situation so desperate. When he was taken off the picture he got in a funk, he was kind of out of sight, out of mind from Hollywood, and he started drinking again. He felt he was once again being forgotten (as he had felt at the end in California).

Something's Got to Give (produced as *Move Over, Darling*) was written for Marilyn Monroe, a remake of *My Favorite Wife.* It was another financial disaster for Fox, and the picture that led to Marilyn's suicide. Henry Weinstein was the producer and George Cukor the director, "a really overwhelming man." At first Marilyn was afraid that Nunnally wouldn't want her because she had once turned down a script he wrote. To convince her that nothing could be less true, he met her at the Polo Lounge of the

Beverly Hills Hotel for "the most enchanting three hours with her. We drank three bottles of champagne. Well, I thought I owed it to the company. She asked if I had been trapped into the project like her, and I told her I had chosen it over several other things. She was trying to figure if I was in on the plot or something. By the time we finished that third bottle we were very close friends and she believed everything I said and I believed everything she said. I told her what I wanted to do, since I hadn't written it then.

"I wrote the script and then went down to Ensenada to do revisions [being a resident abroad, he couldn't work in the United States]. Cukor and Marilyn seemed to like it, but Marilyn didn't have the courage to say so till she'd called Dean Martin, who was to play the man. Like many actresses, she had no confidence in her own judgment. Martin said, 'It's a first-rate script. I read fifty pages and I signed.' That was enough for her, she was very enthusiastic by then. When she left there she was soaring, she was so happy. She saw herself doing a picture that was funny and would bring her back from this slipping.

"As I was leaving for England Henry Weinstein said, 'George wants a writer on the set just for little things.' I said, 'You can do what you want, but let me tell you something. You've done only one picture here. You give a director a writer on the set, no matter what he tells you, you've lost your picture.' The minute the wheels of my plane were off the ground, George had another writer changing stuff. Henry just didn't have the strength. When the blue pages began coming in, it was just like hitting Marilyn with a hammer. Not that these pages were worse, they may have been better, but they were different. And her opinion turned out again not to be worth anything. Even if Dean Martin had agreed with her, there was Cukor. Most of these young actresses always think that the director is God, and he was making these changes. It shook her right down to the bottom, to the point where she wouldn't get out of bed. She was terrified, she dreaded Cukor, and he loathed her. He told me so.

"Then she tried to get me to take over the direction of the picture. This was impossible. I couldn't work in the United States and I didn't have the standing or the talent of Cukor. She was absolutely infatuated with me. Not romantically, nothing like that. She believed me and thought I could handle anything. But the girl was neurotic beyond description. Even if they were nutty enough to let me take George's place, two weeks later something would happen and she would come to hate me as much as she hated him. Marilyn kept retreating farther and farther from reality. They tried to slip the pages in on white paper, but she was too smart, she saw that they were alterations. Every time there was an alteration, it was just like slapping her face again for having an opinion. When I heard that Levathes, then head of the studio, was going to take her out of the picture, I cabled him and said, 'If you're going to take anybody out of this picture, shouldn't you decide first who brings the people in, George Cukor or Marilyn Monroe? You should remove George because they are so antipathetic that that's what's causing Marilyn's disturbance. But he took Marilyn out and eventually called off the picture. It was sold to Doris Day's company and she made it.

"That was the end of Marilyn. She never recovered. I thought she really had been saved. The whole thing was quite sad for me. I had come to know this girl and had found how vulnerable she was, how helpless and how lonely. She had nobody except some girl who might have described herself as a secretary, but she was from the publicity department. She just didn't know how to cope with life at all. She was never promiscuous, or as much as I could hear about her, I mean in the sense that she was laying any and everybody. From the time she fell in love with Joe DiMaggio I'm sure she was faithful to him.

"I think she bored the hell out of everybody. She just didn't have the intelligence, but she was aware she didn't have it . . . my guess is she just wasn't enough for Arthur Miller. After you've married the sex goddess—nobody finds it very difficult to talk before you get into the hay, but what do you say afterwards? Marilyn was like a child, she thought a lay was the answer to everything. When Miller began to lose interest, she went out and had an affair. She thought if she made the man jealous she would win him back. It wasn't true. When she died, she had nobody around."

Six months later, Nunnally was the only unflattering critic in a story about Marilyn in *Esquire* (quotes from Cukor were all

highly complimentary). He had said, some time before, that trying to make contact with her was like trying to talk to somebody
under water. Laurence Olivier found her infuriatingly dense in
The Prince and the Showgirl, which he directed and played in
with her—at the end of a scene she would turn not to him but to
Arthur Miller. "She was just downright rude in a kind of stupid
way," Nunnally said. "But when she was dead it was sad to think
that you might have had Clarence Darrow explaining her the
way he explained Leopold and Loeb, that they were conditioned
as children or in their youth to do these bad or strange or im-
proper things."

The three Jimmy Stewart comedies were directed by Henry
Koster and cut by Marge, when Nunnally was living in England.
Marge says, "We got along fine on all three pictures, but on the
last one [*Dear Brigitte*] Hal Kanter kept appearing and rewriting
scenes. They became slam-bang situation things instead of the
humor that came out of people. But I think Koster presented the
scripts very well." I saw *Mr. Hobbs Takes a Vacation* ('62) and
Take Her, She's Mine ('63) but *Dear Brigitte* ('65) seems to
have sunk (mercifully) out of sight. The first two are broad family comedies bordering on farce. They aren't wonderful, but
they're fun for us kin to watch because they're full of intra-family
humor. (They are part of his "children period.") In *Mr. Hobbs*
nobody dances with Lauri Peters because she has braces and
won't smile, and that's Roxie. There is a daughter with a surly
husband and one with an unemployed husband (me? Marge?
Chris?) and with house-wrecking, screaming babies (me, Marge,
Chris). In *Take Her, She's Mine* Sandra Dee's adventure as a
waitress, folk singer and ban-the-bomb sitter are Chris. In both
pictures Jimmy flails between helpless adoration of the females
of his family and the deep and growing conviction that they are
all out of their minds—alone, or partially aided by one small son
(Scott), he tries vainly to stem an onrushing tide of feminine
madness. He is straight and old-fashioned and preaches the traditional virtues to his daughters. As he puts Sandra Dee-Christie
on the plane to college, shouting over the heads of her boy
friends, he reminds her that marriage is a girl's highest goal and
then comments, as she checks tons of luggage, "I wouldn't be
surprised if the plane taxied all the way to Chicago." He adores

her, he is terrified of separation. As sparse, enigmatic letters arrive, his fantasies grow, and finally he rushes off (to Paris, where Zanuck insisted part of the picture be filmed for save-tax-money reasons) to save her virtue. But she doesn't want it saved, she's in love. But it's Jimmy's love we pay attention to as she dresses in a cootie-ridden Daniel Boone costume for a party on a *bateau mouche* to meet the chap's parents, and does everything wrong in a heroic attempt to leap the generation gap, to accept the kind of love that wasn't allowed his generation. (Throughout he crabs continually that the French speak French.) When he has accomplished this remarkable change of mind, he returns home to notice his younger daughter—who was previously a child—popping out of her bikini in a poolful of horny young men. He turns ashen and collapses into a chair—is there no end to it?

Mr. Hobbs was adapted from a story by Edward Streeter (author of *Father of the Bride,* an *SEP* writer of Nunnally's vintage) and *Take Her, She's Mine* from the Broadway play. As for *Dear Brigitte,* he had allowed himself to be persuaded to do an idea he didn't really like. When Henry Koster, the director, hit upon the odd idea of having one of the characters address the audience directly, as in *Tom Jones,* Nunnally asked that his name be taken off it, which it was.

And after that came *The World of Henry Orient,* an adaptation of my novel, which he had bought in 1961.

New York   1958–1962

It took Len over a year and a half to find a job. His specialized talents in Arabic, desert geography and the ability to negotiate with sheikhs didn't interest anybody in New York—it was before anybody took Saudi Arabia very seriously. We lived in a railroad flat on Morningside Heights; Paula was born in January '59, and oh, God, we were poor. We had some money that we had saved in Arabia, but as the months passed with no income (except the little I earned) it shrank terribly and both Len and I, instead of drawing together during this period of hardship, retreated to separate areas of misery. Len went around to his interviews and I put Marion and Paula in a stroller and sat with the other local mothers around a sandbox on Morningside Drive. The other women were wives of St. Luke's interns or young Columbia professors, and we were all broke. We talked of how to stretch a pound of hamburger and we passed beat-up baby clothes around to each other. There seemed to be hope for some of us, but some you knew would always be living at Broadway and 112th, buying bruised melons and packages of oxtails. Occasionally somebody moved to the suburbs or the East Side, when a resident-husband went into practice or a doctorate-getting husband left Academe and went into the ad business. I pined for the East Side, which as I remembered it was free from the atmosphere of struggle we all lived in, then scolded myself for being such a snob. It was worse because Len had grown up poor, and deprivation didn't make him feel—as it did me—so insulted, like a slap in the face from a friend. I simply couldn't manage any life Len provided for me, and I never stopped blaming myself and pretending to be strong and brave and cheerful.

At night after the little girls were in bed I sat down at the typewriter and wrote. *Henry Orient* had come out in 1958 to very respectable reviews full of first-novel adjectives—"touching," "poignant," "bittersweet" and sometimes "hilarious," and Judith Crist on the *Tribune* pointed out that I had written about nothing but adolescents so far and it was to be devoutly hoped that I would move on to adults. There was also a flurry of gratifying letters to Pop from his friends, which I suppose would have turned my head (as my mother would put it) if I had had a normal amount of confidence, or if I had not been so suspicious of praise delivered through a parent—how often had I told a friend how bright and wonderful her child was, when in fact I couldn't stand the little bastard? As it was, I only felt too heavily the responsibility of turning out another one as competent, which I knew was the real test. Like a child who had been pushed into growing up too fast, I missed my amateur standing—I never really lay back and purred over all this praise, there was no time for that, the road to professionalism was long and rough and rocky and the compulsion to get on with it so strong I was almost unable to enjoy the pleasures along the way. I devoured the reviews but only half believed them, as though they were a diversion, a trick to keep me from slogging on with the real stuff. Not only that, but the pleasure I did have over the book was a guilty secret—it could only make Len feel worse. So under the rock (where it was getting rather crowded) went that too.

But I was in a good period for work and I sold to magazines steadily. "I read the *Sports Illustrated* story [really a non-fiction article] with pleasure and amusement," Nunnally wrote. "You may very well have tapped a new vein of subject matter. The vein is ignorance. When I heard you were going to do a story relating to football I could only say to myself, Whatever has come over *Sports Illustrated!* Nora on football! Well, sir, Scotty and I, deep in record books when I'm not throwing him passes in the back yard, had many a hearty laugh over that one. Why did I never think of this approach to writing? I've got more ignorance on more subjects than almost anybody you know. Somebody mentions electronics and I say something like, oh, boy! and let it go at that. You say, okay, sir, and go back and write a respectable, readable, salable story about it. To take just sports alone, how many do you not know about? Hockey? Jai alai? Ninepins?"

When I wrote three articles for the *Atlantic Monthly* about love, sex and marriage, he refrained from comment. Saying in 1961 that marriage was a trap women imposed upon themselves, with a lot of help from men, was new enough to make him nervous.

"What's marriage for if it isn't for two people to be peacefully at ease with each other? After dinner Dorris and I sit and read and drop our books or papers from time to time as something occurs to us to talk about. We talk about the kids, about somebody we saw during the day, a picture or a book, a show, vague plans for the future, something we read and thought was amusing or interesting or surprising. We argue. Occasionally she denounces me as an intellectual or a cynic which means only that I liked (or disliked) something and she did not. We go back to our Confederate childhoods for recollections that amuse us . . . the marriage is doomed that you have to work at continually. That may be the way it is at first, for both characters are playing new positions, but when you realize marriage is not a time bomb, and that the perfect man or woman has yet to be born . . . Dorris and I have falling outs, sometimes on very fundamental things, but I'm sure she knows as well as I that in the bottom of our hearts this is a better, warmer, sweeter relationship than any other we can think of. (This doesn't go if I get home this evening and find that Dorris has packed her bag and gone.)" It sounded peaceful and wonderful, but at that time I hadn't heard Dorris' side of it.

In 1961 my second novel, *A Step Beyond Innocence*, came out. Throughout the reviews ran a flicker of disappointment that I had never really gotten a grasp on what I wanted to say. The subject—college girls and their work vs. marriage conflicts—baffled me as much now as it had before. It was said to be "too sociological," that it lacked "conflict and a point of view." Pop wrote from London, "I suspect you've been disappointed by the reception of *Step* . . . these things do happen, honey. It's part of the business. But the *Herald Tribune* fellow [John K. Hutchens] paid indirect tribute to you by the suggestion of something like impatience all through his review, as if he had a right to expect better from you than this. . . . I've got praise and I've got some awful shellackings, really vicious ones, but after a while they were both just memories, and rather faint ones at that, because I became enthusiastic about another story. At once I forgot everything else. Once when she was little, either Christie or Roxie said, 'Why don't you try for an Oscar, Dad?' I said in effect, 'Listen, you little punk, I never typed a sentence that I wasn't trying for an Oscar.' Only mediocrity is consistent. That's because mediocrity takes no chances. Mediocrity plays it very, very close to the vest. Other writers lunge at something else. . . .

"You have proved that you're a writer of consequence. You have only to point to the evidence. Two or three stories ranking with the best that I know, and a novel of such freshness and sensitivity that everybody who has read it has been completely won by it. The stuff is there . . . some years ago I was alarmed by the long run on the ground before take-off of a plane at Shannon. I got to wondering if we'd ever get up, but just dive into the Irish Sea. A little later the pilot, an Englishman, came into the lounge and sat down by me and I asked him if there was any problem about taking off. He looked at me as if I were nuts. 'Look,' he said, 'with X speed, X square feet of wing surface, X wind, X humidity etc., there is no way on God's earth of keeping a plane from taking off.' That's the way I figure it with you—with X ability, X seriousness, and X confidence, there is no way on God's earth of keeping you from writing good stories."

It was around that time that I began to go crazy. Nobody recognized it as that—it wasn't the kind of thing I had ever been expected to do. But it was time to pay the price, not only for avoiding whatever I really was, but for refusing to even try to find out. I had become more and more convinced that the truest things I felt, the deepest feelings, were dangerous and inadmissible; that the occasional flickers of longing I felt for any life but the one I was leading were signals of the blackest treachery that must be held down at all costs. The energy that this took was beginning to wear out, and what I had left I used for the children;

there was little left for Len beyond an arm's-length sympathy and a certain automatic behavior. Len by this time was working at a bank, starting all over again, which took all his energy, and we barely had a marriage. I don't know why I was so hard on myself, why any of my friends were better able to admit their miseries than I. I had some idea I was entrusted with talent, success and the fulfillment of the American dream, I was going to take off like the plane. I was going to do it all better than anybody else. I had been brought up to despise weakness, amateurishness, wasted time and talent. Do it well or forget it. And underneath this was increasing, like a spreading stain, a growing sense of weakness and incompetence, along with panic that I was losing control, I was dropping the balls, I couldn't keep up this juggling act any longer.

I began to get strange sensations, curious floating feelings in the head that in another time and place would have been called "spells." Nora is having one of her spells, they would say, get the spirits of ammonia. She has them during the hot weather, they pass away by dinner, they run in the family. Her brain runs over. It would have been a pleasure to have them, say, in Columbus, the explanations would have been so comforting, there would have been a big, warm cushion of family to fall back on. But on Morningside Heights they were dreadful. My family was gone: my mother and Rogers were in South America that year, and Pop and Dorris were by then living in London. I went around from doctor to doctor with my spells, until I found one who diagnosed them as neurological. He told me I must go into the hospital for certain uncomfortable X-ray procedures and to find out if, by any chance, I had a brain tumor—in which case I might possibly be saved by surgery.

I went home and collapsed in terrified tears. So this was what I had done to myself, rotted my own brain. It never occurred to me that I might survive this; there was no doubt in my mind that I would die or turn to a vegetable on the operating table as the surgeon cut gobs out of my head, tossing them aside and saying, "There go the French lessons." But it wouldn't stay a joke, no matter how hard I tried to make it into one—this was my head, my hopes, my life. Could the man mean it? No human being had cut through to me as completely as that doctor, however unintentionally; nobody had reached out and grabbed my feelings like that and, by doing so, proved that I still had some. He was marked, that man; and to avoid thinking about my head, my marriage, myself, and what kind of a mother I was, and because I was lonely and afraid I was going to die, I fell in love with the neurologist. He was an attractive man, easy and pleasant and usually willing to make us a cup of tea at his home/office and sit around chatting for a while after he had tapped my knees. In between visits (I made a lot of them) I floated about in a champagne haze. This was it, I had found love at last. Len and I would get a friendly divorce and I would marry the neurologist, who didn't seem to have a wife already. When I told him how I felt I was a little surprised that, rather than taking me in his arms, he told me (quite good-humoredly) that it was a "transference" and I should go to a shrink. I demurred, having already found my doctor, who would solve everything, including my rotted brain. I went into the hospital and underwent his dreadful procedures without a murmur of protest, which worked to both of our advantages, particularly since he fouled up one pneumoencephalogram and had to do it all over again. Anyone less besotted would have yelled like hell, but I only smiled with pleasure that he would again stick his foot-long needle up my spine in our symbolic act of love.

Since the tests were negative it was assumed that my problem was insanity, and he persuaded me to go to his friend Charlie for analysis. Now I had two doctors, I was safer than ever. But peace and safety were the last things I wanted, really, and to make a little trouble I wrote of my neurologist love in a diary which I left for Len to find. Len, who had been fairly patient throughout all this besides being terrified about my condition, snapped at this one and went to the neurologist for an interview I will never know about but which caused the doctor, who had been good-natured up to this point, to turn pale and tell me he wouldn't treat me anymore. "Go home," he said in dreadful tones, "and work on your marriage." Never had he been like this, angry, shuffling papers around. He wouldn't even smile and would hardly meet my eye. He was racked with something—possibly guilt. At any rate, I wept about it all to Charlie, eighty per cent of whose fee was covered by Len's Major Medical.

By late '61 I knew the marriage was over, as really it had been for a long time. When I wrote this to Pop, who had been worrying about my head and my life, he got on a plane and came to New York, where he took a suite at the Plaza and set himself up as a kind of intermediary. Len and I took turns going down (on the subway) for conferences.

Him: You know, honey, there isn't any such thing as a perfect human being.

Me: It isn't that, it's that I have to find myself. I have to understand who I am.

Him: Can't Len help with that?

Me: No, because it was he who caused me to falsify myself, though he didn't mean to.

Him: It takes time for two people to really understand each other.

Me: I suppose it sounds terrible but I don't even care about understanding Len because I don't understand myself.

Him: That's what the therapy's for.

Me: As a matter of fact you don't understand me either. Neither does Len. Neither does my mother. Nobody does. You've never been in analysis.

Him: You're goddam right.

Me: You just go along saying "Who, me?" while everybody else in your family lies on the couch and talks about how you screwed up their heads.

Him: Well, that's not the first time I've been told that.

Me: You really have a lot of insecurities. I'll bet you're threatened by your unconscious homosexuality.

Him: This is a fine time to tell me. Just an aging nance.

Me: As a writer, you really should have taken the trouble to find out about yourself.

We had tea. We had drinks. We had lunch, ordered in the room. When I was a child and he had come to the Plaza and ordered our meal in the room, I had felt deprived—I wanted filet mignon in the Edwardian Room, where the celebrities were. Now I treasured the privacy and the privilege of being served a meal I hadn't cooked. As it had been with Marge, I'm sure he had no idea how poor we were, and if I looked shabby, he probably just thought I was a slob or else too busy with the kids to go shopping and buy myself clothes.

> *Him:* You must take your therapy very seriously. Never mind about me. I can't change any more. But you have someone you can talk to with no fear of being judged. Nobody will tell you you're bad or wrong for your thoughts or behavior.

My psyche's lovely, dark and deep, and I had miles to go before I understood it. I had to make the descent into this abyss by myself. It was hard for him to understand that I wasn't leaving Len for another man or with my eye fixed on another relationship (now that the neurologist had broken my heart), for he suggested I experiment with one before getting a divorce. And it was hard for him to understand why I couldn't make this trip into the darkness while I remained married. I hardly understood it myself but knew it had to be.

> *Him:* I suppose I don't need to point out that this has to have an effect on the little girls.
> *Me:* It would be worse for them if I stayed.
> *Him:* You're going to find out what I can't even begin to tell you, what the separation of two people with children means.
> *Me:* I survived.
> *Him:* Well, I hardly did.

But we had, and with my help the girls would too. I was going to bring it off, this *geste* of self-fulfillment. I would teach them to be strong women, forgetting that I was anything but that myself and collapsing under the load even with Len's help. It was extraordinary how quickly I forgot my own limitations, pathological in fact.

Pop then made his extraordinary, unexpected proposal—that he should buy *The World of Henry Orient* and make it into a picture. As an independent producer he could now do that sort of thing. He had thought of it on and off since he had first read it, and now seemed to be the right time. He also wanted me to take a crack at writing the script, which I had never done. It had never even occurred to me that this might happen and when he

said it the clouds parted, trumpets blared. Out of all the conferences came this wonderful gift. It was a vote of confidence as
well as badly needed money delivered in an acceptable way—
through a piece of work. I would have wept over a simple handout, hated him for offering it and myself for taking it. But he had
saved my pride while saving my life.

Back in London he wrote my mother: "I don't think that anything is going to alter Nora's determination to extricate herself
from this marriage. It is not unreasonable to look for specific
causes for the breakup of a marriage but sometimes the causes
are almost indefinable, no more than a feeling perhaps, an insist-
ent irritation, a lack of synchronization of emotions . . . this
could describe almost all marriages at one time or another. An
older woman might accept them philosophically. All marriages
that last are compromises and concessions. If Nora were prepared to give her marriage another five years, it would probably
end only with their deaths. But she isn't prepared to do that . . .
as she approaches thirty she has become panicky. Is this to be
all? She still dreams of romance and excitement with a man who
stimulates her. As she approaches thirty every year lessens her
chances. . . . I think it a waste of time (and I wasted quite a bit
of time at it when I was there last month) to point out to her
that the odds of finding a better substitute for Len are pretty
long. You and I are older, more skeptical, less hopeful of such a
quest. We probably share a philosophy that says there is no ideal
state, no ideal mate; one adjusts; who is to say that the next one
won't turn out to be worse? . . . Nora is not prepared to settle
for less already. And I find myself sympathizing with her and
hoping that by God she will make it. May I suggest that you not
reproach her? She'll have all the standard advice and common-
sensical reproaches that she can take. But don't you think she
knows all that already? She's no dope. And she didn't come to
this decision without long and painful thought. Now let's let her
know we are with her, win, lose, or draw."

The next thing, he told me, was to get to work, on the *Henry
Orient* script. The story, about two thirteen-year-old girls and
the fantasy world they build around an eccentric concert pianist,
was too thin for a picture. "You should give some thought to fat-
tening the character of Henry himself. Presently he should dis-

cover the puzzling fact that two kids seem to be trailing him. Perhaps they actually follow him home. He gives no sign of knowing anything about them until he enters the apartment house and then (shooting inside the vestibule) we see him crack the door and peer out and then turn with a puzzled expression. What the hell is this! . . . Maybe he is a womanizer and his current favorite is waiting for him in his apartment. When he tells her he thinks he's being followed, she gasps. Detectives? No, a couple of kids, young girls. They're detectives, she insists. Panic, etc. It would be just like her husband to pull a trick like that! . . . Henry might be a nervous, fidgety man nearly driven out of his mind by the idea of being followed by two children. Maybe you can think of an actor (Keenan Wynn?) who would help you in your characterization. . . ."

In February, when I moved to my own apartment with the little girls, I wrote the script. God knows how I did it—or anything, as a matter of fact. I still had my "spells," which remained undiagnosed; I went five times a week to the shrink and spent a lot of time writing down dreams and having "breakthroughs"—at least once a day there was some clarion call of truth, some Gordian knot that came undone. The girls were unsettled and needed a lot of attention (which was also true of me, as a matter of fact), there were troubles at school and bouts of weeping, and those haunting questions: Did I love Daddy any more? Was I angry at him? Would I ever be married to him again? When other men began to appear (which they did, rapidly) each one was asked if he was going to marry Mommy (they all hastily said no). How could marriage still be in the air, hadn't the world changed at all? And how could I do it all anyway, for God's sake? I was still a little crazy—the anger of years was coming out, a bubbling of rage that seemed endless. I was changing at a faster rate than I had since adolescence—I could hardly keep up with myself. The tape, as Charlie called it (my job was to read it to him), was going so fast I became almost frantic trying to keep up with it, afraid to miss one small piece of this jigsaw puzzle that I was trying so hard to solve.

But the analysis was replacing the process that caused me to write fiction. That energetic probing into my own past was now done, over and over, on the couch, where a terrible logic ex-

plained what had once been magic. The poet's arsenal of metaphor, intuition, suggestion, chance, all of life's most literary moments were translated into a dreadful inevitability which had
been programmed in during the first six years of life. It threw
too much light on the half-shadows of fictional truth; science had
to triumph if the cure was to work, and I was too hooked on the
cure to notice how dreadful the loss, how inexorably the intellectual balance was shifting away from a way of expression
which had always been part of me.

Pop wrote me: "The end [of *Henry Orient*] is the No. 1 concern. For a picture it wouldn't be dramatic to let it be a series
of explanations as it is in the book. It must reach some sort of
visible climax and close without delay. It is important to have
the end in mind from the beginning. It stabilizes the telling of
the tale . . . the finale must be the farewell between Val and
Gilbert [the two girls]. The Henry Orient stage is over and they
both know it. This done (leaving not a dry eye in the house),
the end might be like this: Gilbert being escorted reluctantly into
Mrs. Leopold's dance class by her mother. She is dressed for it
and sullen and rebellious. This is defeat. This is surrender to the
Establishment. The music starts and she shuffles out on the dance
floor with a Trinity boy . . . as the boy talks to her, as the female
in her begins to respond, slowly she begins to smile. He says
something that makes her giggle. She answers. A little of the
flirtatious begins to show in her eyes. By the time we fade out
we know that Gilbert is entering a new world, a world of males
and females and excitement—and sex."

Nervous as I was about the size of this project, I stuck very
close to the book, like a lifeline.

"Nora did a screenplay," Nunnally said years later in an interview. "I hoped she would be able to do it, but she'd never done
a screenplay. She'd never dramatized anything. Just the pure mechanics, you just can't do it the first time you go at it. As I told
her afterwards, if she ever did any kind of dramatization, that
you can't be faithful to the book. She was faithful to her book. I
said, 'You can't afford to do that. The person for you to please is
the audience. They don't care anything about the book, only
what they're seeing on the screen.' Maybe that's why these authors never speak to me again."

It wasn't a very courageous piece of work. I had fattened the character of Henry—but only a little. I had "opened it up"—but not very much. I didn't understand about making it visual and I clung to my own fiction, whose sources were starting to dry up, too much. It was strange about Henry Orient—I thought I could never do it again. Nothing else that had happened to me seemed to have that untouched quality, the uniqueness of a story agitating to be told. The rest of my life seemed so recycled in comparison, so predictable, so like everybody else's. It was depressing to be hung up on being thirteen—worse than the aging college graduate who goes back to the football game every year and gets drunk, trying to go back to the only time in his life he was ever happy. I wanted to be back at the time when the possibilities were infinite, before all the roads started to close down—which they had the minute I started smiling at that boy at dancing school—when I could still create my own life, write my own script. I had not handled interference from other people well—I had proved to be a bad collaborator, most inept at co-operative effort, for I blamed the failure of my marriage entirely on myself and was frightened of being unable to bring up my children. Charlotte was right, I had failed to grow up. And *Henry Orient,* this memorial of childhood, was going to be turned into something else before my eyes, transformed to fit that suspect medium that chewed up stories and spat them out shorn of their freshness and poetry and the authentic burnish of feeling.

In October, Pop's revision arrived with a note saying, "You will probably never speak to me again after reading this . . . [but] I can only say that I have never worked harder on a script to make it attractive to a player" (Hayley Mills, his first choice for Val). I simply have no memory of what I thought of the script, for by then I was in trouble again—I had blacked out a couple of times and now there were to be more tests with new, less desirable neurologists. Back in the underwater world of fear, everything collapsed—he could have written the script in Russian and I wouldn't have cared, or even noticed. I was, from morning till night every day of my life, afraid of dying. Everything I did, making coffee in the morning, reading a story to the girls at night, going out to dinner with a man, everything was a cover, a massive effort to appear as though nothing was wrong.

The fact that I accomplished it was testimony to how expert I had become at dissimulating, how seamless a façade I could maintain. I thought I was becoming very liberated about sex and relating to men and openness and being in touch with my feelings but I couldn't face the possibility of my own demise, couldn't even entertain the thought for a moment without almost screaming. If I could hold it down for a while, go out and drink and screw and forget it, it blew out with double force, like an explosion that blows the insides out of houses, leaving only the shells.

I went to Boston in November for more tests (dangerous ones, it turns out, for they are no longer given). I was glad to go for a hospital stay that might clear up the dreadful ambiguity in which I lived. The tests again were negative, the "spells" undiagnosable but apparently harmless. I went back to New York to Jack, whom I married two years later, and who happened to be a psychiatrist.

London—New York   1962–1965

In 1962–1963 most members of my family went a little crazy. While I was in New York trying to persuade my neurologist to waltz me off to happiness so I wouldn't die of a brain tumor, everybody else, in separate locations, was coming a little unhinged. In London Dorris suffered a "collapse of functions," partially attributable to trying to create American perfection in barbarian England; at Ecolint, her boarding school in Geneva, Roxie collapsed with a kidney infection and was rushed to England for surgery, putting a dent in her education that took years to recover from—afterward she more or less curled up into a ball, gained weight, and gave up, for years. Scott, fearfully out of place at Andover, spent the miserable winter with his legs in casts for a knee disorder, unable to participate in any sports (which at Andover is social death), and ended up in such a misery of uncharacteristic depression that he was fetched home in the middle of the year; and Christie, always the rebel, was, as Scott put it, "swinging from the rafters at some worthless New England institution" (Sarah Lawrence), twanging with dissatisfaction and NoDoz, which effectively ended her education. She went back to London and shortly married a Swedish boy who turned out to be just as unsuitable as everybody had said, besides taking her off to a place called Göteborg. "I hate to think of her exiled out there with all those Swedes and reindeers," Nunnally wrote, and Dorris, who has certain conflicts about higher education for women, said Sarah Lawrence would have done better to teach her herring salting and glogg making.

Change was taking its toll, though of course the roots had been there for years. Christie had always suffered a peculiarly Southern California hangup—she thought she wasn't pretty, she thought Roxie was prettier than she was, and Dorris too, and as a matter of fact almost every woman who walked into the house, and when it's Lauren Bacall who walks into the house, and Mary Healey and Nan Martin and Marilyn Monroe and Ava Gardner, and Joanne Woodward and Ginger Rogers, it's hard to make a case against such a conviction. Roxie, on the other hand, thought Christie was smarter than she was, and since Christie was putting Groucho Marx down at the age of five ("Old comedians never die, they just stop being funny," for which she was sent to her room) and can think rings around most people, it's hard to fight that one too. Scott, the only boy, was born unenvious, bright and serene; as Dorris says, "How could he not? The whole world rotated around him." In search of a cure, Dorris took herself and the children, to the Neihans clinic in Montreux for injections of unborn lamb. "They stabbed us with these huge syringes full of wiggling fetuses," Scott says. The results remain undocumented.

Of course Nunnally wouldn't go near such a place any more than he would go near a psychiatrist. (Dorris once persuaded him to go with her to Montecatini, where, he said later, they drank mineral waters and peed to the sound of Beethoven symphonies. And it was dull—"everybody was so old Dorris and I were practically the Natalie Wood and Warren Beatty of the place.") His style, which we all inherited, didn't include self-scrutiny—you joked, you kept cool, you avoided confrontations. When cornered you let fly with a *mot*, which disarmed your attacker with laughter (hopefully) and finished the conversation. (I remember yelling, when I was young, "Daddy, *don't joke*.") In all exchanges Nunnally was in control—he led and you followed, particularly if you were his child. If most of his colleagues found him easy to get along with, there were some of us (wives, children) who found his personality a mine field. Scott says, "Everybody said that . . . I didn't have a single friend who wasn't stricken with fear by him. All my close friends spent years riddled with fear—I mean they liked him very much, everybody liked him, but he was scary. Somehow the easy chair always turned into a seat of power. We were never hit or spanked or anything like that, but the withering glare . . . it could be the subtlest thing, you'd sense that he was upset and withdrawn and it was a fearsome thing." To please him, to avoid his wrath and disapproval, you learned to do something well. Of course you could please him by being charming and amusing and agreeable, but you could please him a lot more by accomplishment—so those of us who could accomplish did, and those who couldn't suffered in comparison. (All five children have gone into either writing or some aspect of show business, and so far it's even true of the grandchildren old enough to go into something—three out of seven.)

If Marge was the only child who ever developed a working relationship with Nunnally, I was the only one who ever made a deal with him. The purchase of *The World of Henry Orient* was of course to be totally professional. The price was a thousand dollars against a purchase price of ten thousand dollars, with five thousand for writing the script—"Chris Mann [Nunnally's British agent] says that these figures are practically standard for these circumstances," Nunnally wrote in a letter. If this sounds simple, this purchase, in it lay the seeds of what might be called the most emotionally complex deal of our lives. Nunnally said prophetically, in a letter to his lawyer, "This is the last deal in the world I want to get mixed up with." But we were both in up to our necks the day he told me he wanted to buy *Henry Orient*. Of course no deal is as cold a transaction as it is supposed to be, particularly in show business. ("The screams of theatrical hagglers approaching a deal have some resemblance to the screams of cats approaching a love affair," Nunnally said once.) It is a kind of orgasm of talent, money, and hope, all tumultuously coming together in one perfect contract, after which everyone collapses exhausted.

The *Henry Orient* deal—and the adaptation of the novel into a movie and a Broadway musical (*Henry, Sweet Henry*) was really one long two-stage deal—started late in 1961 and ended in 1967. It was—I think—supposed to save all of our lives. In the beginning mine was most visibly in need of saving (no husband, two kids, no money, and crazy) and though Nunnally's career was lively enough at the time (in February of 1962, just after he bought the movie rights from me, he was working on *Stranger in Galah, Something's Got to Give,* and *Henry Orient,* with *Take Her, She's Mine* assigned for production) his situation in the next few years became increasingly difficult, just as mine later improved by acquiring an affluent husband. But the initial sale, when he was up and I was down, had something of the aspect of a *grand geste,* a generous act of salvation by a benefactor who had found a most tactful and ego-saving way of making a handout. *Henry Orient* was, after all, not exactly hot. It had been well received for what it was, a first novel written by a twenty-two-year-old, but no movie company had shown any interest in it until Nunnally came along. There was also something strangely romantic about his wanting to do it. In his own script, Henry Orient (Peter Sellers), the lecherous and seedy concert pianist, uses a similar device to lure his skittish suburban girl friend (Paula Prentiss) to bed:

Henry: You want me to set your poem to music, don't you?

Stella: Oh, so much!

Henry: And why shouldn't you! It's unquestionably the finest poem for music since "Only God Can Make a Tree." It can't fail to become a classic!

For the most part all went well during casting and filming. Possibilities for the two fourteen-year-old girls (Val and Gilbert) were: Hayley Mills (whose refusal took almost a year), Patty Duke, Sue Lyon, Laurel Goodwin, Portland Mason, and dozens of unknowns, from whose ranks were chosen Merrie Spaeth (Gilbert) and Tippy Walker (Val). Mentioned at one time or another for Henry Orient were David Wayne, Robert Preston, Gig Young, Rex Harrison, Tony Randall, and Dick Van Dyke, before Peter Sellers was chosen; and Bob Parrish, Garson Kanin, Joshua Logan and Henry Koster were all considered for director before George Roy Hill got the job. The final cast also included Angela Lansbury, Paula Prentiss, Tom Bosley, Bibi Osterwald, Phyllis Thaxter, and Peter Duchin.

Before the deal was made with George Hill, Jerry Hellman and United Artists, there was a brief go-round with Fox which ended in a row with Zanuck. While United Artists negotiated for the purchase of the script, Henry Koster, Fox director, asked Nunnally if he might read it, which Nunnally let him do as long as he understood that it was not officially submitted to either him or Fox. Koster liked it so much he showed it to Dick Zanuck, who had just started at Fox, and Dick Zanuck liked it so much he sent it to his father. But Darryl took his time about reading it, and in the meantime United Artists made a definite and satisfactory offer which Nunnally accepted. Nunnally returned to Jamaica, one of the offshore places in which he lurked during that period when he couldn't work in the United States without losing his overseas tax status, and shortly received from Zanuck one of his four-page cablegrams recounting their long association and denouncing him for double-crossing him and the studio by selling the script to someone else. Nunnally wired back that he had been misinformed, that the script had never been formally offered to Fox, to which Zanuck replied with another thousand-word cablegram ("He was wrong," Nunnally said, "and I think he knew it") but it was the end of the relationship with Zanuck, and a year or so later, when Nunnally tried to contact him in New York, the word came that it was better that he should not try to see him. Outside of a chance encounter at a restaurant, they never met or spoke again.

As usual the director made some changes in the script. One thing that George Hill took out, mercifully, was something called the "whorehouse framing." I suppose it was in Nunnally's script when I first read it, but if I was sane enough at the time to notice its inappropriateness, which is doubtful, it would never have occured to me to question what he had written. The whorehouse framing meant two scenes, one in the beginning and one at the end, showing that Henry Orient, onetime avant-garde concert pianist, had ended up playing the piano in a whorehouse. Nunnally said he wrote it in case "more exposure was needed to keep Sellers happy" but George found it jarringly out of tune with the story of the little girls and its quite different kind of nostalgia. Fortunately it went. Other changes suggested by George were readily accepted by Nunnally, who had great faith in his director —with good reason, considering his later track record. (*Butch Cassidy and the Sundance Kid, Thoroughly Modern Millie, The Sting, Slapshot.*)

But George's real magic came out on the set. This was a New York story (the exteriors were done around the city and the interiors at the Meyerberg studios on Long Island) and George fitted the scene like a glove—he lived in a brownstone on the East Side, he had daughters at Brearley, and he dressed like an Easterner: floppy Shetland sweaters and gray flannel pants, a lanky just-off-the-campus look, and he looked so young that with a little stretching he could have been a Yale date of Val's or Gilbert's. Tippy Walker (Val) and Merrie Spaeth (Gilbert, the me character) were both Eastern prep school girls and it wasn't long before he had them in the palm of his hand, which was essential in this case because both were untrained. "You have to manipulate your actors," George says. "You tell them anything you think will elicit the response you're looking for." With kids "you can improvise a lot, that's one of the things I was nervous about with Nunnally. If a line came awkwardly to them I would have to change it or improvise a scene . . . when you work with actors you find out basically what they need to feel secure and try to supply that. Since every actor needs something different you do anything that works. With little girls it was easier for them to make believe. I wouldn't let anybody talk to them about their performances. Wouldn't let the cameraman tell them where to move, wouldn't let them stop a take for position, I would not let them be given marks, I tried to make it as much between them and me as possible. I kept it fairly loose, I gave them quite a lot of scope to improvise, gave them things to play with. You say to a little girl, 'I want you to pretend you're mad, and really convince me you're mad. That's all acting is, it's make-believe and making the other person believe . . . then they became very loose, acting became a game in which they could convince somebody they were sincere. They didn't pay attention to anybody else on that set. After every scene they both turned to me like puppy dogs, and I'd say yes or no or change it or whatever."

With adult actors "it's more editing what they bring you than to have to create it. You have to create with non-professionals. With professionals you edit their skills. You cast them right. On *Butch Cassidy* the basic problem with Paul [Newman] that I never saw until after the first week's shooting was his concept of

Butch. Paul wanted to play it like a comic, and he kept saying, 'If I don't do it this way people won't laugh.' I said, 'I don't care if people laugh, that's not the point, they've got to be convinced. You can't play him like a comic, in the first place you're not a comedian and in the second place *Butch Cassidy* is not a comedy so you've got to play it absolutely straight, so if the laugh doesn't come you're not going to have egg on your face.' It took me a week of hard talking to convince him and the first week's editing was quite a job, he still had the rolling eyes, all this terrible stuff. Once he got it, it was just a matter of setting off in the right direction. That bicycle ride— I have a habit in my pictures of popping in a montage or something like hat I did it for a script reason curiously enough, I had no real relationship between Butch and Etta and no way of establishing their closeness, the whole relationship was between Etta and Sundance, so I hit on the idea of making it visual, having him show off for her and so forth. It was Tom Sawyer and Becky and the fence. If you have established a relationship it doesn't need dialogue."

Another reason *Henry Orient* worked so well, according to Merrie Spaeth, was that "it just flowed—of course the two of us were remarkably like the characters we played as personalities. Tippy was off into those wild flights of fantasy and I was sort of two steps behind. . . . I don't know how you were as a child but I think my main qualification for George was that I'd manage to come into a room where there was very little in the way of furniture and trip. I was fourteen and Tippy was sixteen, I was a very gawky private funny fourteen-year-old. I think one of the reasons George was interested was that I was on the periphery of social life. Most fourteen-year-olds had even at that time found things like transistor radios. And Tippy was very peculiar, in a nice sense."

One of George's most effective tricks was putting certain scenes—of the girls running through the streets and "splitsing" whatever is in their way, fire hydrants, kids on tricycles, et cetera —in slow motion, so they seem to float through the city air. "That was the first time slow motion was used in an American feature motion picture. And I stole it from Leni Riefenstahl, a German Nazi director who did divers in the '36 Olympics. She photographed them so you never saw them take off and you

never saw them hit, they just floated through the air. And I
didn't want to let people know I was stealing this from Leni
Riefenstahl. I shot thousands of feet of little girls in slow motion.
I took the film editor to the Museum of Modern Art and showed
him the Leni Riefenstahl and said, 'This is what I want.' So we
got it together."

I had made a few trips to Long Island to watch some of the
filming, and then when it was finished George had me to see a
rough cut of the whole picture. I thought it was wonderful and
charming, I thought he had captured my incandescent New York
and put it on the screen with sureness and magic—but Henry
Orient, played by Sellers, jarred me to the roots. My Henry, in
the novel, had hardly existed outside of the little girls' minds, but
Nunnally's Henry was broad, farcical, rolling his eyes, losing his
pants, haunted by visions of jealous husbands, a comic-book
figure in a landscape of daydreams and fantasy. I had known
Henry had been "fattened" but I did not like the nature of his fat
in this picture, though I would have laughed at his antics in another context. My Henry, what there was of him, had had a little
soul, a hint of tragedy, a suggestion of lonerism that would have
endeared him to two bright waifs such as Val and Gilbert, but
the appeal of this pants-falling-down Henry condemned the girls
to a typical teen-age ordinariness which was exactly what they
were not, which was one of the whole points of the book . . .
well. That was why writers whose books Nunnally adapted never
spoke to him again. But I couldn't do that, and besides, I understood the reasons for the changes—without them there couldn't
be a commercial picture, and if it wasn't commercial, it wouldn't
exist. Pop wrote:

"This is one of the proudest moments of my life, to have collaborated with you in a project of such size and promise. The
fact is, you've given me many occasions for pride, and not one
for unhappiness, but this was one that I was a part of. You had
written a book that had never received the excitement that it
was worth, a book of such imagination and gentle, tender humor
that I can think of few I would compare to it. This does happen,
in all the arts, a work that is swept past too quickly by the flood
of stuff that overwhelms their fields unceasingly, and while I la-
ment the unfairness whenever I feel it, it outraged me when it

happened to your book. Rarely can anything be done about it. The world moves too fast. But this was an exceptional book, a rare work . . . the enthusiasm people have shown for the script is for that lovely story of the two little girls finding a world of their own in a daffy piano player. That's what makes them well up with affection and warmth for it. Hill: 'Now for God's sake, don't do anything that will hurt the two kids.' Bob Parrish: 'You didn't do anything to the two little girls' story, did you?' And that's the story that makes the script something better than anything I have ever done. Orient is okay and all that; he's a good character devised by an old professional; Val and Gilbert are creations that never existed before. Orients I can write, have written, by the dozens; Val and Gilbert I couldn't manage if I wrote for another fifty years."

The World of Henry Orient didn't make any money. "The trouble was the title," George Hill says. "People heard Sellers and they thought it was something Chinese. It was the least successful of all my films, but it's still my favorite" (spoken after *Slapshot*). "People ask me about it constantly. For a film with that many fans, its being so unsuccessful is startling." It wears well, and last year, when I saw it at the Museum of Modern Art, I was no longer jarred by the Sellers comedy, it had all somehow blended like old wine. The audience was adoring though the print was lavender and distorted (CinemaScope squeezed onto a non-CinemaScope screen), the magic was still there, and during the scene of Val's fantasy about Gilbert's parents somehow getting together again ("he'd take her in his arms and rain kisses on her upturned face . . . he'd simply love her to death right there in the door"), as the camera closes on Gilbert's face ("she smiles ruefully at the lovely, foolish idea"), there was not a dry eye in the house, as there had not been, Merrie Spaeth told me, on the set the day it was filmed.

Jack and I were married around the same time *The World of Henry Orient* came out (Easter of '64 at the Music Hall). We were sorely tried right from the beginning. My divorce took over two years to get. Marion and Paula, when I told them they were going to have a stepfather, immediately burst into tears. After our wedding we missed our plane to Puerto Rico, had to spend the night at the Ramada Inn and lost the underwater

camera I had given Jack for a wedding present in a taxi at
Kennedy. On paradisaical St. Bart's I was bitten by a monkey
(possibly rabid) and on Guadeloupe Jack was felled by an
abscess which caused his face to swell like a cantaloupe. Apparently we were not blessed by the gods. Why not, what had
we done wrong? We had been honest and faithful and brave.
We had our analysts' approval. We were in love, all we wanted
was happiness, the fulfillment of the American dream. And we
were supposed to be so smart, the two of us, a writer and a psychiatrist. Not a hidden motivation could escape us, phony façades
peeled away before our sharp eyes. I probably was no longer
crazy (I had guaranteed against that by marrying a psychiatrist)
and no longer constantly afraid of dying (my tests continued to
be negative). But I had so little faith in my own head that I
handed it over to Jack (who never asked for it) for care and cultivation—he would put ideas in it, tell it what to think, and instantly detect any signs of madness, in which case I would run
back to Charlie for a retread. After what had seemed like a
plumbing, devastating search for identity, a fight for personal
freedom, I was still in the habit of capitulating to whatever man
was dominating my life—Nunnally, Len, Charlie, and now Jack.
Of course I had learned that penis envy is sick and that I should
revel in being a woman. I was full of feelings that six or seven
years later would have been easily translatable into early fem-
inism, but they were diffuse and baffling, and though I wrote a
little about these things I was never a crusader and they just sort
of bubbled around without taking hold. I had made a private
deal with myself—I could be a serious writer as long as I
brought my husband his martini, agreed with whatever he said,
and discussed my work with friends as though it were a pleasant
little hobby that kept me off the streets, like macramé. I convinced myself that this would work, and for a period I suppose it
did. I put myself down, back in the kitchen, and when I burst
out, ten years later, I was twice as angry because really nobody
had insisted I go there but myself.

Around this period I threw out Nunnally's letters, the only
time I ever did that. I think I was trying to exorcise him so I
could really be married to Jack, rather an analytic concept and
ineffectual at best—exorcising Nunnally was more complicated

than that. But it was the first time I really felt the conflict, felt the weight of my father somehow grinding against the other parts of my life, pulling at me, asking things I couldn't give. What he was asking I hadn't the faintest idea. Possibly I was just tired of his putting my poem to music (I had by then finished another novel and was getting tired to death of *Henry Orient*), which he was about to do again, because now there was talk of turning it into a Broadway musical. It was fun, it was flattering, and the money couldn't be ignored, but it underlined his success and my dependence on it, a lifetime of thank-you notes—for money, for love, for summers in the sun and screen credits and rewriting my first novel. He made it difficult for anybody else to give me anything I would value and almost impossible for me to value anything I acquired myself, even including husbands. And this marriage, unlike the first one, demanded a lot of time, and attention, the whole relationship was more intense. I couldn't keep Jack at arm's length as I had Len, fending off the real involvement. We were at some deeper level of primitive threats, and somehow Nunnally was one of them. On the day we were married, at the house of friends in Darien, Nunnally phoned from London before the ceremony had actually taken place, which we were holding off till all family members had arrived. "My father," I snapped at the surprised lady who had answered the phone. "I won't talk to him until I'm married." I was surprised at my own rage. Possibly I thought he could stop the wedding, though he seemed to approve of the entire venture. Possibly I wanted him to stop it, or at least to fight for me a little. Or else I was furious that he hadn't come, and had sent, instead, two cases of Piper Heidsieck. God knows what it was, and I forgot it for years. After the ceremony was over he called back, or else I called him, and we pretended nothing had happened.

All these half-conscious things came out in fiction form. Some months later I finished a new novel, *Love Letter in the Dead-Letter Office*, about a daughter raging against her Hollywood-producer father. Nunnally predictably didn't like it, which I knew because his comments dealt with style and avoided content. I hadn't expected his enthusiasm, the book was too angry. It was, for me, experimental, more ambitious than anything I had done before, and it failed because the anger was too unintegrated. Nunnally said later it hadn't worked because I had been trying to write about Hollywood without really understanding it, but I think what he meant was that I had been trying to write about him without understanding him, which was true enough. Of course I had been trying to tell him something— *let me out of your grip*—but my message did end up in the dead-letter office.

Henry, Sweet Henry

At first Nunnally was skeptical about the idea of turning *Henry Orient* into a musical—he said Broadway was for masochists not interested in earning money, which didn't describe him. But it was the talk of a man trying to tell himself he no longer found an old love exciting. He had been burned by his last encounter—*Park Avenue* in 1946, written by Nunnally, directed by George Kaufman, music by Arthur Schwartz and lyrics by Ira Gershwin, with Leonora Corbett, a gavotte of divorces and remarriages which ran for only six weeks in spite of all that talent. At first he went cautiously. But Jerry Hellman, the producer, and Bob Merrill, composer and lyricist (*Take Me Along, Carnival,* lyrics for *Funny Girl*), were enthusiastic, as was George Hill, who was to direct for the stage as well, and by the fall Nunnally had written the book (the libretto, that is, not the script, and not the novel) in Bermuda, another offshore hovering place, and there was talk of offering it to Victor Borge or Alan Arkin. At the same time he wrote the book for *Breakfast at Tiffany's,* also in collaboration with Bob Merrill, and was hoping for a spring production. The atmosphere was one of hope. "When he discovered writing for the stage again he was so happy," Roxie says. "He and Mama used to talk about the joy of finding a whole new form that he left long ago."

By this time he was ready to try something new. *Dear Brigitte* had been "a dismal experience from beginning to end," and interesting projects were coming in rather slowly. He had gone to work again on *Stag at Bay*, a play about John Barrymore first written in 1939, whose production was canceled in '42 when Barrymore died. Now he converted it from stage play to screenplay, but it was turned down in October by Ray Stark at Seven Arts. Everything was on spec. That of course was show biz, but it was a little nerveracking for an old studio employee well into his sixties. Besides, being an independent producer involved a certain amount of producing, and "Unfortunately, I haven't one single piece of talent as a producer," he said once in a letter to Garson Kanin. "I'm like the guy who couldn't make a dame in a whorehouse. My general approach to a star is, 'You wouldn't like this, would you?' And of course he wouldn't. If I were Sam Spiegel, I'd be sitting on Harrison's doorstep until he said yes. I'd push that little girl Hayley into a corner and twist her arm till she gave in. But when Mills wrote me that Hayley now wants to play older parts, hug-the-boy parts, I could hardly wait to get him on the phone and tell him I didn't blame that kid for one instant and that she would be insane to even consider my script." He told George Hill that moving to England had been a mistake. "I'm an employee," he said, "a writer on order, not a self-propelling operator. [At Fox] I'd finish an assignment and there'd be three or four books on my desk and that would be my next assignment. But prompting and doing my own digging and writing my own originals . . . a mistake."

Initially we all went toward the second phase of our deal in a springtime spirit—the movie that was captivating New York couldn't fail as a Broadway musical. In Bermuda the writing of the book was going well and Bob Merrill was writing songs that had everybody humming. A show was being born, carried forward (as always in the beginning) by a wave of hope. But there was the first spot of trouble. Jerry Hellman made a "deal" with Nunnally, George Hill and Bob Merrill for what he, or his lawyer, Mort Leavy, called "the entire Johnson interests." Since my agent was away at the time and hadn't been consulted about any of this, I dispatched a lawyer friend, Howard Solomon, to register an objection. Howard told Leavy there wasn't any deal, Leavy said there definitely was and if I objected to any of the terms I should work it out with Nunnally. Jerry, who was new at the game at that time, had made a natural enough mistake—he assumed that since I, like Athena, had sprung from the brow of my father, I could be counted on to agree with whatever he said. Well, if you accept the family history of the entire world, this was a natural enough assumption—father knows best. Even if you only accepted the history of our family it was true enough, except that I had been told, for as long as I could remember, that I must be a professional. There was never any question for Pop or me that we should be separately represented in these negotiations, that when it came to deal-making our relationship was irrelevant—and I think we both actually believed that.

Nunnally wrote that he had never considered this deal firm and final, it was only an arrangement in principle. "To me a deal becomes firm only when it is examined in detail by somebody better qualified than myself to have an opinion about it. In other words, an agent or a lawyer." Besides "it never occurred to me that Jerry could accept this as a definite commitment for you. . . . Collins (my agent) has every right to contest any point that he does not think fair or equitable, without consideration of me. I see no reason why he shouldn't ask for a cash payment or a larger percentage, neither of which I would object to . . . if Collins thinks he can get more he should by all means have a go at it up to the point of jeopardizing the production. In the last analysis the fact remains that the stage rights are still yours. As a result of Hellman's lawyer's naïveté, you are sitting in the catbird seat." Around the same time he wrote his agent, "Hellman seems to be having some difficulty with Nora. . . . I must say Jerry deserves it. It was naïve of him to assume that I spoke for Nora except in principle. A more experienced producer wouldn't have dreamed of taking my word for it. He would have checked immediately with Nora's agent. Now he'll have to deal with an agent who is resentful of being ignored."

One of the problems was that, in all the excitement, nobody had optioned the property for the stage, which is rather like moving into an apartment without signing a lease. I still owned it, which made all the guys nervous and frightened me to death. It was all very well for Pop to tell me so briskly to get in there and fight, but he might as well have handed me a gun and told me to shoot him. How could I fight my father for more money, which was what it came down to? It would be like attacking Santa Claus, guilt would stay my sword. It would be greedy, and I didn't even have the excuse of being poor any more. But if I didn't do it, I would continue in what was now beginning to feel like a paralysis, this habitation of my life by my father, the weight of what he thought I was—which was stronger because he had been physically present so little.

It was easy for us to embellish each other. He once said I was the only one of his children who never disturbed him. But if this was true I was a fantasy daughter, a productive Barbie doll who turned up every once in a while for doses of approval, the kid who had alleviated his own guilt by turning out to be all right— for if he'd felt bad about Marge he'd felt worse about me, I was the product of the second failure. No wonder I'd always tried to be so perfect when I was with him, no wonder Christie had the nerve to get mad and I didn't, that Roxie had the nerve to fail and I wouldn't have dared. No wonder I buried my demons so deeply. My sins would be doubly visited on my father. I wasn't smart enough to know all this at the time, but I did know that our relationship was, in a large sense, a fraud—that he didn't even begin to know me, all he knew was a cheery, appreciative façade, grateful for being invited, each summer, and writing Dorris a thank-you note each September. There were times when I thought we must both be bored with this—God knows I was, but I had no idea how to be myself with him, to rage, to cry, to reveal my seamy and human side. I wanted to pay him back for putting me in this impossible position, for leaving me without knowing I loved him enough to be angry about it.

Other problems arose with *Henry, Sweet Henry*. Jerry Hellman was turning out to be a do-nothing. In early '65 Nunnally wrote to Bob Merrill, "Jerry once described himself to me, only half facetiously, as a 'dynamic and creative producer.' So far, this dynamic and creative producer has distinguished himself by going nowhere near Victor Borge [a possibility for Henry] and now 'having reservations' about the only other serious candidate [Alan Arkin]. I think he has confused his role with that of a goalie on a hockey team. He is not so much interested in scoring as preventing a score. Time is passing and it is not enough for our peerless leader simply to shake his head at every suggestion." Nothing much happened for a while, and in November the whole project seemed threatened when Nunnally's agent suggested to him that Hill and Hellman might drop out of the project entirely. Nunnally immediately jumped on the agent. "I am shocked by what you say . . . is it possible that you accepted this lofty disposition of an important project without protest? Bob Merrill and I gave up time and money to prepare a book and a score. (Hellman and Hill, as it happened, were not called on to give up anything.) Merrill and I are professionals who could very well have applied our effort to other purposes. . . . I am a member of a partnership, not a chump who has become entangled in an idiot arrangement. Nearly a year has passed during which Merrill and I have waited without either impatience or resentment while he [Hellman] and George engaged in other profitable activities, a year during which he gave us not the slightest sign that he was preparing to dishonor his agreement with us . . . so far I have won not even a skirmish on the Broadway front [and] I do not like to face complete defeat in New York through a lack of resolution or action on the part of my agent." The agent, Marvin Josephson, replied that if Hellman and Hill were not enthusiastic they should be taken out of the project at the cheapest price. He also reminded Nunnally that when he had entered into this arrangement, he and Bob Merrill had been "totally unprotected and were doing a great deal of work for a producer who had no previous producing experience" and that the fact remained that Nunnally still did not control the basic property. Not only that, but Nunnally was in the same situation with *Tiffany's* (which David Merrick was producing) because the basic property was controlled by another.

But both George and Jerry Hellman reaffirmed their commitment to the *Henry Orient* project. The whole scuffle was put down to bad communication, but now the project was laid aside while George finished directing *Hawaii* ("a beast"). Then in March Nunnally read that George had signed for another picture (*Thoroughly Modern Millie*) and lashed out again, frightened at this newest threat. "It was stupid of him to believe anything that comes out in *Variety*," George says. "He sent me a very harsh note right out of the blue. I was planning all along to do *Henry Orient*. I sent him a note saying it was untrue." George's hurt reply again reaffirmed his interest in *Henry Orient* and *Tiffany's* as well. At the same time Hellman, never very enthusiastic, dropped out, which didn't seem to bother anyone very much. The concomitant project, *Breakfast at Tiffany's* (also with Nunnally, Merrill and Hill), was said to be threatened because Nunnally's demands were too high, to which he replied "that was one of the oldest and feeblest threats ever used in negotiations." David Merrick had turned the *Tiffany's* book over to Abe Burrows and now wanted Nunnally out of the project completely.

The trouble was that Nunnally, for the first time, was no longer busy and sought after, and Merrill and Hill were; that Nunnally had put in the time and done the work, which threatened to go down the drain if Hill, for instance, under no real obligation to anybody, dropped out; that Nunnally's only (professional) income at this time was from the *Henry Orient* project (another aborted project, a remake of *You Can't Take It With You*, died in September '66 because Jimmy Stewart cooled on it); that now he was out of *Tiffany's* everything, really, hung on *Henry Orient*, and still nobody had optioned the property.

Another producer, Bobby Fryer (*Sweet Charity, Mame*) was found almost immediately, and with him came a new injection of hope. There was renewed casting talk (suggested Henrys: Danny Kaye, Peter Lind Hayes, Jack Cassidy) and the agents and lawyers got back on the telephone. There was a slight snarl about my representation. The previous summer I had left Collins and Curtis Brown (for a variety of reasons) for an old Smith friend in a new business, Helen Brann at James Oliver Brown. Helen and Jim Brown inherited the "Nunnally-Nora complexity" including Jerry Hellman's fantasy deal for "the entire Johnson interests," which they set about trying to put in order, now that we really seemed to be going toward production. They restated my terms, all of which had been stated two years before by Collins. There were immediate howls of anguish from Bobby Fryer, who had thought he was inheriting the father-knows-best arrangement. He told Pop I was being "absolutely unrealistic" and Pop, rather than telling me again to get in there and fight, now set about persuading me to give in.

As his involvement with Broadway increased, London made no sense any longer, and neither did hovering about on offshore islands—the physical beauty that might have caused creativity to gush in another writer passed through Nunnally's consciousness like wind through a screen. He once wrote about Jamaica, "I had some daffy notion that Montego Bay was a resort like Palm Springs or Miami Beach. It's nothing but a collection of colored folks' shacks and funny hat stores. The only reason they didn't laugh when I asked for the typewriter rental store was that they didn't know what a typewriter rental store was." Alistair Cooke says, "I suggested Bermuda to Nunnally—I thought of the light and the marvelous water, boats and fish and so on, he lands up in the Princess Hotel way downtown in a room on an alley, and he could have been in Detroit." There were certain family troubles that made them want to be back in the States. Christie, now the mother of a young son, was going toward a divorce, and Roxie (twenty), that summer in Beverly Hills, had caused a certain amount of terror in the family by becoming the constant companion of Groucho (seventy-nine). "He liked me because I knew all his references," Roxie says. "I was in his crowd already. He began to talk about marriage—it was unreasonable and unthinkable on any level whatsoever. He'd say, 'You can have fellows in.' This was not my idea of a first marriage—or any marriage. I couldn't handle the position I was put in. He could be awfully tiresome, incredibly obtuse, and he could be cruel, but everybody laughed anyway because it was Groucho. But when we were alone he could be dear and kind and charming. He gave me little gifts—he would send somebody to pick them out, but he sent them to Gucci. I liked going to places where people had known my parents and then could accept me." She says now that she thinks Dorris took this more seriously than Nunnally. "Dad knew it wasn't serious, that we were both just two lonely people who needed each other for different reasons—Grouch liked to have a pretty girl to take out, preferably a blond, blue-eyed WASP." But Dorris wasn't taking any chances and eventually Roxie was packed off to Boston. By December '66 Nunnally was in New York at the Berkshire Hotel, and early in the year he and Dorris took an apartment at Sixty-third and Third, across from where I had grown up.

By this time his Broadway venture hardly looked promising. He was out of the ill-fated *Tiffany's* (renamed *Holly Golightly;* when in a desperate move Mary Tyler Moore was replaced by Diahann Carroll, Nunnally suggested they call it *Holly Godarkly*), which was so badly panned in Philadelphia and Boston (with Edward Albee's script) that David Merrick closed it after one night. By then he was working on *Darling of the Day*, an adaptation of his own *Holy Matrimony*, a project clouded with doubt from the beginning, so all hopes—far too many—hung on *Henry Orient*, which I appeared to be fouling up.

In New York, he told me that it was my stubborn insistence on unrealistic terms that was holding up the deal with Bobby Fryer and that I was, in fact, threatening the entire production (that oldest and feeblest of threats). When I told him that my agents had assured me that there was nothing out of line about my terms (which hadn't changed in two years) nor was the production at all threatened, in fact as far as they were concerned things were moving along nicely with Bobby Fryer, he told me it wasn't true, Fryer was impatient, and my agents were not only inexperienced but dishonest.

I have never felt so desperate as during those interviews. He came over two or three times in the evening, after dinner. He looked tired and old and was alternately stern (do as you're told) and very, very persuasive. There was little talk of family matters or anything else, and his interest in Justin, the new baby, was brief.

I don't remember if Jack was around, but if so he rather wisely kept out of it. Pop and I sat in the living room and I listened while he asked me to cut myself in half. I could no longer do whatever he told me to do just because he said so—on the contrary I was inclined to do just the opposite, a rebellion I should have gone through fifteen or twenty years before but never did because I was so afraid of falling into disfavor, because in some veiled way I was aware how dreadful it would be for us both. Now he was asking me to do the impossible, to sign without reading the small print, to jump into the river without knowing how to swim. The more he talked the more determined I was not to give in. The worst part was that he was actually coming to me and asking for something, which had never happened before. I had always gone to him, for advice, for love, for money, or to laugh, and it infuriated me more that now that he had at last come to me it was for something impossible. Did he need nothing from me that I could give without destroying myself? Wasn't there something smaller, something I could give with pleasure? If this was the price it was too high.

Him: What you don't understand is that your terms are impossible.

Me: But they're no different than they were before, and you told me to ask for them. Why don't you leave all this up to the agents?

Him: Because your agents are way out of line. They know nothing about theater deals. Neither do you.

Me: (desperate) But they're all I've got. And they tell me your people refuse to meet with them and even discuss it.

Him: Look, honey, they're going to blow the whole deal. Can't you understand that? That's why I'm here, to try and get you to understand that you're being represented by irresponsible people.

Or he would outline new terms and ask me if I would accept them.

Me: I can't. I don't know. I can't answer these things myself.

Him: You haven't contributed anything to this. Bob Merrill and I have worked for two years without a penny to make this happen. You haven't done a thing.

Me: But why should I do a thing?

Him: I'd like to know now if you accept these terms. George and I can't go any farther.

Me: Yes. No. Stop, I don't know!

Him: It pains me to say this but I must remind you that I am sixty-nine years old and am facing the end of the road. I can't risk the loss of this production.

Me: (trying to be soothing) We're not going to lose it. Everybody wants to do it.

Him: Then for God's sake stop blocking progress.

It would have been so easy to give in to anything he wanted, but I couldn't have done it without feeling I had wronged myself in a way I could never make up. I was like the shoe repairman on the corner of Sixty-first and Third who refused to be evicted when they wanted to build the high-rise. Everybody else had been bought out, the grocer on the corner, the Armenian rug dealer, the truss shop, the stationery store. Every building was torn down except the shoe repairman's, a surly type, who scowled among his innersoles while continuing to impede progress. I had always hated him but I slowly began to admire him. He saw no reason to leave his shop, which was the last one on the corner. They could do nothing to get him out. Finally they had to build the high-rise around his little building. (It is now the Tapemeasure shop on the northeast corner, a monument to stubbornness.) But the building had gotten built anyway. What drove them mad was simply that this lousy little Wop wouldn't give in, and no doubt the more he understood what power he had the more he dug in his heels. I was making them crazy because I was so unimportant and because I had such control and everybody had assumed I wouldn't be a problem. It had been a reasonable assumption, I had never been one before. If I had been they would have found some other way of dealing with me.

The deal was really all about love, I had always known that, but I hadn't known it would also be a test of who was going to survive, a mosaic of guilt and greed and rejection. Of course love is always about these things, but remarkably enough I didn't know that yet. In order for one of us to survive the other had to be struck down. It was an odd arrangement, and God knows I hadn't known about it in the beginning. But if this was the choice, it wasn't going to be me. The strangest part was that Nunnally talked as though I was crippling him financially. If that had been true I would have given in long before this. But there was no way I could believe he was poor, he and Dorris had too many flats and orange groves and supermarkets and whatever else they had. When they talked of being poor it meant they might have to go into capital. When I talked of being poor it meant there was nothing left in the bank. Probably they did get frightened about money, but it was fear of a strange nature. Somehow capital didn't count, you erased it from your mind. It wasn't there to use, it was there to make you feel secure, except that it didn't seem to even do that. In a strange way it didn't exist. It took a twist of the mind I was barely able to manage and had very little sympathy with, and it was based on the assumption that, by putting what I understood to be a fair price on my book rights, I would be somehow going into his capital. Screw his capital, that was no concern of mine.

During the proceedings Helen consulted constantly with Flora Roberts, a top theatrical agent (*West Side Story, Chorus Line, Side by Side, Ain't Misbehavin'*). "Nothing you were asking was out of line," Flora said later. "If you'd been a nice little girl you'd have taken one per cent. But we weren't off base asking that much (one and a half per cent). You go between one and two per cent. Nunnally made a mistake in not getting the option right at the beginning, and he knew it. He was the old pro of the movie business but he didn't know the Broadway theater." But that was logic, that was reality, as were the orange groves and the supermarkets. What was really going on was Nunnally's fear that this production might never come to being and that he might be through professionally, on Broadway, this final front —and that I, of all people, might be the one to shoot the bullet. His rage went far beyond the exigencies of the moment, I threatened him more than I ever knew. (It never is easy to pass the torch on to the next generation. I watch with mixed feelings the success of my own children. I love them, I want them to triumph, and every one of their successes moves me slightly nearer the exit door.) What I thought of as integrity appeared to him as ingratitude, what I called principles he saw as stubbornness and selfishness, nails in his coffin.

Right after Christmas Bobby Fryer dropped out (for reasons of his own, it turned out, that had nothing to do with me) but was almost immediately replaced by Norman Twain and the late Ed Spector, the producers with whom a deal was finally made. By this time all communication between Pop and me had ceased. A few days after Christmas he returned some little gifts I had sent over to the Berkshire, with a cold little note, and it was then I knew how angry he was, far angrier than I had ever known he could be. It frightened me out of trying to make peace, or doing anything, in fact; and so for the next nine months there was only silence from him (and Dorris and the rest), a silence as complete as death, as cold as the winter. For the first time that I could remember my father and I lived in the same place, only nine blocks apart, and never, during that time, did we cross each other's doorsteps. It was what happened when, for the first time, I said no.

Three months after Nunnally's death, Dorris gave me a letter he had written me at the same time but never sent.

At the top it says, "Written in anger and never sent. In fact, no letter or explanation of any kind to Nora. I don't believe she would ever understand."

"Dear Nora:

"Assuming that I must spell it out for you, your conduct for the past month has been callous and selfish, not to say stupid, beyond anything I would ever have believed. Out of a greediness that was shocking, you have put me through as agonizing a month as I have ever known, and you did it knowingly, cold-bloodedly, after I explained not only my own desperation but the desperation of the project. I found myself reduced to reminding you of my age and of my actual need for this production, a shameful moment indeed for me, and after reassuring me as you might reassure Paula when she complained about a teacher, you continued precisely as before . . . it was George's opinion, though he used politer words, that you had been a dope who fell into the hands of ignorant and unscrupulous bandits." He went on to spell out examples of the dishonesty and ignorance of my agents compared to his and George's (Sue Mengers) and to tell how they had almost botched the deal. "During this ordeal you have broken your word time and time again. You repudiated the agreement we all made two years ago [father knows best]. It is all very well to say you didn't feel bound by anything Collins negotiated. That is, to say it now. But at that time he was unquestionably your agent. You even asked me if he shouldn't be called in on the matter. I saw no reason why he shouldn't be, but assumed that it would simply be to be informed of the terms to which we all agreed in our brave little start. Each of us was to get minimum royalties. The rest of us simply informed our agents that we had agreed to this arrangement and needed no contracts; we were prepared to accept what is laughingly called a gentleman's agreement. We all worked (not you) off and on over two years. I put in something like eight months altogether on the script, Bob possibly four months, George less, for his duties were not preparatory. Bob and I spent thousands of dollars travelling back and forth between New York and London, living in hotels. You were called on to spend nothing. We were working for you as well as ourselves. So at the end of the two years what happens? Having invested time and money and talent into a script and score, we honored our agreement. What did you do? You disavowed Alan Collins. You denied accepting the terms I heard you accept. You dishonored your agreement. Do you know that we could have done that too? We had nothing on paper. We could have broken our word to each other and repudiated our agreement. But we didn't. Only you did. But neither George nor Bob ever mentioned this to me. They knew they didn't have to. They were able to imagine my shame. . . .

"But beyond all this deviousness and bad faith, what cut me, what I don't see how I can ever forget, is your willingness to watch me suffer, your indifference to my desperation, your dismissal of all I had done to prolong the life of your work for your benefit as well as mine. Do you know what my work on this play script turned out to be? It turned out to be the means by which you could blackmail me. Together with George and Bob, I was creating something that you could use to put me through the meat-grinder. No? Then tell me if you would have demanded such terms two years ago when there was no script or score?

"Last night I was too sick at heart to attend that dinner [for the two new producers]. How could I face those people knowing that my daughter, for whom we had worked so hard as well as ourselves, had proved to be dishonest, dishonorable, a liar, an ingrate, and a destroyer of other people's work. I was sick because a daughter I was once so proud of, I was now ashamed of. Because she had betrayed not only me but my friends. I was sick because I could think of no excuse for her, no way to justify her behavior. She had betrayed me out of the lowest and most vulgar of reasons, greed. Not privately, but publicly. For everyone to see. I was sick because I felt I had done everything I could think of to help her, had never lied to her in even the slightest detail, but she had defected from my love and concern and placed her faith and belief in other hands. You can now look to them for any further concern.

"Pop"

I took the letter back to the bedroom (Pop's room before he died) and read it and cried and read it some more and cried some more. Dorris had asked me if I minded sleeping in Nunnally's bed, and I had told her I rather liked the idea. (Charlie would have said that was where I always wanted to be.) I wasn't afraid of ghosts, no ghost could have been as bad as this.

It was some months after his death but his clothes were still in the drawers and the familiar odds and ends still on his desk—the familiar pictures, the brass scissors he said nobody would let him have. There was a blue glazed ashtray I had made him when I was a child. What had passed between us was so strange, its violence so veiled—nothing was overt, only the silent surface like the soundproof, cloudy glass that I was always straining to see through when I was a child. This seemed to be how we all functioned in my family; if it was important you put it on paper and either left it around or gave it to somebody else to deliver, only if things were written down did they have any reality. I had been told by more than one exasperated male that I didn't know how to fight, that I couldn't just come out and say I was mad, and it was true, I was afraid if I did the world would stop.

The night was silent, out in the driveway the four parked cars were black shadows, the breeze from the window smelled of gardenia. Out in the living room sat Dorris, who had delivered this racking message. I had also learned from Charlie that, no matter how much you try to hide anger, it never goes away—it will lurk around, curling the gut and lining the face, until it can fly out and make its presence known. I don't know why I was so surprised to find Dorris was angry at me, to hear the rage in her voice when she told me how adamant Nunnally had been about buying that tepid property, *The World of Henry Orient,* how he had taken less than his usual price for a screenplay, how the agents had warned him of the dangers of pricing the Nunnally Johnson name and script so low, of lowering his value by doing the project at all. But he was determined, she told me, to help me with money and a screen credit, I was flat and I needed bailing out. I didn't appreciate what he had done for me, I didn't know the value of sharing a screen credit with Nunnally Johnson. My work had been worth nothing, and instead of thanking him for all he had done for me I turned around and knifed him in the back.

He had expected me to thank him. But children are never grateful, there is no reason for them to be, they are too occupied with fighting for their own identities. Since I had liked my own book I had assumed Nunnally had bought it for its quality, and I didn't know what there was to thank him for. It wasn't that I was under any illusions about my marketability, but I knew my father, and he wasn't going to buy anything he didn't think was good, nor was he going to make a movie out of something he didn't think was going to make money—particularly not as an independent, when the risk was his. Marge had said, "Nunnally never helped his children unless they could perform," and I had simply assumed that I had performed—I had to assume that, anything else would have been unbearable.

Dorris' message might have been diffuse, but it was there—I had been a thorn in her side ever since that day she walked across the lawn on Camden Drive. There wasn't anything personal about it, really we liked each other quite a lot. But on some darker level she could have embedded my feet in concrete and sunk me off Catalina. Well, that wasn't the first time one of us thought that. The relationships in our family were too complex, the guilt and rejection had to burn off somewhere. There had been so many of us vying for Nunnally. As Auden said, not only did we want to be loved, but we wanted to be loved alone. I thought of the graves in the Columbus cemetery, of all those ancestors who stayed together and died together, and how far, and by what strange paths, we had come since then.

Henry, Sweet Henry (Don Ameche, Carol Bruce, Louise Lasser, Robin Wilson, Neva Small) opened September 25, 1967, in Philadelphia at the Shubert Theater. Jack and I went down for the opening with friends. We were all very done up, and I was so nervous I could eat none of a very elegant French dinner and made everybody leave in the middle.

At the theater there was a certain amount of flurry and we sat in our VIP seats, a moment to be cherished if I had not been looking around so frantically for my father. At length when the theater had quieted down he came down the aisle. When I saw him I began to cry quite uncontrollably. I must have been sitting near the end of the row, for we embraced. He said, "No more, no more," while I continued to weep and Jack and the others pretended I didn't exist—it was, I suppose, an unusual demonstration. I had never cried like that over Jack. When Pop went to watch the show from the rear I still couldn't stop, though the lights had dimmed. When I became aware that they were probably holding the curtain until I controlled myself, I managed to stop. I was so flooded with love and its complexities, I saw the play only dimly. Now he was back in my life, he had to be fitted in somewhere, but not, for either of us, in the space we had occupied before. A day or two later he wrote:

"Nora darling, Is it possible that we can take it that I've been away, without ever mentioning why, and catch up on each other when I get back? I've missed you terribly.

"Love,
Pop"

New York—California
1967–1977

Whatever *Henry, Sweet Henry* had been for Pop and me, it wasn't the hit everybody had expected. It had been loved in Detroit and Philadelphia, but New York was harsher. The entire family—all of it—gathered for the Broadway opening: Nunnally and Dorris and Chris, Roxie and Scott, Marge and Gene and their two kids, Mike and Kim, Marion, escorted by Cecil, who came to town for the occasion, Jack and I and Marion and Paula. Even June was there, my old friend upon whom I had modeled Val. At the opening-night party after the performance, we waited, quite cheerfully, for reviews. A couple of the early TV comments were favorable, but then there was a bleak turn for the worse. Clive Barnes of the *Times* found the music too feeble and old-fashioned—times had changed, the Beatles had happened. The two girls were good, but Don Ameche wasn't (which was true enough). It was just all too diffuse and derivative. Other reviews were not much better, though Walter Kerr, on Sunday, was kind. It ran for ten weeks at the Palace, so it couldn't really be called a flop. But it didn't make anybody rich. When it closed, early in '68, it was the end of an idea that had germinated in my head around 1955. We had wrung it dry and been wrung out ourselves by it. I had had my name in lights at the Palace, which I used in later years to remind myself that I was not passing through this life unnoticed.

Nunnally's third play, *Darling of the Day*, went into rehearsal.

"He had ominous misgivings about it," Alistair Cooke says. "He said it was going to be the only play on Broadway with two leading ladies" (Patricia Routledge and Vincent Price). Though he had adapted his own greatly loved material, *Holy Matrimony* (from Arnold Bennett's *Buried Alive*), it was beset with misery from the start. He wrote me from Toronto, "As forecast exclusively in these columns, this is a mess. I can't decide who is more to blame, Vincent Price or Vinaver, the director. (You certainly don't expect me to say *I'm* to blame!) On top of everything else we are playing in a theatre about the size of Yankee Stadium and little can be seen and next to nothing heard. So this is the end of the Grand Old Man of the Silver Screen in the theatre. Three up, three down."

Accompanying him was Roxie ("an excellent secretary when I can get her up. I take all her calls and deliver messages accurately"), who says, "It was a horrible experience for Dad. In Toronto he was so unhappy with it, he said the best he ever saw was a run-through for backers in a bare room in New York. From then on it went downhill. There was Jule Styne for the music, Yip Harburg for the lyrics, Nunnally for the book, veterans all three, and the director was twenty-three or twenty-four with only one credit, *The Mad Show*. . . . Dad thought he totally did not direct. The more he backed away from controlling anything, the more hell broke loose. Nobody else could control Vincent Price and nobody had the power the director would, so the show was let like a child to go rampant and run wild. I think everybody got self-indulgent there." The show got to New York but lasted only a week or two.

The year before he had written the script for the last picture he ever made, *The Dirty Dozen* (Lee Marvin, Ernest Borgnine, Telly Savalas, Donald Sutherland, directed by Robert Aldrich), which came out in '67. It was adapted from a big, sprawling book but, he said, "it wasn't on as high a level of literature as *Grapes of Wrath* and it was about one fifth as hard to do." But he was taken off the script. Monica Kemberg, a close family friend, says, "I went to see him one day and he was terribly upset, the most upset I had ever seen him. He said, 'For the first time in my life I've been fired. The director felt the script was not right, another writer came and did it.' He was terribly

thrown by it, somehow that was the last straw." After arbitration
by the Screenwriters' Guild, he shared credit with Lukas Heller,
the new writer. "I didn't go see it, it was like the expectant father
getting intimations that he isn't the father of the baby, so he
doesn't look forward to the birth with great excitement." The
other writer injected more violence, for which the picture was
criticized in reviews. "Robert Aldrich is a he-man director, he
must be harsh and cruel and tough and all that," Nunnally said.
"War is a dreadful thing and if people are going to be killed and
their bones broken and their heads busted open, you have to go
along with that. The people who criticize it—their criticism, I
think, was not on the grounds of the brutality, but the reason for
it . . . they don't object to explicit violence if they think that the
purpose is understandable or acceptable. They took *The Dirty
Dozen* simply being no more than a melodrama, and they didn't
think that melodrama justified this much blood and all that sort
of thing."

By the summer of '68 Nunnally and Dorris had made the decision to leave New York and move back to California. He had
written the *Dirty Dozen* script in London and had been assigned
The Frontiersman, but movie work was coming too slowly and
the Broadway chapter was closed. In a farewell letter to agent
Bob Coryell in '67, he had written, "Since you and Meta have
often explained to me what a difficult person I was to peddle
(through circumstances, of course) I can't help believing that
this decision may come as something of a relief to you. There
can't be much satisfaction in hawking an apparently immovable
commodity." The reply was, "The problem was you worked in
London." They had been glad to leave England. Dorris was
bothered by the "anti-Americanism (over the Vietnam War),
the marches on the Embassy. We were reviled and belittled,
and it made me wretched. But there was a certain amount of
culture shock when we returned to the States."

They rented a house in Hollywood, "this place that had white
fake ormolu around all the doors," Alistair Cooke described it,
"looking like soft meringue, icing, you know. In fact the whole
place looked like a meringue, and to see Nunnally in there was
preposterous. It had a lot of mirrors on doors and things and he
said, 'Back into any room, otherwise, you'll smash your face in.'

Oh, that was a ludicrous house. And then of course they moved
to what I called the Disney Castle on the hill." I never saw the
meringue house, about which Christie said, "I always expected
to open some closet door and find a skeleton in a leather bikini."
Then after some house hunting (which even included the house
on Bedford Drive in Beverly Hills where Nunnally and Marion
had lived when I was born) Dorris went to court and bid for the
Disney castle, which was an estate sale. Pop wrote, "I wasn't
there but Roxie said her mother gave a magnificent performance,
cold and merciless, a veritable Katy Hepburn, as she drove her
opponent to penury, social ruin, and possibly suicide. But when
an actress gets her teeth into a scene like that I don't have to tell
you what the outcome will be. She is not going to make an exit
until she stands alone on the field of battle. In the meantime,
whatever became of that figure that we had agreed was as high
as we could afford? We are now on the hook for a sum that can
only lead to the poorhouse."

Meanwhile Nunnally was on the Warner's lot in Burbank
finishing *The Frontiersman,* "Jack Warner's swan song," planned
to be a big picture with a twenty-million-dollar budget. It was a
long and difficult job, for there was no novel or story to base it
on, just an enormous, formless amount of research material about
Ohio and Indiana in 1770 and 1780.

"There was one character, Tecumseh, who had all the qualities
of a great man," Nunnally said, "so I had to fashion a story of the
Lost Cause. Tecumseh tried to get the Indians to stop fighting
with each other and unite as an Indian nation, a red nation. He
came very close to it and he justified such an examination in dramatic terms."

The story is long and complex and took eight months to write,
the longest he ever spent on any script. "But the worst problem,"
he said, "was to get the producer to leave me alone." He had
fought off Kenny Hyman while writing *Dirty Dozen* and was
fighting off this one, who kept asking him to lunch. He liked
being left alone entirely during the period when he was writing
a script and nobody had really understood that the way Zanuck
had. But it was never produced. Later that year he wrote me,
"*The Frontiersman* was a desperate measure. There was no story,
I didn't care much about the material or the period, and if there

had been anything else, even a small thing, I would have passed it up. Even now I have little to hope for. By the time I finished it, apparently to everyone's satisfaction, revolution broke out in the studio. It's either bought or sold or merged by rumor every day. Adding to which, Jack Warner, who engaged me for this personal production, fell out with the Hymans, who now run the place, and it may take months for anything to be decided, whether Jack is to make the picture, or Warner's Seven Arts, or neither. They may still be speaking but it's certainly not about *The Frontiersman.*"

Around the same time he finished an adaptation of *Scuba Duba,* Bruce Jay Friedman's "wild, obscene and very funny play." In it Nunnally breaks all his old scriptwriting rules—scenes run on for pages, speeches are endless and circular, and not much happens really. "It was so loose, if you found a good funny scene or a speech on page 82 and it sounded like it fitted on page 32, it didn't alter it at all," he said. "I mainly had to edit it because he writes too much."

Friedman was disappointed when he read it—he missed every cut and winced at every change in wording. "Nobody speaks to me after I've adapted his stuff," Nunnally said. The story is about your basic New York middle-class cuckold whose wife has run off with "a goddam spade scuba diver, a black phantom of the depths." It all takes place on the Riviera. "You're a little shocked when you read it first," Nunnally said, "but it actually wasn't dirty." It isn't, only blissfully funny. Psychiatrists do wild fandangos and zaftig girls peel off their shirts for no particular reason. The wife and the other woman become immediate fast friends, landlords rush off to bed with prospective tenants, everyone free-associates and nobody ever answers a question. New York audiences (of course partly black) found nothing offensive in the racial talk (and there is hardly a race that doesn't get the shaft) because this talk is only a device used for comedy—Harold, the cuckold, would hate Scuba Duba no matter what color he was. But Walter Matthau, when offered the part, backed away from it. Black problems were prominent and heavy at the time and the studio was unwilling to make the picture. It ended up on the shelf.

The first few months at Warner's gave Nunnally a little burst of optimism. "I seem to have settled into this studio about the way I was at 20th Fox," he wrote me. "I am hardly through one assignment before I am being urged to take another, to follow. It's extraordinary what being seen around does for a screenwriter. For a time in London I was becoming resigned to the sad fact that I was finally through, that my age had brought me down at last, and we'd have to begin figuring how we would be able to live, much more simply, when work stopped altogether. The end of the trail. In many ways a Hollywood producer is like a small child who assumes that when a person is not in the room with him that person no longer exists." Once upon the lot, the work appears like magic. He did a third script after *Scuba Duba, The Hundred Million Dollar Snatch* (a bank-robbery picture), which was never produced either. But early in '69 the direction of *Scuba Duba,* which he had hoped for, was withdrawn from him—he was too old, his health was too bad (he had had two light coronaries in London). It was a dreadful disappointment. "Six projects broke Nunnally," Dorris says, "the three plays and those three last scripts that never got made." There were other aborted projects and possibilities during that time but none as demanding as these, none that he had fastened his hopes on so.

In one way his age forced him to stop, but in a larger sense it was really the aging of the movie industry, which was in its terminal stages when he came back from London. "You have never seen such a hopeless place," he wrote to Bobby Dolan, a close friend, in '69. One studio after another was going broke. "Warner's is another of those sad studios where nothing happens and nobody knows whether anything will ever happen again or not. The general view about Kenny Hyman's regime is that it was total calamity, as if a sturdy old organization had been left in the hands of a retarded child. One after the other most of the brass found reason to fly out to New York and London a month or so ago. When the lone vice-president, about seventh in line of command, was asked why he was still here he replied that he had been left behind to negotiate with the Japs. As I see it, Kenny reduced the studio to a shambles and then went over the hill." At MGM, "the minute I get set the studio collapses. On the same day that I was lined up to do the script for *Taipan,* an old-fashioned blockbuster to be produced by Marty Ransohoff, a messenger arrived and fell prostrate at our feet, his dying words being that the new Kerkorian management [of MGM] had scrapped the whole project. Sic semper!"

Now agents have rushed in to fill the vacuum which used to be occupied by people who were essentially creators, like Zanuck or Dore Schary. Now the policy and decision making and deal making are done by agents, Jay Kantor and Alan Ladd at Fox, Ashley at Warner's, Shepherd at Metro. "The stars have become very big and hard to do business with," says Sol Siegel. "Agencies are way out of control. The cost of picture making has gone up so high it's a near tragedy if one misses."

"TV is a murderous business," Nunnally said in an interview. "I don't see how anybody has any inclination to fun or joy. It is awful. The deadlines and the whole gripping control of business . . . the movie business now is episodic. A picture like *Midnight Cowboy* and the two fellows in it give wonderful performances, Voight, a superb performance, Hoffman a good performance. In the old days if that had been done by a studio Voight would have been made for life or for a long time, but where has Voight been since then? Nothing was done for him. You have no continuity of interest in an actor any more. Hoffman will never be the star that the old stars were. The old stars did the same role over and over and it made them fortunes and world fame. George Arliss used to say you're crazy to change your act. In the old days there was a security about it that was conducive to fun, it's necessary for fun. That was true of writers too. For a long time I had three- or five-year contracts. I didn't have to worry a bit about security and if you were a writer who was able to deliver and showed some talent they reached out and grabbed you. I'm glad I don't have to scramble in it."

He wrote to Bobby Dolan, "I saw George Seaton at Groucho's the other night. As with all of us out here these days, we keened over the hard times. For fortyniners like George and me, it is doubly tough. Not only are all but a couple of studios flat broke and planning no productions, but even if they were George and I doubt that we could cut the mustard these days. We've seen *Midnight Cowboy* and *Bob and Carol and Ted and Alice* and we are not sure that we are capable of that sort of thing. To tell the truth, I enjoyed both pictures, but this halfway point between clean and downright dirty would probably be quite beyond me."

The new Hollywood, which is mainly television, is strangely grim compared to the lightheartedness of the old days. "We laughed more then," George Seaton says. Nunnally said, "I miss the evenness of life at the time I was the most successful. I never did anything tremendously important, but . . . the things I was turning out were most of the time financially successful, a good deal of the time critically successful—sometimes neither. But on the whole the batting average was high enough so that I didn't have to worry."

The price was having your soul owned by the studio, but possibly that wasn't a bad price, all things considered. "You gave up quite a bit for what you got paid," he said. "What you wrote never belonged to you, it belonged to the company. That's never true with the stage or with a novel. A novelist sells certain rights but he retains others. I wrote the script for *The Grapes of Wrath*. It seems to run on TV every third week. If I had owned it I would be a very rich man. But I have no claim on it."

Considering the way things ended up, most of them didn't do too badly. "We'll live through it," says Sol Siegel from his Beverly Hills home, "in our tattered garments, and the little hovels we live in."

Nunnally's and Dorris' little hovel, the Disney castle, was the most spectacular place they were ever broke in. On an upper edge of Beverly Hills, an area of insanely inflated land values where mansions jam against mansions and houses on stilts hang over cliffs, the Ridgedale house and grounds had a sort of trompe-l'oeil effect—from the french doors in the living room no human habitation was visible, you looked out over what seemed like a fifty-mile perspective. From the pool and its row of matched cypresses the lawn tumbled away down the hill to a wrought-iron gate which led out to reality (or whatever was out there). On the grounds there were two smaller houses which were occasionally rented out. As always, there was an enormous living room nobody ever sat in because the small study was pleasanter and nearer the kitchen.

There really is nothing like a house in Beverly Hills. They are so clean, so quiet and they smell so good, of newness and jasmine from outside and whatever Dorris is cooking. They are never musty, they never shiver or creak. If they are rootless (since they need no furnaces they have no basements) they feel solid under the feet, they are built flush on the earth. They are lined with pale soft carpeting which flows everywhere, up staircases and into closets and bathrooms. To walk barefooted from one end to the other is a sensuous experience, a light and silent flight of pure pleasure. My daughter Marion, a film student, talks of "live rooms" and "dead rooms." Live rooms rattle, shake, echo with street sounds and murmurs from next door, tremble with taps and clicks on the carpetless floors. They are hard to work in, they distract, they demand an attention of their own. Beverly Hills houses have dead rooms, silent and soothing. In them voices are louder and clearer and words double in importance, sometimes even take on an importance they don't really have. In a live room you have to fight to be heard, in a dead room your mumbled sentence trailings are stamped on the air like hallucinations. It gives everything a strange importance, trivia is elevated to epigram status.

Outside, up above Beverly Hills, there is no climate of sound which demands attention. There is the gentlest of breezes from the distant hazy sea, cars roll silently up and down the white streets. Drivers are polite and patient, they do not bear down on their horns in a frenzy of rage and frustration, they never lean out their windows and scream "fuck." There is none of the tacky garishness associated with this part of the world, instead there is majesty and restraint in the Mercedeses with their famous drivers rolling slowly down Benedict Canyon, between the towering palms and the occasional sweatless jogger. Even the freeways are almost dreamlike, they have no ruts or holes or sudden twists, instead they are embedded with small metal buttons which create a soothing buzz in car and body as though some benign supernatural force has taken over the wheel. Over everything the smog shimmers, blurring outlines and colors like the patina of an old painting, muffling sound and pain and ugliness.

In 1970 Jack and I went to the Ridgedale house for a visit. By then we had another child, Jonathan, and had moved from Manhattan to a seven-bedroom Victorian house in Larchmont in a sort of fruitless pursuit of the American Dream. That it wasn't going to work became apparent almost immediately, and we lived with our failure for years, unable to either solve it or get out of it or even admit that the failure lay not in the house but in the marriage. Before this became glaringly obvious, we each became furious at the other's inability to fit into suburban life. Jack hated puttering around the house and wouldn't go near a lawn-mower, I hated loading up the station wagon with groceries and children. We belonged where we had left, in a New York apartment where you could press a button and the super came to solve everything. At first we blamed it all on money, we couldn't afford to improve the house, we were in over our heads, which is exactly what Nunnally and Dorris were saying about their house. But in Beverly Hills the effect was far different. We lay by the pool near a hedge of blooming roses, the tips of the cypresses swayed in a gentle breeze. Nunnally sat in a lounge chair and talked while we listened. It was the way it had always been, no one would ever know that he and I had grappled, struggled, and that I had won—if indeed I had. We had never talked about it and by his direction we never would. It was like some phantom sea battle, the ships had sunk and the survivors were sworn to silence, it might as well never have taken place. The surface of the water didn't even ripple.

Around that time I was contracted by a New York producer, Hale Matthews, to adapt Jane Bowles's *In the Summerhouse* for the screen. I don't think I had ever gotten such pleasure from an assignment, which arrived just when I was feeling the most housebound, the most isolated and out of touch with whatever sources there were which made me able to write. I was writing non-fiction pieces for *Cosmopolitan*, which was all right, but it wasn't enough, and turning this strangely stiff and daffy play into a movie script was such fun I could hardly believe I was being paid to do it. Nunnally wrote, "I am going to read the Jane Bowles play again but I don't think I will do more than venture a few guidelines, as they say in Washington. Such as: Do as little as possible with the play. Too many screenwriters feel compelled to 'contribute' to the story. Somebody asked David Brown at Fox if Ernie Lehman was worth all that money they paid him. Lehman wrote the screenplays of *Who's Afraid of Virginia Woolf?* and *Hello, Dolly*, among others. 'Well worth it,' Brown said. 'He's one of the few writers in this business who doesn't try to improve a hit.' . . . Write as if you yourself had to pay for every word out of your own pocket . . . try to decide whose story you are going to tell. This doesn't mean changing it, for God's sake, but for an emphasis on one or two characters . . . in a play, scenes are sometimes (on account of the limitations of the stage) actually two or three scenes rather arbitrarily united. Don't hesitate to split it up, and in different locations. That's what they'll look for—'opening it up.' The stage is confining, a picture should be mobile . . . your script ought to run around 130 or 135 pages. I am mailing you one of my scripts as a kind of pattern for typography. I never use anything but DISSOLVE TO, to indicate a passage of time or a distant location. Everything else is direct cuts, which means continuous action. The longer you can go with direct cuts, the better it will read and play. Come to a DISSOLVE reluctantly.

"To me Mrs. Bowles is very stiff and mannered. Say your stuff over out loud before setting it down, to see if it comes out easily and naturally . . . if she has long speeches, don't hesitate to break them up. The best dialogue should sound as if it were overheard, not just heard . . . have the characters clear to you, so that they will always speak in character. If it is definite that the girl killed the other girl, that's a big high point. Talk it over with the producer first, so you'll both see eye to eye on it. Have an understanding with him as to what actually happened on that cliff. To be in agreement will give you more confidence in what you're doing. Don't run the risk of surprising him. Your job is simply to tell that story that you both agree on, and tell it effectively."

Hale and I talked and seemed to see things the same way, and then I went home and thought of Ernie Lehman and wrote a draft that clung closely to the play. But the trouble was that *In the Summerhouse* wasn't any hit, it is a peculiar little cult play full of bumps and awkwardnesses that disguise the good qualities that I was supposed to bring out. Hale was very nice about it, but we both knew I had goofed. It appeared that Nunnally had been wrong. He had, God knows, been wrong before, but I felt so protective of him that I could hardly bear to admit it, because it seemed to shift some unbearable responsibility onto me, and I wanted very badly for him to be right and redeem himself for *Henry, Sweet Henry*. With a lot of tactful help from Hale, we blew some of Nunnally's thinking out of my head so that I could write the script he had hired me to do, looser and wider and more inventive. It seemed extraordinary that Hale had hired me for my own talents rather than warmed-up Nunnally Johnson, which it might be assumed I had taken in with my formula, and even more extraordinary that by doing what Nunnally said I was fouling myself up. Nunnally himself admitted defeat—he read the finished script "with pleasure and bewilderment—pleasure because I found it a thoroughly professional translation of the play into a screenplay, and bewilderment because the thing still baffles me. When I said this to Audrey Wood [theatrical agent] when she was out here a few months ago she simply said, 'It's not your kind of thing, you wouldn't understand it.' Ordinarily this wouldn't satisfy me, but whatever my obtuseness, assuming that's what it is, the fact remains that some very considerable people see it not only clearly but favorably. Not only you and Hale Matthews but Truman Capote, Gar Kanin and Ruth Gordon, and those who accorded it respect when it was a play on Broadway. Since it is impossible for me to dismiss their opinions I can only assume that I've got some kind of inexplicable hang-up about it."

Then in November he wrote, "It will probably come as no surprise to you that, as it must to all screenwriters, the end has come for me. I'm having to pack it in, as we say in London. No more offers and not likely to be. The movies out here have hit the bottom, on top of which the business has passed into the hands of Youth, and next week I will be 72, and only people with bad eyesight can't tell it by looking at me. I've lost confidence and vigor and the impulse to write anything. Not that I have any great complaint; I've been around a long, long time, longer than almost any other writer out here, and for the most part have had a reasonably satisfactory professional life. Dorris and I have enough if I never work again, but it is still depressing to realize that the party's over."

It was strange and terrible news—what would rush in and fill that vacuum? Would he dictate his memoirs, would young screenwriters sit at his feet? Illness and pain rushed in almost immediately, in the form of a series of back operations for a skin cancer which had become infected, and of the slowly advancing emphysema which had by then announced itself. He had stopped his heavy cigarette habit, but it was too late. The emphysema cut his energy down bit by bit, inexorably, leaving more and more time for brooding and reflection. He wrote, "More and more it has been brought home to me that the biggest emptiness in my life is that I have had so little time with you and your kids. Every time I see the kids I ache at the thought that our homes have always been so far apart that I haven't been able to enjoy them as much as I would so want to. But a nice thing is that when I was last there they all imprinted themselves on my memory, even tiny little Jonathan, so that I can almost literally see them at any time. And that's quite often, believe me."

In the summer of '71 Scott caused a great deal of excitement by getting married (to Amy Cohen, a Brandeis classmate) at the Ridgedale house. Pop wrote, "It isn't easy arranging things to suit an anti-Establishment couple. For example, at one time Amy thought that the ceremony should be performed by 'a freaky monk.' This suggestion resulted in a profound hush. When the bride's mother asked her if she were going to carry flowers to the altar the bride said that she would prefer carrot tops and celery. Sometimes I wonder why I was ever born. . . . The bride says she is making her own wardrobe and for a while there was a staggering rumor that the groom was making his. But this was obviously too ridiculous to be believed and now it appears that the bride is making herself responsible for both outfits."

I went to the wedding with Marion and Paula, now fifteen and twelve and bug-eyed over the most exciting social event of their lives. Besides the old Hollywood (represented by Groucho, the Mercers, the Negulescos, and a rumor of Katharine Hepburn, which never materialized) there were what Pop called "the love couples," Scott's and Amy's friends, who arrived by car or on foot for the celebration. They brought, along with their pot and their little bags of granola, the winds of change. At that time I was thirty-eight and a resident of Larchmont, New York, and I found them rather startling. "I'm not sure what to tell Marion and Paula," I said to Pop, "when they ask me why they all sleep in the same room before they're married." "Tell them it's dreadful and disgraceful," he snapped. He had once told Jack, only half jokingly, that it was hard for him to accept Scott's getting for free what he had had to pay dearly for.

In the late afternoon sunlight Amy, in a beribboned dress, walked barefoot from the little house where they had been staying on a path of fern fronds to stand with Scott before a not very freaky judge. Alex, Christie's son, then about six, was supposed to have been a sort of attendant but he hid under the hedge and was replaced by Paula. Afterward there was a reception held around the pool with stereophonic music chosen by Scott and a buffet catered by Chasen's. After dinner most of the love couples, exuding clouds of marijuana, took off their clothes and jumped into the pool. Waves of shock went through the older generation, and I watched in pain as Paula sat by the pool ogling a naked young man who was trying to hand her a lighted joint. My old friend Avery, now thin and beautiful and between marriages, said, "I've been everywhere and done everything but I've never been to a party like this." We watched the beautiful young bodies, who didn't even swim around discreetly, but who leaped off the diving board, everything floating and flying. Most of the older generation left—this might have been Hollywood, but good God. Nunnally, sitting at a table with his cronies, pretended to be unimpressed. "So what's new? We did it forty years ago." At the height of the excitement the bride and groom stripped and descended into the shallow end amid thunderous applause, while Marion and Paula almost fell into the pool with excitement. There went any notions of protection I might have had, and there, in some subtler way, went my marriage. We were so earnest, Jack and I, so grim really, so burdened and so angry at our chosen lot. He had refused to come to this wedding or to let me bring the little boys, as though the whole experience were some sort of threat. And he had been right, it was. The house in Larchmont had never seemed so musty, so hopeless, so drab and out of repair, so joyless. It sucked at us like quicksand.

We made periodic efforts to try and get out of it. In '71 we thought everything could be solved by moving back to New York and we looked at apartments and enrolled all four kids in schools in the city. In '72 we decided that what we really needed to be truly happy was Scarsdale, and we found a house in Scars-

dale and didn't buy it. Early in '73 we were definitely going back
to Manhattan. But since we knew the trouble had almost nothing
to do with where we lived each little effort at change ended up
in nothing.

I hardly need to document the misery of a dead marriage. The
air in our house was heavy with failure, the kids' questions went
unanswered because nobody knew what to say. We ate in silence, after dinner we went our different and lonely directions.
Sometimes, after everybody was in bed, we sat down in the
kitchen and tried to talk about whatever was wrong. For two
smart people who had undergone psychoanalysis we did remarkably badly. Possibly we had never learned to talk to each other,
or to tell each other what we needed. We might have found out
ages ago whether or not we could supply these things to the
other. Now it seemed that we couldn't, we were both too
wounded and wary. What once would have been a pleasure to
give now took almost impossible effort. Everything was loaded
with meaning, we could never be guileless with each other again.
There was no longer such a thing as a spontaneous gesture, we
could no longer give each other anything new or pure. We were
impaled on our own metaphors. Jack couldn't tell me he wanted
to try again without my injecting it with dark motives. I couldn't
tell him I loved him without him thinking I was lying. If he
reached over and took my hand my first thought was that he
wanted to bury all our problems under a blanket of sex. We
were beyond even the accusations, those were a litany, even accusations have a certain life to them, they are made with the
hope of bringing about change. They are presumed to hold some
truth, but in the dark halls where we now moved truth had been
replaced by suspicion. Since neither of us believed anything the
other said we were truly finished, with a finality that nothing
could ever reverse. It was dreadful and sad, for we had been in
love—I had at least, and I believed he had. I had had a second
chance, I had let my feelings loose on him, and it seemed now
they had burned both of us up.

That year I made two more trips to California, to interview
Pat Loud of "An American Family" fame for an as-told-to book,
and the slow process of separation continued. That I could survive without Jack had hardly seemed a possibility, so completely

had I abnegated myself, but now it seemed that I might be able
to, even with four children. It was a fantastic thought, frightening and exhilarating, and it fitted one of my two chronic fantasies about the way I would end up living. In the divorced-
woman fantasy, I would live in a wonderful apartment in New
York, do interesting work, have love affairs, and generally be
chic, classy and unforgettable, rather like Edith Haggard,
though the lady of my imagination never had children and I
seemed to have four. The other fantasy, which I still have (as I
muddle through the first one, which isn't quite as wonderful as I
expected), is rather like a Seagram's Christmas ad. I live in a
large, pleasant and rather old-fashioned house in some country
place where it is always snowing and people are always arriving
for some hearty occasion like Christmas dinner. Fires crackle in
fireplaces, my charming but faceless husband mixes drinks and
says amusing things. A small number of well-behaved children
appear occasionally while the guests and I carry on clever and
interesting conversation. When it isn't Christmas, I spend my
days working in a paneled study and my faceless husband, who
is ever agreeable and co-operative and kind, goes off on some
vague business or errands, but is always back for dinner (we
have a cook) and nights of perfect love. It is dreadfully sad, it is
what Larchmont was supposed to be and never was. The longing
for a family is intense and dies hard, harder when its achievement seems so infuriatingly close. We had everything but a good
relationship, and since we couldn't manage that the trappings
meant nothing.

By that summer Nunnally and Dorris had managed to sell the
Ridgedale house and had moved to a one-story house on Tower
Road in Beverly Hills. Nunnally's condition had deteriorated so
that it was difficult or impossible for him to climb stairs, and he
could negotiate this house without discouraging bouts of breath-
lessness. The house is approached by a winding driveway and it
sits on the top of a hill which looks down on the neighbors'
(Danny Kaye, George Hamilton) pools and trees, and in the distance Beverly Hills as far as Century City. The rooms are "dead"
and lovely, and a tiny breeze blows in from the terrace. In the
study (as usual no one sits in the living room) in a leather chair
in the corner, Nunnally sat next to the gas fire, that strange Cali-

fornia phenomenon, and talked with some difficulty, for his breath came harder and harder. When he became too tired he got up, leaning on his cane, and shuffled slowly back to his bedroom. Or else he would leave the dinner table after a few minutes, too tired to go on. The rest of us, whoever was there, would rush into the vacuum he had created, free of the restraints he put on us. You couldn't really talk when he was around, or some of us couldn't. Even in his breathless silence he was too much of a presence.

In his room at the end of the hall, he brooded, usually about his children and grandchildren. Since there are twelve of us, he had quite a lot of material. As a group we haven't done too badly, but to him our faults and failures burned in his brain, our miseries tortured him. In some fashion he saw them all as his fault. He wrote to my mother, "Having nothing to do but brood I spend a lot of time worrying about the various members of my family, probably unnecessarily. Oddly enough, in one of her *New Yorker* stories Nora scolded me for trying to live other people's lives. It was an acute observation, and now that I have little else to do I am more given to it than ever." "I think he was absolutely destroyed by the fact that he had three marriages instead of one," says Monica Kemberg. "I think he felt for the rest of his life guilty, he was a bad father, he broke people's lives." He had bad insomnia and dreadful, haunting nightmares (often about words and puns) that took until early afternoon to shake off, then he began to be frightened about what would come the next night. "He was deeply depressed in his last years," says Dorothy Cameron Disney, mystery writer and old friend. "He was afraid of everything, of being poor, of going crazy, of dying. He was losing one word a day and then by the end it was ten words a day." His obsession for work had warded all this off, and now the demons crept in and took over.

During the last years there were periodic flickers of interest in a movie career which had gone on for over forty years. In '71 he was offered, and turned down, a Harold Robbins story about the auto industry in Detroit (presumably *The Betsy*). "I returned the Robbins book because the only parts of it that I could understand were the pornographic sections and I figured that it would be too difficult for me to tell the story of the Edsel in terms of

two or three writhing naked bodies. As I have always been the
first to acknowledge, there are limits to my talents." Around the
same time he was offered "a fat advance" by Doubleday for an
autobiography, which he turned down. When I said, "But *why?*"
he told me he simply couldn't do it. "It's hard to explain to anyone not headed for the last roundup. It's actually an inability to
function successfully, much as a fading ball player is unable to
make the plays he once handled with ease. I tried time and time
again and finally had to pack it in." In 1972 he was honored by
the American Film Institute for a series on screenwriters. For
years he had wanted to make *Roxie Hart* into a Broadway musical for Gwen Verdon, which happened (*Chicago*) but with her
production company and another writer. But in '73 that long-
unproduced play, *Stag at Bay,* was at last put on by an amateur
group at Florida State University in Tallahassee. It was a gala
occasion, but if anybody thought (which they did) that it might
lead to Broadway, they were mistaken. By '76 efforts to resusci-
tate Nunnally's unproduced works were largely in the hands of
"a small cottage industry in my house" whose occasional efforts
have so far come to nothing, but which marches bravely on.

His love and gratitude to Dorris were greater than ever—she
had devoted her life to him. If she had, as he once said, threatened to leave him about fifty times, he would never have left
her. One can stand only so much divorce. In the later years
Dorris took up cooking with an intensity and seriousness which
bordered on the nerve-racking. One's heart skipped a beat when
she entered the kitchen. Nunnally, in the leather chair by the
fire, wanted her to sit by him as much as he wanted what she
produced in her pots and skillets, but the two things weren't possible. Dorris turned out to be a feeder. "Food was always a big
thing in our family," Scott says. "The best way to get the parents
was with a hunger strike." "She's like a Jewish mother," Betty
Bacall says. "You come in, 'Eat, baby,' this and that, nine thousand different things. The house was always terrific to walk into."
It's true, there were three refrigerators full of pâte, cold soup,
chocolate mousse, roasts, fruit, shrimp, Pinot Chardonnay, avo-
cados, cold chicken, homemade mayonnaise, God knows what
else, in eternal preparation against famine or unexpected guests,
who, since they knew the customs of the house, were likely to

materialize. But this plenty could not be prepared casually, and Dorris emanated non-interference. "Honey, for God's sake get a cook," Nunnally said occasionally. They did, but it bothered Dorris to be out of the kitchen, and she ended up telling the cook what to do. Presently the cook would leave. The kitchen was Dorris' territory, and she wouldn't give it up.

In '74 I moved with the children into a rented house in Larchmont, a kind of hang-in period of a couple of years before I moved back to the city, and was finally divorced in '75. It was a long and painful business and Nunnally sat in California and fretted over what turned out to be an endlessly frustrating legal maneuver. On the fever chart of which children were creating how much anxiety, I went right off the top. My life was measured out in court adjournments and though I was assigned another script (*The Book of Eve,* a Canadian production which never came off) Pop wasn't happy about the way I talked about it. "The way you talk about the movie script makes me very uneasy. I have never heard of a script being written in a month, not even for a quickie production, and I don't believe it can be done . . . a good job and a good picture could lead to other and higher-paying jobs. Your concern and responsibility do not end when you turn in the script, you can't just turn in a script of 100-plus pages and say to yourself, 'Now I've done my part, from now on it's the producer's business.' You did a script a few years ago that never got a production . . . a big part of the blame for this failure was yours. Your script didn't sell itself to the money people. After reading it they dropped the idea. For this reason or that, you blew it.

"Don't think I don't know what I'm talking about. In my final year or so at Warner Bros. I did three scripts that were shelved. There were several contributing reasons why this was done, but I had to accept a major part of the blame. In other words, I blew it. I blew it three times. And there weren't many producers interested in me after that . . . a producer at MGM instructed George Kaufman to turn in a certain sequence by Thursday. George replied, 'Now let me get this straight. Do you want it Thursday, or good?'"

Not that the rest of us were doing so wonderfully, except Scott, who was, that spring, nominated for a Tony award for his set design for *Dance with Me*. ("He never took my work seriously until then," Scott says, "then it seemed more real. This may sound horrible but I feel a weight lifted with his dying. Never in my life did I do anything awful and have his judgment. He had a very strict concept of right and wrong. I don't feel now the heavy weight of those principles.") Christie was still in the lower reaches of the long apprenticeship to become a film editor, which caused Nunnally to sigh fretfully, and Roxie, though she had met her now husband Michael Lonergan, was still suffering from night blindness about his suitability as a husband. By this time my oldest daughter Marion was at the film school at USC, determined to crack the industry like everybody else in the family, and Nunnally saw all of us as husbandless women struggling against impossible odds in a discouraging profession. He wrote my mother, "The reason I worry about Nora is this: the day of the short story is just about gone, it's a dying art form. And in this era not much better can be said of the novel. A few biggies can make it but not one in a thousand first novel writers. Writing a screenplay is not enough. It's not a credit until it's produced. And Hollywood is now some kind of wildcat game, dozens of gypsy campfires all over the whole area. I suppose that TV is the likeliest field left, and that, I'm told, is a real rat race. Still, it's enormous, with hundreds of companies turning out half-hour shows all the time. So far as the writer is concerned, TV is one enormous anonymous field. In the whole history of TV there haven't been more than five writers whose names would be recognized even by other writers." When he fussed to me about young Marion, saying, "I wish she'd just marry some nice affluent young man," I said, "I married two nice affluent young men and look where I am." We looked at each other over a vast distance, a span of time that had turned my thinking around. There had been a time when I would have agreed with him, now I knew that you are always on your own really, and I hoped Marion knew it too.

That summer I took Justin and Jonathan, then nine and seven, to California for a visit to their grandpa. His condition continued to deteriorate and I knew that if I didn't arrange this meeting now it might never happen. Nunnally found them enchanting if exhausting (a not unusual opinion). He wrote my mother, "Everything here excites them and I seem to be a kind of tourist sight for them. They love to come into my room and are forever asking the others if they don't think Grandpa needs more orange juice, or a magazine, or personal attention of this sort or the other. Last night they just about reached the bottom when Jonathan led Justin in by the hand and said, 'Grandpa, this is Justin.' It was a pretty feeble excuse but it served."

He was quite alone now among the local senior citizens. His old friend Harry Ruby, the songwriter, had died in '74, and Arthur Sheekman was alive but in a nursing home. Dave Chasen, the restaurateur, had died in '73. Occasionally Groucho came for a visit. "The nurse wheels him in and he says, 'Hello, Nunnally,' and falls asleep. I read or write letters, and then the nurse comes back and he says, 'Goodbye, Nunnally,' and she wheels him away. We've had several visits like that."

Now he sat most of the time in the chair in the corner of his room. Next to him was his desk, which he only used to reach into a drawer to get something, a pencil and paper or an address book, or, if the occasion warranted, which it often did, a checkbook. Nearby was the oxygen tank with its breathing mechanism that did so little good. In his camel-colored bathrobe he looked gentle, tender really, his face pink and his white hair combed back, his hands quiet in his lap. The strains were gone, the lines of anger and pain diffused in some eleventh-hour semblance of peace. He had become at last an angel. I knew he was sad, I knew he fought to stay alive another day or another week, but since I couldn't bear the thought of his pain I blocked it out, I only wanted to see contentment. Every time I walked into that room I felt a great wash of unexpressed love of the kind whose nature was kept pure by its very incompleteness. He was the first one, the beacon, the one by whom all the others were measured, the one who had come back even after I had hurt him as badly as I have ever hurt anybody. He had not given me up. The last Christmas of his life, I had been moved to write him and tell him he had done well by me, that he had been in fact one hell of a father. He called me in New York and told me that this little paragraph, far too little, was his most treasured Christmas present. It was so easy to do and I had said it so little, we had all said it so little.

He made a major effort for Roxie's wedding, in December of
'75. If it lacked the abandonment of Scott's, the occasion was
beautiful and splendid. He didn't go to the pre-wedding party,
at the Beverly Hills Hotel (but was visited that evening by Betty
Bacall, who stood outside his door and said, "If there's anything
you want, just pucker up your lips and . . . whistle"), but
gathered all his strength to give Roxie away at the church and to
go to the reception at Chasen's. The effort was almost superhu-
man and was the last one he was able to make. A few months
later he took to a wheel chair, the effort of walking from one end
of the house to the other had become too much.

When Dorris phoned in March of '77, to say that he had gone
into the hospital again, I went into a cold paroxysm of indeci-
sion. If he were going to die I should leave immediately. But if
he weren't I shouldn't. He had gone in with pneumonia and had
almost no chance of surviving. But I decided he was not going to
die, even though I knew he was going to. I suppose it just
seemed like a frightful thing to assume, I might cause it to happen if it were not going to anyway. By the time Scott phoned, a
couple of days later, to tell me it was over, I was half packed
and had made arrangements to leave the boys with Jack. It was
around six or seven in New York and I was frantic to leave that
night, as though there might yet be some wisp of life left there,
like a vapor. There were no seats on any plane that night and
Scott, Amy and I flew out the next morning. Amy was rather
quiet but Scott and I might have been going off to a picnic. We
chattered and joked all the way across the country. We made fun
of the movie and drank Bloody Marys. We were going to a
good funeral, what was the difference really, other trips had
been made for good weddings or gatherings of some sort. Nunnally had been barely there in recent years, now he was barely
gone. When we arrived at the house and embraced a great many
tearful people I began to realize I was splitting in half, something was very wrong.

Marion arrived from USC and Paula from Redlands, where she
was in her freshman year. Marion was red-eyed and broken-
voiced, Paula was cheerfully expressionless like her mother. She
had learned dissimulation from me, it was the family talent. Six
months before I had delivered her at her new college; another

child would be three thousand miles away from home. The decision had been a mistake and we both knew it, and after we waved slowly good-by I went back to the house, sat down by Pop and burst into tears. "My God," he said. "I haven't even got the strength to hug you." I sat in his lap and cried some more, it had been so long since I had been able to. I told him that I had screwed up everything, my life, my talents, and I was now making considerable inroads on my children. He said, "Sometimes I wake up at three in the morning and I see my whole life as a failure." I appreciated his not contradicting me. So you didn't get over it, you lived with it, probably you died with it. It had nothing to do with what anybody else thought, it was a private cancer. I didn't even understand what I wanted that I had not been able to get or exactly what I had failed to accomplish. Sometimes it seemed that it was always having love come out so badly, but it was possible that my notions of love were as unworkable as his (and those perpetrated by his industry) and I had spent my life trying to make human beings fit into impossible outlines. It could have been the price of change, the painful residue that came of trying to make things better. Whatever it was, it had little to do with logic, it was just that we both had the same miseries.

A plan was made, shortly after we arrived, to go to the funeral home to "see him." I thought of *The Three Faces of Eve*, whose heroine's personality split into pieces when she was forced to kiss her dead grandmother; I thought of Jack's father, his face painted into a mask unlike any he had ever worn, as we all trooped around and tried not to stare at him. I thought of my mother after Rogers' death a few years before, a new freedom in her walk and expression now that it was all over. I didn't really understand any of it, but I did know there was something terribly wrong with the way I was standing around in the hall chatting as though I were at a cocktail party, that I would pay later for this numbness, and Scott would too. Down at the end Pop's room looked the same as ever, but it frightened me to look at it. Of course, that was what was wrong—I didn't believe he was dead. I remembered hearing of a crazy person whose whole illness came from never having actually seen the corpse of his fa-

ther and so, on some level, believed him to be still alive, and I
knew I had to see for myself.

A group of us went to the funeral home where we went one or
two at a time into a rather large chapel. In the back Nunnally
lay covered with a sheet. I suppose I had expected him to be
dressed up, possibly in one of those George Raft suits with
suspenders and peg pants and clock socks and a pair of Mr.
Cleverly's custom shoes, and a hat probably with a small feather
in the band, and a raincoat tucked next to him, like the old
newspaperman he was. It might have been the sheet, it might
have been the heart-stopping stillness, but there was his face,
there was the proof, the eyes were closed for good to me and to
everybody else, and I cried then, yelled and wept and shuddered
and had to be half carried out. It was hard to leave that place,
because immediately he was going to be burned and then I
would have only absence to deal with, an empty space that
could be filled, at last, only by me.

NUNNALLY JOHNSON PICTURES

1927:

Rough House Rosie (Paramount). A silent, adapted from a Nunnally Johnson short story of the same name, with Clara Bow.

1933:

A Bedtime Story (Paramount). Screenplay by Nunnally Johnson, Waldemar Young, and Benjamin Glaser, directed by Norman Taurog, produced by Benjamin Glaser, with Maurice Chevalier, Helen Twelvetrees and Edward Everett Horton.

Mama Loves Papa (Paramount). Screenplay by Nunnally Johnson and Arthur Kober, directed by Norman McLeod, with Mary Boland and Charles Ruggles.

1934:

Moulin Rouge (Twentieth Century). Screenplay by Nunnally Johnson and Henry Lehrman, directed by Sidney Lanfield, produced by Darryl F. Zanuck, with Franchot Tone, Constance Bennett and Helen Westley.

The House of Rothschild (Twentieth Century). Screenplay by Nunnally Johnson, directed by Alfred Werker, produced by Darryl F. Zanuck, with George Arliss, Loretta Young, Boris Karloff, Robert Young and Helen Westley.

Bulldog Drummond Strikes Back (Twentieth Century). Screenplay by Nunnally Johnson, directed by Roy Del Ruth, produced by Darryl F. Zanuck, with Ronald Colman, Loretta Young, Charles Butterworth, Una Merkel and C. Aubrey Smith.

Baby Face Harrington (MGM). Screenplay by Nunnally Johnson, Edwin Knopf and Charles Lederer, directed by Raoul Walsh, with Charles Butterworth and Una Merkel.

Kid Millions (MGM). Written by Nunnally Johnson, Arthur Sheekman and Nat Perrin, directed by Roy Del Ruth, produced by Sam Goldwyn, with Eddie Cantor, Ann Sothern, Ethel Merman and George Murphy.

1935:

Cardinal Richelieu (Twentieth Century). Screenplay by Maude Howell, Cameron Rogers and W. P. Lipscomb (N.J. had his name taken off), directed by Rowland Lee, produced by Darryl Zanuck, with George Arliss, Halliwell Hobbes, Maureen O'Sullivan, Cesar Romero.

Thanks a Million (Twentieth Century-Fox). Screenplay by Nunnally Johnson, directed by Roy Del Ruth, produced by Darryl F. Zanuck, with Dick Powell, Ann Dvorak, Fred Allen and Patsy Kelly.

The Man Who Broke the Bank at Monte Carlo (Twentieth Century-Fox). Screenplay by Nunnally Johnson and Howard Ellis Smith, produced by N.J., directed by Stephen Roberts, with Ronald Colman, Joan Bennett and Nigel Bruce.

1936:

Prisoner of Shark Island (Twentieth Century-Fox). Written and produced by Nunnally Johnson, directed by John Ford, with Warner Baxter, Gloria Stuart, John Carradine, Joyce Kay and Harry Carey.

The Country Doctor (Twentieth Century-Fox). Written by Sonya Levien, directed by Henry King, produced by Nunnally Johnson, with Jean Hersholt, June Lang and the Dionne quintuplets.

Dimples (Twentieth Century-Fox). Screenplay by Arthur Sheekman and Nat Perrin, directed by William Seiter, produced by

Nunnally Johnson, with Shirley Temple, Frank Morgan and Helen Westley.

Road to Glory (Twentieth Century-Fox). Screenplay by William Faulkner and Joel Sayre, directed by Howard Hawkes, produced by Nunnally Johnson, with Warner Baxter, Lionel Barrymore and Fredric March.

Banjo on My Knee (Twentieth Century-Fox). Written by Nunnally Johnson, directed by John Cromwell, produced by Darryl Zanuck, with Barbara Stanwyck, Joel McCrea, Helen Westley and Buddy Ebsen.

1937:

Slave Ship (Twentieth Century-Fox). Screenplay by Sam Hellman, Lamar Trotti and Gladys Lehman, directed by Tay Garnett, produced by Nunnally Johnson, with Warner Baxter, Wallace Beery, Mickey Rooney and Elizabeth Allan.

Cafe Metropole (Twentieth Century-Fox). Written by Jacques Deval, directed by Edward H. Griffith, produced by Nunnally Johnson, with Loretta Young, Tyrone Power, Adolphe Menjou, Gregory Ratoff and Helen Westley.

Nancy Steele Is Missing (Twentieth Century-Fox). Written by Hal Long and Gene Fowler, directed by George Marshall, produced by Nunnally Johnson, with Victor McLaglen, Walter Connolly, Peter Lorre and June Lang.

Love Under Fire (Twentieth Century-Fox). Written by Gene Fowler, Allen Rivkin and Ernest Pascal, directed by George Marshall, produced by Nunnally Johnson, with Loretta Young, Don Ameche and John Carradine.

1939:

Jesse James (Twentieth Century-Fox). Screenplay by Nunnally Johnson, directed by Henry King, produced by Darryl F. Zanuck, with Henry Fonda, Tyrone Power, Randolph Scott, Nancy Kelly, Henry Hull, Brian Donlevy, John Carradine and Donald Meek.

Wife, Husband and Friend (Twentieth Century-Fox). Written and produced by Nunnally Johnson, directed by Gregory Ratoff, with Warner Baxter, Loretta Young, Binnie Barnes and Cesar Romero.

Rose of Washington Square (Twentieth Century-Fox). Written and produced by Nunnally Johnson, directed by Gregory Ratoff, with Alice Faye, Tyrone Power, Al Jolson and William Frawley.

1940:

The Grapes of Wrath (Twentieth Century-Fox). Written by Nunnally Johnson, directed by John Ford, produced by Darryl Zanuck, with Henry Fonda, Jane Darwell, Charley Grapewin, Dorris Bowdon, John Carradine, Russell Simpson. (Oscar nomination.)

Chad Hanna (Twentieth Century-Fox). Written and produced by Nunnally Johnson, directed by Henry King, with Linda Darnell, Henry Fonda, John Carradine and Dorothy Lamour.

1941:

Tobacco Road (Twentieth Century-Fox). Written by Nunnally Johnson, directed by John Ford, produced by Darryl Zanuck, with Charley Grapewin, Gene Tierney, Marjorie Rambeau and William Tracy.

Roxie Hart (Twentieth Century-Fox). Written and produced by Nunnally Johnson, directed by William Wellman, with Ginger Rogers, Adolphe Menjou, George Montgomery and Nigel Bruce.

1942:

The Pied Piper (Twentieth Century-Fox). Written and produced by Nunnally Johnson, directed by Irving Pichel, with Monty Woolley, Ann Baxter, Roddy McDowall, Peggy Ann Garner and Otto Preminger.

Life Begins at 8:30 (Twentieth Century-Fox). Written and produced by Nunnally Johnson, directed by Irving Pichel, with Monty Woolley, Ida Lupino and Cornel Wilde.

1943:

Holy Matrimony (Twentieth Century-Fox). Written and produced by Nunnally Johnson, directed by John Stahl, with Monty

Woolley, Gracie Fields, Laird Cregar, Una O'Connor and Eric Blore (Oscar nomination).

The Moon Is Down (Twentieth Century-Fox). Written and produced by Nunnally Johnson, directed by Irving Pichel, with Cedric Hardwicke, Henry Travers, Lee J. Cobb, Dorris Bowdon and Peter Van Eyck.

1944:

The Keys of the Kingdom (Twentieth Century-Fox). Written by Joseph L. Mankiewicz and Nunnally Johnson, directed by John Stahl, produced by Joseph L. Mankiewicz, with Gregory Peck, Thomas Mitchell, Vincent Price and Rose Stradner.

Casanova Brown (International). Written and produced by Nunnally Johnson, directed by Sam Wood, with Gary Cooper, Teresa Wright, Frank Morgan and Anita Louise.

Woman in the Window (International). Written and produced by Nunnally Johnson, directed by Fritz Lang, with Edward G. Robinson, Joan Bennett, Raymond Massey and Dan Duryea.

1945:

Along Came Jones (International). Written by Nunnally Johnson, directed by Stuart Heisler, produced by Gary Cooper, with Gary Cooper, Loretta Young, William Demarest and Dan Duryea.

1946:

The Dark Mirror (Universal-International). Written and produced by Nunnally Johnson, directed by Robert Siodmak, with Olivia de Havilland, Lew Ayres, Thomas Mitchell and Richard Long.

1947:

The Senator Was Indiscreet (Universal-International). Written by Charles MacArthur and Nunnally Johnson, directed by George Kaufman, with William Powell, Ella Raines, Peter Lind Hayes, Arleen Whelan and Ray Collins.

1948:

Mr. Peabody and the Mermaid (Universal-International). Written and produced by Nunnally Johnson, directed by Irving Pichel, with William Powell, Ann Blyth, Irene Harvey, Andrea King and Clinton Sundberg.

1949:

Everybody Does It (Twentieth Century-Fox). Written and produced by Nunnally Johnson, directed by Edmund Goulding, with Paul Douglas, Linda Darnell, Celeste Holm and Charles Coburn.

1950:

Three Came Home (Twentieth Century-Fox). Written and produced by Nunnally Johnson, directed by Jean Negulesco, with Claudette Colbert, Patrick Knowles, Sessue Hayakawa and Florence Desmond.

The Gunfighter (Twentieth Century-Fox). Written by William Bowers and William Sellers, directed by Henry King, produced by Nunnally Johnson, with Gregory Peck, Jean Parker, Millard Mitchell and Helen Westcott.

The Mudlark (Twentieth Century-Fox). Written and produced by Nunnally Johnson, directed by Jean Negulesco, with Irene Dunne, Alec Guinness, Finlay Currie and Beatrice Campbell.

1951:

The Desert Fox (Twentieth Century-Fox). Written and produced by Nunnally Johnson, directed by Henry Hathaway, with James Mason, Luther Adler, Cedric Hardwicke and Jessica Tandy.

The Long Dark Hall (Twentieth Century-Fox). Written by Nunnally Johnson, directed by Anthony Bushell and Reginald Beck, produced by Peter Cusick, with Rex Harrison, Lili Palmer and Tania Held.

1952:

Phone Call from a Stranger (Twentieth Century-Fox). Written and produced by Nunnally Johnson, directed by Jean Negulesco, with Shelley Winters, Gary Merrill, Michael Rennie, Keenan Wynn and Bette Davis.

We're Not Married (Twentieth Century-Fox). Written and produced by Nunnally Johnson, directed by Edmund Goulding, with Fred Allen, Ginger Rogers, Marilyn Monroe, Paul Douglas, David Wayne, Zsa Zsa Gabor and Eve Arden.

My Cousin Rachel (Twentieth Century-Fox). Written and produced by Nunnally Johnson, directed by Henry Koster, with Olivia de Havilland, Richard Burton, Donald Squire and Audrey Dalton.

1953:

How to Marry a Millionaire (Twentieth Century-Fox). Written and produced by Nunnally Johnson, directed by Jean Negulesco, with Lauren Bacall, Marilyn Monroe, Betty Grable, David Wayne, Rory Calhoun and Cameron Mitchell. (Writers' Guild nomination.)

1954:

Night People (Twentieth Century-Fox). Written, produced and directed by Nunnally Johnson, with Gregory Peck, Buddy Ebsen, Rita Gam, Anita Bjork, Walter Abel and Casey Adams.

Black Widow (Twentieth Century-Fox). Written, produced and directed by Nunnally Johnson, with Ginger Rogers, Van Heflin, Peggy Ann Garner, Gene Tierney and George Raft.

1955:

How to Be Very, Very Popular (Twentieth Century-Fox). Written, produced and directed by Nunnally Johnson, with Betty Grable, Sheree North, Robert Cummings, Charles Coburn and Orson Bean.

1956:

The Man in the Gray Flannel Suit (Twentieth Century-Fox). Written and directed by Nunnally Johnson, produced by Darryl Zanuck, with Gregory Peck, Jennifer Jones, Keenan Wynn, Marisa Pavan, Lee J. Cobb, Fredric March and Ann Harding.

1957:

Oh, Men! Oh, Women! (Twentieth Century-Fox). Written, produced and directed by Nunnally Johnson, with David Niven, Barbara Rush, Dan Dailey, Ginger Rogers, Tony Randall and Natalie Schafer.

The Three Faces of Eve (Twentieth Century-Fox). Written, produced and directed by Nunnally Johnson, with Joanne Woodward, David Wayne and Lee J. Cobb.

1959:

The Man Who Understood Women (Twentieth Century-Fox). Written, produced and directed by Nunnally Johnson, with Henry Fonda, Leslie Caron, Cesare Danova and Myron McCormick.

1960:

The Angel Wore Red (released by MGM). Written and directed by Nunnally Johnson, produced by Goffredo Lombardo, with Ava Gardner, Dirk Bogarde, Joseph Cotten and Vittorio De Sica.

Flaming Star (Twentieth Century-Fox). Written by Nunnally Johnson, directed by Don Siegel, produced by David Weisbart, with Barbara Eden, Steve Forrest and Dolores Del Rio.

1962:

Mr. Hobbs Takes a Vacation (Twentieth Century-Fox). Written by Nunnally Johnson, directed by Henry Koster, produced by Jerry Wald, with James Stewart, Maureen O'Hara, Lauri Peters, Fabian and John Saxon.

1963:

Take Her, She's Mine (Twentieth Century-Fox). Written by Nunnally Johnson, directed by Henry Koster, produced by Frank McCarthy, with James Stewart, Sandra Dee, Audrey Meadows and Robert Morley.

1964:

The World of Henry Orient (Pan Arts). Written by Nora and Nunnally Johnson, directed by George Roy Hill, produced by

Jerry Hellman, with Peter Sellers, Paula Prentiss, Angela Lansbury, Tippy Walker, Merrie Spaeth, Phyllis Thaxter, Bibi Osterwald, Tom Bosley and Peter Duchin. (Writers' Guild nomination.)

1965:

Dear Brigitte (Twentieth Century-Fox). Written by Hal Kanter, directed and produced by Henry Koster, with James Stewart, Fabian, Glynis Johns and Brigitte Bardot.

1967:

The Dirty Dozen (MGM). Written by Lukas Heller and Nunnally Johnson, directed by Robert Aldrich, produced by Kenneth Hyman, with Lee Marvin, Ernest Borgnine, Charles Bronson, Jim Brown, John Cassavetes, Donald Sutherland and Telly Savalas.

INDEX